FUSHIGI YÛGI
GENBU KAIDEN

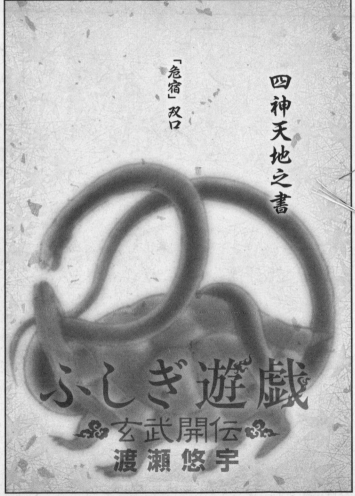

四神天地之書

「危宿」双口

ふしぎ遊戯
玄武開伝
渡瀬悠宇

story and art by **YUU WATASE**　　　Vol. 7

CONTENTS

TRANSLATION OF "THE UNIVERSE OF THE FOUR GODS"

Urumiya: Twin Mouths

Cast of Characters

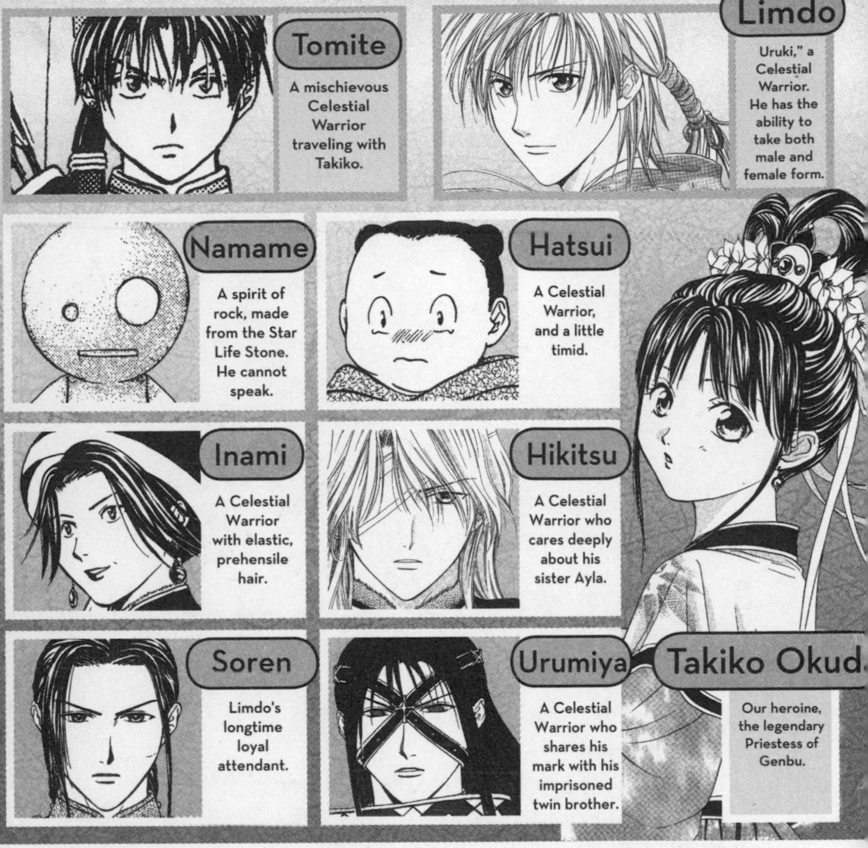
Tomite
A mischievous Celestial Warrior traveling with Takiko.
Limdo
Uruki," a Celestial Warrior. He has the ability to take both male and female form.
Namame
A spirit of rock, made from the Star Life Stone. He cannot speak.
Hatsui
A Celestial Warrior, and a little timid.
Inami
A Celestial Warrior with elastic, prehensile hair.
Hikitsu
A Celestial Warrior who cares deeply about his sister Ayla.
Soren
Limdo's longtime loyal attendant.
Urumiya
A Celestial Warrior who shares his mark with his imprisoned twin brother.
Takiko Okud
Our heroine, the legendary Priestess of Genbu.

The Story Thus Far

The year is 1923. Takiko is drawn into the pages of *The Universe of the Four Gods*, a book her father has translated from Chinese. There, she is told that she is the legendary Priestess of Genbu, destined to save the country of Bêi-jîa. She must find the seven Celestial Warriors who will help her on her quest.

Six Celestial Warriors have joined Takiko, and only Urumiya remains missing. Finally he is revealed to be their powerful adversary Hagus! Takiko discovers that Urumiya is really two people: Hagus and his twin brother Teg, who is imprisoned somewhere in Tèwulán. Captured by the enemy army, Takiko tries to sway Hagus by vowing to rescue Teg...

FUSHIGI YUGI
GENBU KAIDEN

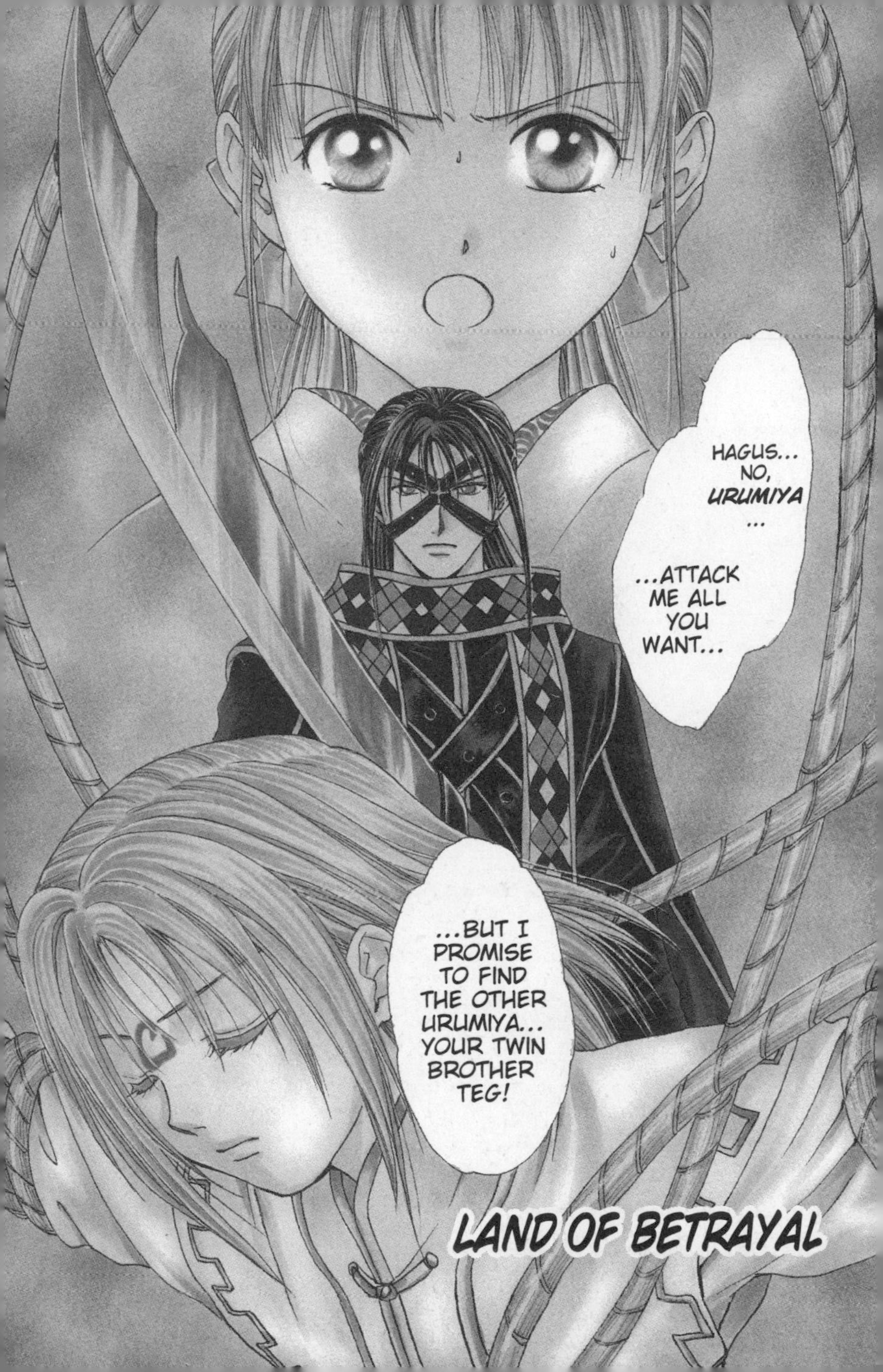
HAGUS... NO, URUMIYA ...
...ATTACK ME ALL YOU WANT...
...BUT I PROMISE TO FIND THE OTHER URUMIYA... YOUR TWIN BROTHER TEG!
LAND OF BETRAYAL

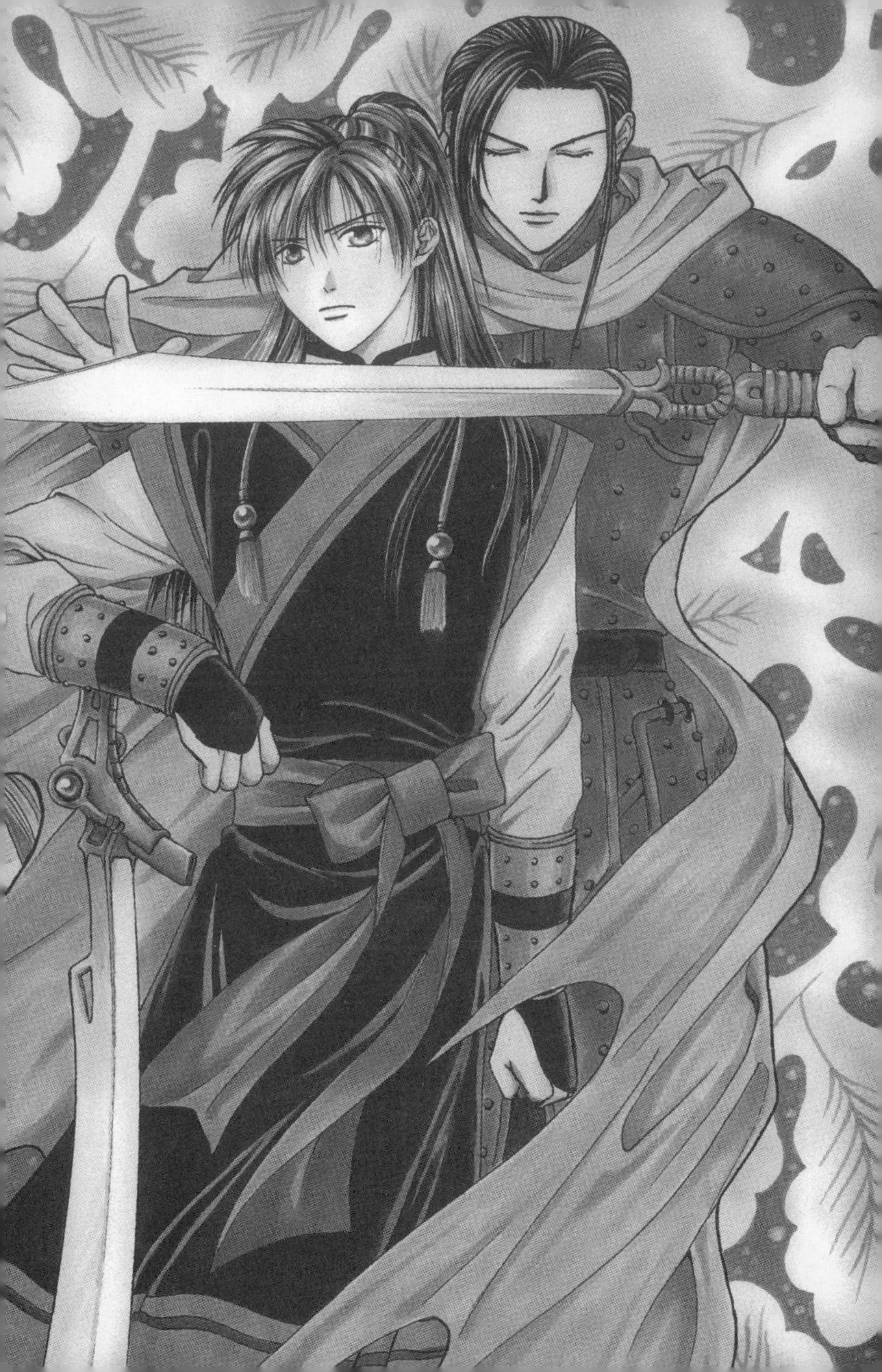

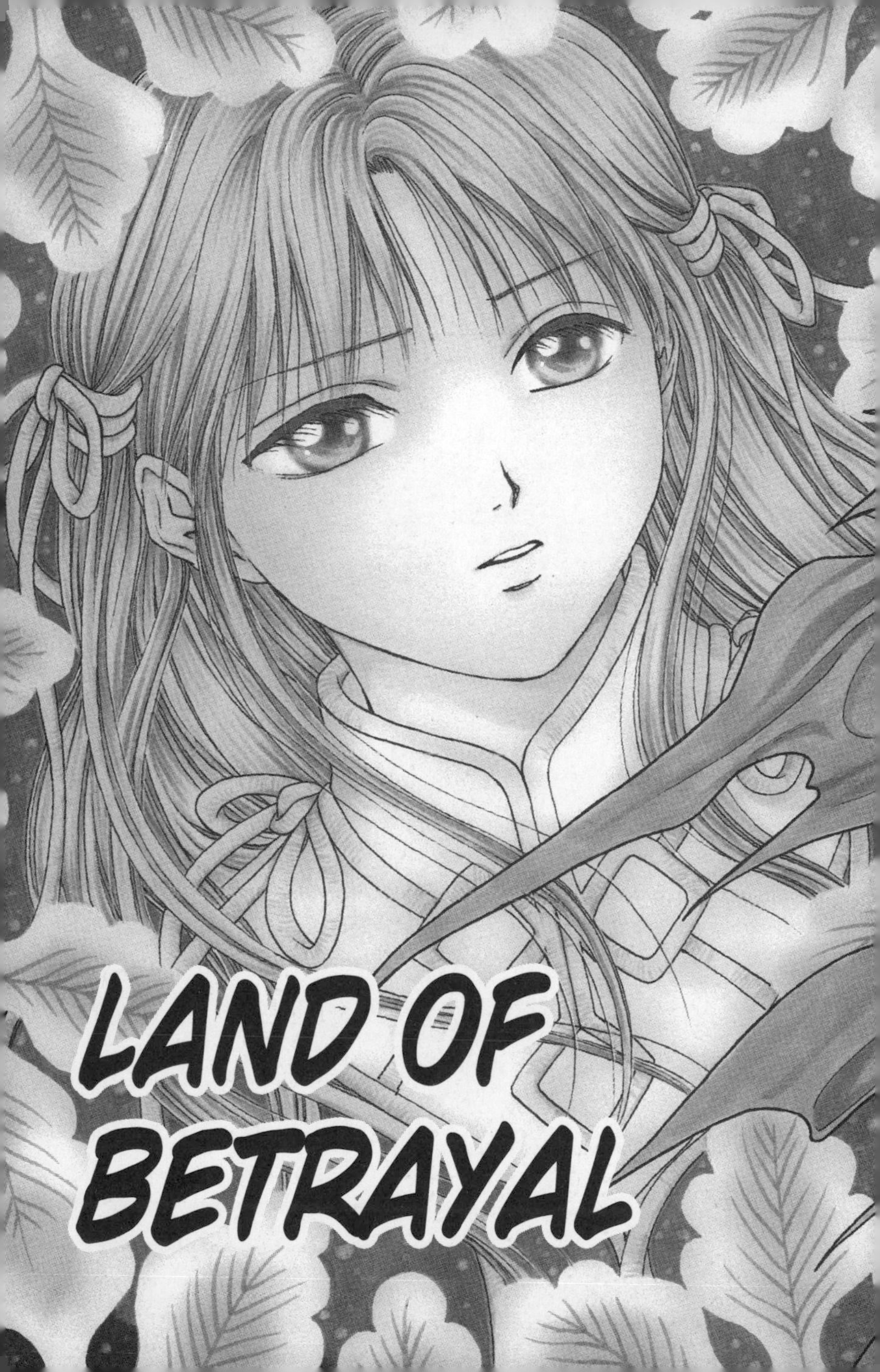
LAND OF
BETRAYAL

一

Siiiiigh... (¯A¯;

It's me, Watase. I have a fever and an upset stomach, and I'm about to collapse. I'm in so much pain that I don't know what to write. Can I even be coherent through this fever?

Anyway, **Genbu** is finally up to Volume 7. It feels weird to **still** be at Volume 7 after all this time, thanks to the publishing schedule of only two volumes per year. The pace picks up in this volume, now that all the Celestial Warriors have shown up (sort of). I'd like to wrap it up around Volume 12 if I can...We'll see what happens. The pace here is very different from the serials in *Shojo Comics*. Maybe it won't fit into 12 volumes...Well, I'll avoid thinking about the future for now. Actually, I don't even have the energy to think for the time being. (^^;) My back hurts too! (I drew 170 pages in April and May!)

I've been rambling in my blog recently, so I can't think of topics to write here. (That, and I'm tired too.)

Oh, I've received letters complaining that, because there have been so many battles, the romance part of the story has fallen by the wayside. Don't worry, it's all good. (I hope...) The romance will be back. I don't have a normal female brain, so I don't feel the need for romance in manga, but I do want Takiko and Uruki to have a proper, bittersweet love story. Even so, I **really** wanted to draw the action in this volume, so I got all worked up about it. **This** is more like my kind of story.

二

Romance always seems limited because the characters are so focused on each other. It's boring...I'd much rather write about ideals like steadfast conviction or devotion or...see, I really don't have a female brain at all. Besides, this is a fantasy. The adventure comes first.

I went out of my way to force more love scenes into the old *FY* to fit in with the tone of *Shojo Comics*. It worked out okay, since the theme for Suzaku was "love." Each of the four gods has a theme. Seiryu's theme, since Yui was the priestess, was "friendship." Genbu's is "life and death." That's exactly what this volume is about. I haven't revealed Byakko's yet, so I won't go into it. But it's not romance. (For some reason, many people seem to be under the impression that *Byakko* will be this passionate love saga. I mean, there will be some love, of course.) Whether I can do the Byakko arc depends on how *Genbu* does, or rather whether *Perfect World* can continue...If it doesn't sell, there won't be room in the current market for *Byakko*.

I **think** it'll work out...

Why am I being such a harsh realist? My brain's in a haze. How do I say this? When your gut is hurting, it takes so much out of you! I haven't had this problem in a while...and I don't have any medicine...

My head hurts!

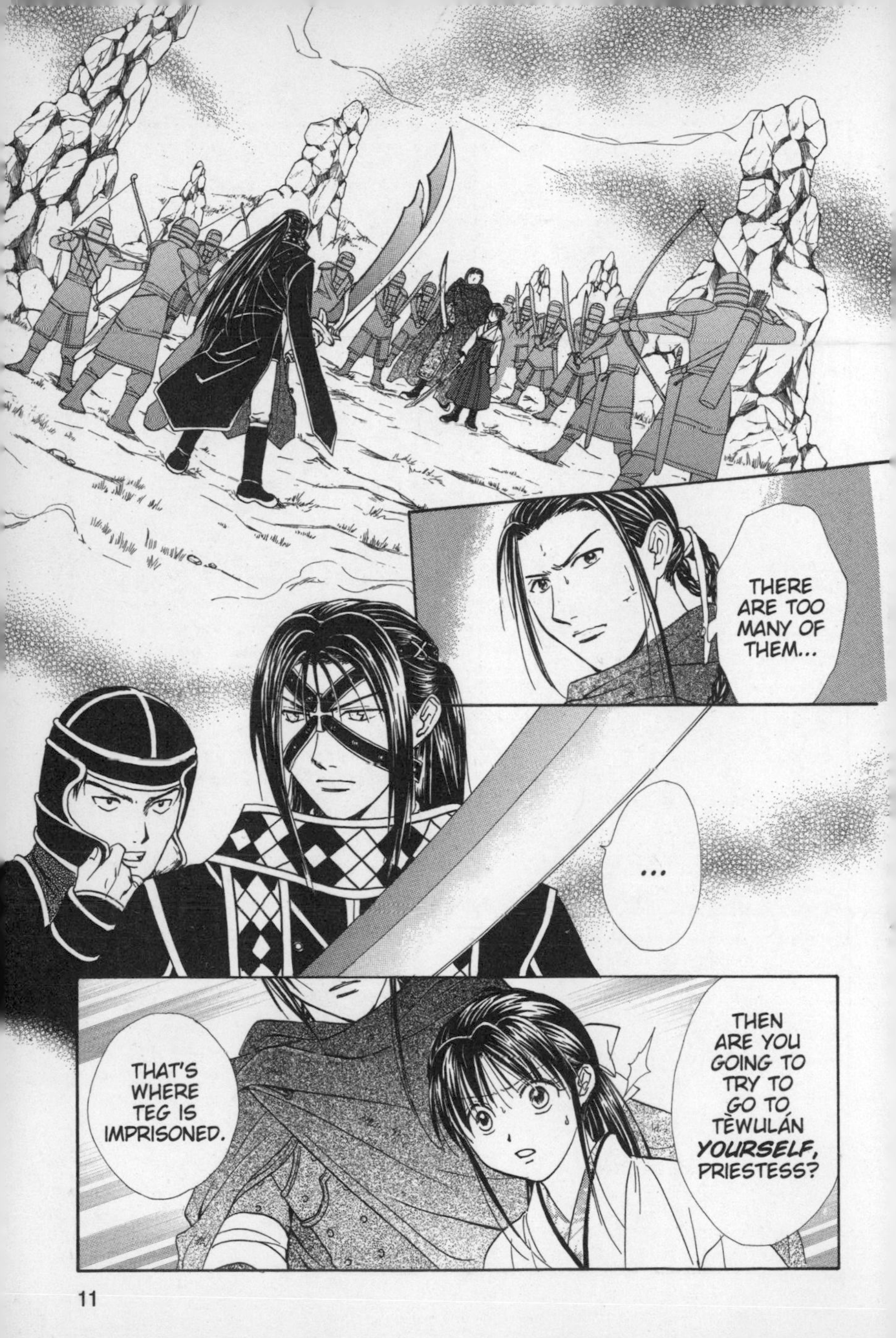
THERE ARE TOO MANY OF THEM...
...
THEN ARE YOU GOING TO TRY TO GO TO TÈWULÁN *YOURSELF*, PRIESTESS?
THAT'S WHERE TEG IS IMPRISONED.

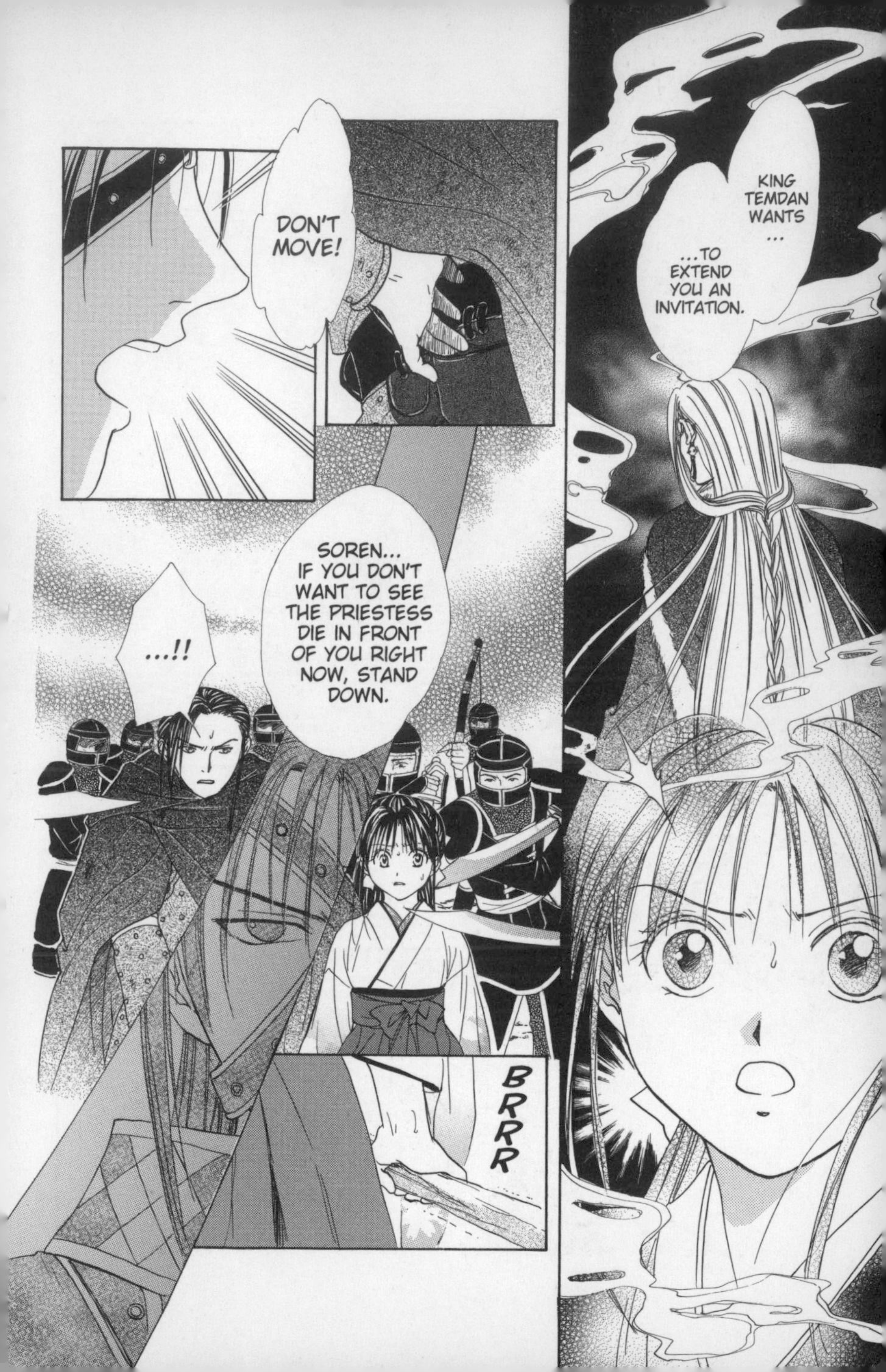
KING TEMDAN WANTS ...
...TO EXTEND YOU AN INVITATION.
DON'T MOVE!
SOREN... IF YOU DON'T WANT TO SEE THE PRIESTESS DIE IN FRONT OF YOU RIGHT NOW, STAND DOWN.
...!!
BRRR

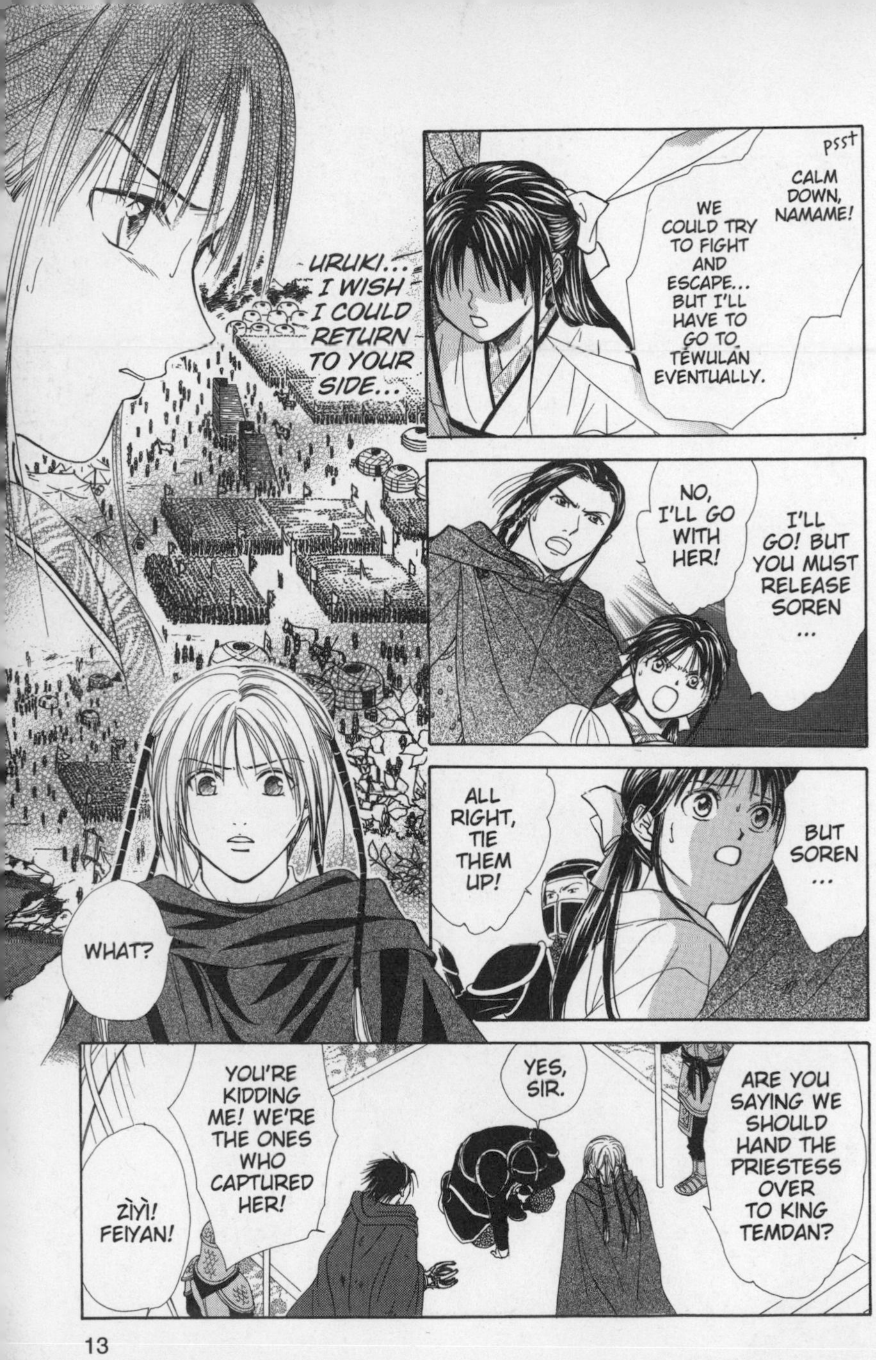
psst
CALM DOWN, NAMAME!
WE COULD TRY TO FIGHT AND ESCAPE... BUT I'LL HAVE TO GO TO TEWULAN EVENTUALLY.
I'LL GO! BUT YOU MUST RELEASE SOREN ...
NO, I'LL GO WITH HER!
BUT SOREN ...
ALL RIGHT, TIE THEM UP!
URUKI... I WISH I COULD RETURN TO YOUR SIDE...
WHAT?
ARE YOU SAYING WE SHOULD HAND THE PRIESTESS OVER TO KING TEMDAN?
YES, SIR.
YOU'RE KIDDING ME! WE'RE THE ONES WHO CAPTURED HER!
ZÌYÌ! FEIYAN!

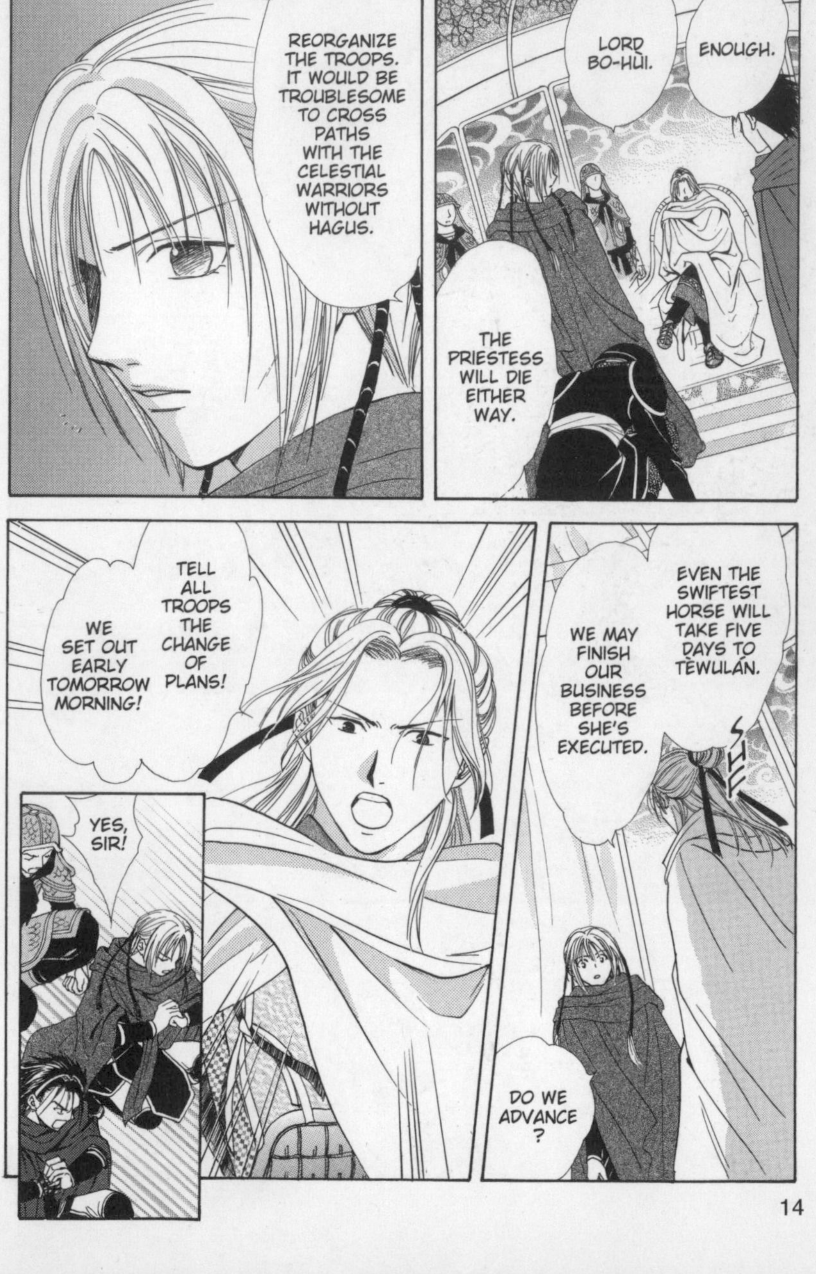
ENOUGH.
LORD BO-HUI.
THE PRIESTESS WILL DIE EITHER WAY.
REORGANIZE THE TROOPS. IT WOULD BE TROUBLESOME TO CROSS PATHS WITH THE CELESTIAL WARRIORS WITHOUT HAGUS.
EVEN THE SWIFTEST HORSE WILL TAKE FIVE DAYS TO TÈWULÁN.
WE MAY FINISH OUR BUSINESS BEFORE SHE'S EXECUTED.
SHF
DO WE ADVANCE?
TELL ALL TROOPS THE CHANGE OF PLANS!
WE SET OUT EARLY TOMORROW MORNING!
YES, SIR!

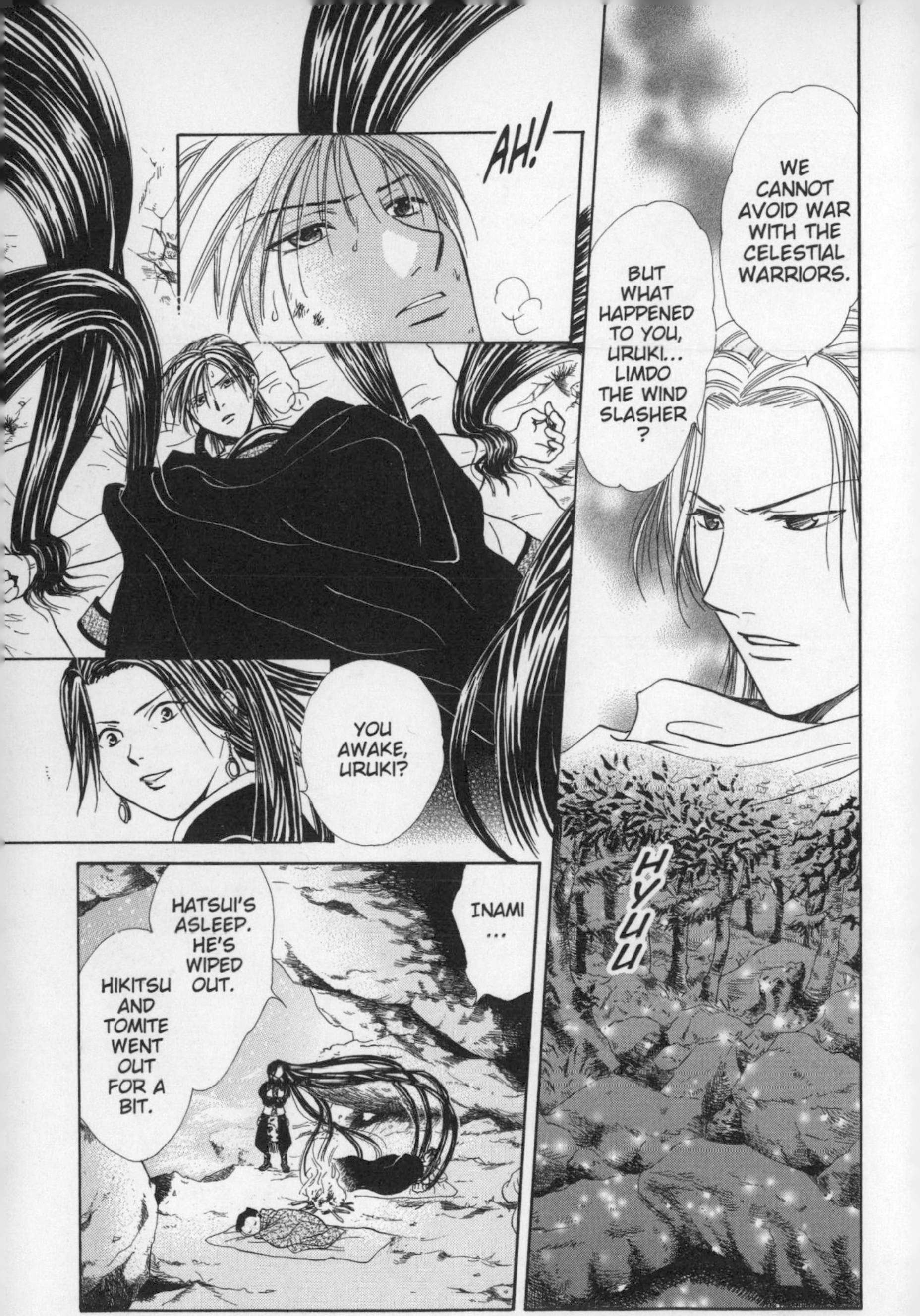
WE CANNOT AVOID WAR WITH THE CELESTIAL WARRIORS.
BUT WHAT HAPPENED TO YOU, URUKI... LIMDO THE WIND SLASHER?
AH!
YOU AWAKE, URUKI?
HYUUU
INAMI...
HATSUI'S ASLEEP. HE'S WIPED OUT.
HIKITSU AND TOMITE WENT OUT FOR A BIT.

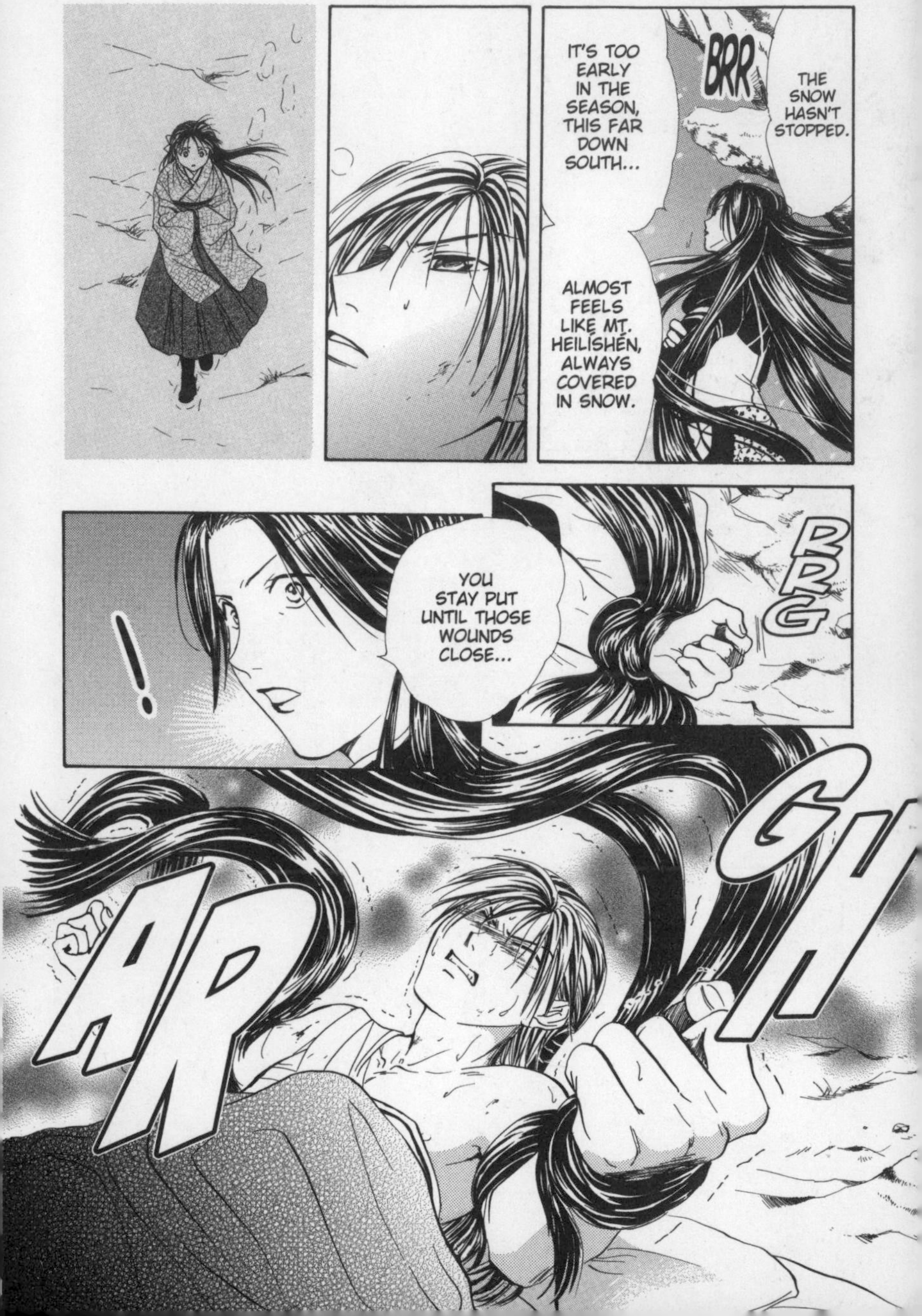
BRR
THE SNOW HASN'T STOPPED.
IT'S TOO EARLY IN THE SEASON, THIS FAR DOWN SOUTH...
ALMOST FEELS LIKE MT. HEILISHÉN, ALWAYS COVERED IN SNOW.
RRG
YOU STAY PUT UNTIL THOSE WOUNDS CLOSE...
!
ARGH

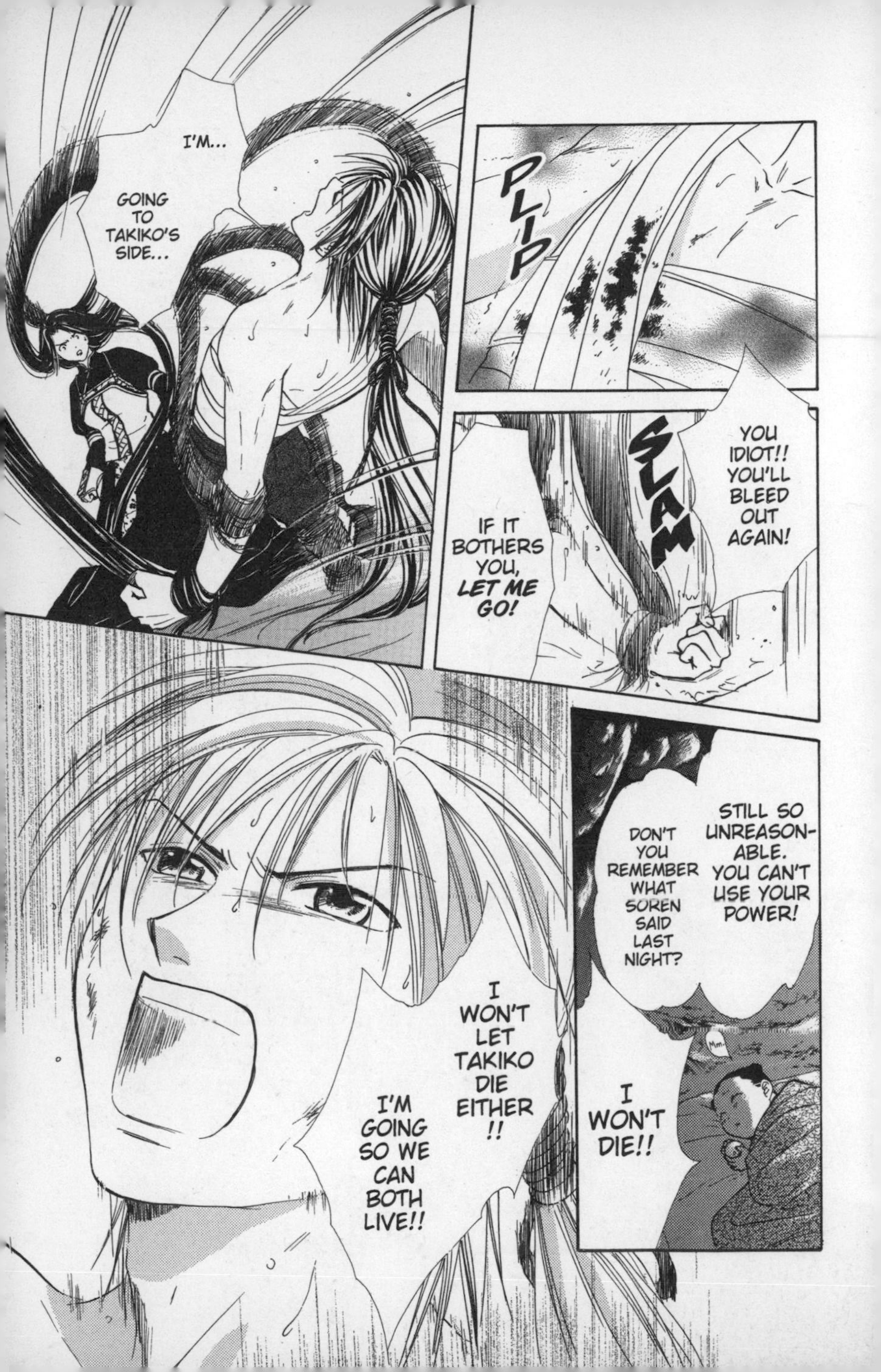
PLIP
SLAM
YOU IDIOT!! YOU'LL BLEED OUT AGAIN!
IF IT BOTHERS YOU, LET ME GO!
I'M...
GOING TO TAKIKO'S SIDE...
STILL SO UNREASON-ABLE. YOU CAN'T USE YOUR POWER!
DON'T YOU REMEMBER WHAT SOREN SAID LAST NIGHT?
Mm-
I WON'T DIE!!
I WON'T LET TAKIKO DIE EITHER!!
I'M GOING SO WE CAN BOTH LIVE!!

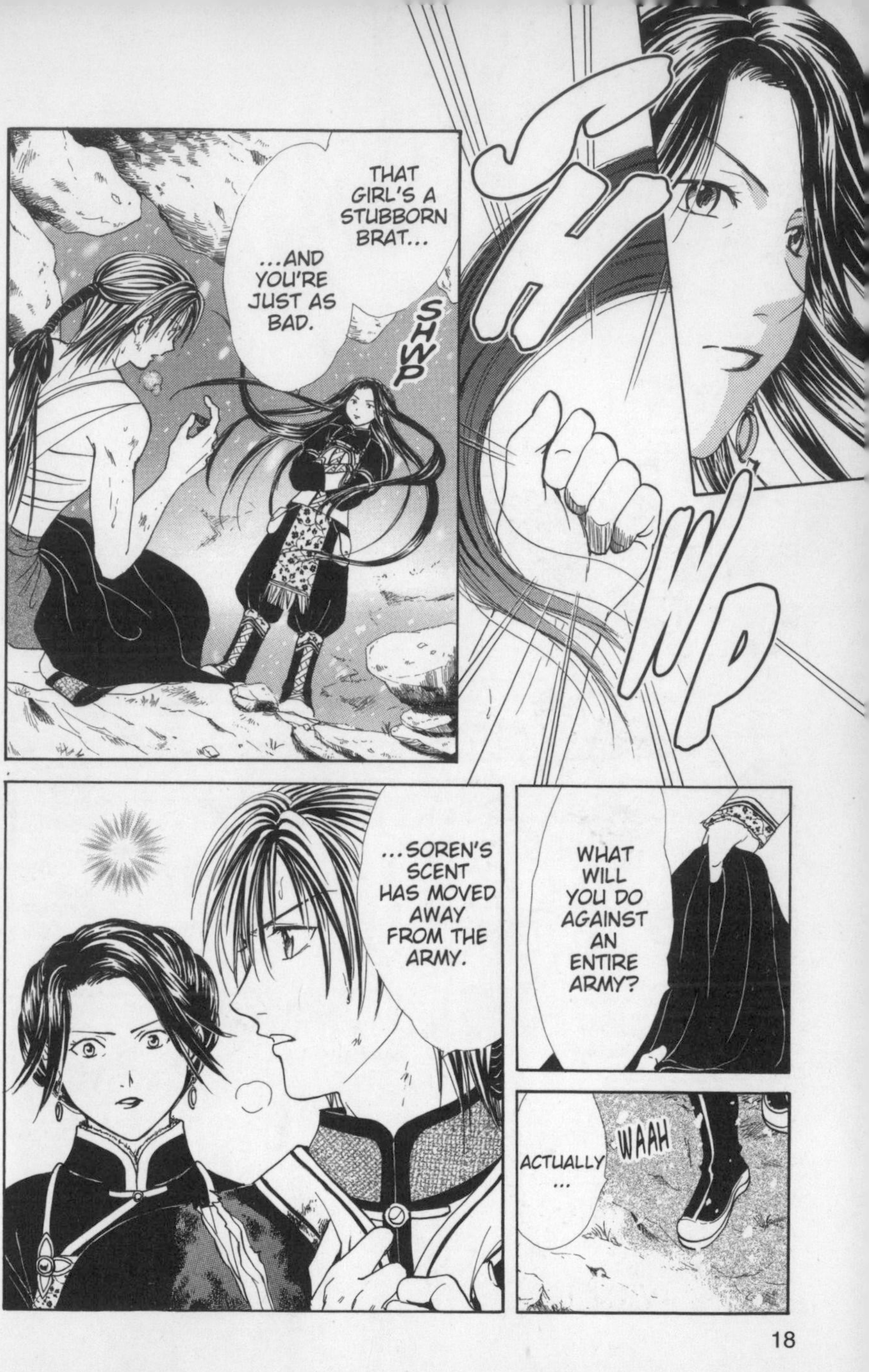
THAT GIRL'S A STUBBORN BRAT...
...AND YOU'RE JUST AS BAD.
SHWP
WHAT WILL YOU DO AGAINST AN ENTIRE ARMY?
ACTUALLY ...
WAAH
...SOREN'S SCENT HAS MOVED AWAY FROM THE ARMY.

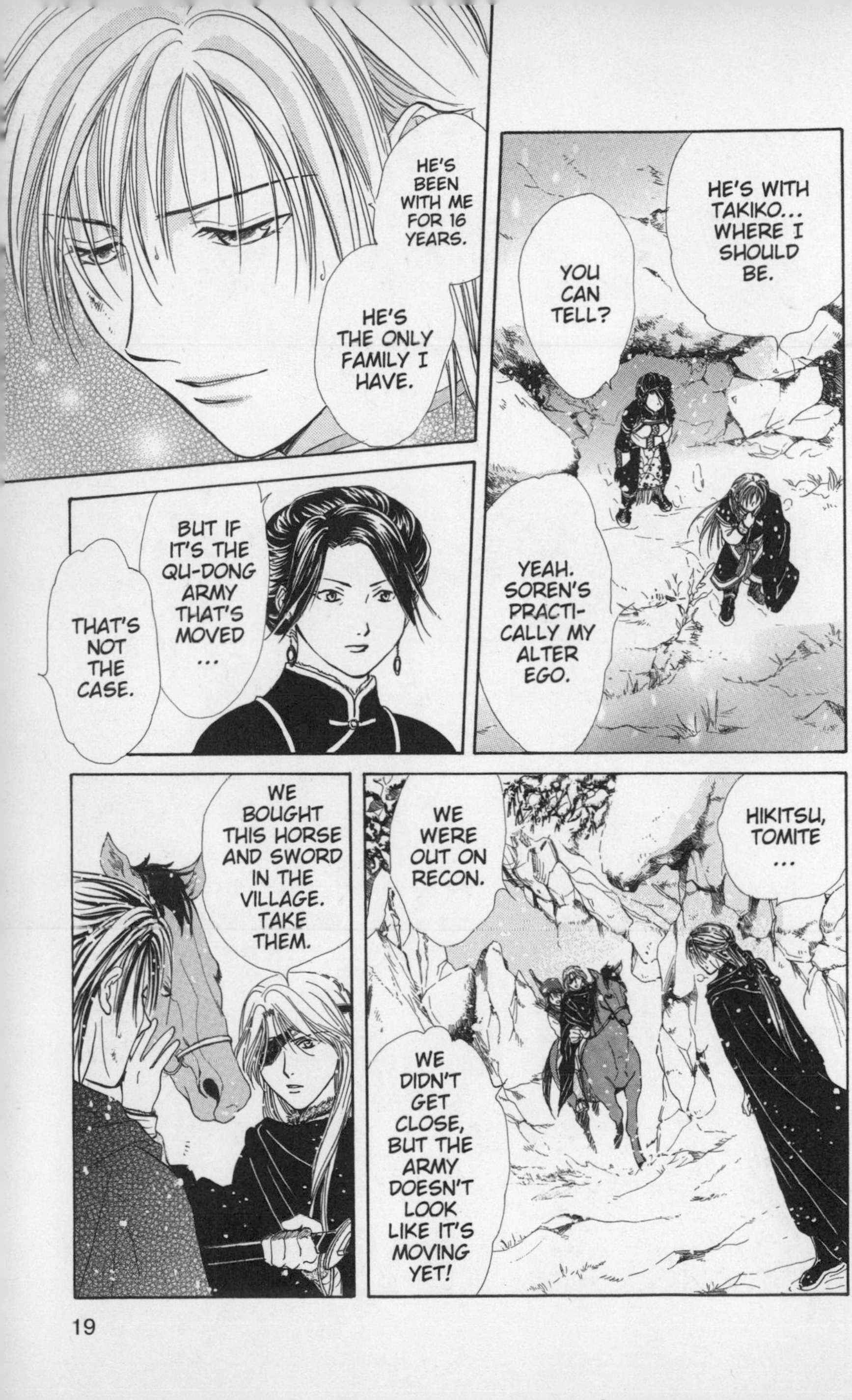
HE'S WITH TAKIKO... WHERE I SHOULD BE.
YOU CAN TELL?
YEAH. SOREN'S PRACTI-CALLY MY ALTER EGO.
HE'S BEEN WITH ME FOR 16 YEARS.
HE'S THE ONLY FAMILY I HAVE.
BUT IF IT'S THE QU-DONG ARMY THAT'S MOVED ...
THAT'S NOT THE CASE.
HIKITSU, TOMITE ...
WE WERE OUT ON RECON.
WE DIDN'T GET CLOSE, BUT THE ARMY DOESN'T LOOK LIKE IT'S MOVING YET!
WE BOUGHT THIS HORSE AND SWORD IN THE VILLAGE. TAKE THEM.

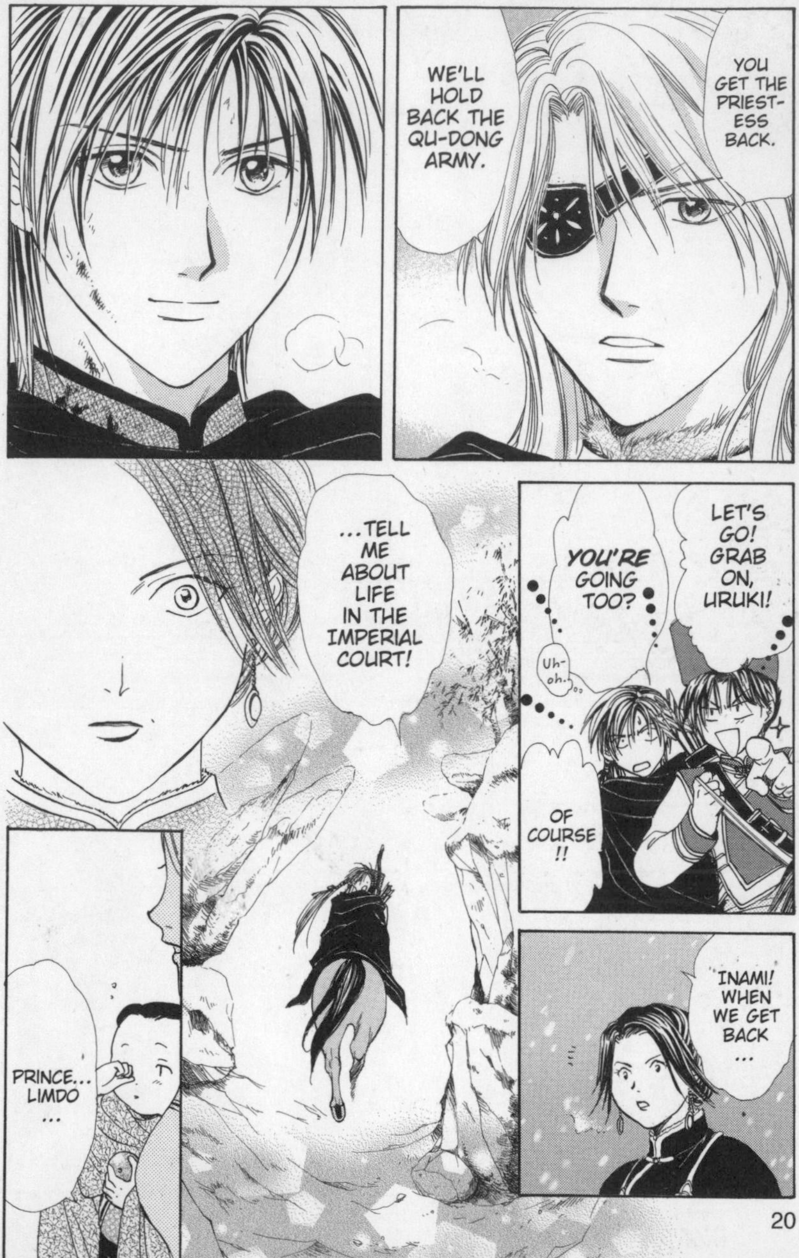
YOU GET THE PRIEST-ESS BACK.
WE'LL HOLD BACK THE QU-DONG ARMY.
LET'S GO! GRAB ON, URUKI!
YOU'RE GOING TOO?
Uh-oh...
OF COURSE!!
...TELL ME ABOUT LIFE IN THE IMPERIAL COURT!
INAMI! WHEN WE GET BACK...
PRINCE... LIMDO...

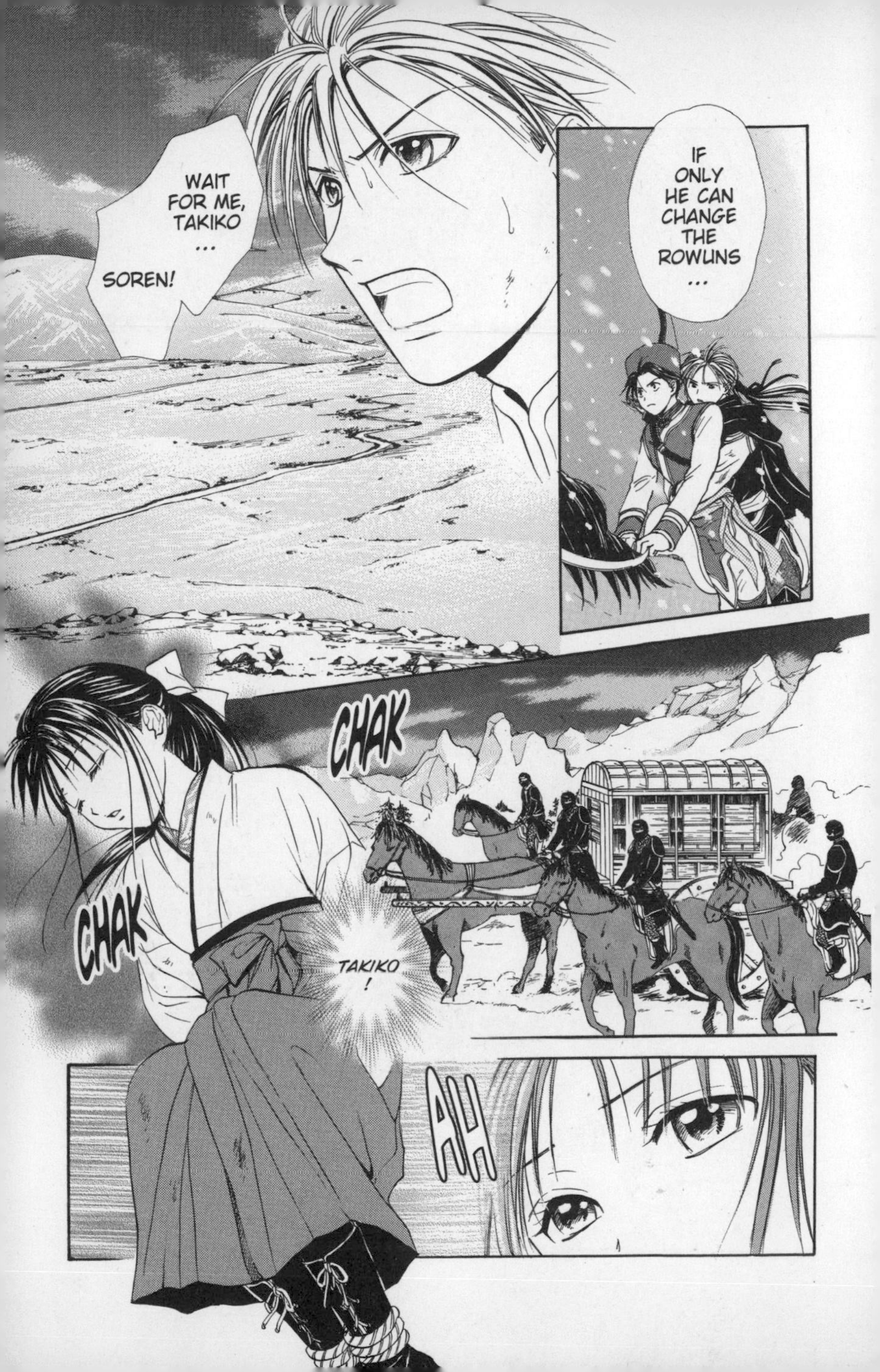
IF ONLY HE CAN CHANGE THE ROWUNS ...
WAIT FOR ME, TAKIKO ...
SOREN!
CHAK
CHAK
TAKIKO !
AH

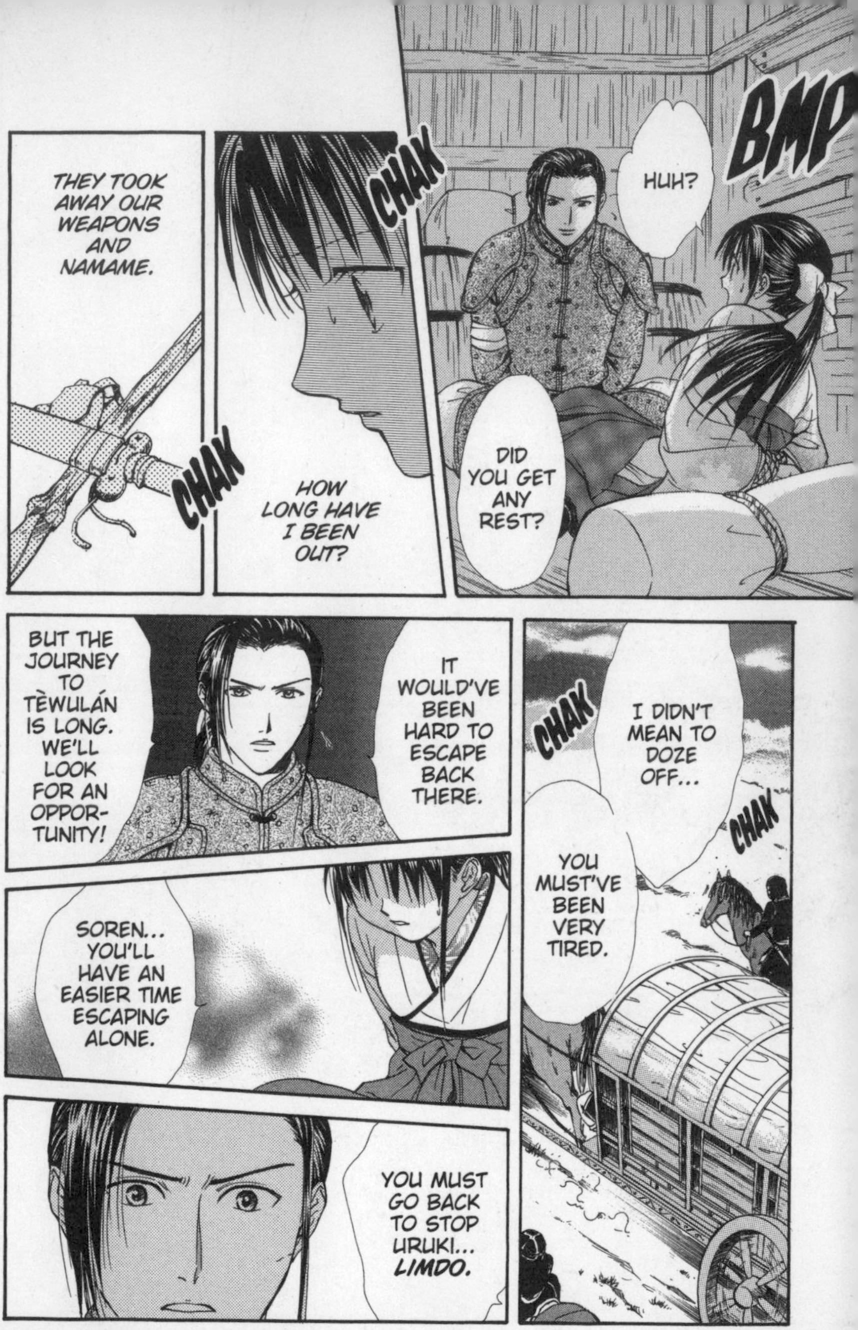
BMP
HUH?
DID YOU GET ANY REST?
CHAK
HOW LONG HAVE I BEEN OUT?
THEY TOOK AWAY OUR WEAPONS AND NAMAME.
CHAK
CHAK
I DIDN'T MEAN TO DOZE OFF...
CHAK
YOU MUST'VE BEEN VERY TIRED.
IT WOULD'VE BEEN HARD TO ESCAPE BACK THERE.
BUT THE JOURNEY TO TÈWULÁN IS LONG. WE'LL LOOK FOR AN OPPOR-TUNITY!
SOREN... YOU'LL HAVE AN EASIER TIME ESCAPING ALONE.
YOU MUST GO BACK TO STOP URUKI... ***LIMDO.***

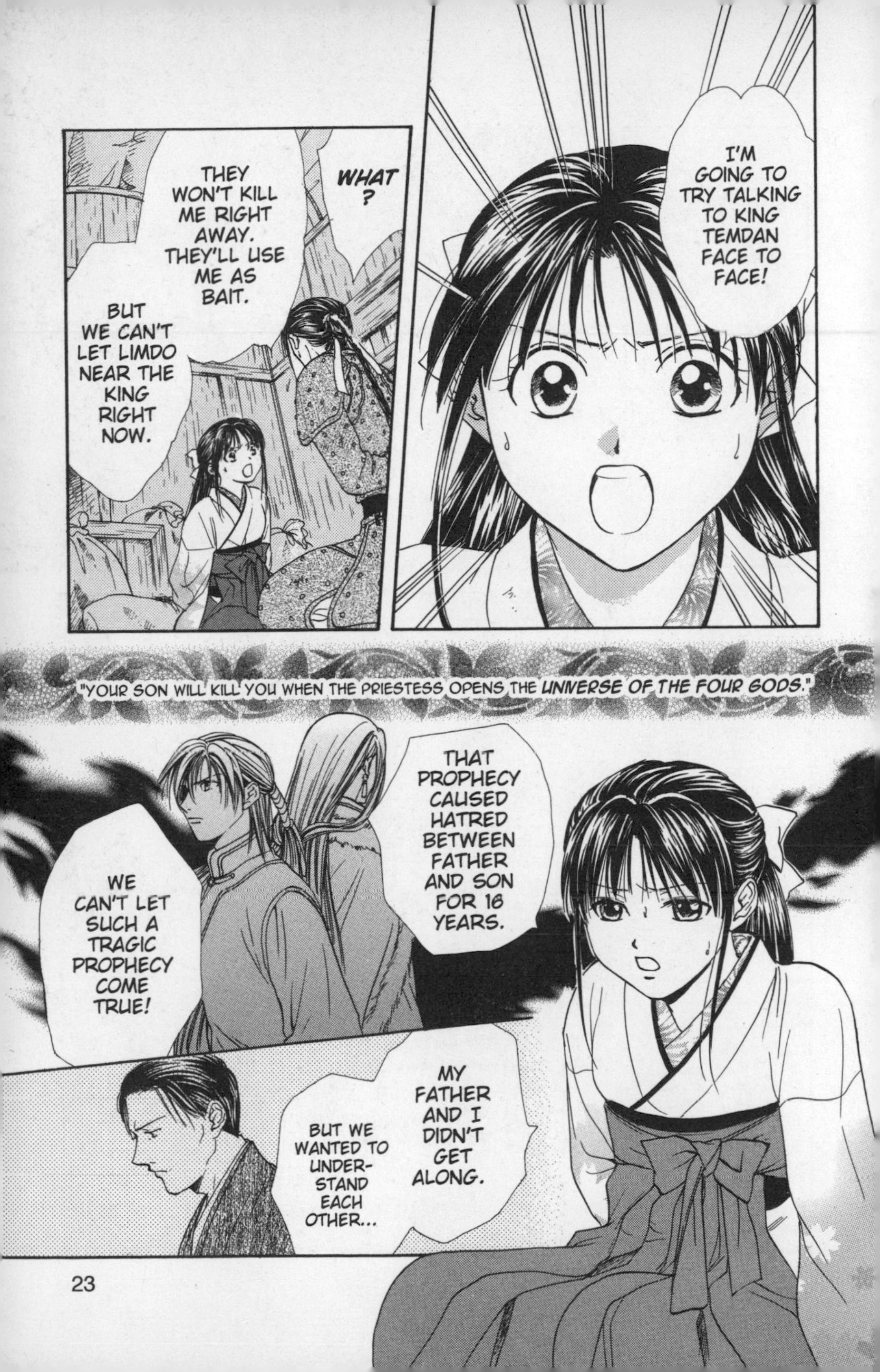
I'M GOING TO TRY TALKING TO KING TEMDAN FACE TO FACE!
WHAT?
THEY WON'T KILL ME RIGHT AWAY. THEY'LL USE ME AS BAIT.
BUT WE CAN'T LET LIMDO NEAR THE KING RIGHT NOW.
"YOUR SON WILL KILL YOU WHEN THE PRIESTESS OPENS THE *UNIVERSE OF THE FOUR GODS*."
THAT PROPHECY CAUSED HATRED BETWEEN FATHER AND SON FOR 16 YEARS.
WE CAN'T LET SUCH A TRAGIC PROPHECY COME TRUE!
MY FATHER AND I DIDN'T GET ALONG.
BUT WE WANTED TO UNDER-STAND EACH OTHER...

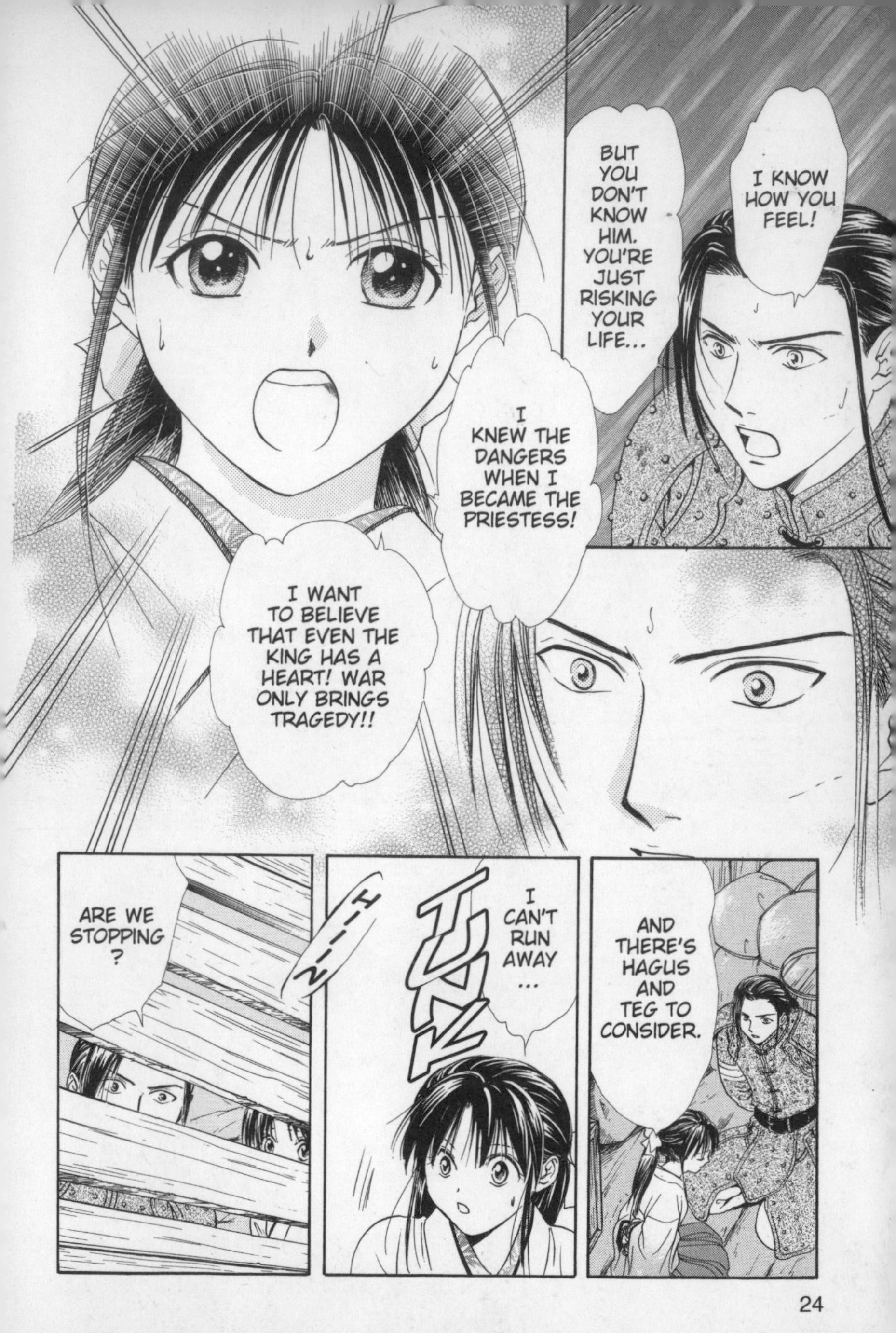
I KNOW HOW YOU FEEL!
BUT YOU DON'T KNOW HIM. YOU'RE JUST RISKING YOUR LIFE...
I KNEW THE DANGERS WHEN I BECAME THE PRIESTESS!
I WANT TO BELIEVE THAT EVEN THE KING HAS A HEART! WAR ONLY BRINGS TRAGEDY!!
AND THERE'S HAGUS AND TEG TO CONSIDER.
I CAN'T RUN AWAY...
TUN
HI-I-IN
ARE WE STOPPING?

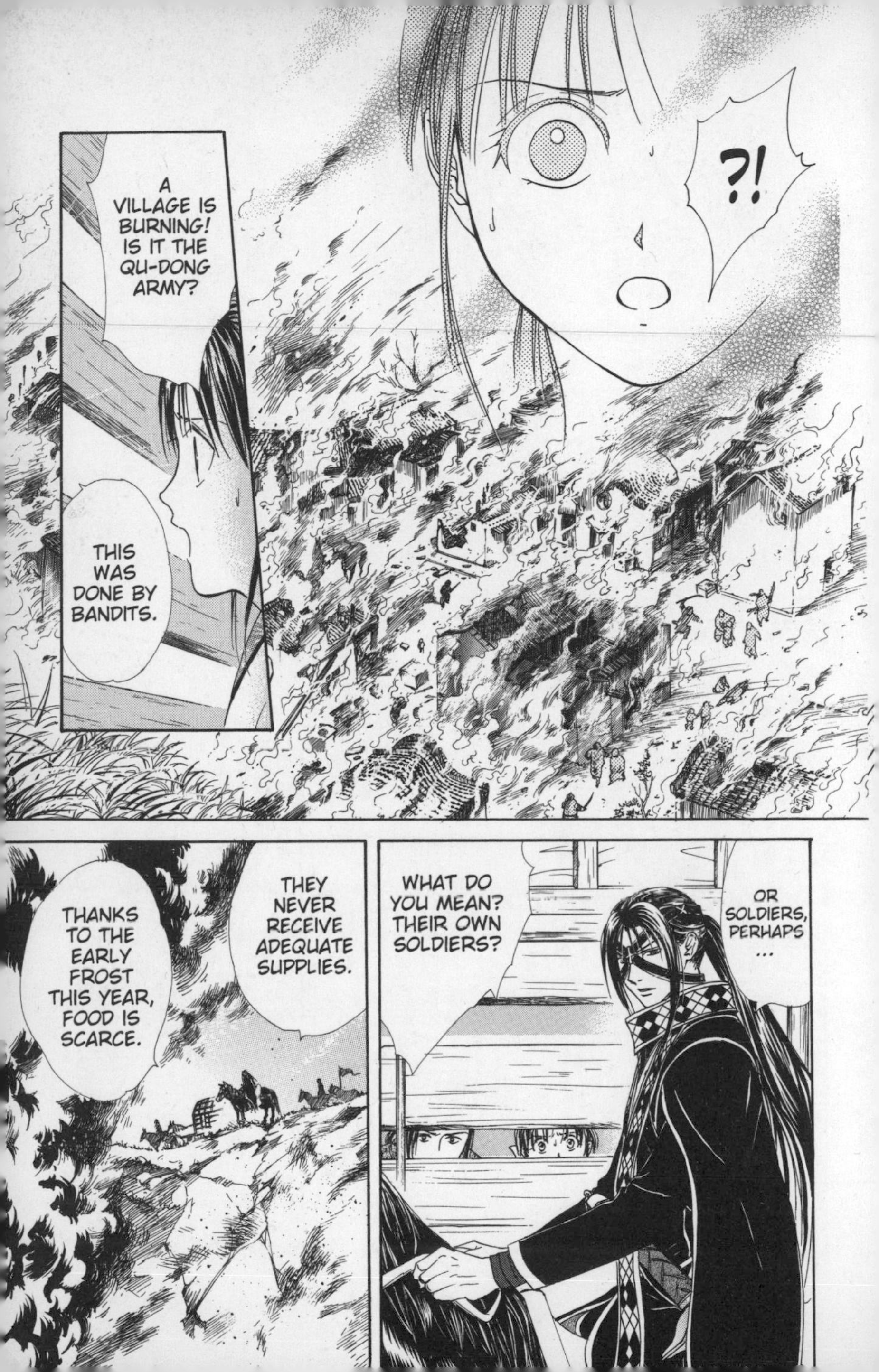
?!
A VILLAGE IS BURNING! IS IT THE QU-DONG ARMY?
THIS WAS DONE BY BANDITS.
OR SOLDIERS, PERHAPS ...
WHAT DO YOU MEAN? THEIR OWN SOLDIERS?
THEY NEVER RECEIVE ADEQUATE SUPPLIES.
THANKS TO THE EARLY FROST THIS YEAR, FOOD IS SCARCE.

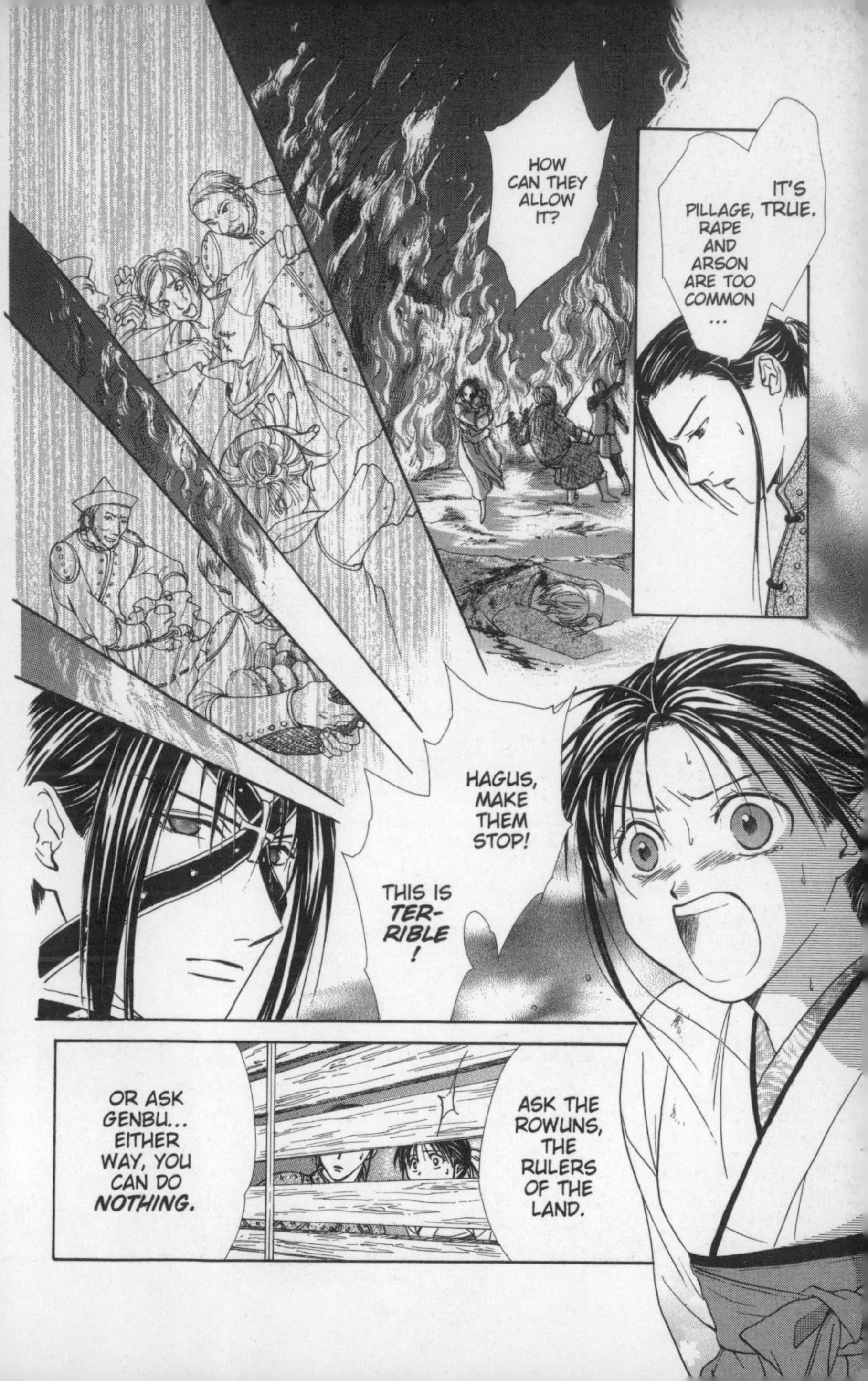
HOW CAN THEY ALLOW IT?
IT'S PILLAGE, TRUE. RAPE AND ARSON ARE TOO COMMON ...
HAGUS, MAKE THEM STOP!
THIS IS *TER-RIBLE*!
ASK THE ROWUNS, THE RULERS OF THE LAND.
OR ASK GENBU... EITHER WAY, YOU CAN DO *NOTHING*.

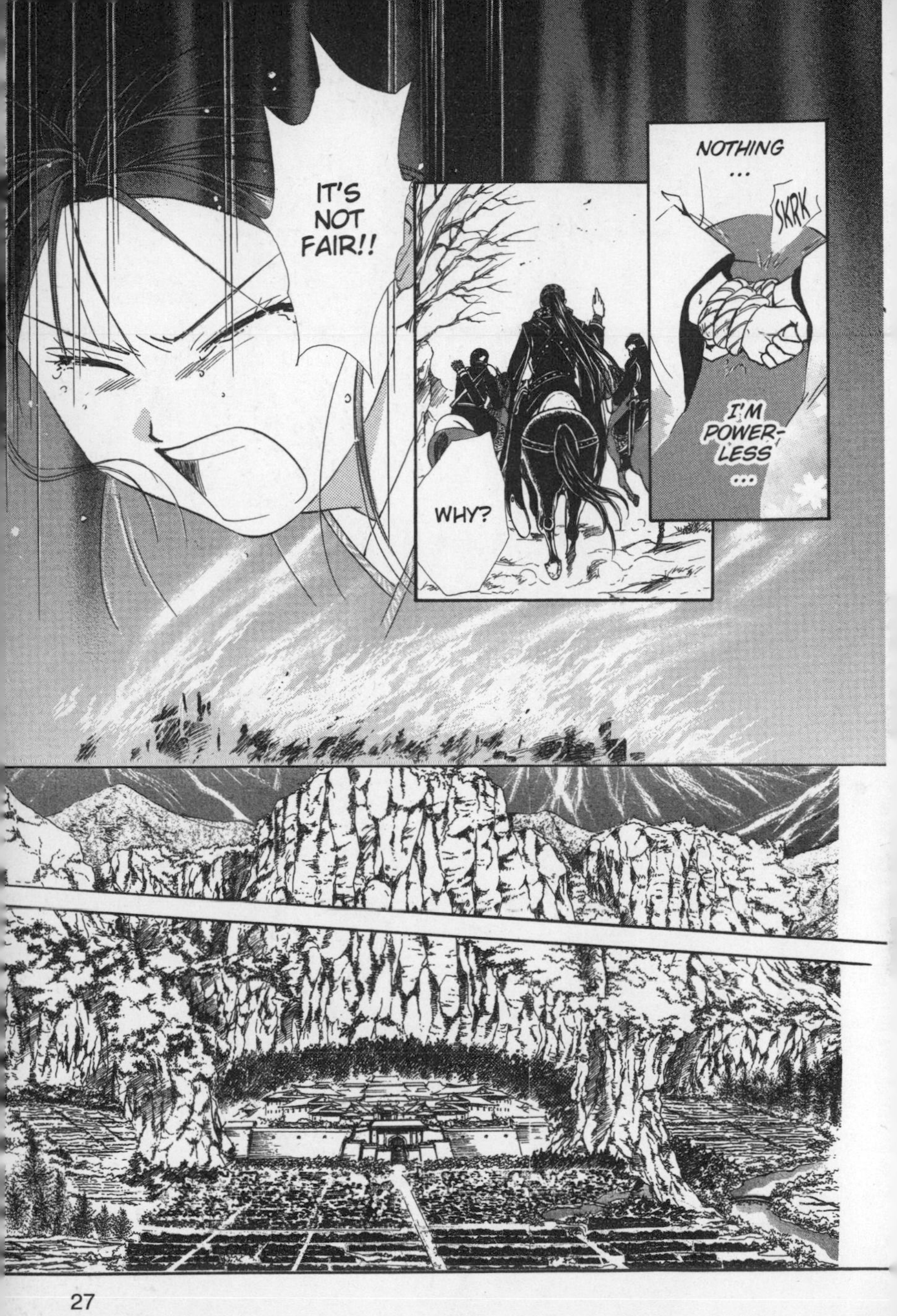
NOTHING ...
SKRK
I'M POWERLESS ...
WHY?
IT'S NOT FAIR!!

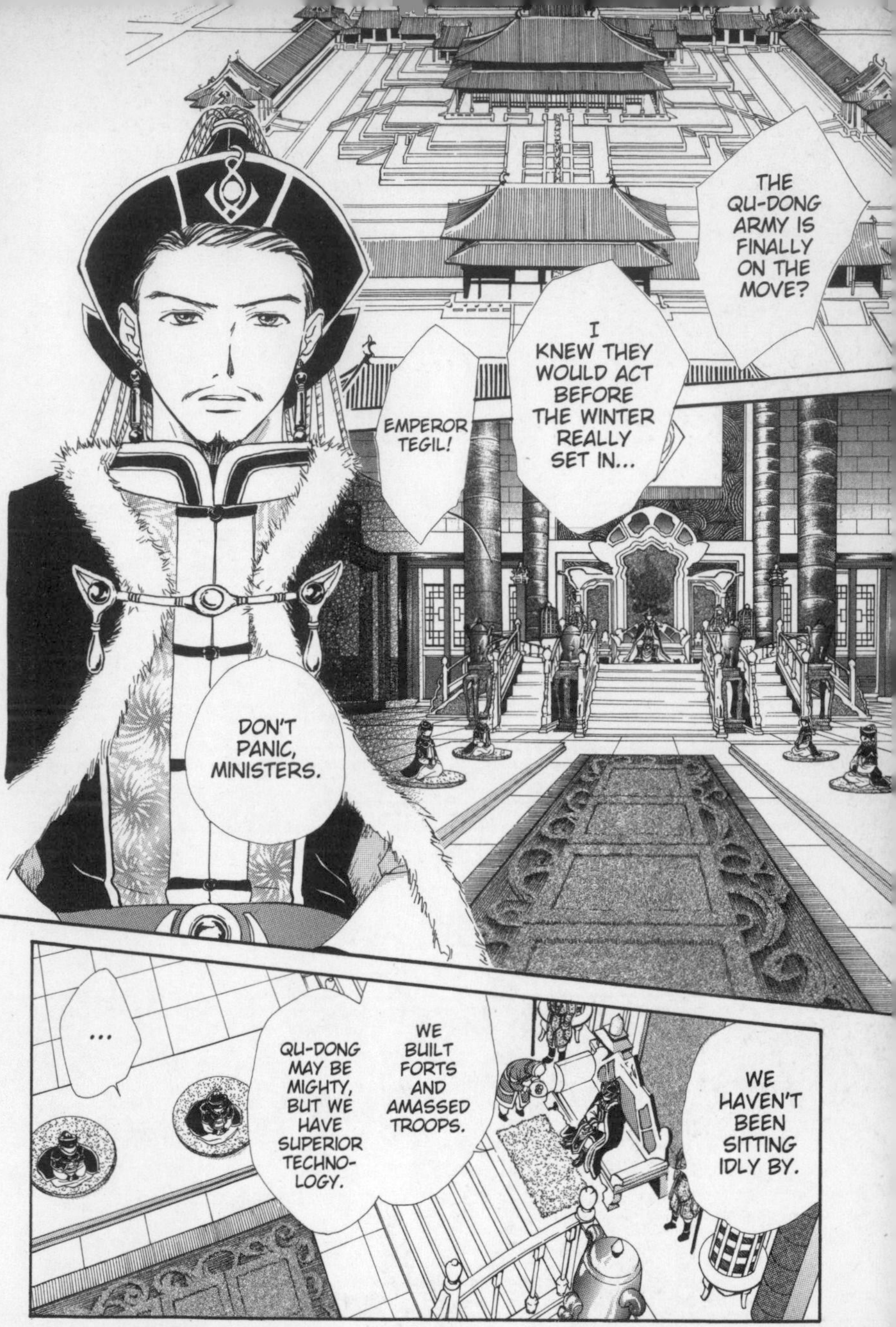
THE QU-DONG ARMY IS FINALLY ON THE MOVE?
I KNEW THEY WOULD ACT BEFORE THE WINTER REALLY SET IN...
EMPEROR TEGIL!
DON'T PANIC, MINISTERS.
WE HAVEN'T BEEN SITTING IDLY BY.
WE BUILT FORTS AND AMASSED TROOPS.
QU-DONG MAY BE MIGHTY, BUT WE HAVE SUPERIOR TECHNO-LOGY.
...

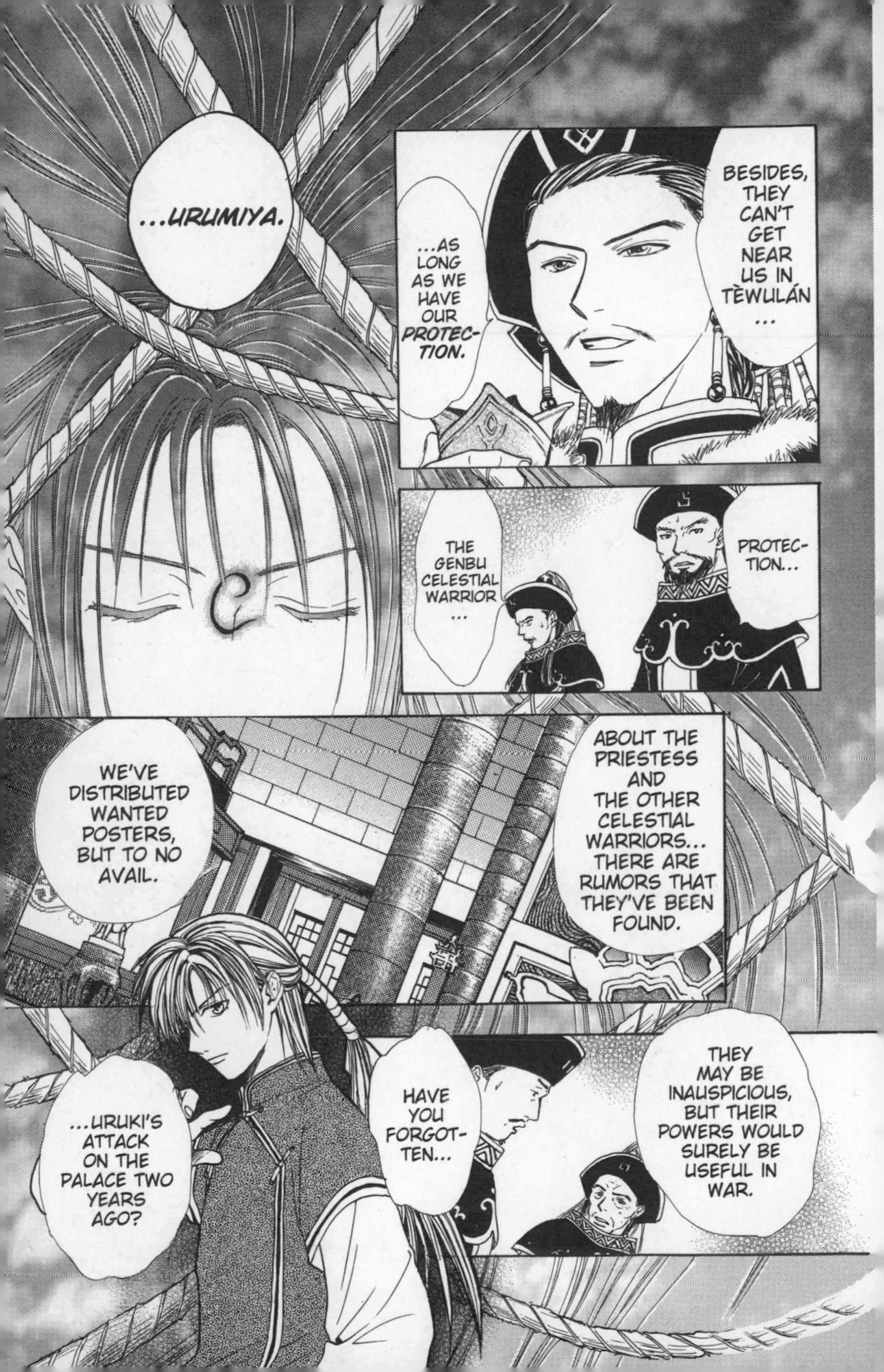
BESIDES, THEY CAN'T GET NEAR US IN TÈWULÁN...
...AS LONG AS WE HAVE OUR PROTECTION.
PROTECTION...
THE GENBU CELESTIAL WARRIOR...
...URUMIYA.
ABOUT THE PRIESTESS AND THE OTHER CELESTIAL WARRIORS... THERE ARE RUMORS THAT THEY'VE BEEN FOUND.
WE'VE DISTRIBUTED WANTED POSTERS, BUT TO NO AVAIL.
THEY MAY BE INAUSPICIOUS, BUT THEIR POWERS WOULD SURELY BE USEFUL IN WAR.
HAVE YOU FORGOTTEN...
...URUKI'S ATTACK ON THE PALACE TWO YEARS AGO?

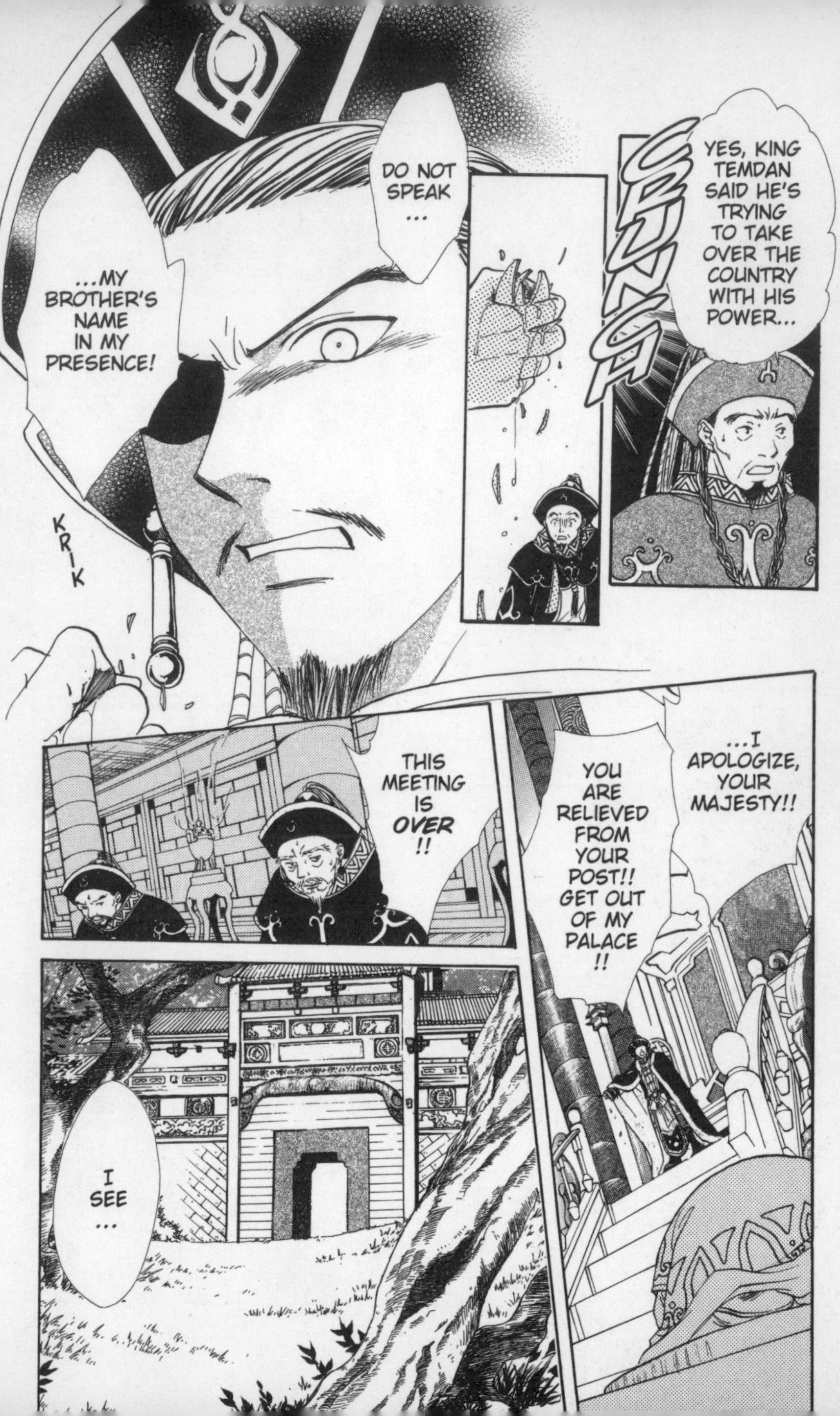
YES, KING TEMDAN SAID HE'S TRYING TO TAKE OVER THE COUNTRY WITH HIS POWER...
DO NOT SPEAK...
...MY BROTHER'S NAME IN MY PRESENCE!
KRIK
...I APOLOGIZE, YOUR MAJESTY!!
YOU ARE RELIEVED FROM YOUR POST!! GET OUT OF MY PALACE!!
THIS MEETING IS OVER!!
I SEE...

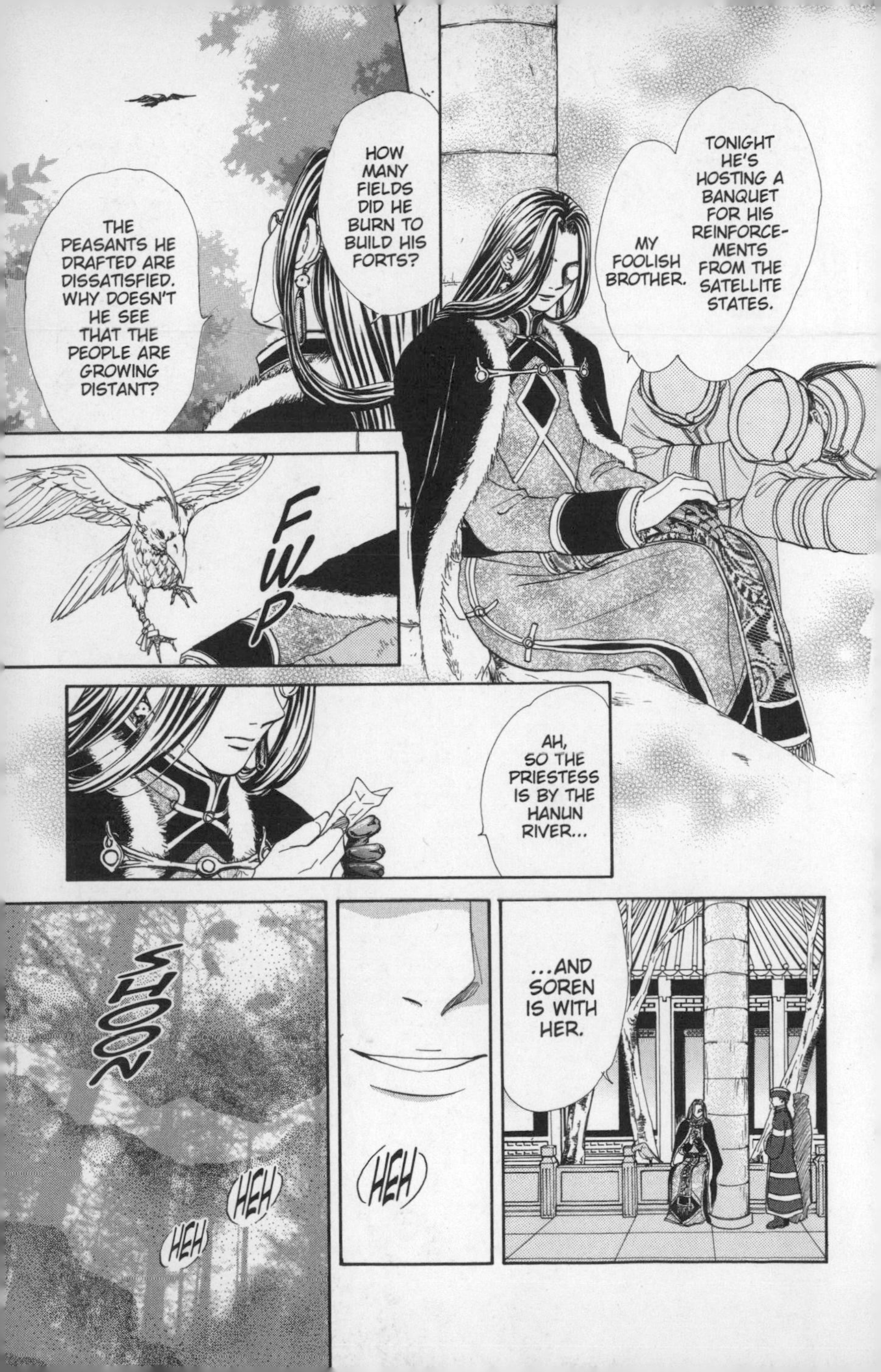
TONIGHT HE'S HOSTING A BANQUET FOR HIS REINFORCEMENTS FROM THE SATELLITE STATES.
MY FOOLISH BROTHER.
HOW MANY FIELDS DID HE BURN TO BUILD HIS FORTS?
THE PEASANTS HE DRAFTED ARE DISSATISFIED. WHY DOESN'T HE SEE THAT THE PEOPLE ARE GROWING DISTANT?
FWP
AH, SO THE PRIESTESS IS BY THE HANUN RIVER...
...AND SOREN IS WITH HER.
HEH
SHOON
HEH
HEH

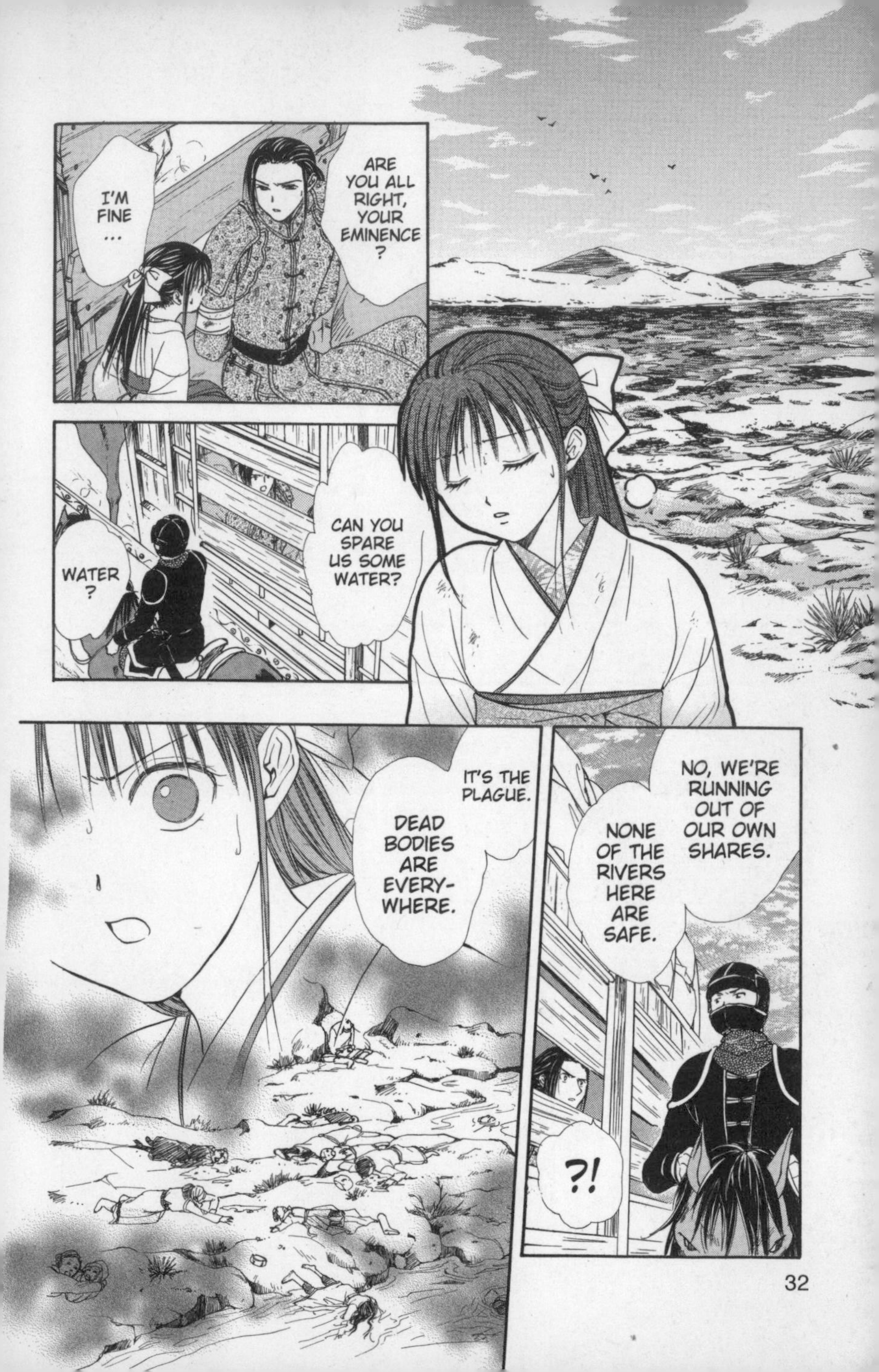
ARE YOU ALL RIGHT, YOUR EMINENCE?
I'M FINE...
CAN YOU SPARE US SOME WATER?
WATER?
NO, WE'RE RUNNING OUT OF OUR OWN SHARES.
NONE OF THE RIVERS HERE ARE SAFE.
?!
IT'S THE PLAGUE.
DEAD BODIES ARE EVERYWHERE.
...

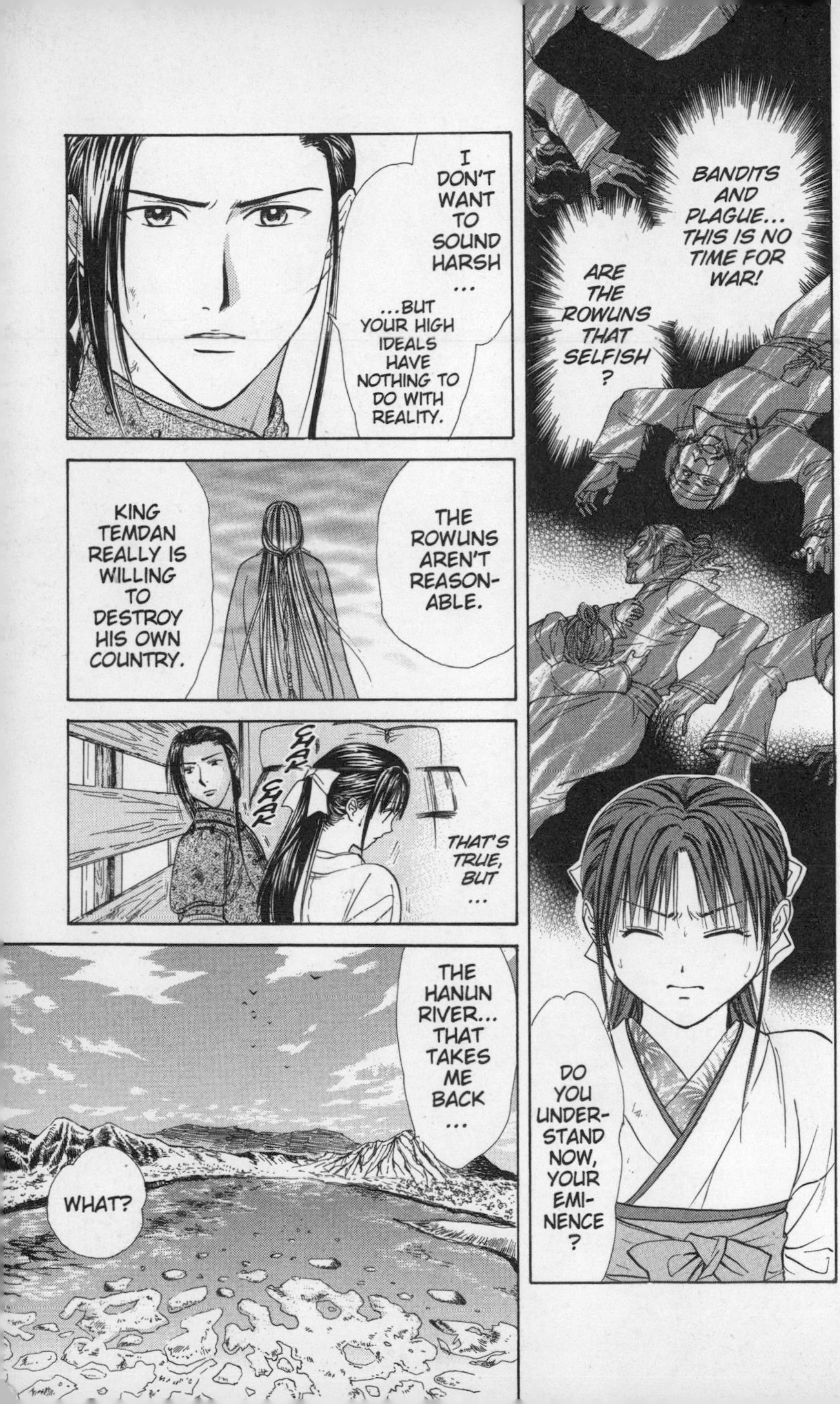
BANDITS AND PLAGUE... THIS IS NO TIME FOR WAR!
ARE THE ROWUNS THAT SELFISH?
DO YOU UNDER-STAND NOW, YOUR EMI-NENCE?
I DON'T WANT TO SOUND HARSH...
...BUT YOUR HIGH IDEALS HAVE NOTHING TO DO WITH REALITY.
THE ROWUNS AREN'T REASON-ABLE.
KING TEMDAN REALLY IS WILLING TO DESTROY HIS OWN COUNTRY.
CHAK CHAK
THAT'S TRUE, BUT...
THE HANUN RIVER... THAT TAKES ME BACK...
WHAT?

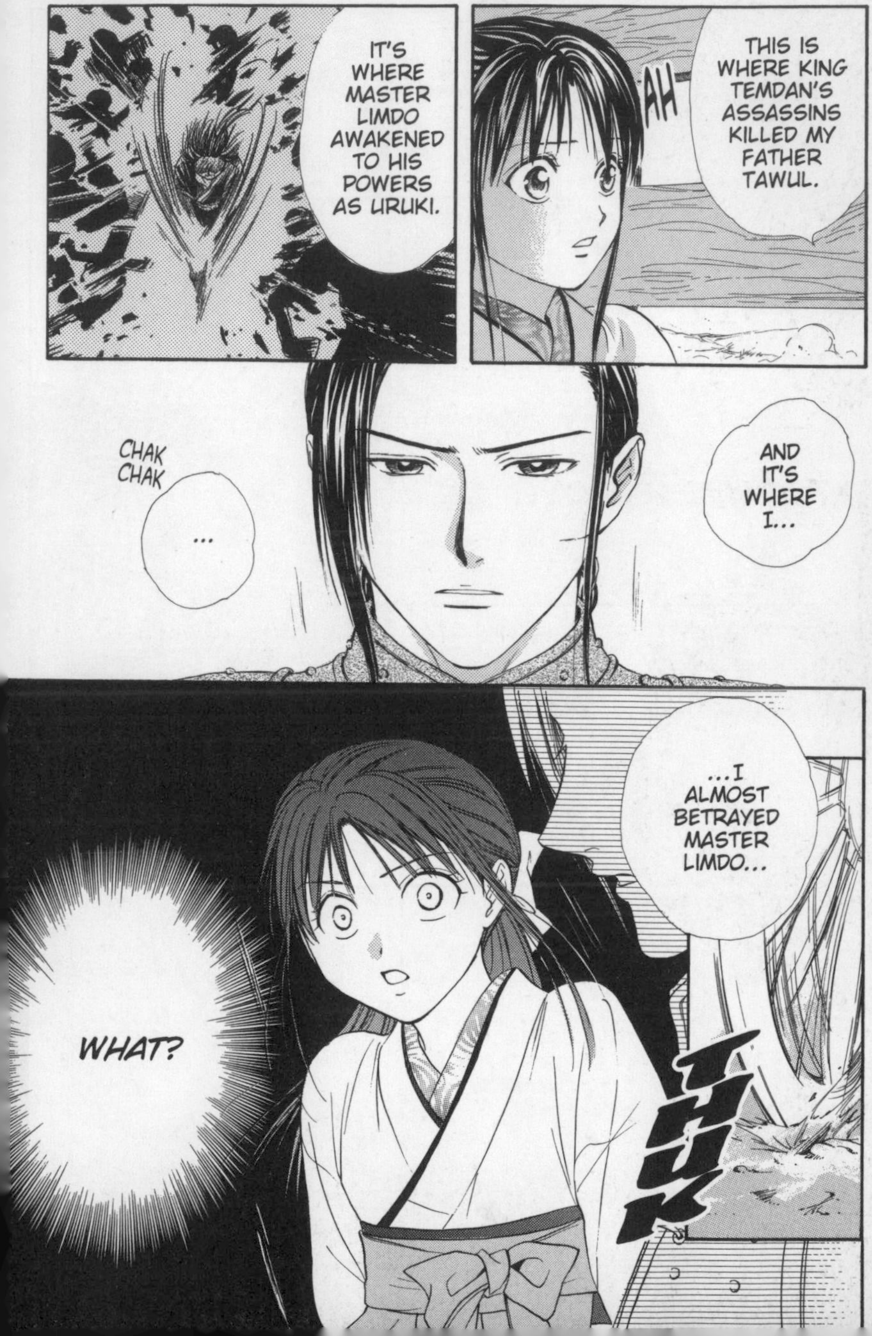
AH
THIS IS WHERE KING TEMDAN'S ASSASSINS KILLED MY FATHER TAWUL.
IT'S WHERE MASTER LIMDO AWAKENED TO HIS POWERS AS URUKI.
AND IT'S WHERE I...
CHAK CHAK
...
...I ALMOST BETRAYED MASTER LIMDO...
HUK
WHAT?

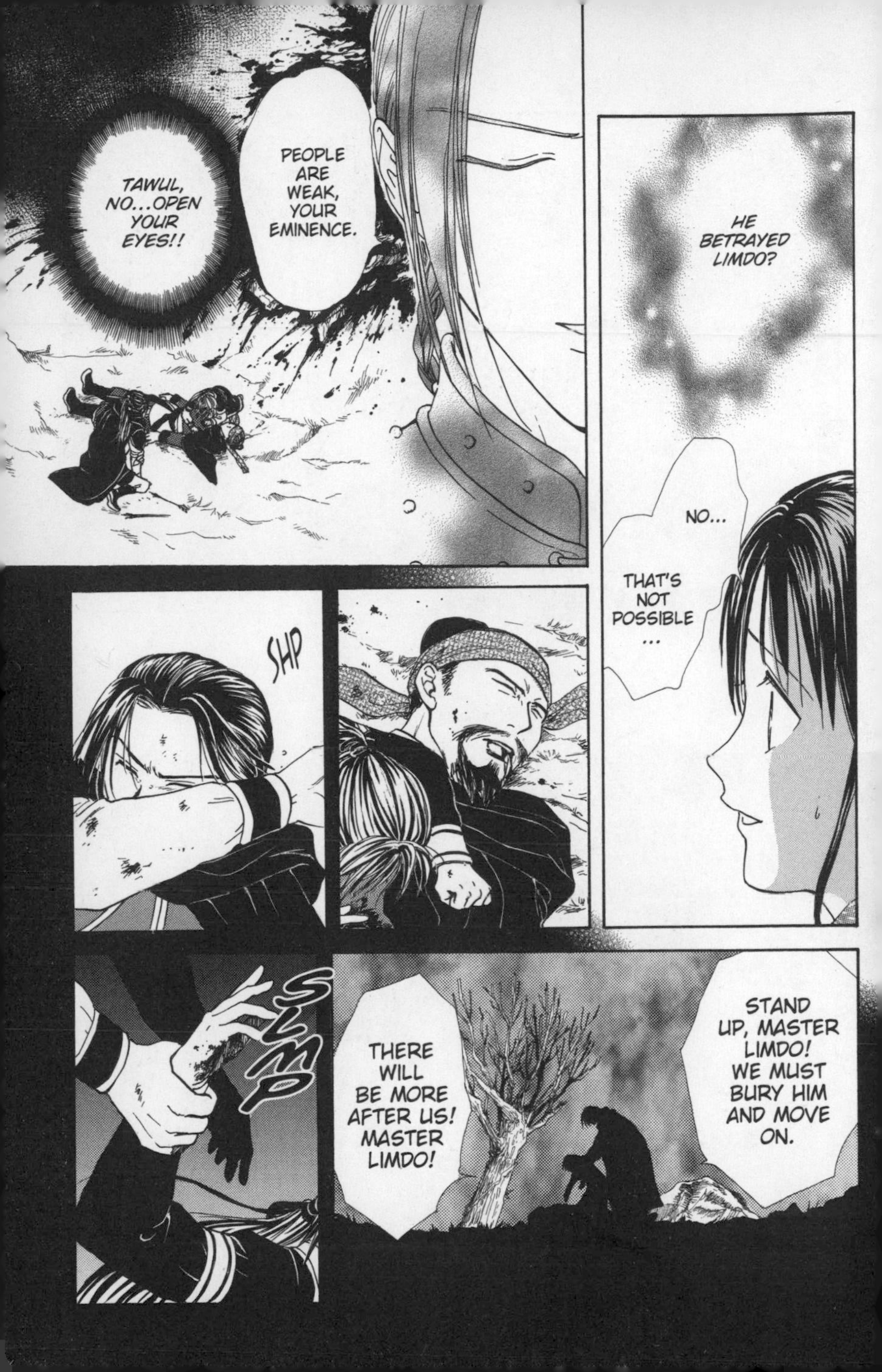
PEOPLE ARE WEAK, YOUR EMINENCE.
TAWUL, NO...OPEN YOUR EYES!!
HE BETRAYED LIMDO?
NO...
THAT'S NOT POSSIBLE ...
SHP
STAND UP, MASTER LIMDO! WE MUST BURY HIM AND MOVE ON.
THERE WILL BE MORE AFTER US! MASTER LIMDO!
SLMP

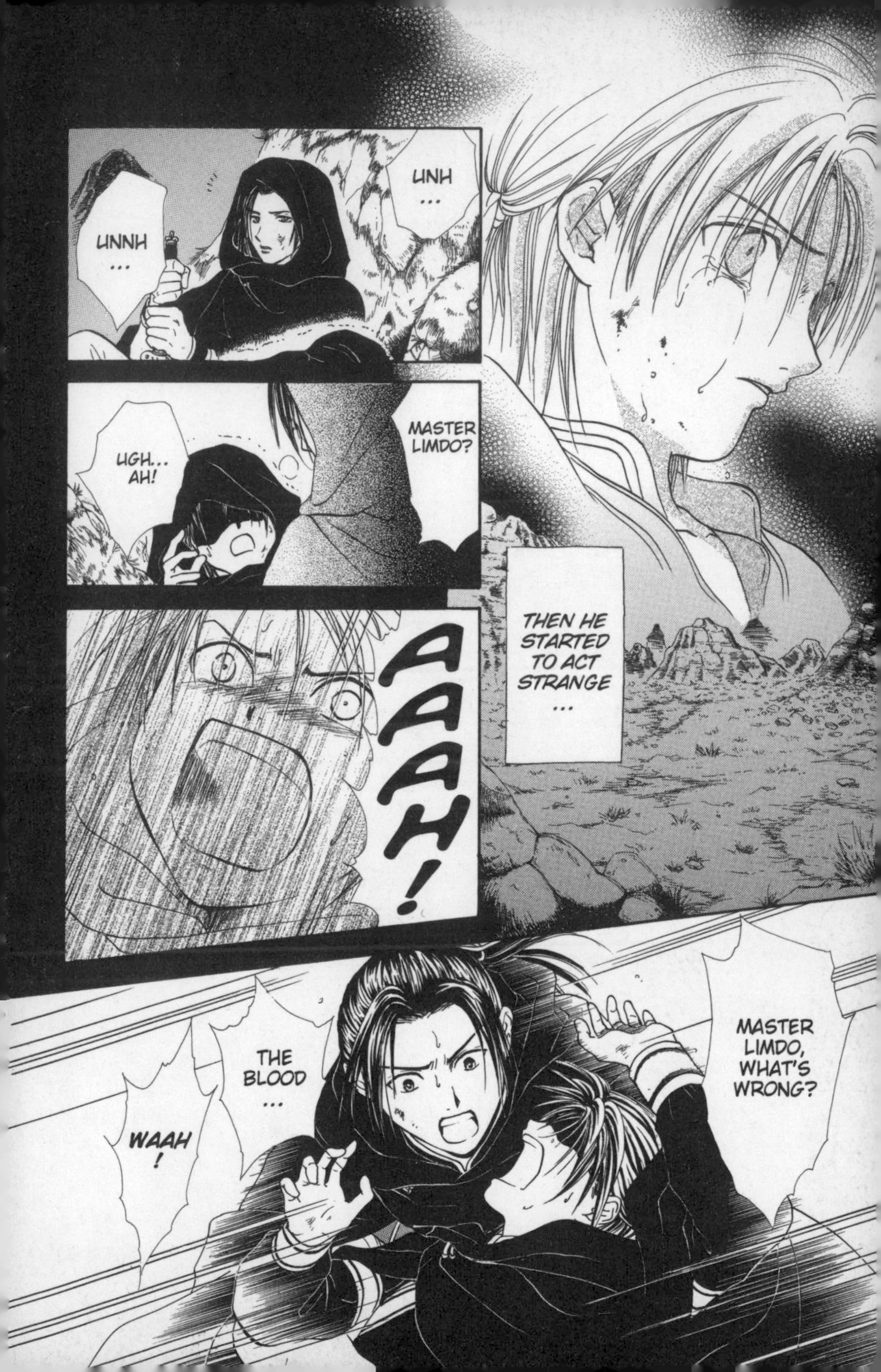

THEN HE STARTED TO ACT STRANGE ...
UNH ...
UNNH ...
MASTER LIMDO?
UGH... AH!
AAAAH!
MASTER LIMDO, WHAT'S WRONG?
THE BLOOD ...
WAAH !

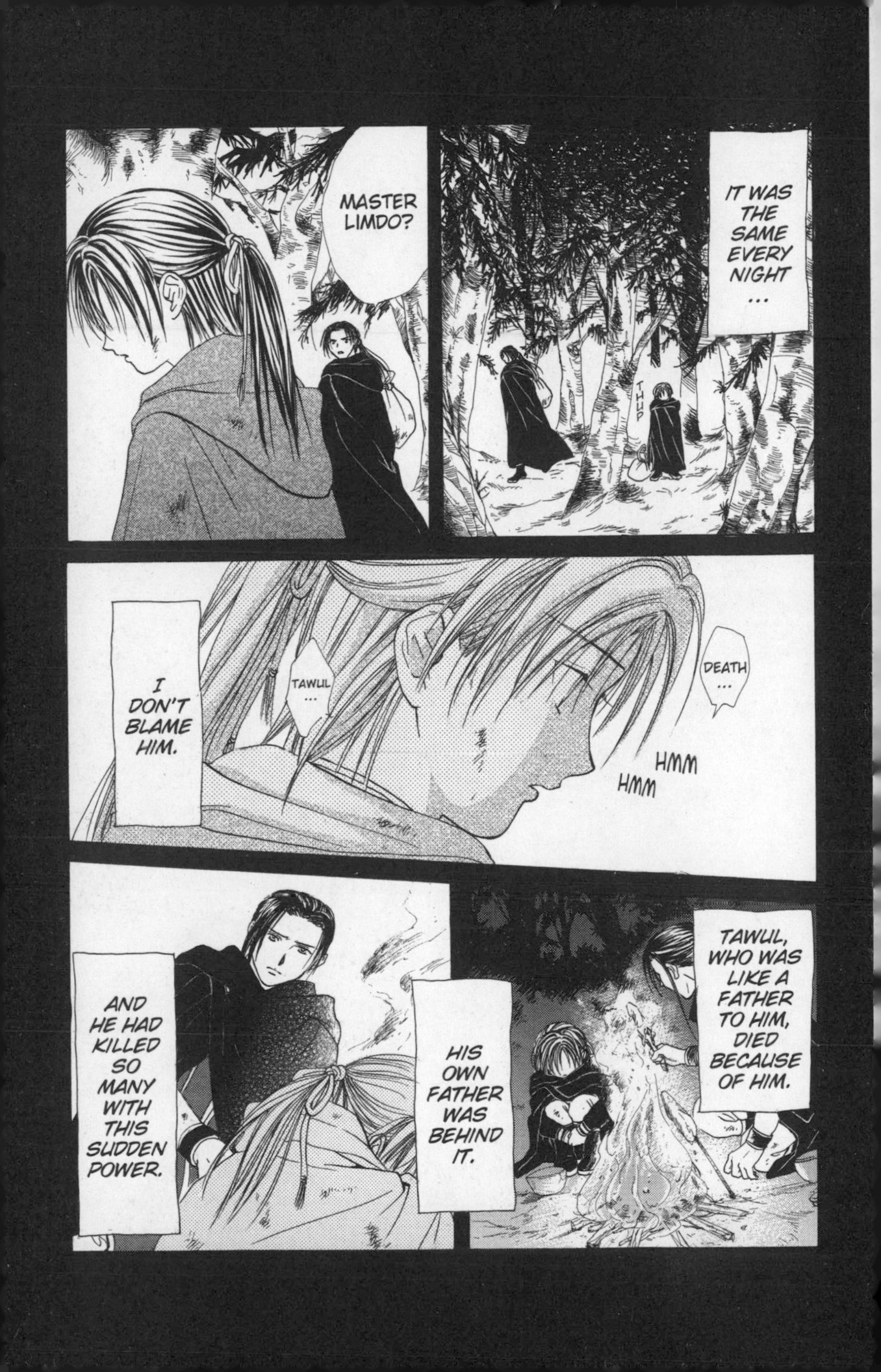
IT WAS THE SAME EVERY NIGHT ...
THUP
MASTER LIMDO?
DEATH ...
HMM HMM
TAWUL ...
I DON'T BLAME HIM.
TAWUL, WHO WAS LIKE A FATHER TO HIM, DIED BECAUSE OF HIM.
HIS OWN FATHER WAS BEHIND IT.
AND HE HAD KILLED SO MANY WITH THIS SUDDEN POWER.

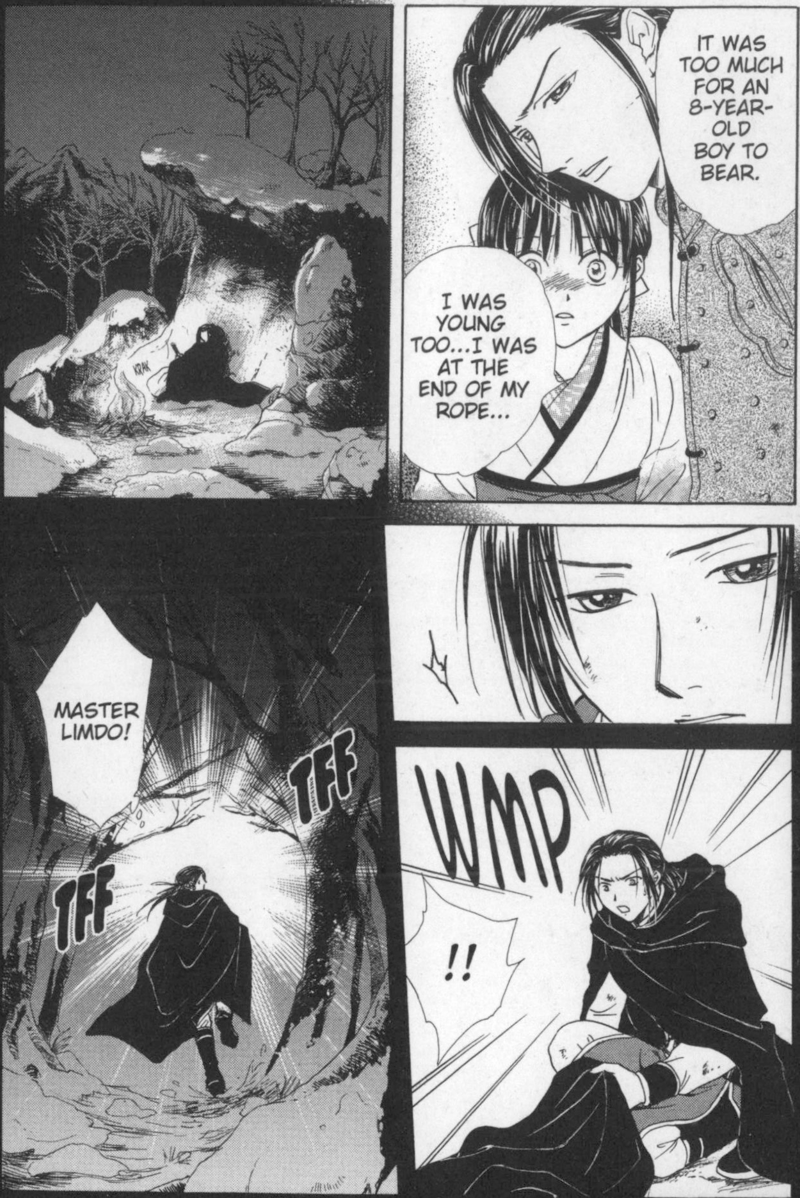
IT WAS TOO MUCH FOR AN 8-YEAR-OLD BOY TO BEAR.
I WAS YOUNG TOO...I WAS AT THE END OF MY ROPE...
KRAK
WMP
!!
MASTER LIMDO!
TFF
TFF

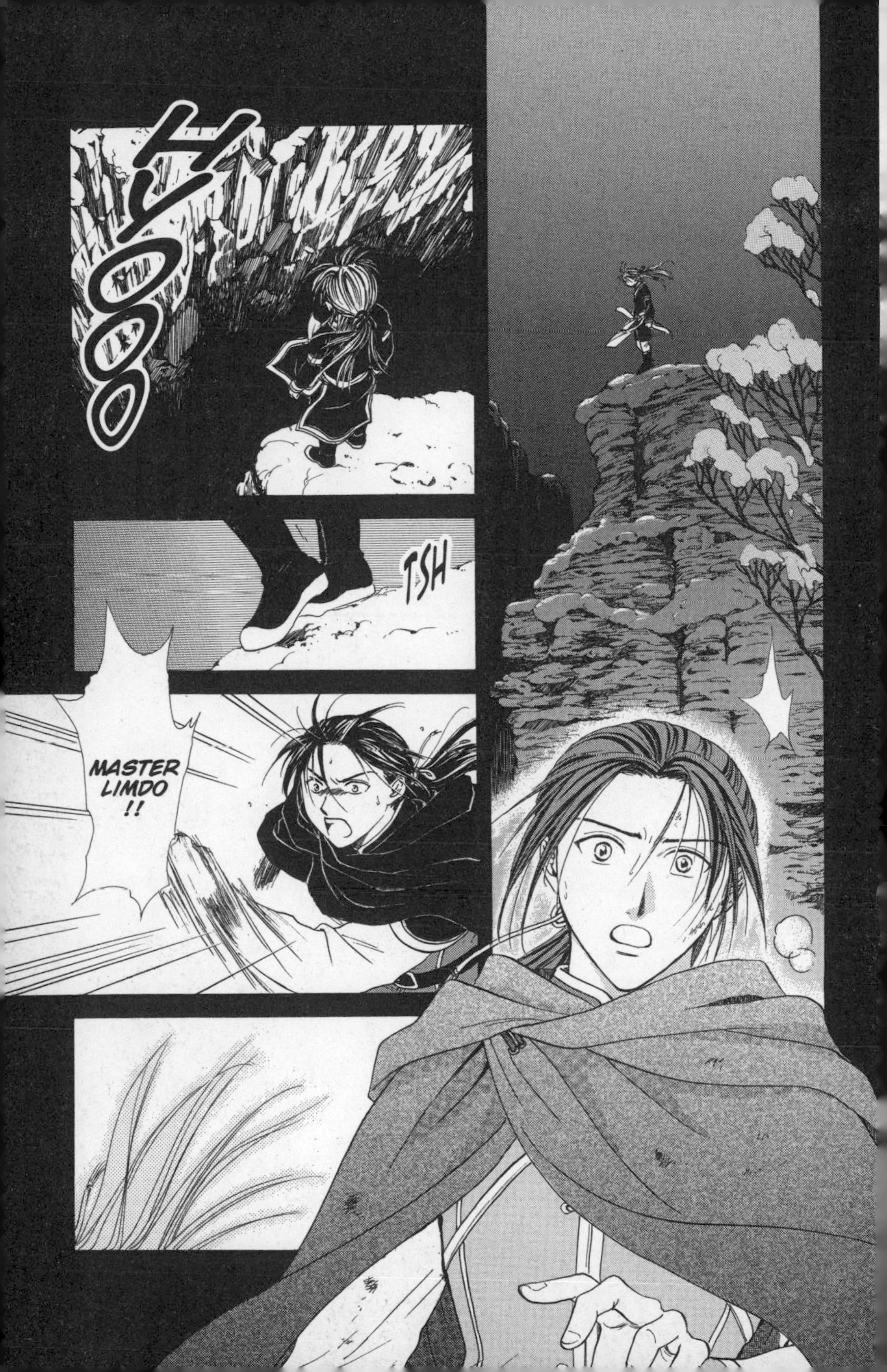
HYOOO
TSH
MASTER LIMDO !!

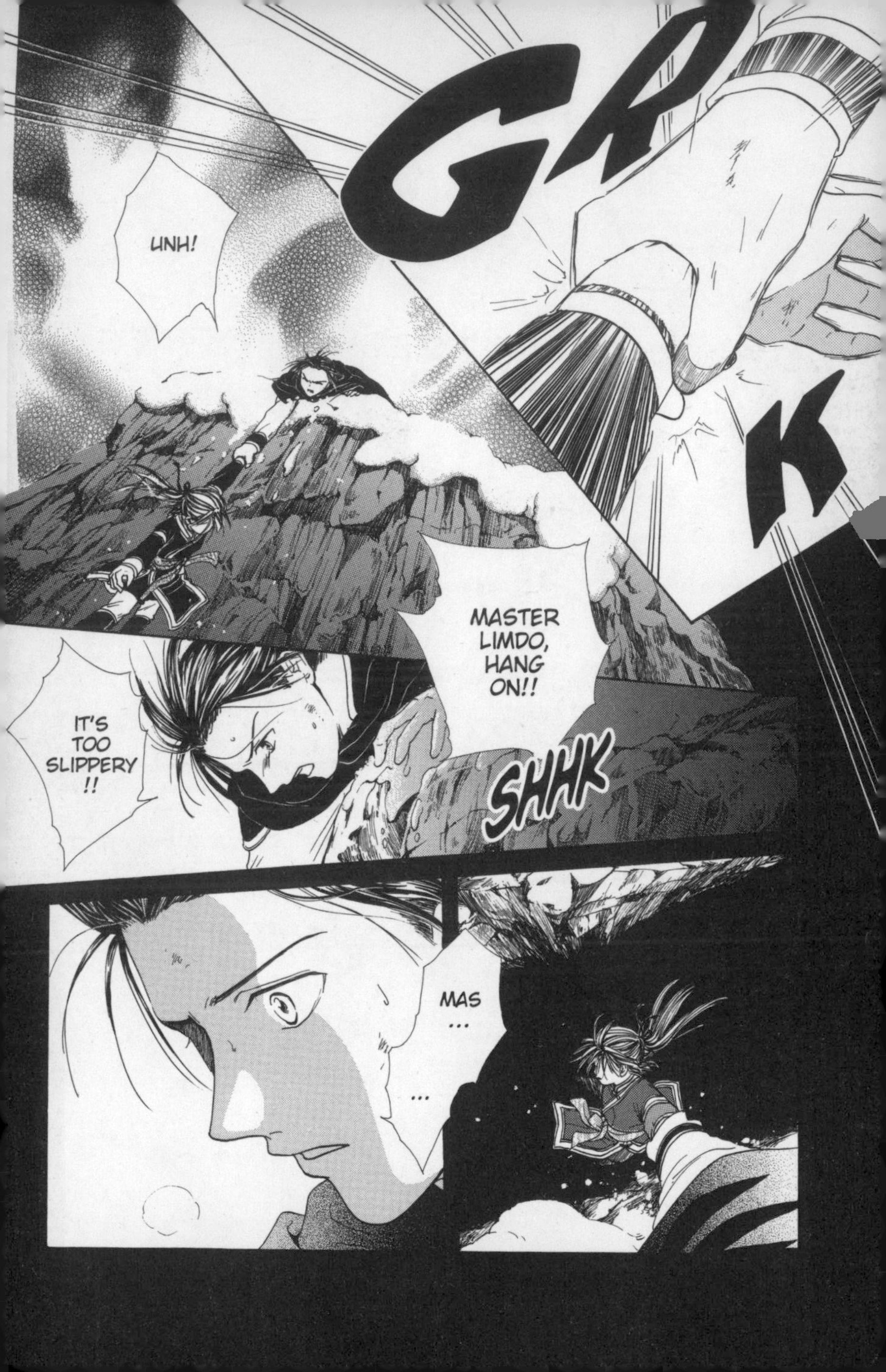
GRK
UNH!
MASTER LIMDO, HANG ON!!
SHHK
IT'S TOO SLIPPERY!!
MAS...
...

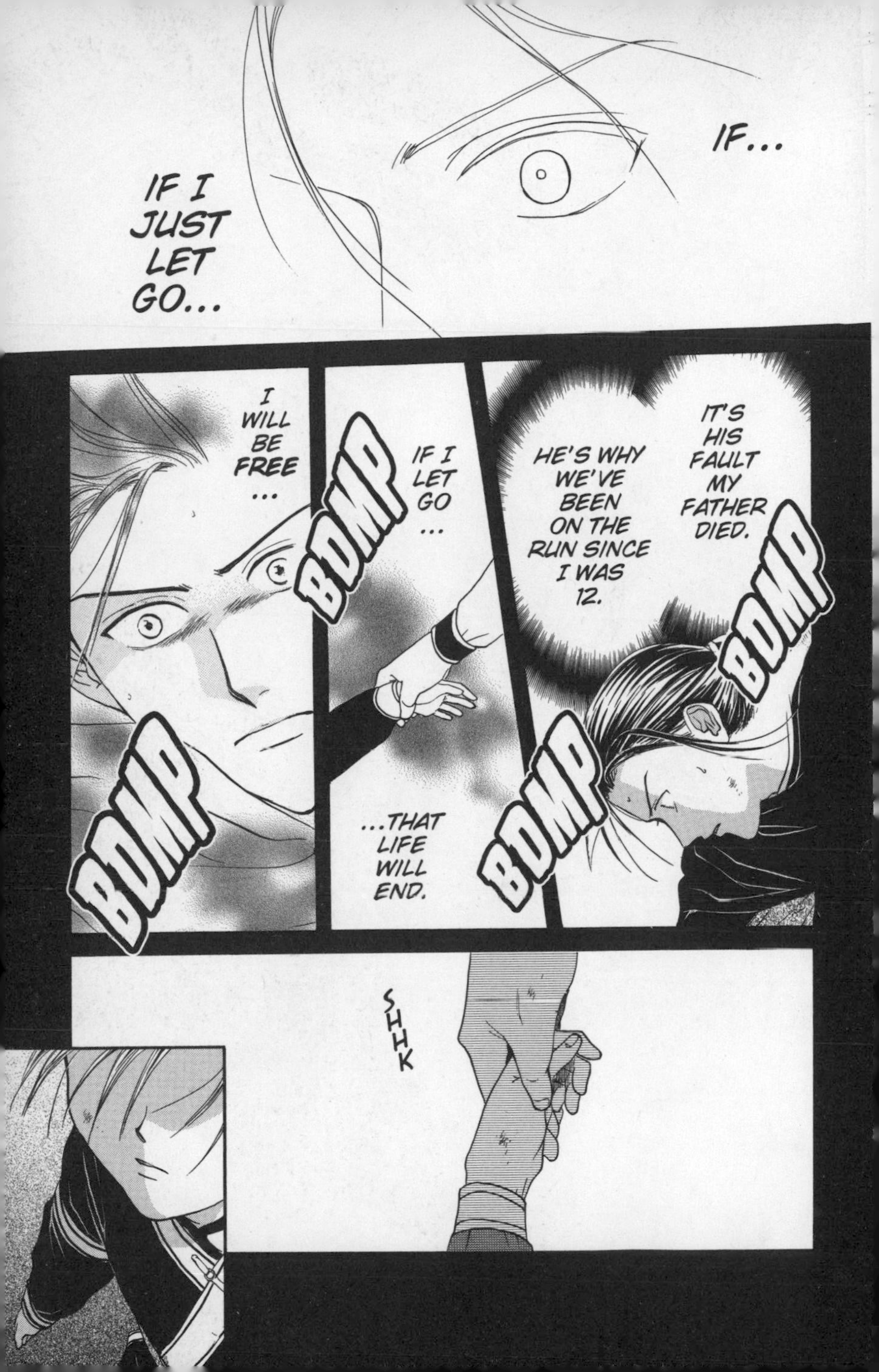
IF...
IF I JUST LET GO...
IT'S HIS FAULT MY FATHER DIED.
HE'S WHY WE'VE BEEN ON THE RUN SINCE I WAS 12.
BDMP
BDMP
IF I LET GO ...
BDMP
...THAT LIFE WILL END.
I WILL BE FREE ...
BDMP
SHHK

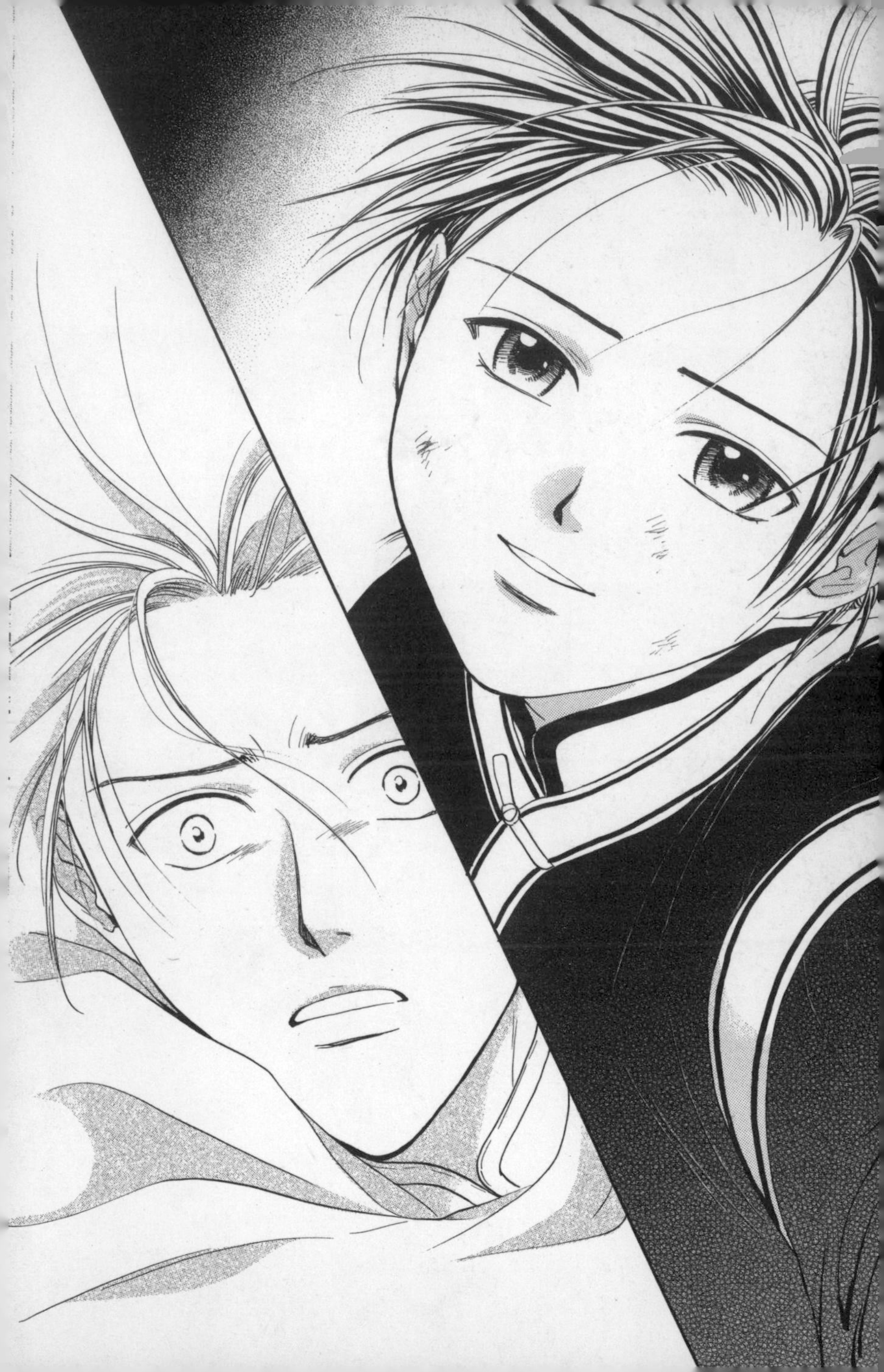

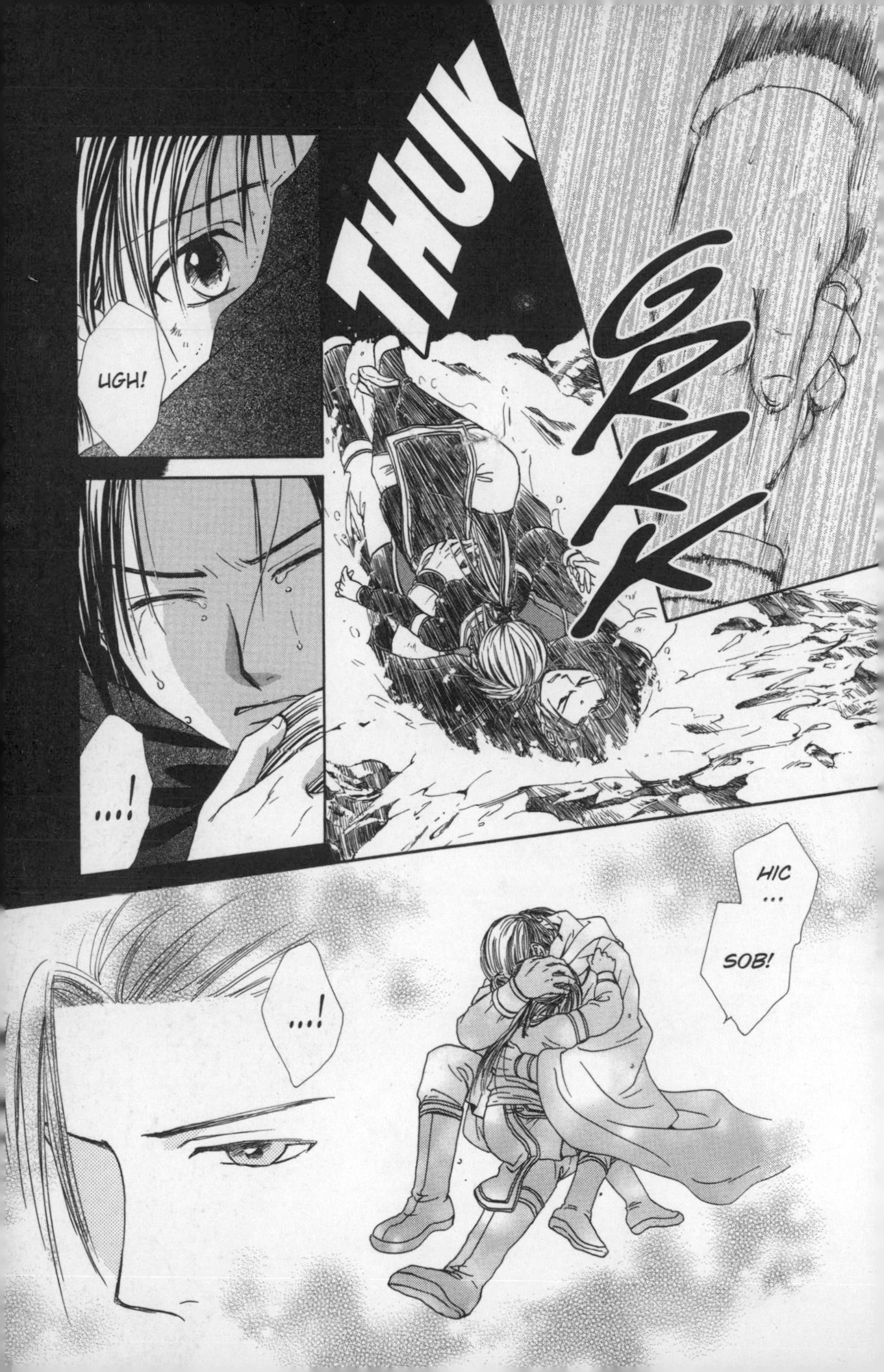
GRRK
THUK
UGH!
...!
HIC ... SOB!
...!

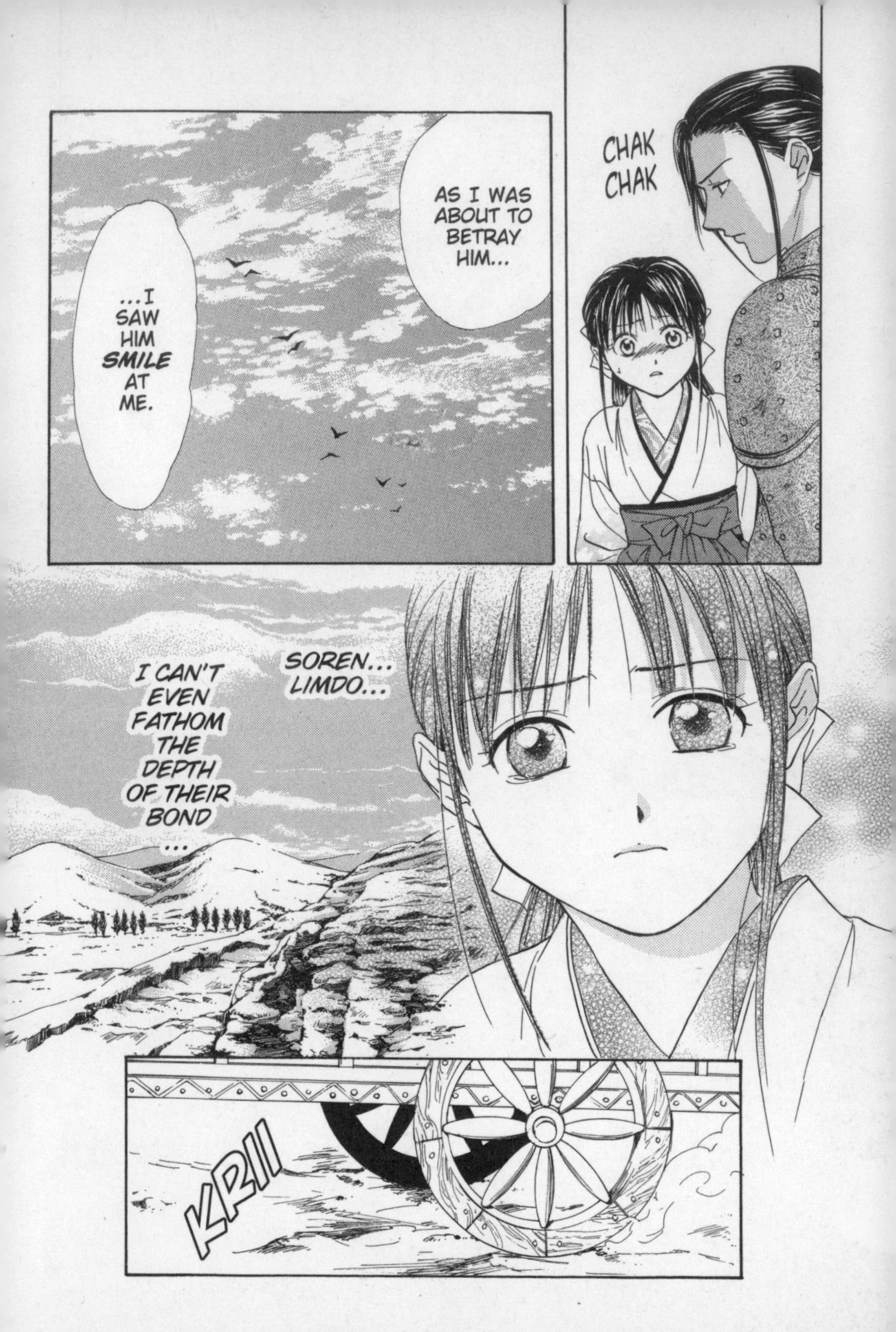
CHAK CHAK
AS I WAS ABOUT TO BETRAY HIM...
...I SAW HIM SMILE AT ME.
SOREN... LIMDO...
I CAN'T EVEN FATHOM THE DEPTH OF THEIR BOND...
KRIII

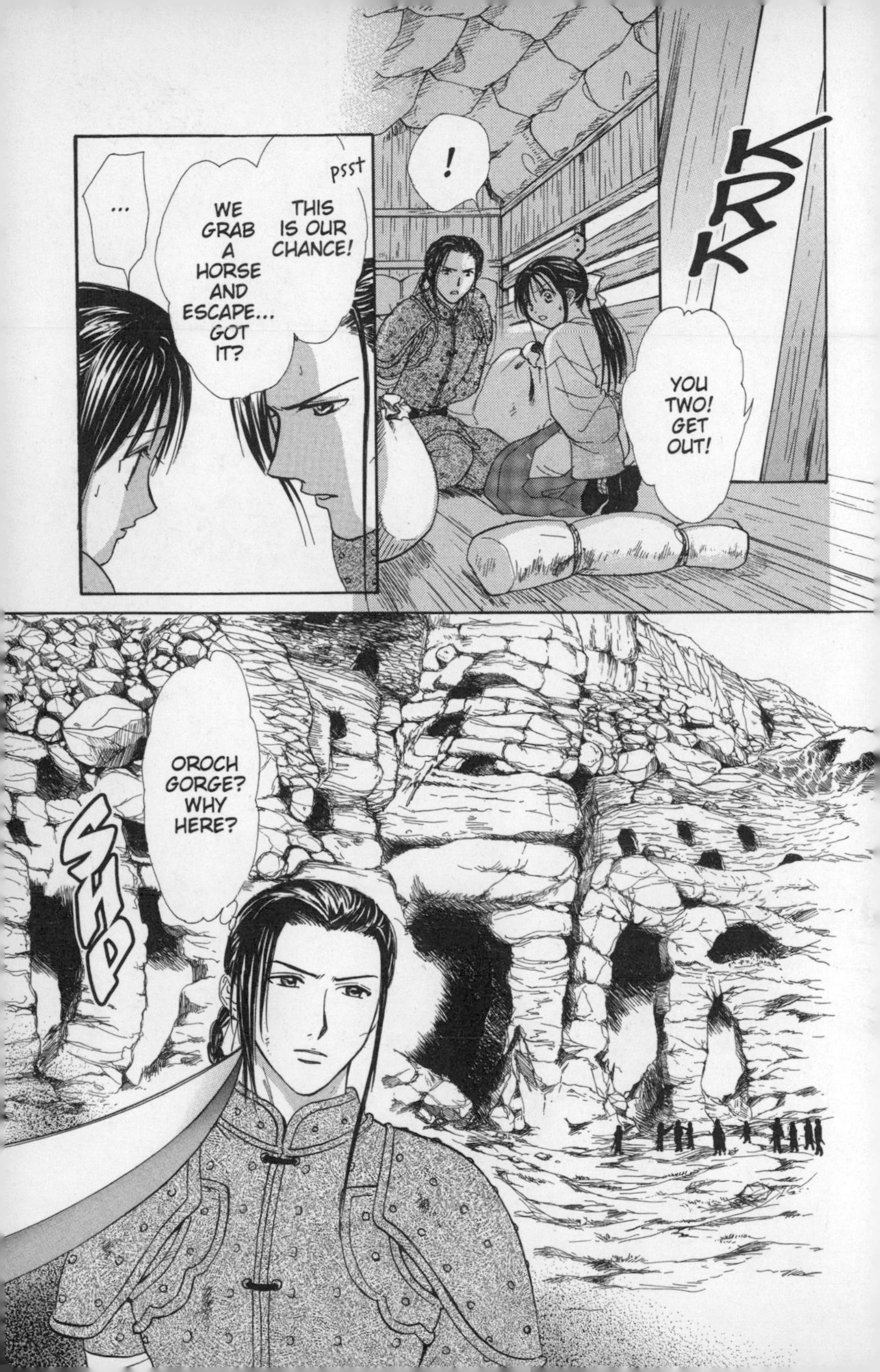
KRK
!
YOU TWO! GET OUT!
psst
THIS IS OUR CHANCE!
WE GRAB A HORSE AND ESCAPE... GOT IT?
...
OROCH GORGE? WHY HERE?
SHP

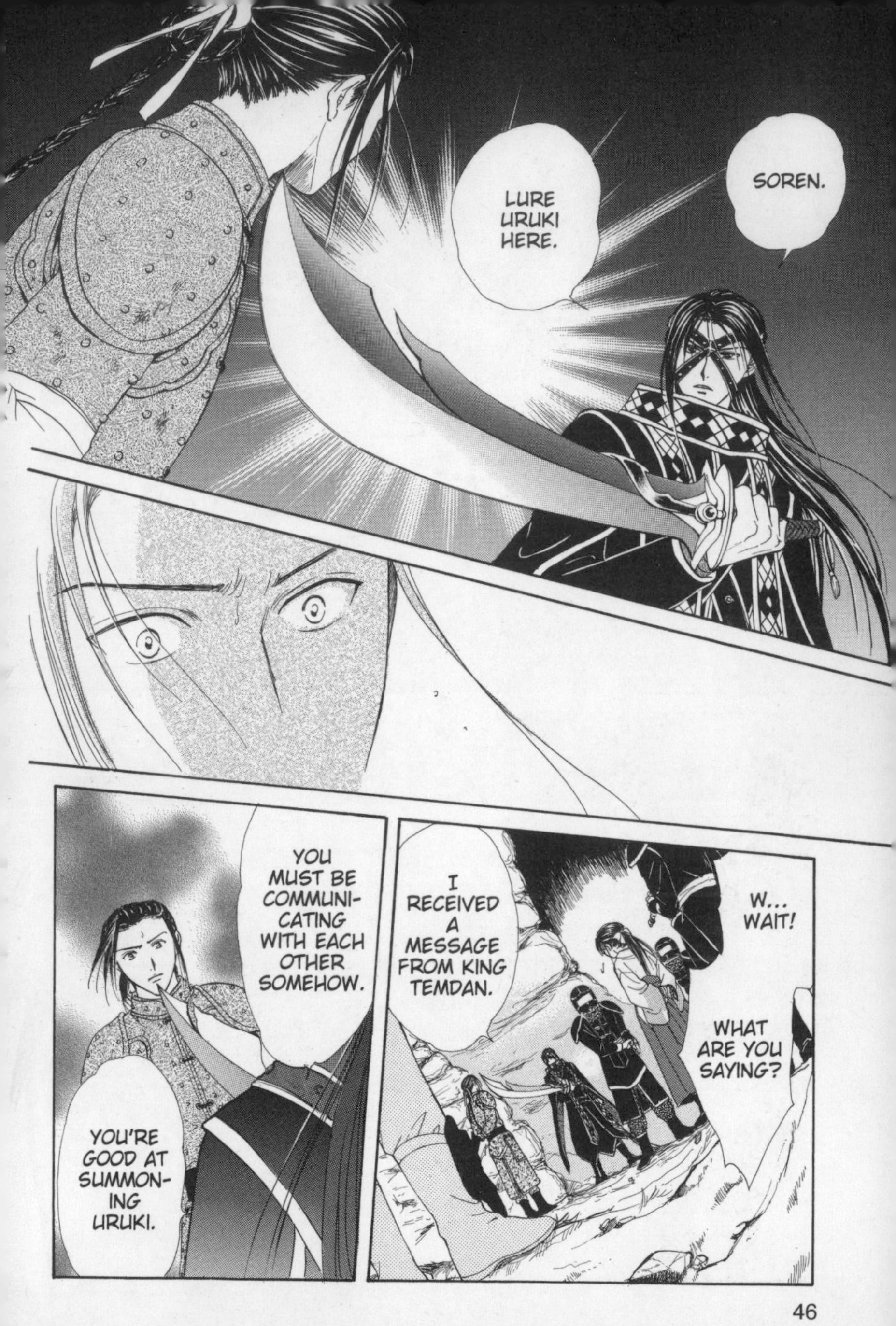
SOREN.
LURE URUKI HERE.
W... WAIT!
WHAT ARE YOU SAYING?
I RECEIVED A MESSAGE FROM KING TEMDAN.
YOU MUST BE COMMUNICATING WITH EACH OTHER SOMEHOW.
YOU'RE GOOD AT SUMMONING URUKI.

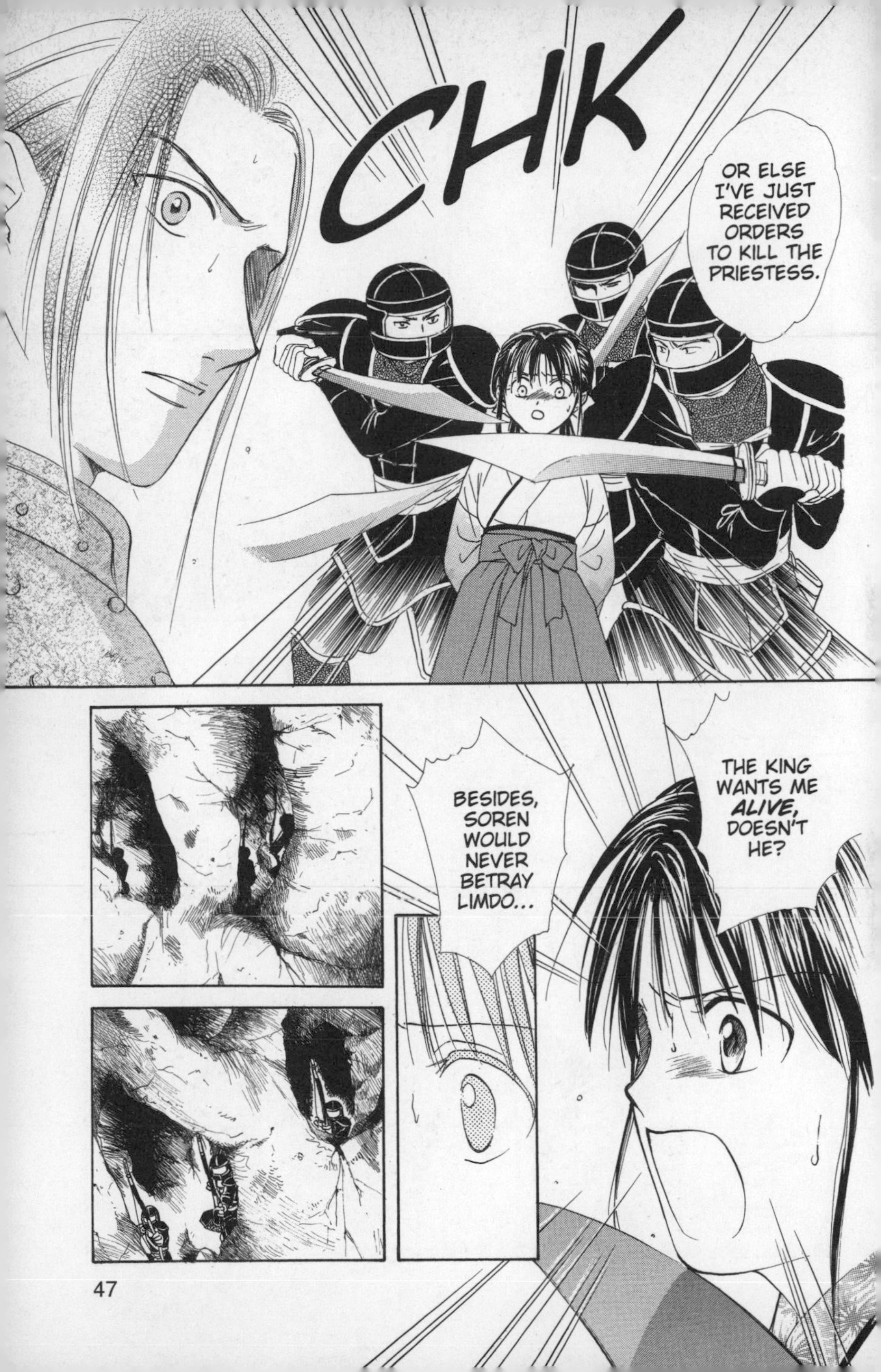
CHK
OR ELSE I'VE JUST RECEIVED ORDERS TO KILL THE PRIESTESS.
THE KING WANTS ME *ALIVE*, DOESN'T HE?
BESIDES, SOREN WOULD NEVER BETRAY LIMDO...

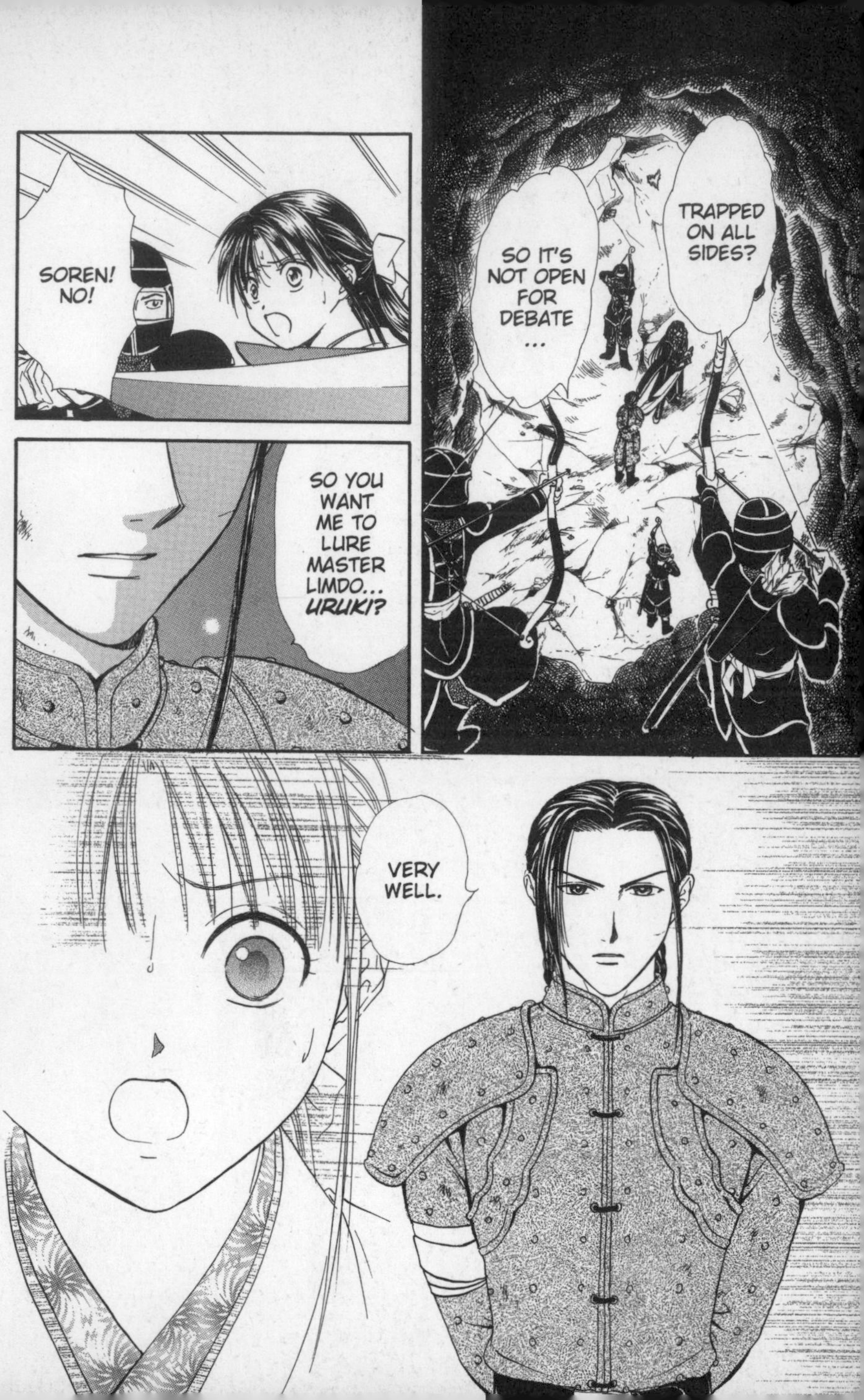
TRAPPED ON ALL SIDES?
SO IT'S NOT OPEN FOR DEBATE...
SOREN! NO!
SO YOU WANT ME TO LURE MASTER LIMDO... *URUKI?*
VERY WELL.

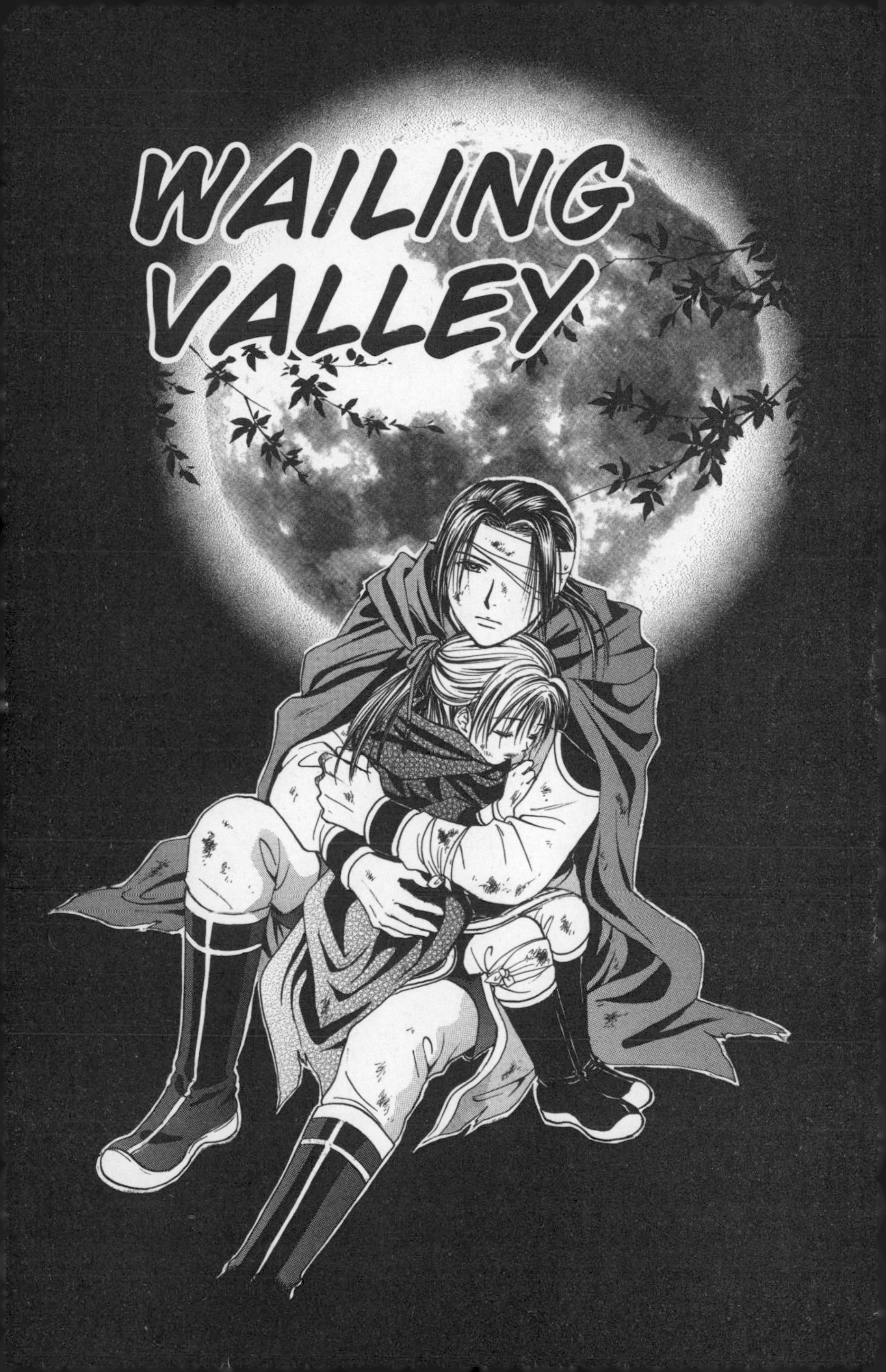
WAILING VALLEY

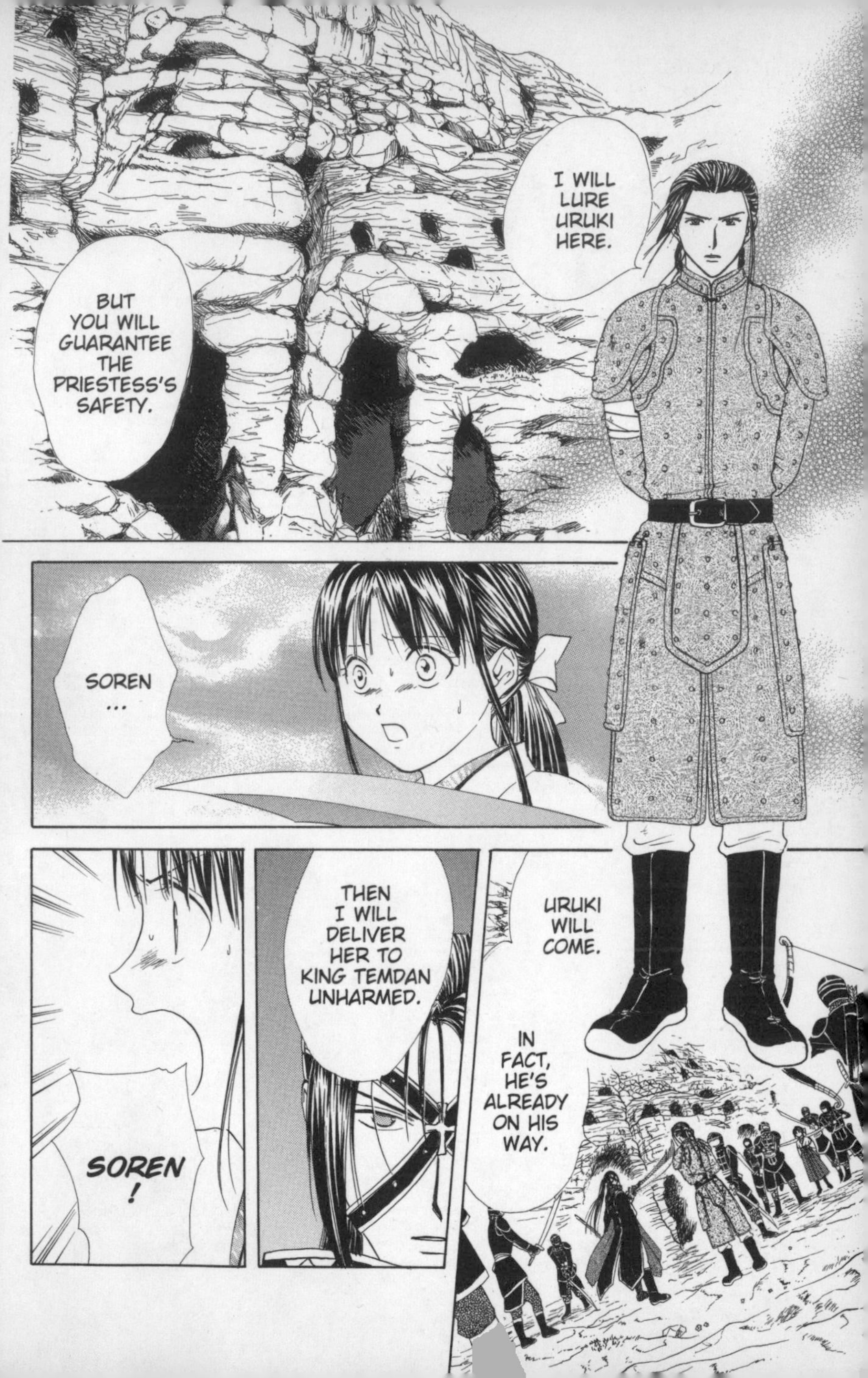
I WILL LURE URUKI HERE.
BUT YOU WILL GUARANTEE THE PRIESTESS'S SAFETY.
SOREN ...
URUKI WILL COME.
IN FACT, HE'S ALREADY ON HIS WAY.
THEN I WILL DELIVER HER TO KING TEMDAN UNHARMED.
SOREN !

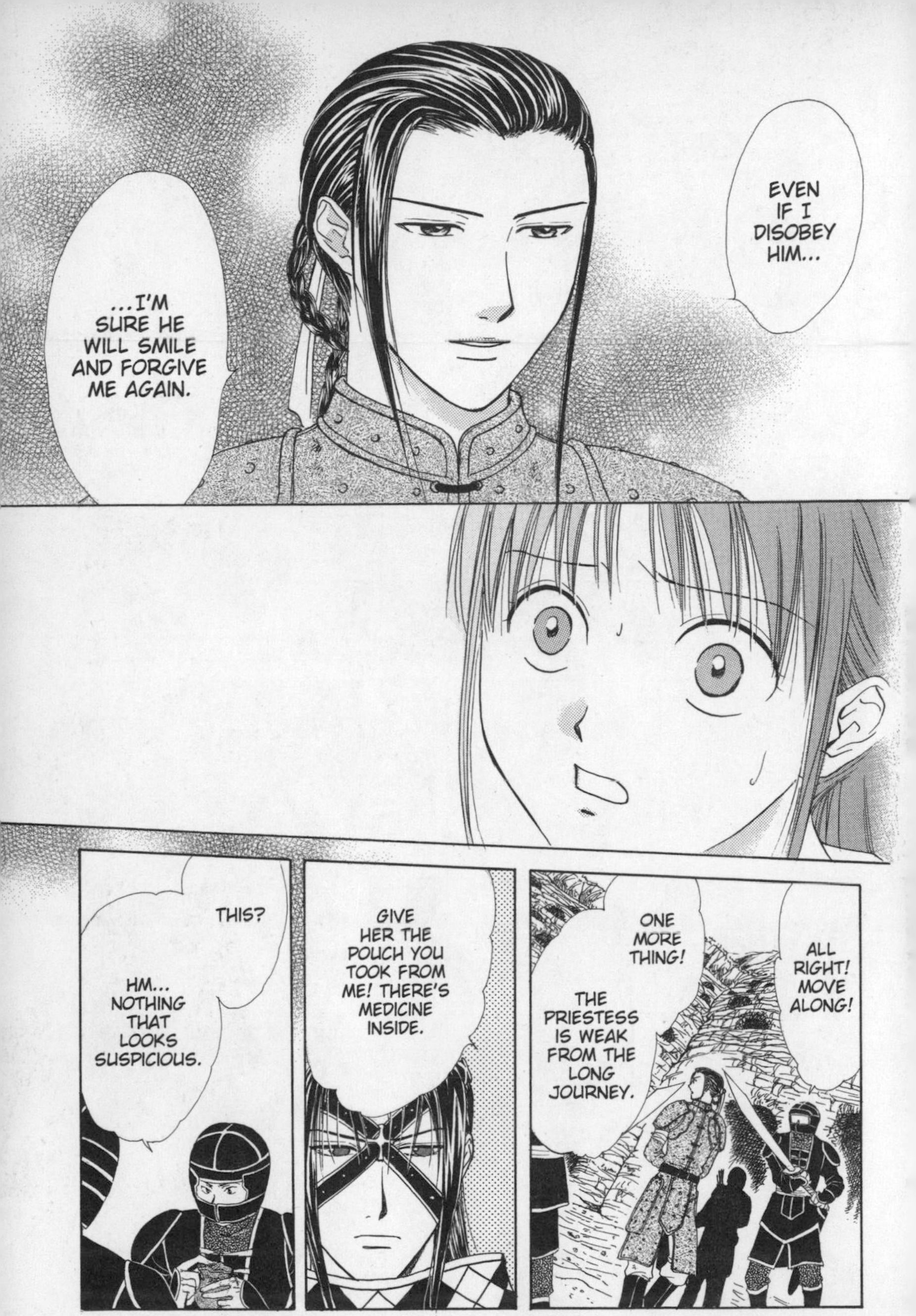
EVEN IF I DISOBEY HIM...
...I'M SURE HE WILL SMILE AND FORGIVE ME AGAIN.
ALL RIGHT! MOVE ALONG!
ONE MORE THING!
THE PRIESTESS IS WEAK FROM THE LONG JOURNEY.
GIVE HER THE POUCH YOU TOOK FROM ME! THERE'S MEDICINE INSIDE.
THIS?
HM... NOTHING THAT LOOKS SUSPICIOUS.

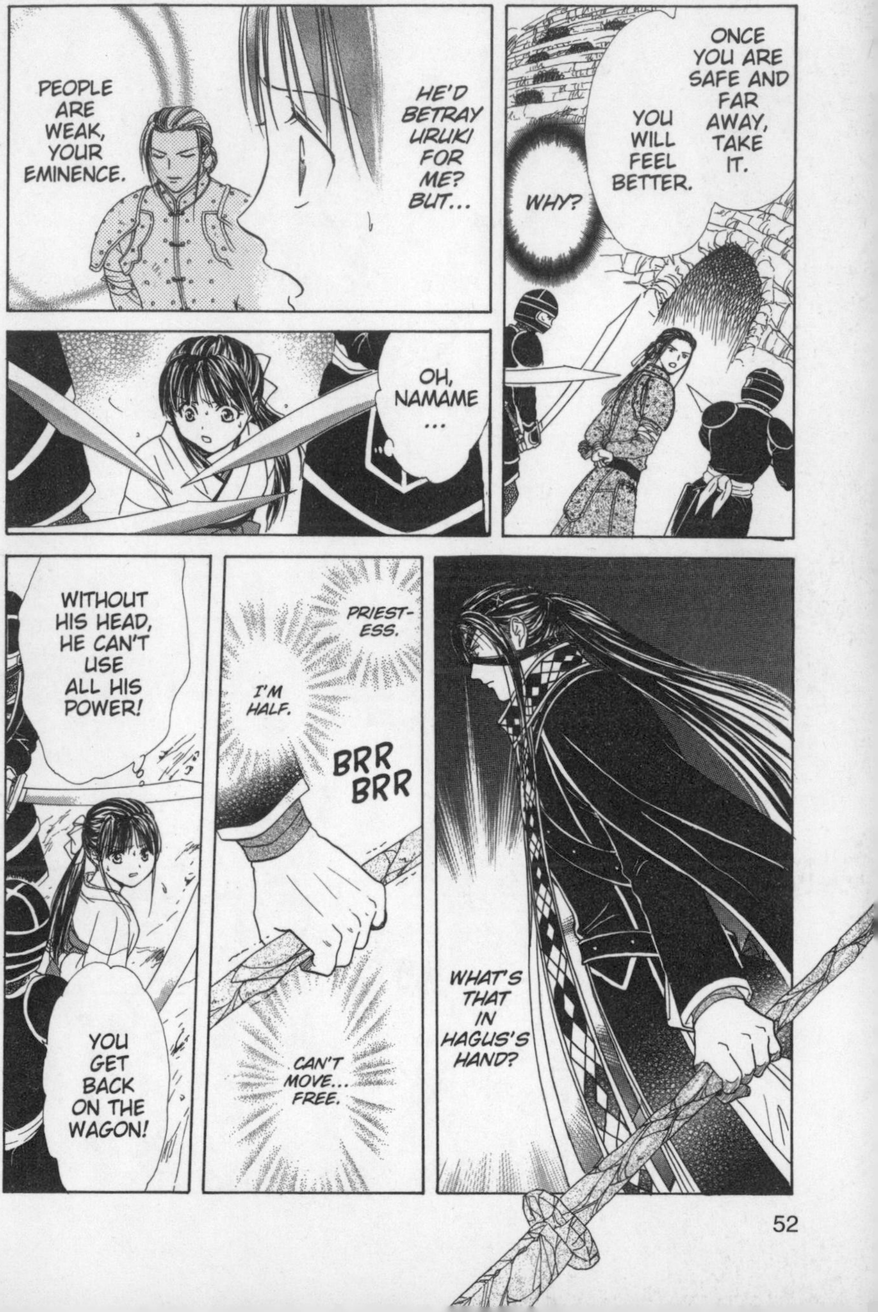
ONCE YOU ARE SAFE AND FAR AWAY, TAKE IT.
YOU WILL FEEL BETTER.
WHY?
HE'D BETRAY URUKI FOR ME? BUT...
PEOPLE ARE WEAK, YOUR EMINENCE.
OH, NAMAME ...
WHAT'S THAT IN HAGUS'S HAND?
PRIEST-ESS.
I'M HALF.
BRR BRR
CAN'T MOVE... FREE.
WITHOUT HIS HEAD, HE CAN'T USE ALL HIS POWER!
YOU GET BACK ON THE WAGON!

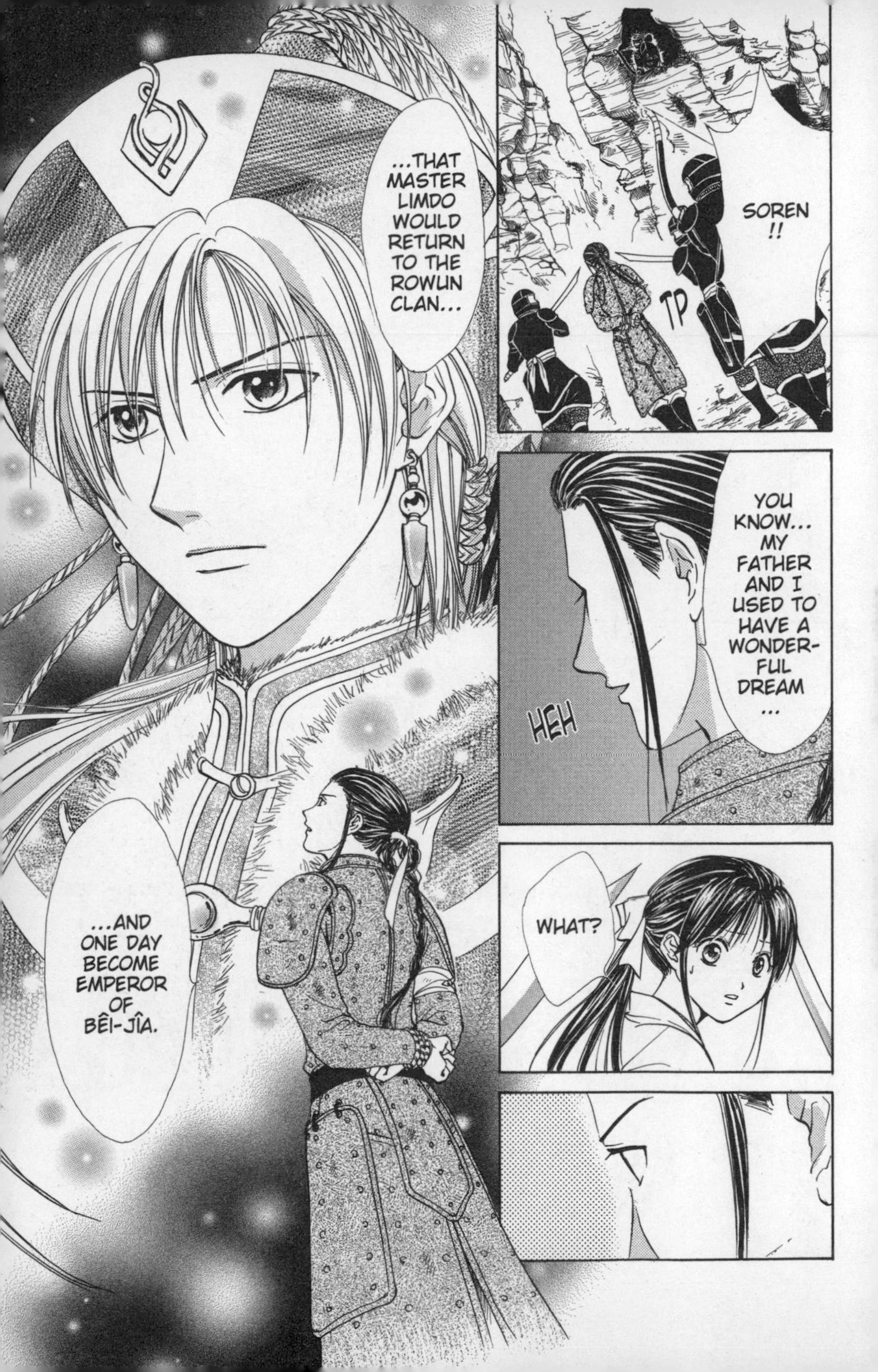
SOREN !!
TP
YOU KNOW... MY FATHER AND I USED TO HAVE A WONDERFUL DREAM ...
HEH
WHAT?
...THAT MASTER LIMDO WOULD RETURN TO THE ROWUN CLAN...
...AND ONE DAY BECOME EMPEROR OF BÊI-JÎA.

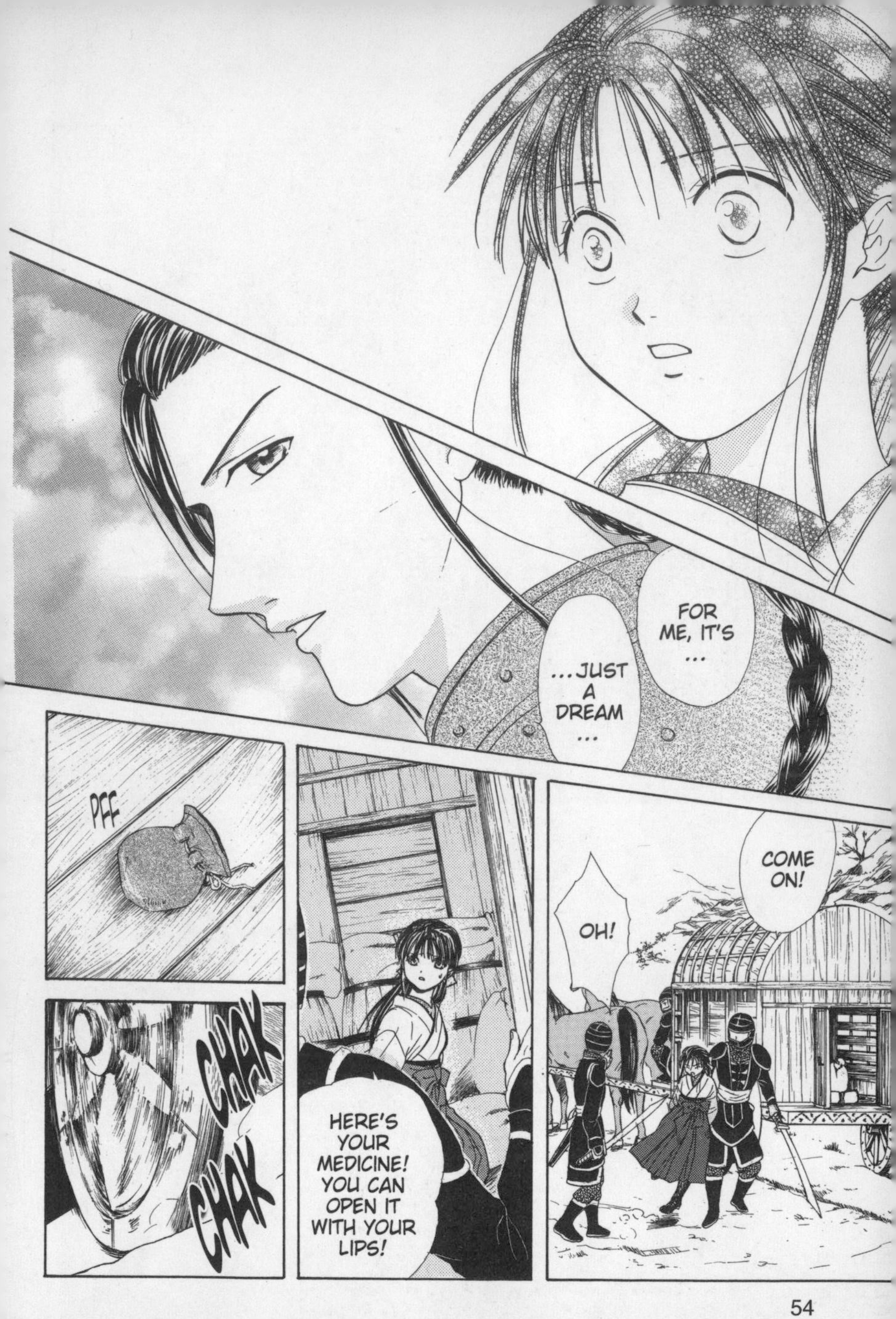
FOR ME, IT'S ...
...JUST A DREAM ...
COME ON!
OH!
HERE'S YOUR MEDICINE! YOU CAN OPEN IT WITH YOUR LIPS!
PFF
CHAK
CHAK

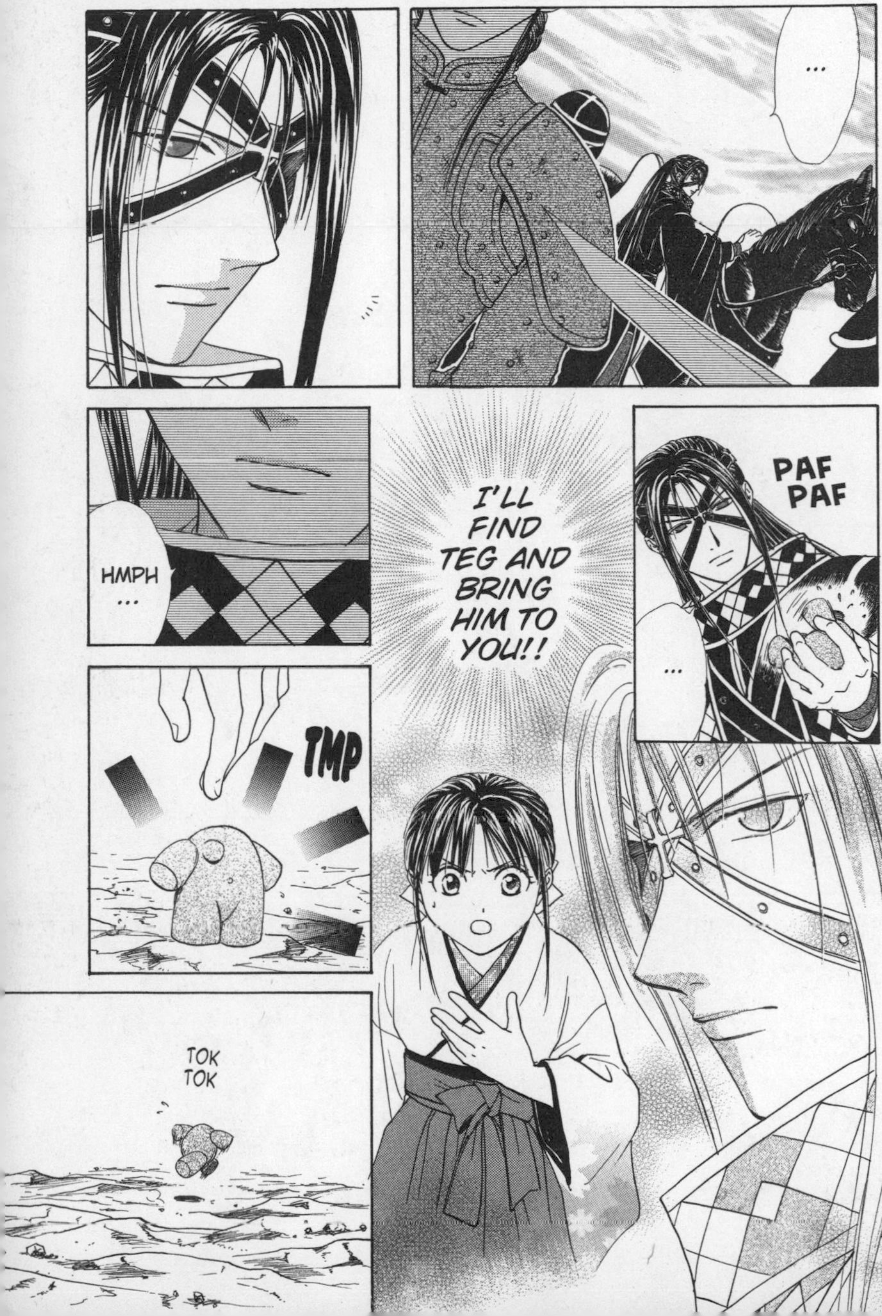
...
PAF PAF
...
I'LL FIND TEG AND BRING HIM TO YOU!!
HMPH ...
TMP
TOK TOK

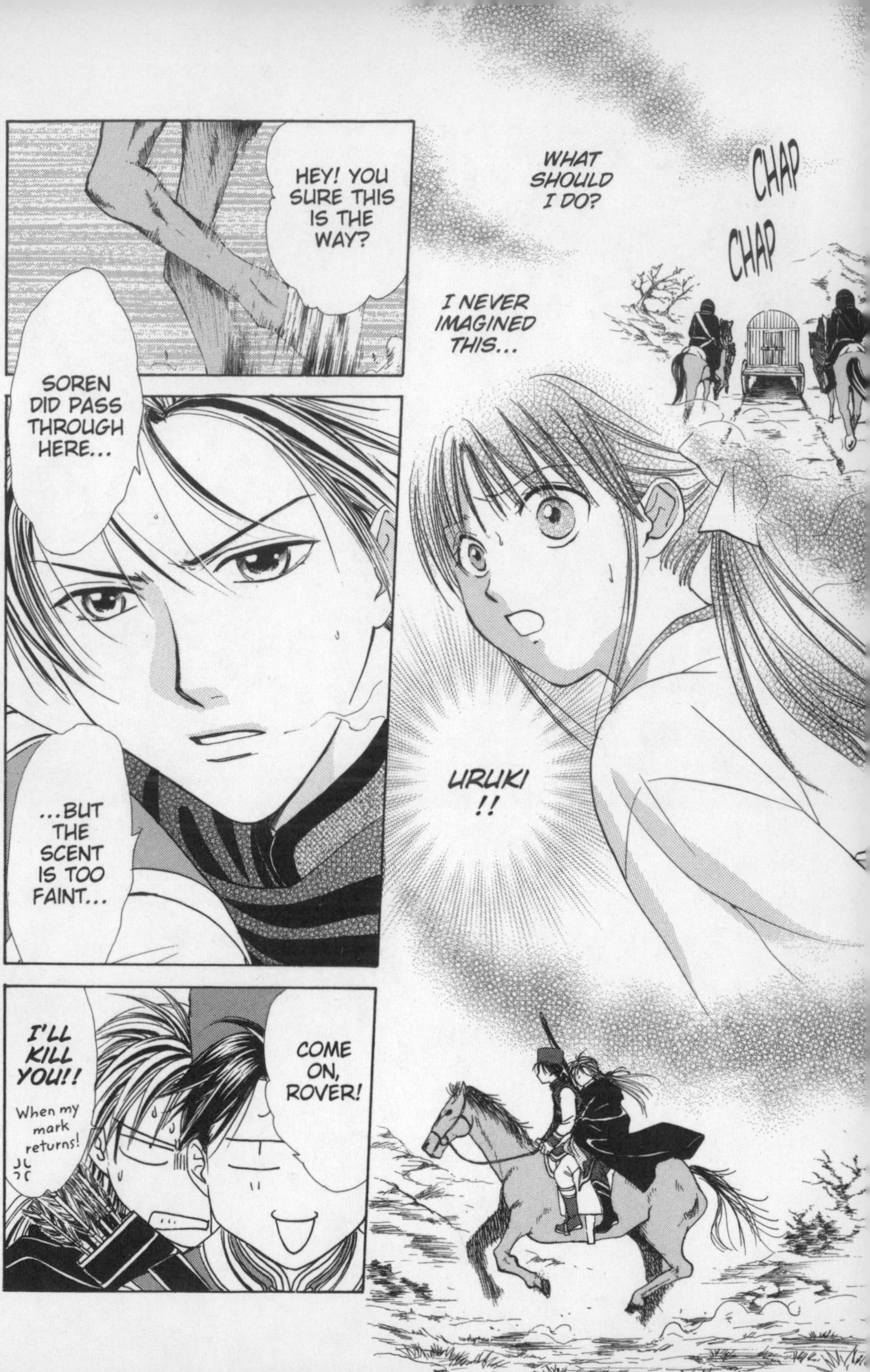
CHAP
CHAP
WHAT SHOULD I DO?
I NEVER IMAGINED THIS...
URUKI !!
HEY! YOU SURE THIS IS THE WAY?
SOREN DID PASS THROUGH HERE...
...BUT THE SCENT IS TOO FAINT...
COME ON, ROVER!
I'LL KILL YOU!!
When my mark returns!

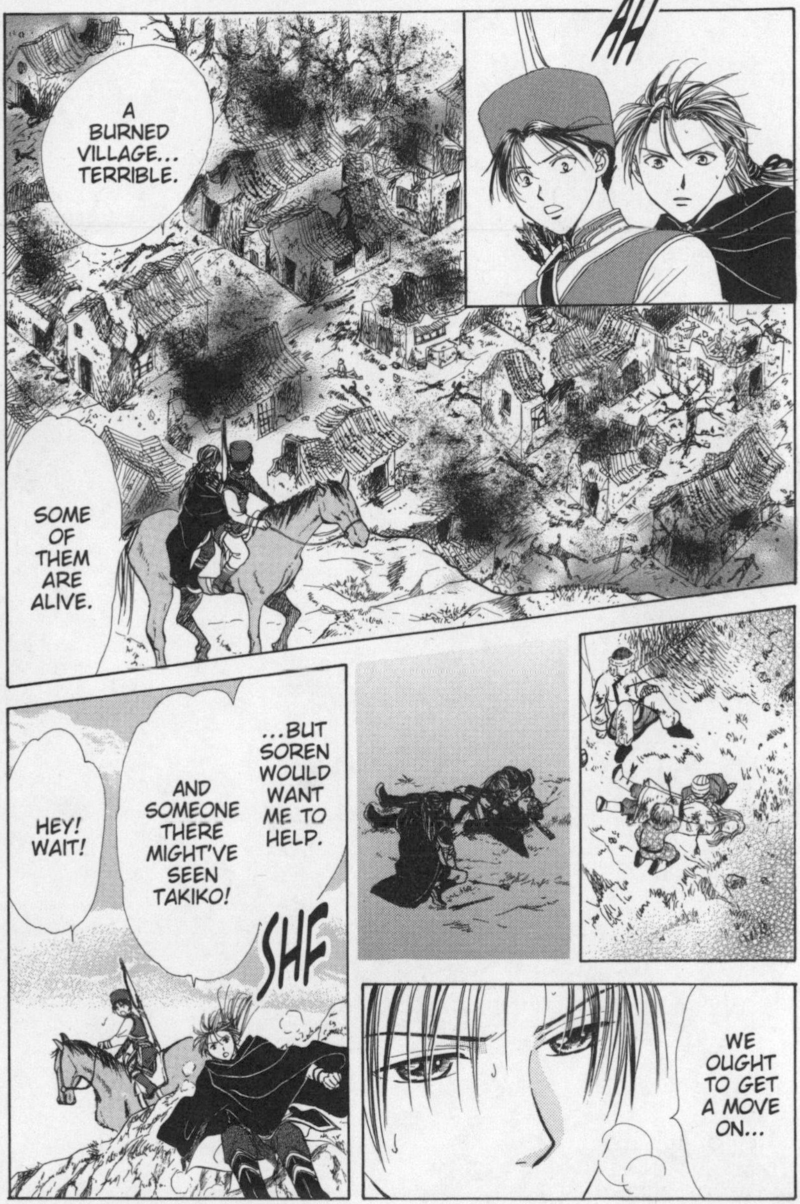
AH
A BURNED VILLAGE... TERRIBLE.
SOME OF THEM ARE ALIVE.
WE OUGHT TO GET A MOVE ON...
...BUT SOREN WOULD WANT ME TO HELP.
AND SOMEONE THERE MIGHT'VE SEEN TAKIKO!
HEY! WAIT!
SHF

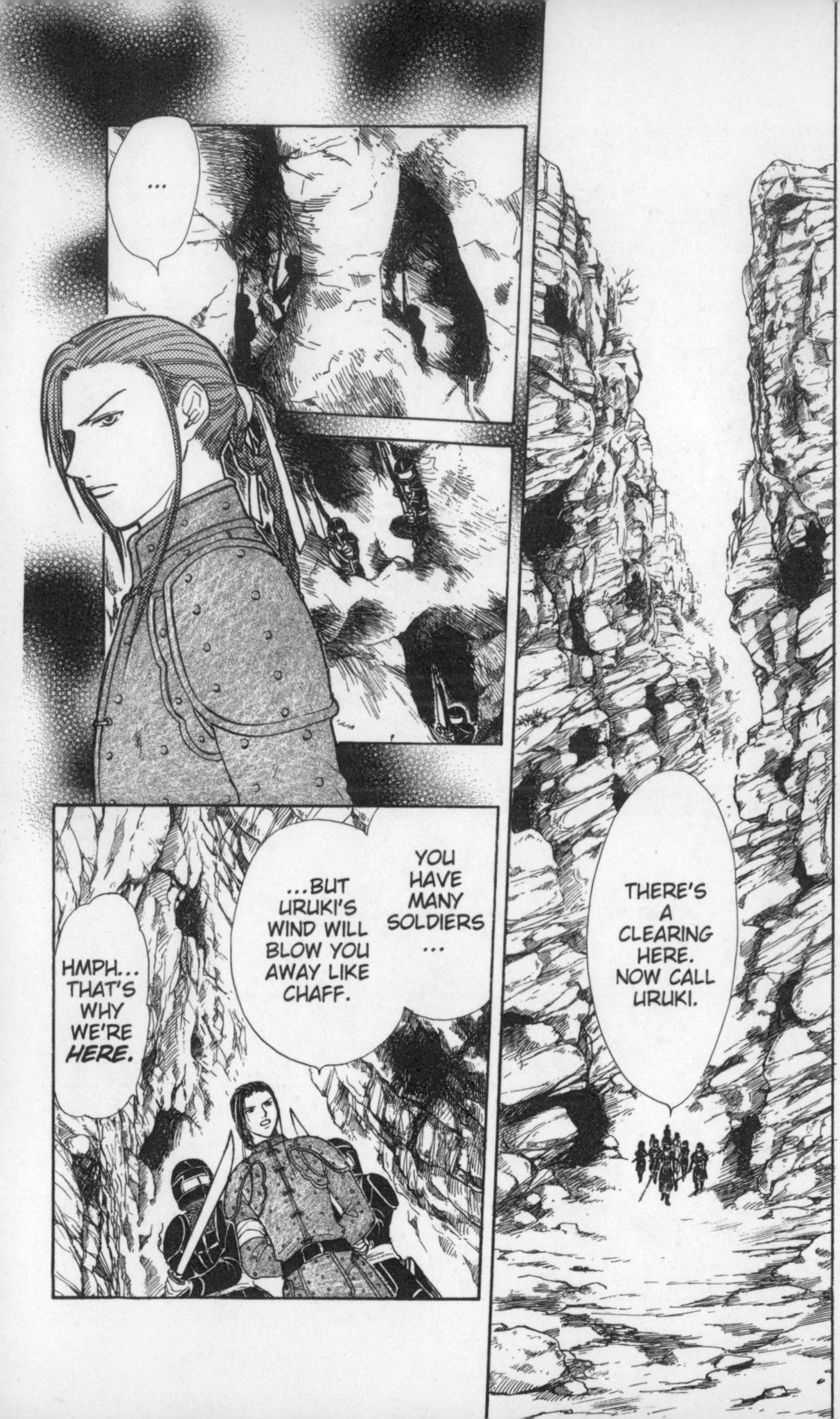
THERE'S A CLEARING HERE. NOW CALL URUKI.
...
YOU HAVE MANY SOLDIERS ...
...BUT URUKI'S WIND WILL BLOW YOU AWAY LIKE CHAFF.
HMPH... THAT'S WHY WE'RE *HERE*.

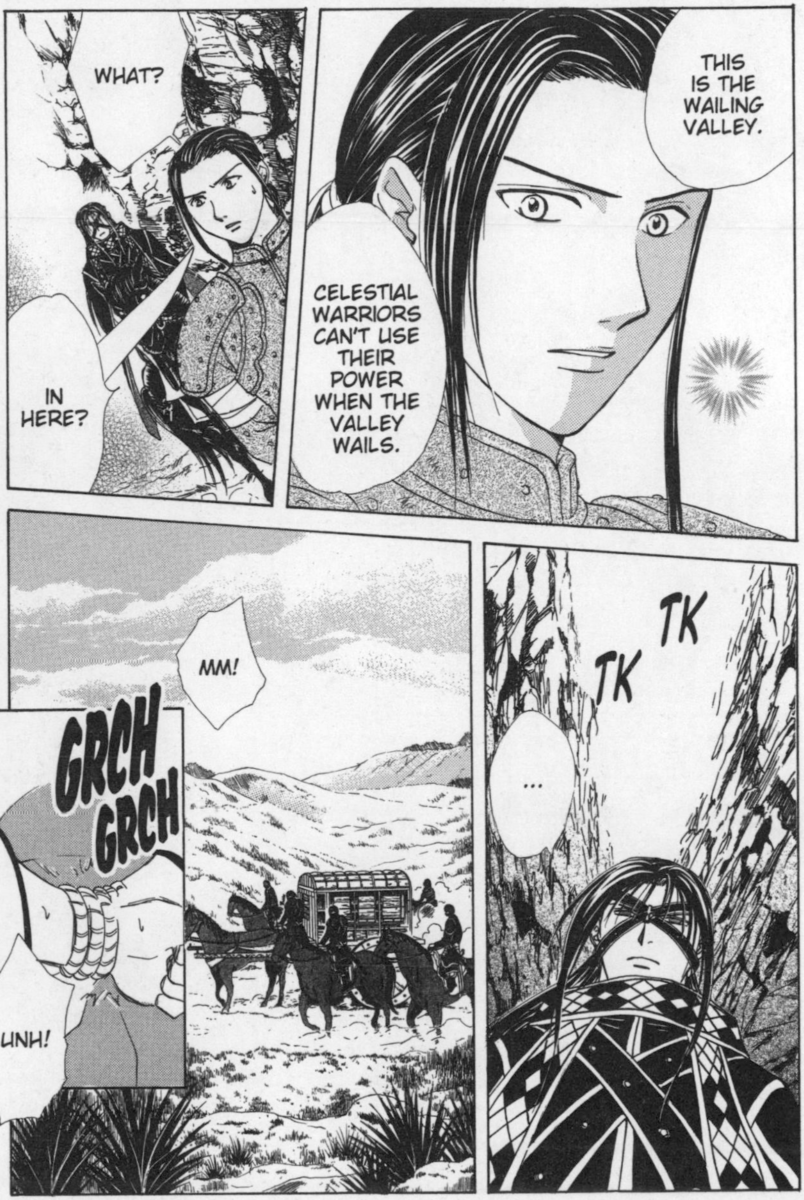
THIS IS THE WAILING VALLEY.
CELESTIAL WARRIORS CAN'T USE THEIR POWER WHEN THE VALLEY WAILS.
WHAT?
IN HERE?
TK
TK
...
MM!
GRCH GRCH
UNH!

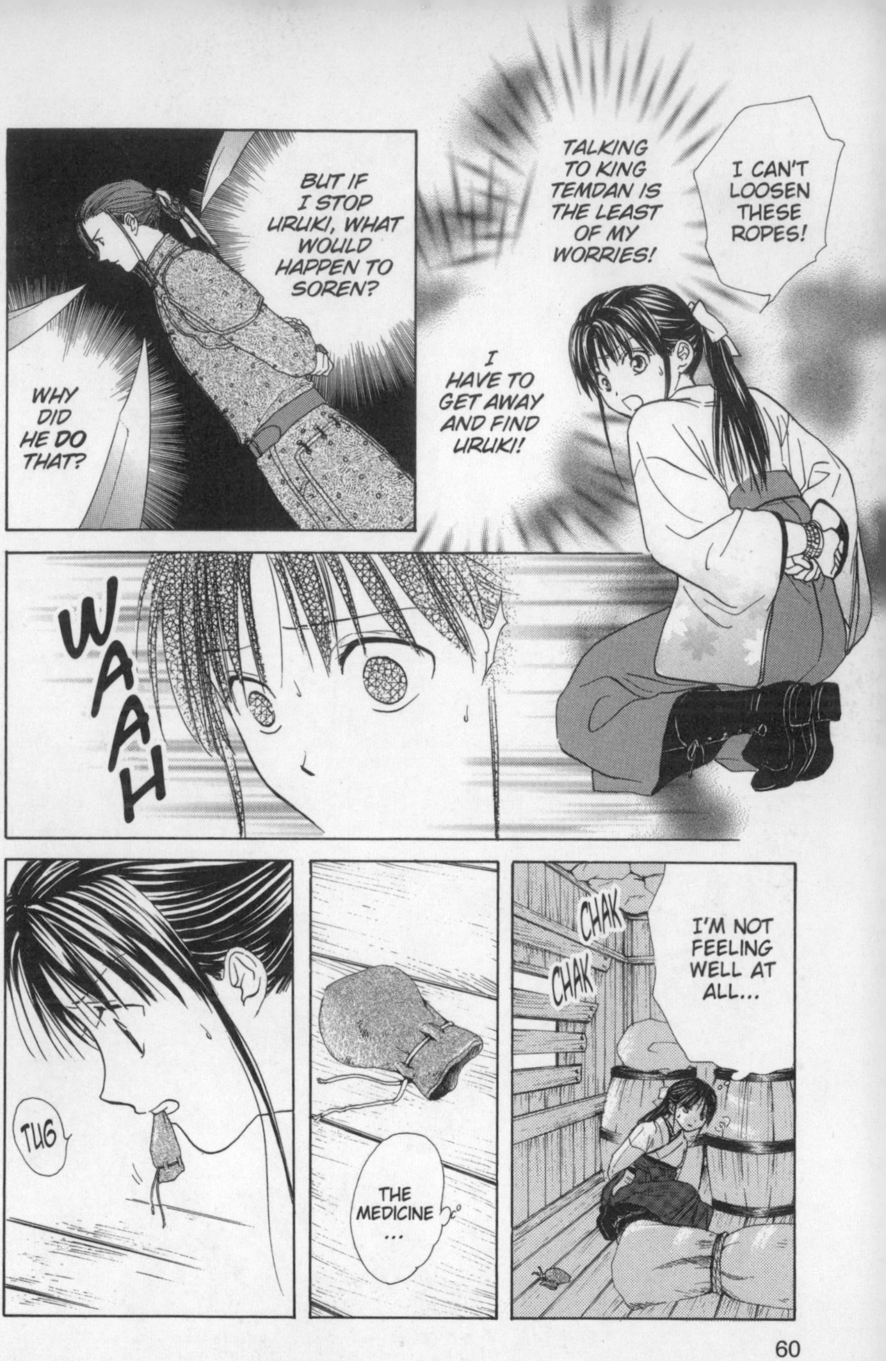
I CAN'T LOOSEN THESE ROPES!
TALKING TO KING TEMDAN IS THE LEAST OF MY WORRIES!
I HAVE TO GET AWAY AND FIND URUKI!
BUT IF I STOP URUKI, WHAT WOULD HAPPEN TO SOREN?
WHY DID HE DO THAT?
WAAH
I'M NOT FEELING WELL AT ALL...
CHAK
CHAK
THE MEDICINE...
TUG

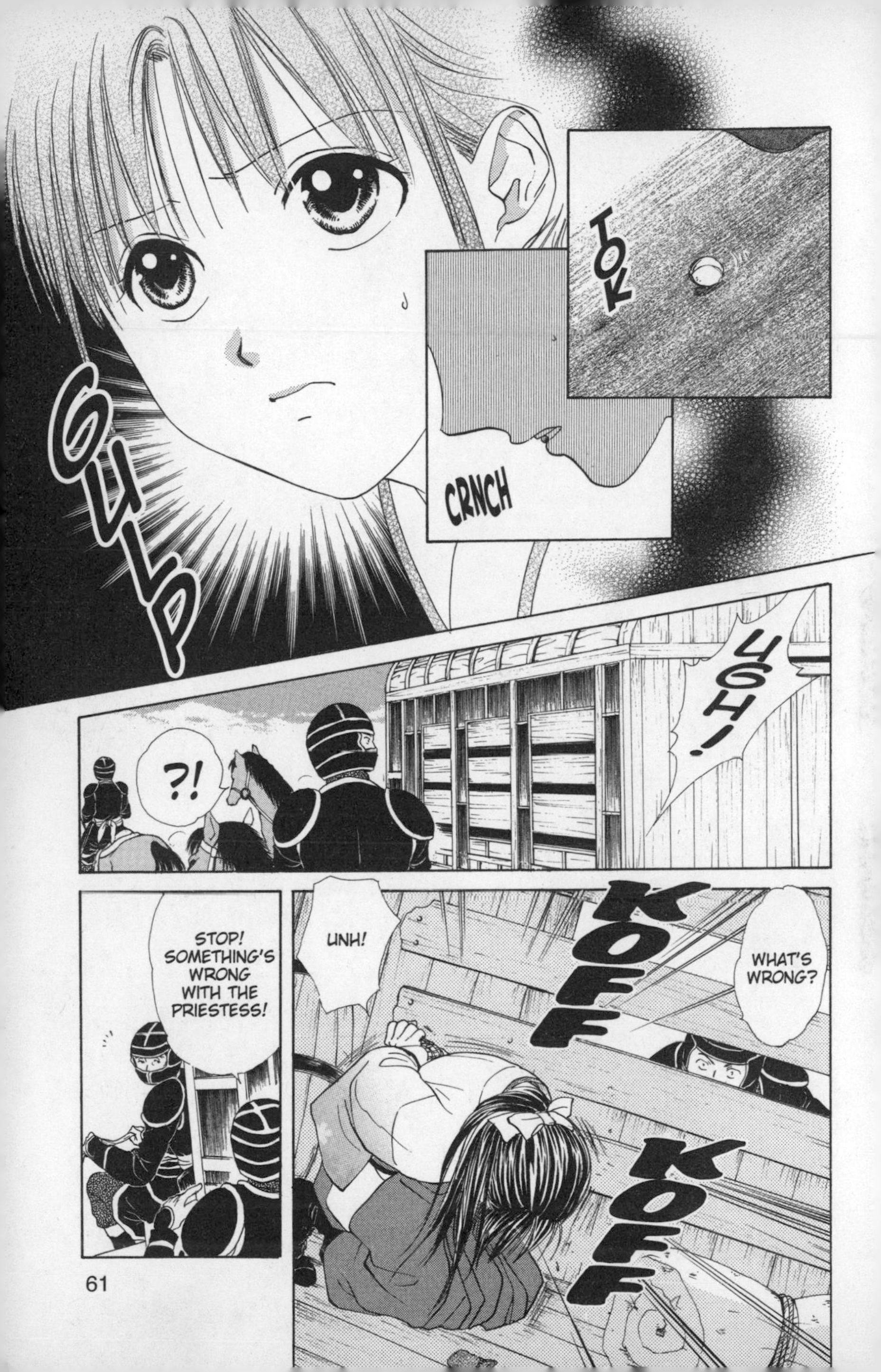

TOK
CRNCH
GULP
UGH!
?!
KOFF
KOFF
WHAT'S WRONG?
UNH!
STOP! SOMETHING'S WRONG WITH THE PRIESTESS!

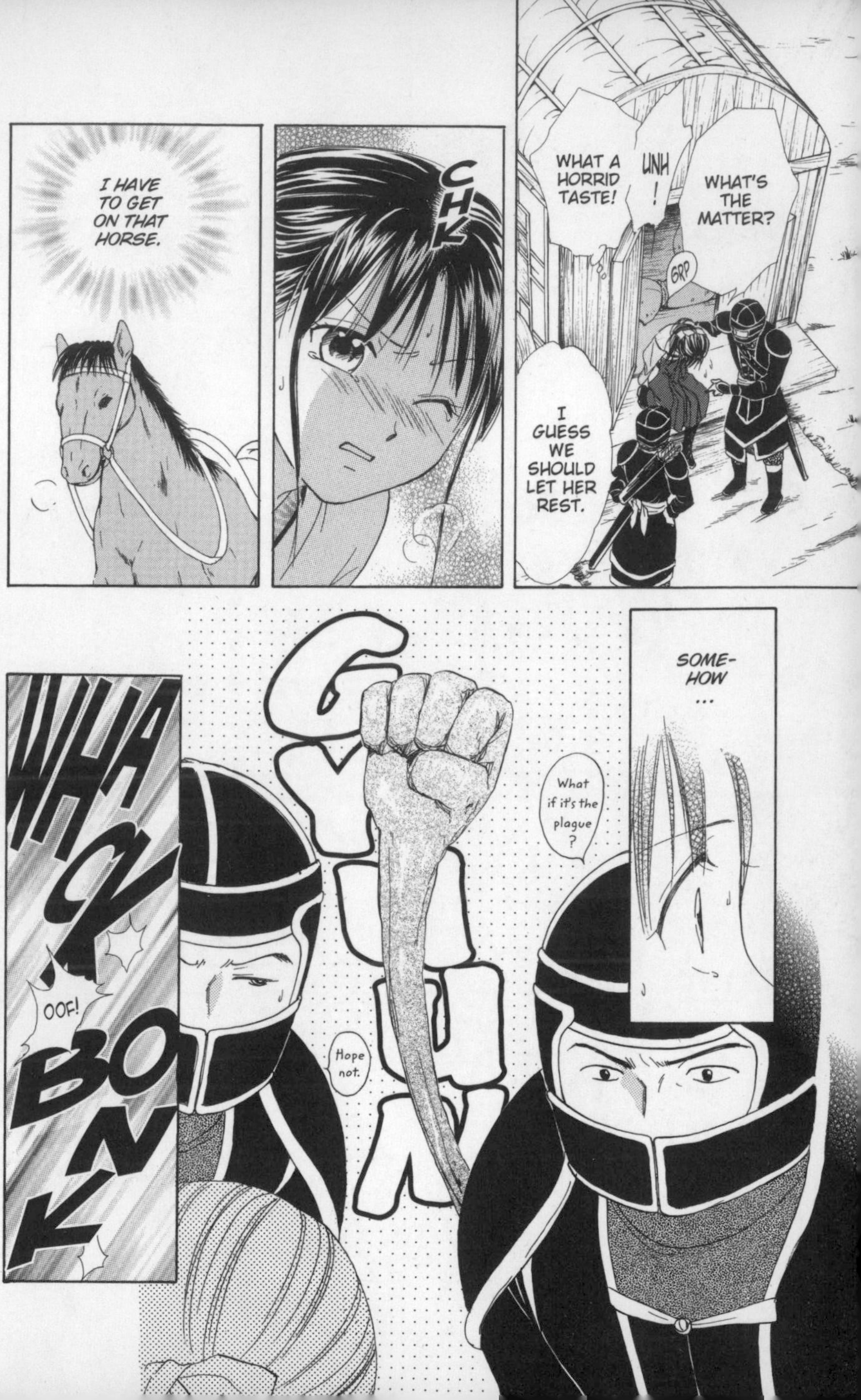
WHAT'S THE MATTER?
UNH!
WHAT A HORRID TASTE!
GRP
I GUESS WE SHOULD LET HER REST.
CHK
I HAVE TO GET ON THAT HORSE.
SOME-HOW...
What if it's the plague?
Hope not.
WHACK
BONK
OOF!

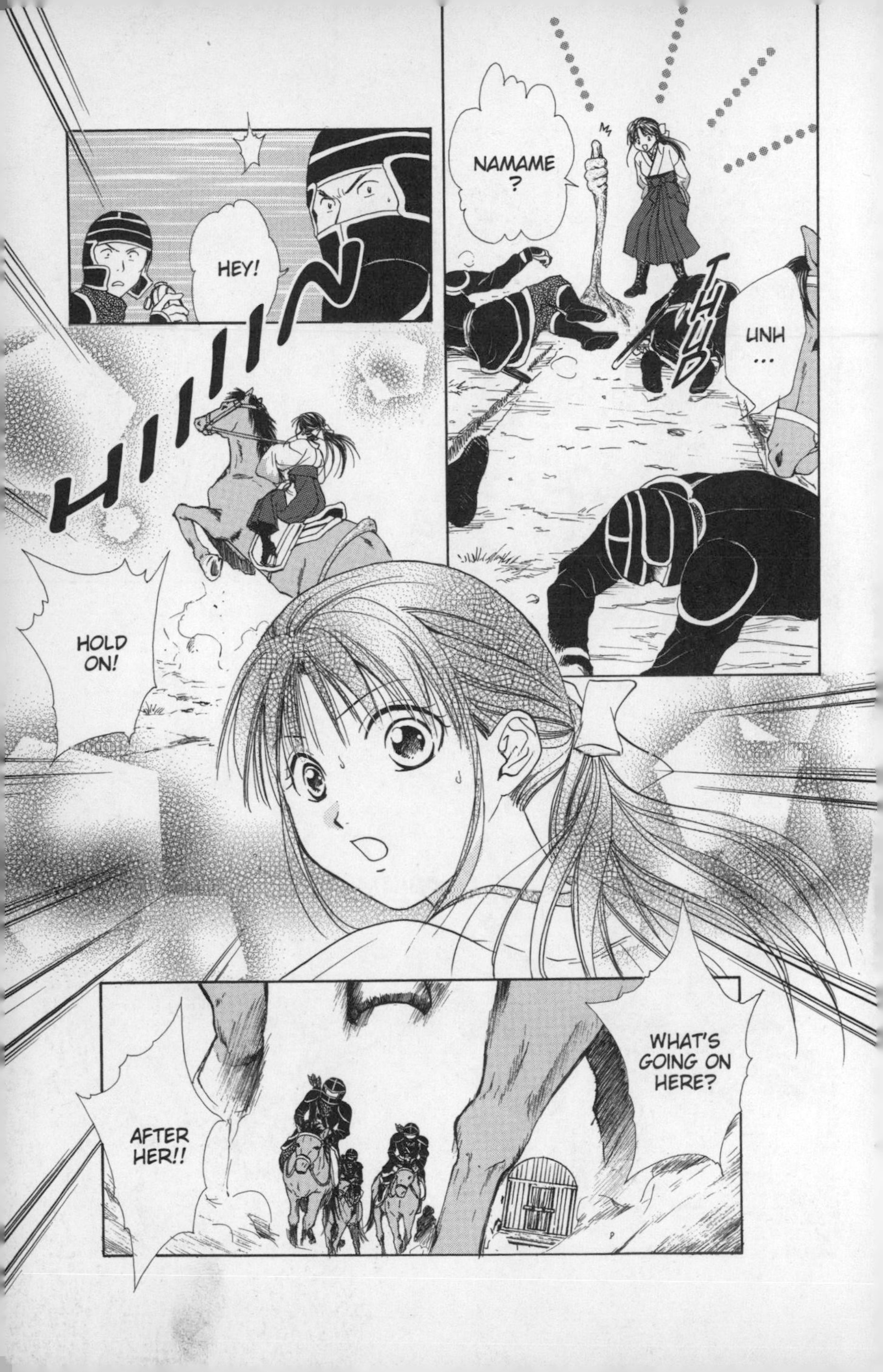
NAMAME?
UNH...
HEY!
HIIIIN
HOLD ON!
WHAT'S GOING ON HERE?
AFTER HER!!

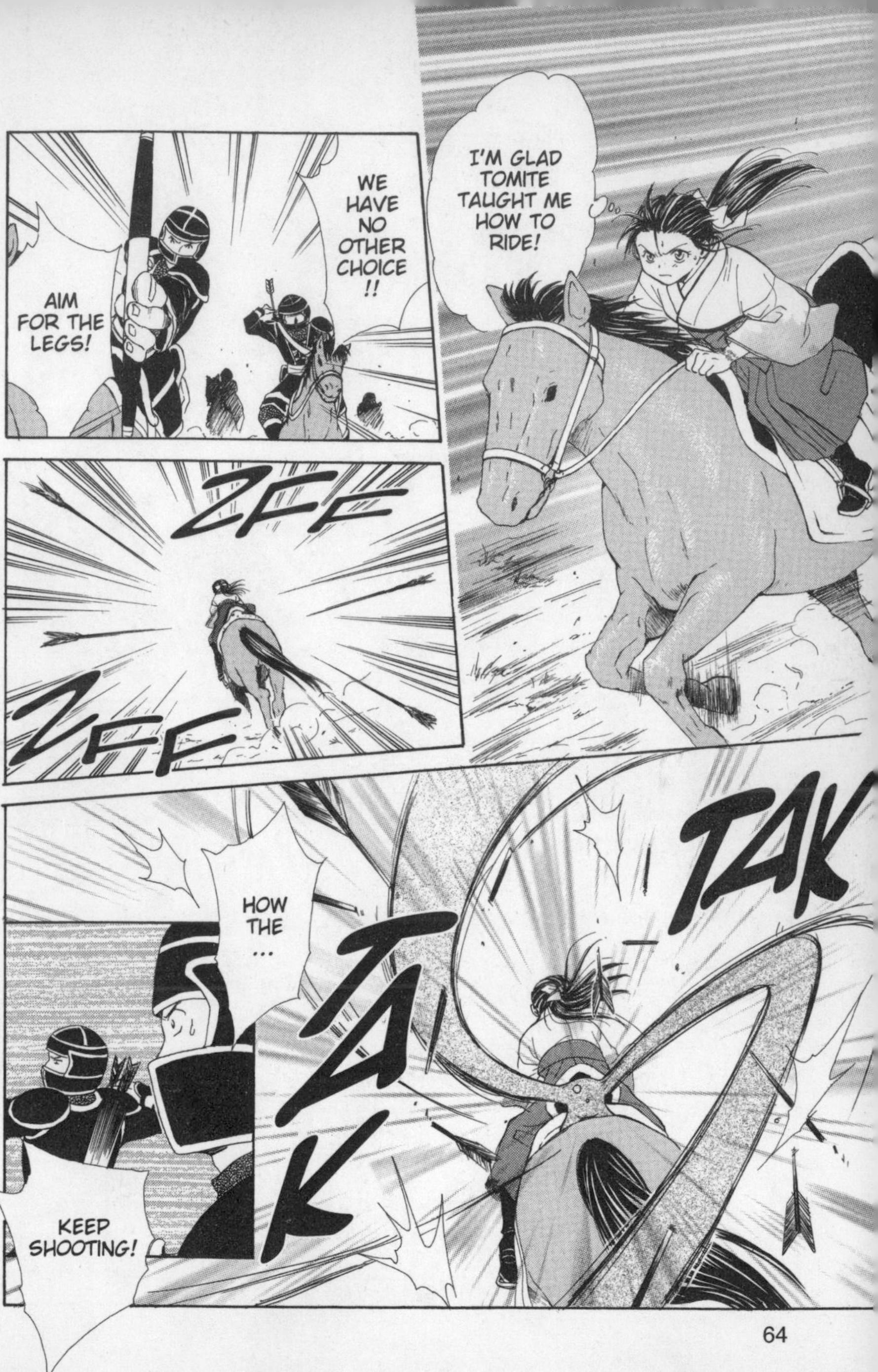
I'M GLAD TOMITE TAUGHT ME HOW TO RIDE!
WE HAVE NO OTHER CHOICE !!
AIM FOR THE LEGS!
ZFF
ZFF
TAK
TAK
HOW THE ...
KEEP SHOOTING!

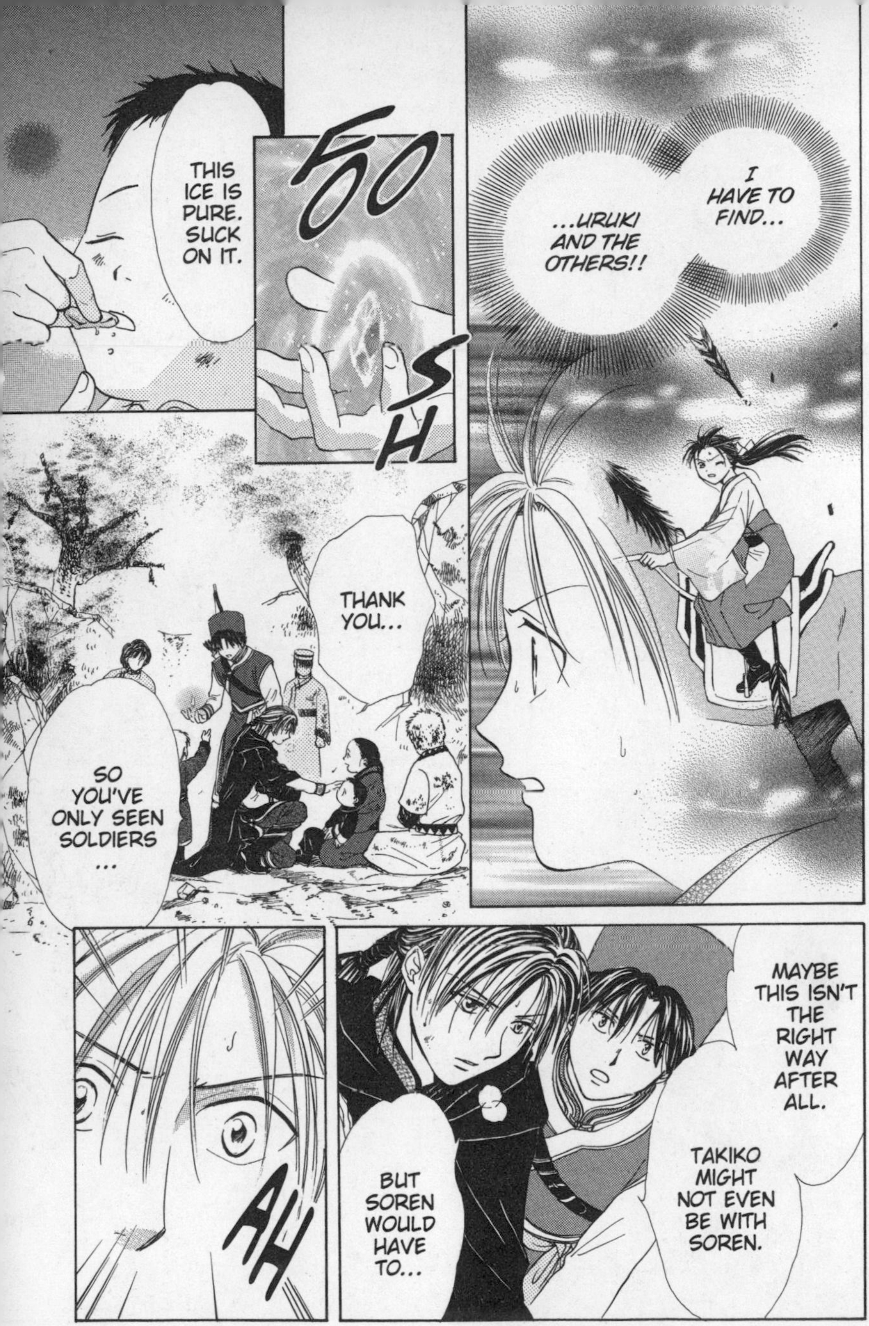
I HAVE TO FIND...
...URUKI AND THE OTHERS!!
SOO
SH
THIS ICE IS PURE. SUCK ON IT.
THANK YOU...
SO YOU'VE ONLY SEEN SOLDIERS...
MAYBE THIS ISN'T THE RIGHT WAY AFTER ALL.
TAKIKO MIGHT NOT EVEN BE WITH SOREN.
BUT SOREN WOULD HAVE TO...
AH

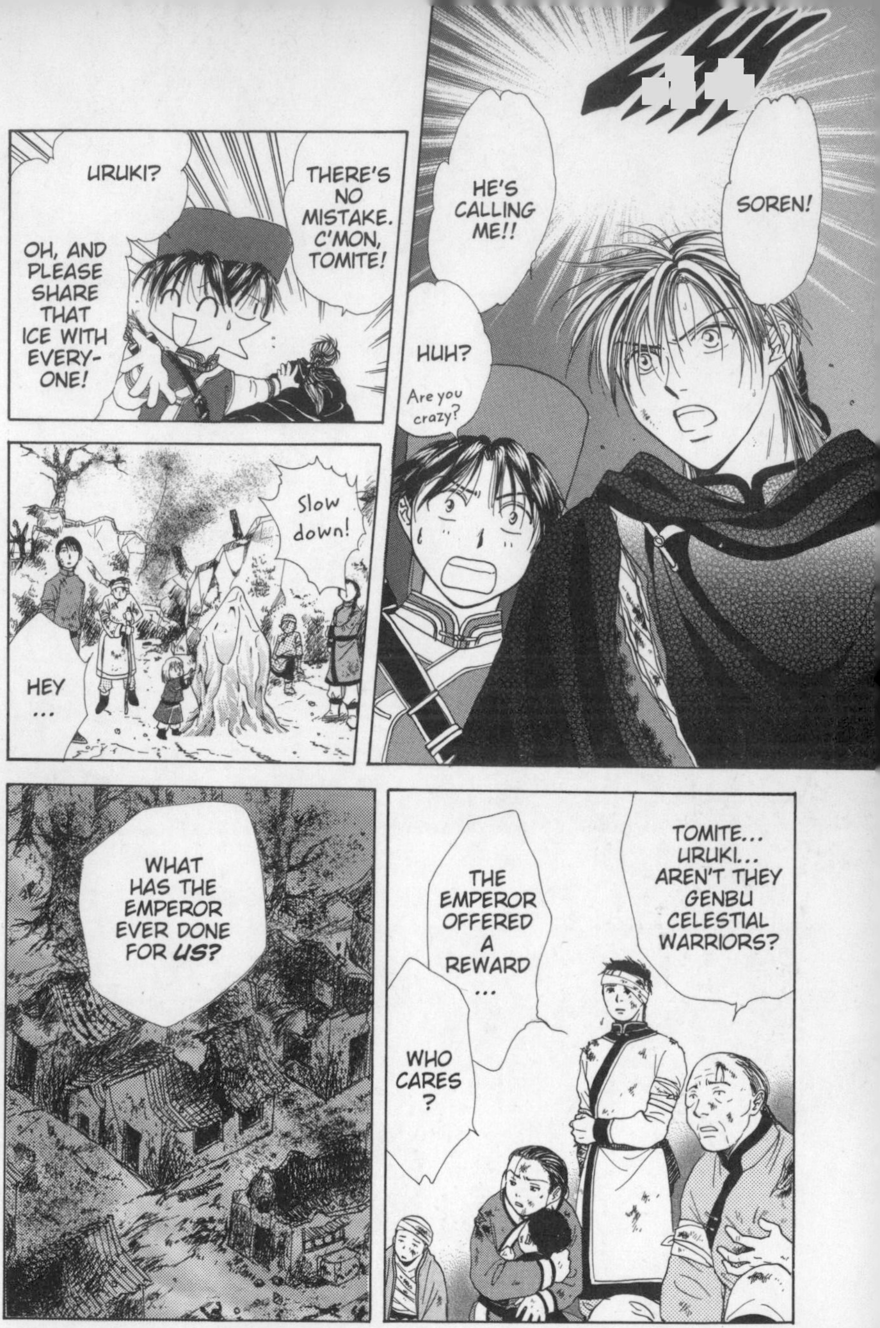
SOREN!
HE'S CALLING ME!!
HUH?
Are you crazy?
THERE'S NO MISTAKE. C'MON, TOMITE!
URUKI?
OH, AND PLEASE SHARE THAT ICE WITH EVERY-ONE!
Slow down!
HEY...
TOMITE... URUKI... AREN'T THEY GENBU CELESTIAL WARRIORS?
THE EMPEROR OFFERED A REWARD...
WHO CARES?
WHAT HAS THE EMPEROR EVER DONE FOR *US*?

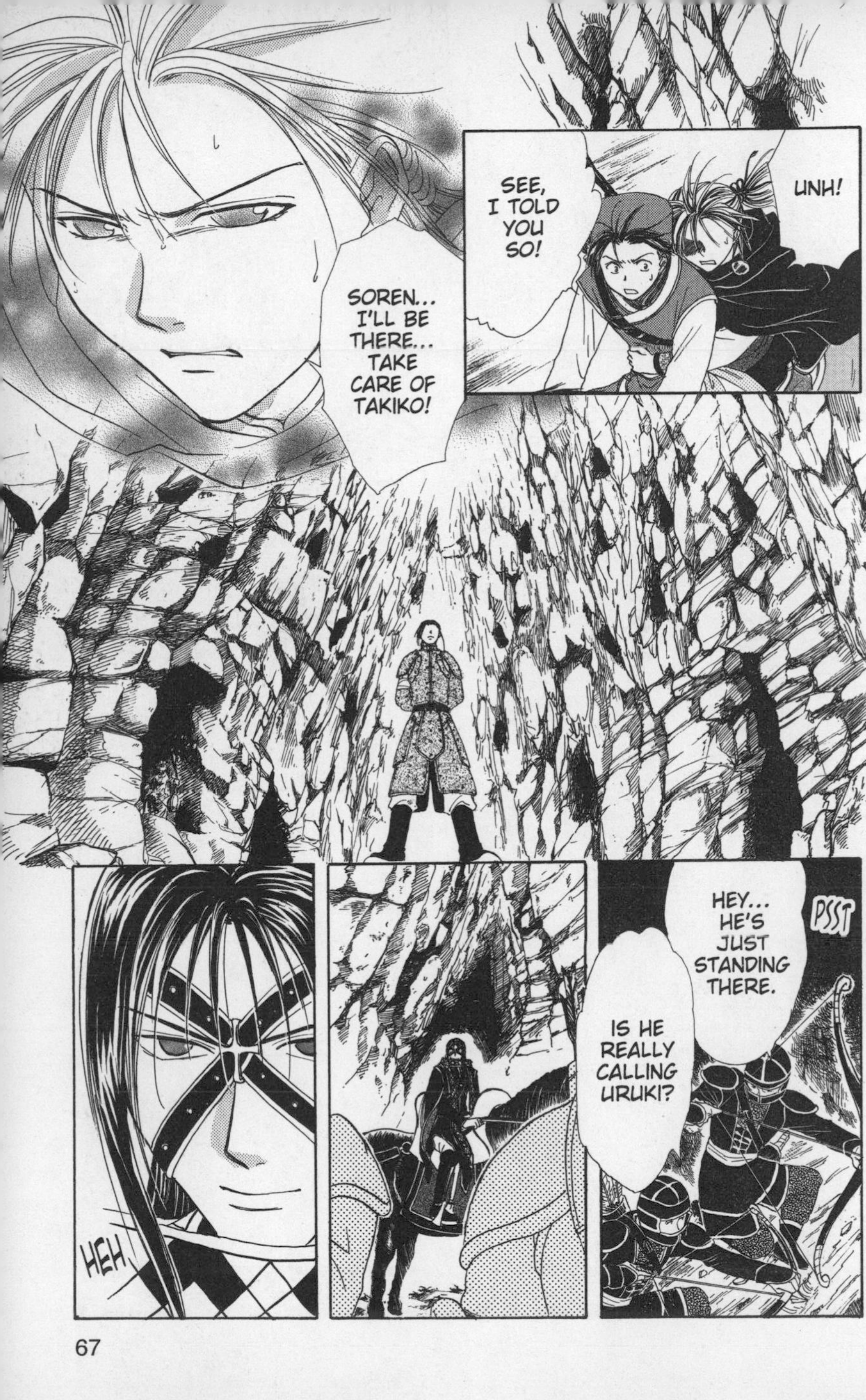
UNH!
SEE, I TOLD YOU SO!
SOREN... I'LL BE THERE... TAKE CARE OF TAKIKO!
PSST
HEY... HE'S JUST STANDING THERE.
IS HE REALLY CALLING URUKI?
HEH

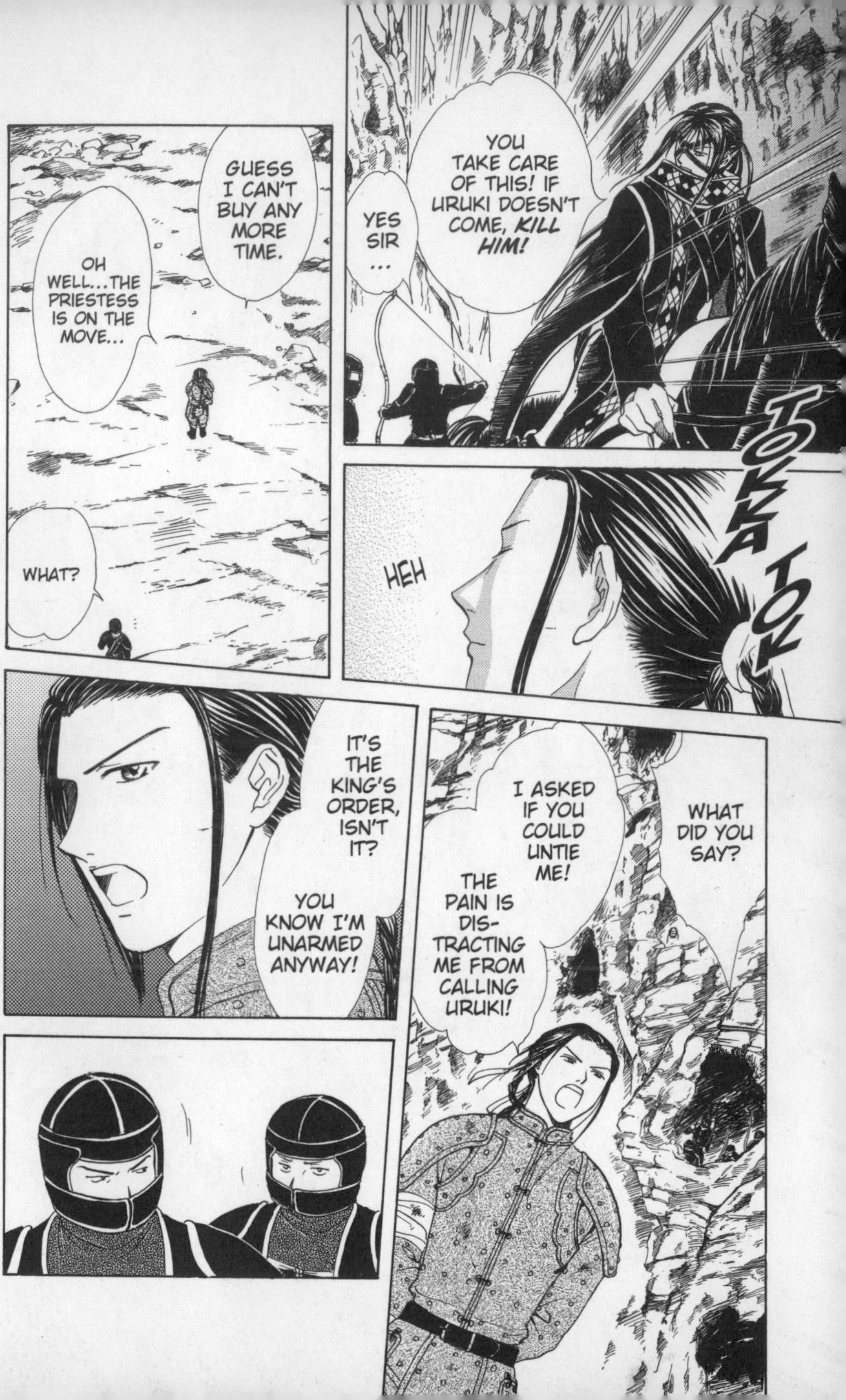
YOU TAKE CARE OF THIS! IF URUKI DOESN'T COME, KILL HIM!
YES SIR ...
TOKKA TOKK
HEH
GUESS I CAN'T BUY ANY MORE TIME.
OH WELL...THE PRIESTESS IS ON THE MOVE...
WHAT?
WHAT DID YOU SAY?
I ASKED IF YOU COULD UNTIE ME!
THE PAIN IS DIS-TRACTING ME FROM CALLING URUKI!
IT'S THE KING'S ORDER, ISN'T IT?
YOU KNOW I'M UNARMED ANYWAY!

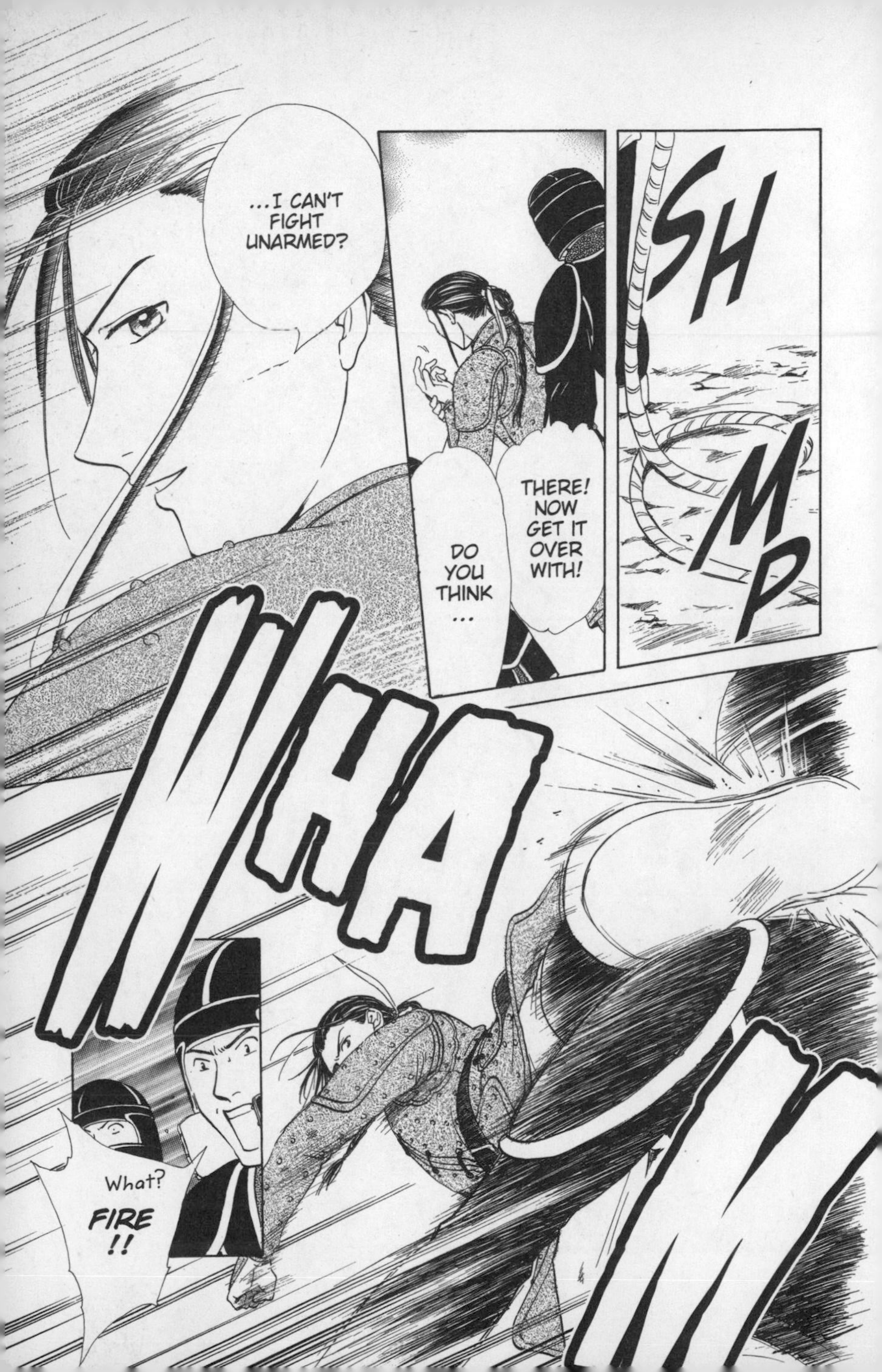
SHMP
THERE! NOW GET IT OVER WITH!
DO YOU THINK ...
...I CAN'T FIGHT UNARMED?
WHAM
What?
FIRE!!

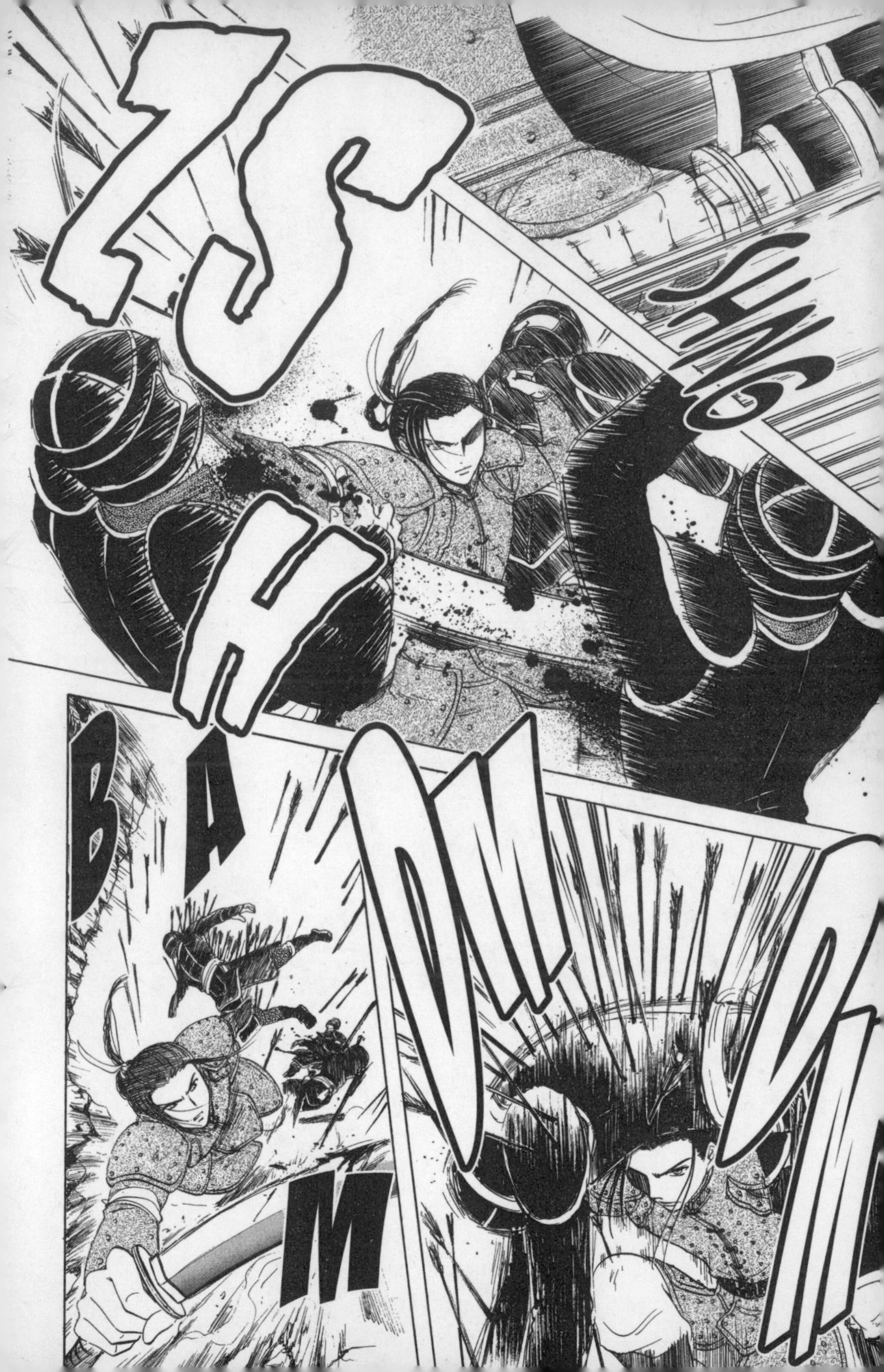
SHING
BAM

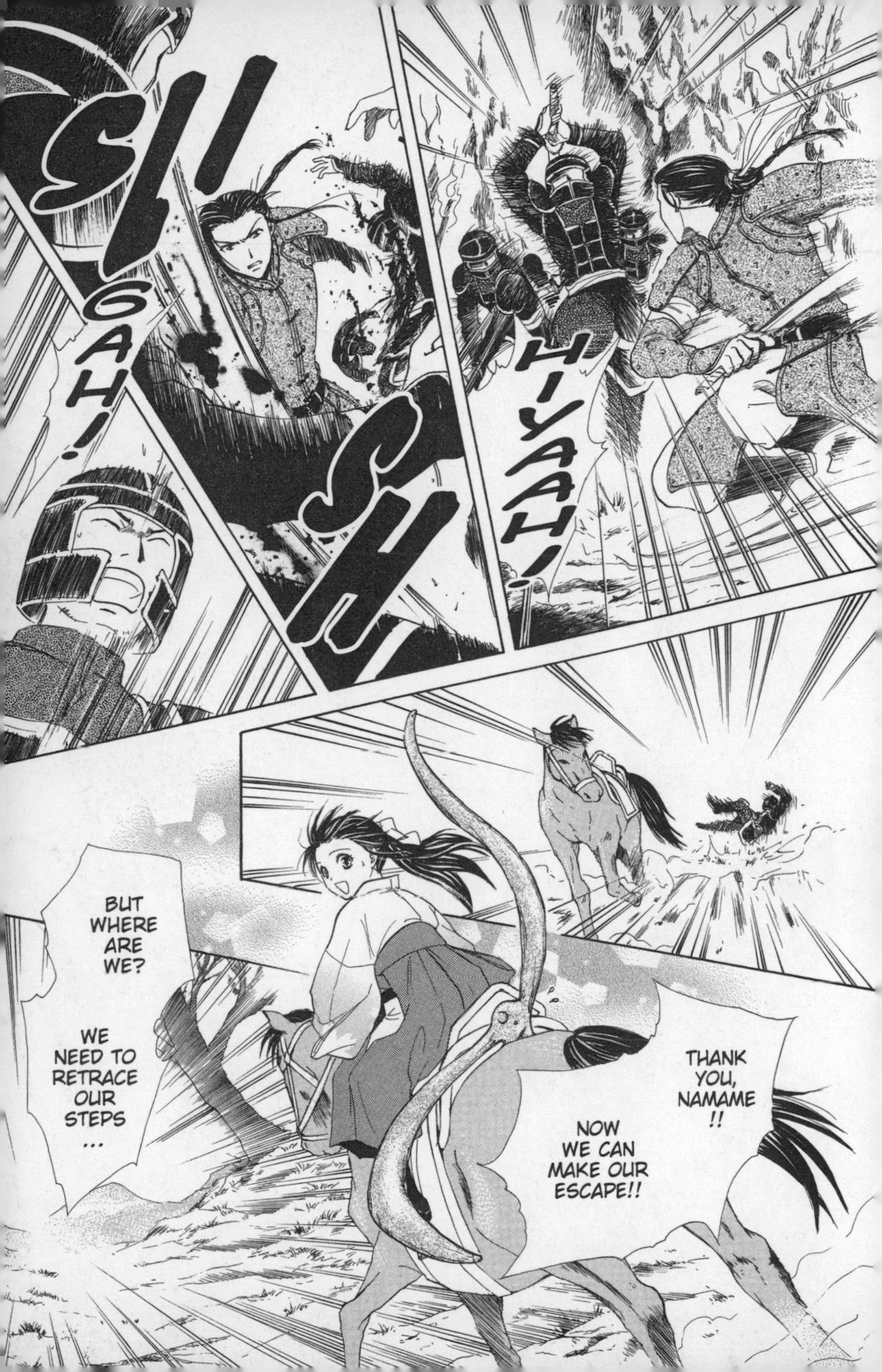
HIYAAAH!!
SH
SH
GAH!!
THANK YOU, NAMAME!!
NOW WE CAN MAKE OUR ESCAPE!!
BUT WHERE ARE WE?
WE NEED TO RETRACE OUR STEPS ...

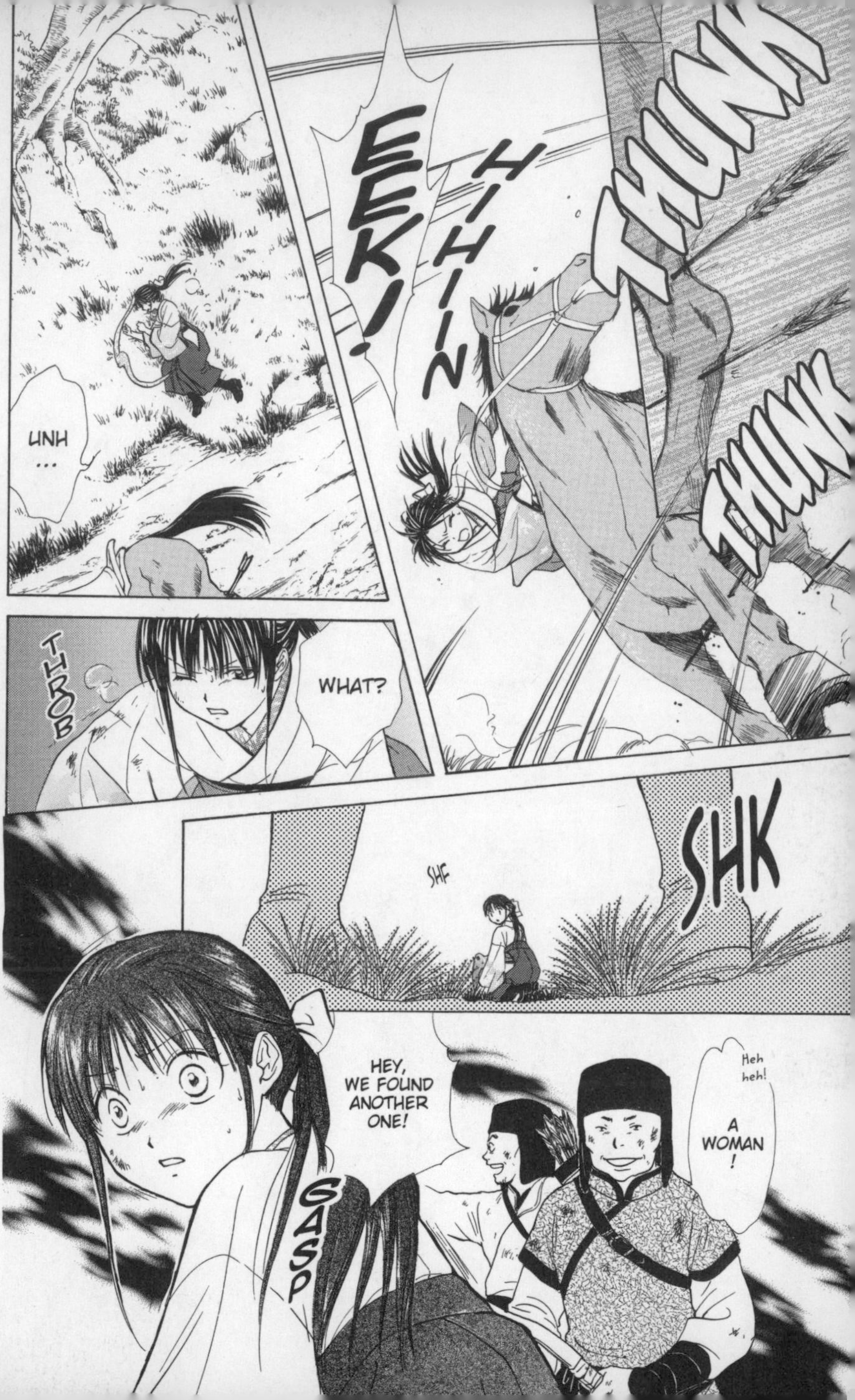
THUNK
THUNK
HIHIIN
EEK!
UNH...
THROB
WHAT?
SHK
SHF
Heh heh!
A WOMAN!
HEY, WE FOUND ANOTHER ONE!
GASP

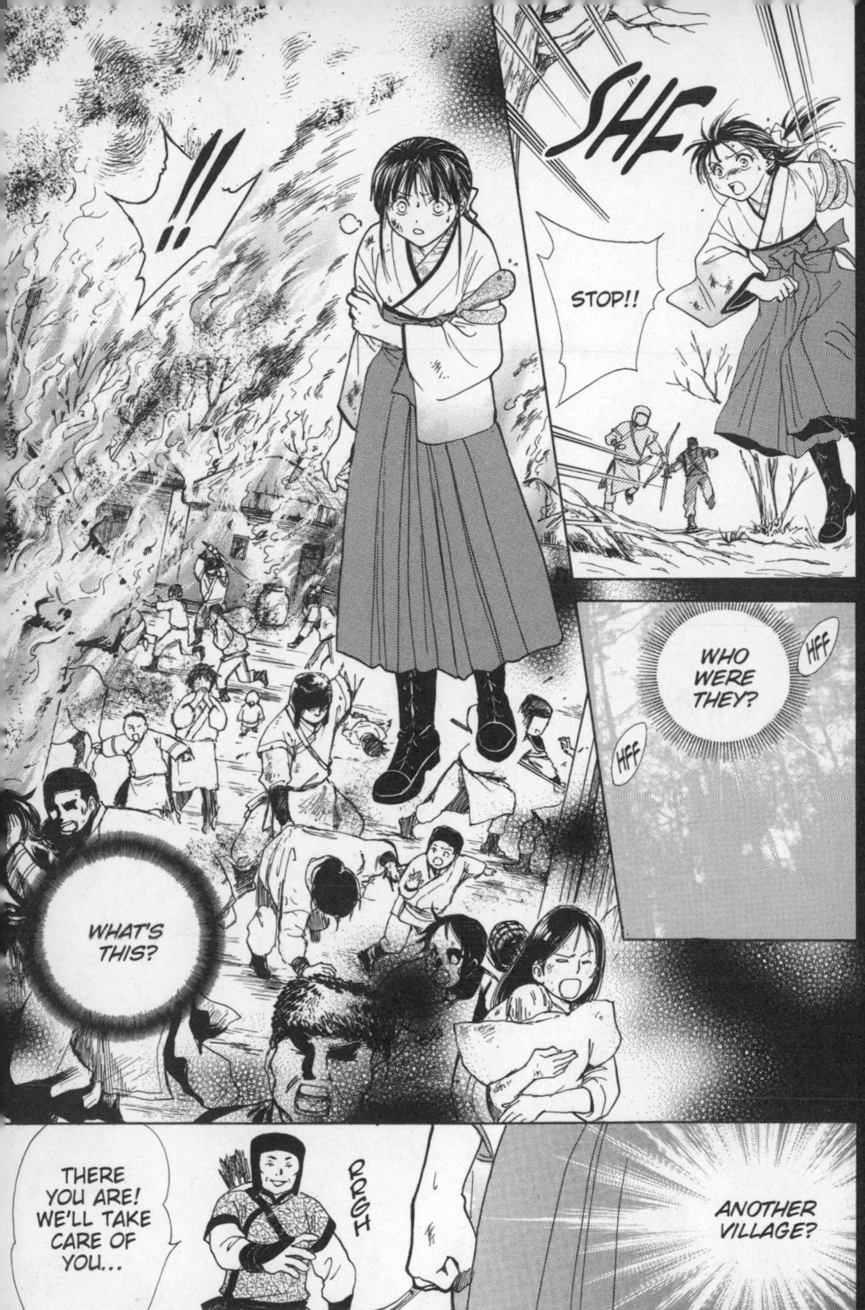
SHF
STOP!!
HFF
WHO WERE THEY?
HFF
!!
WHAT'S THIS?
ANOTHER VILLAGE?
RRGH
THERE YOU ARE! WE'LL TAKE CARE OF YOU...

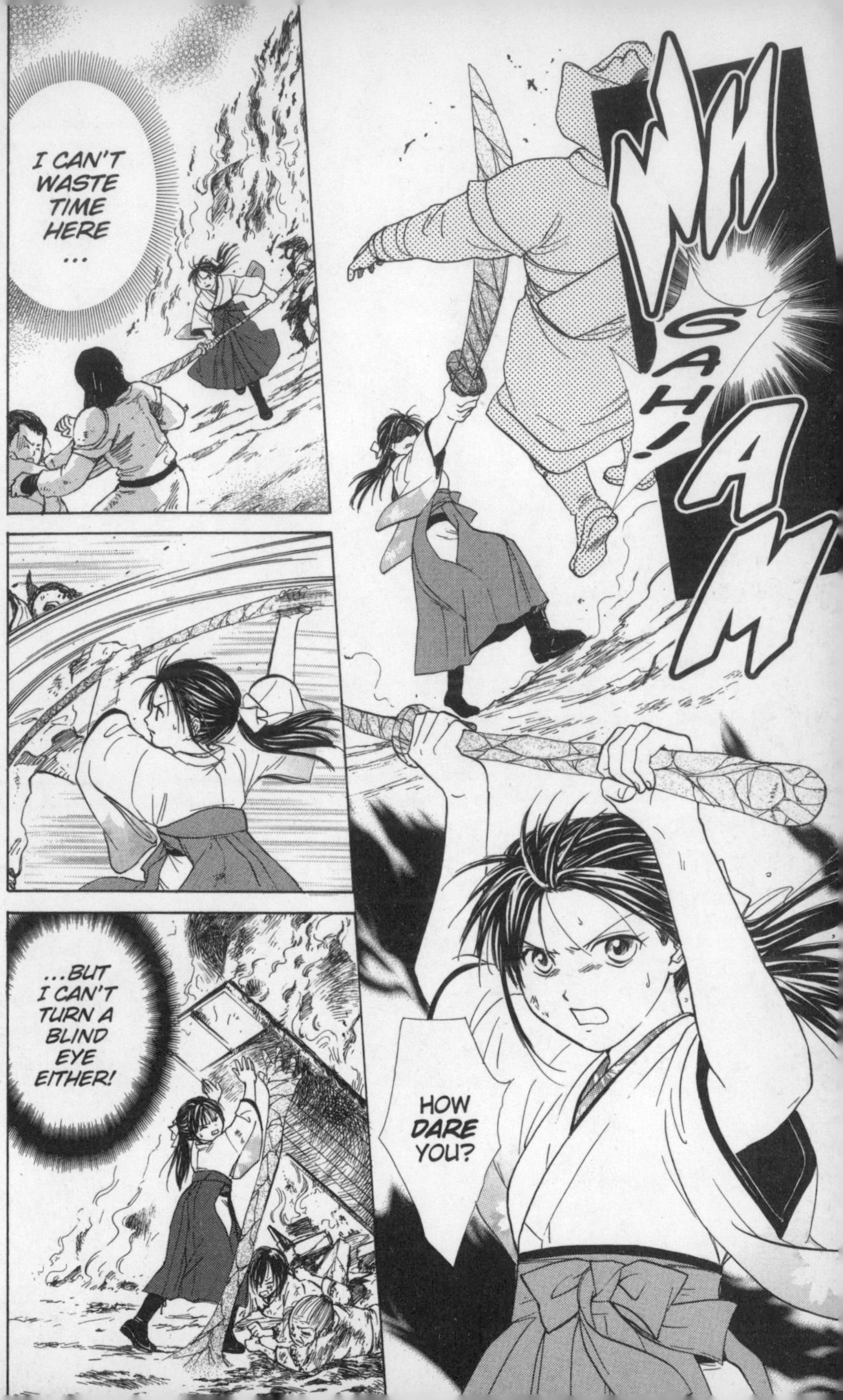
WHAM
GAH!!
HOW DARE YOU?
I CAN'T WASTE TIME HERE ...
...BUT I CAN'T TURN A BLIND EYE EITHER!

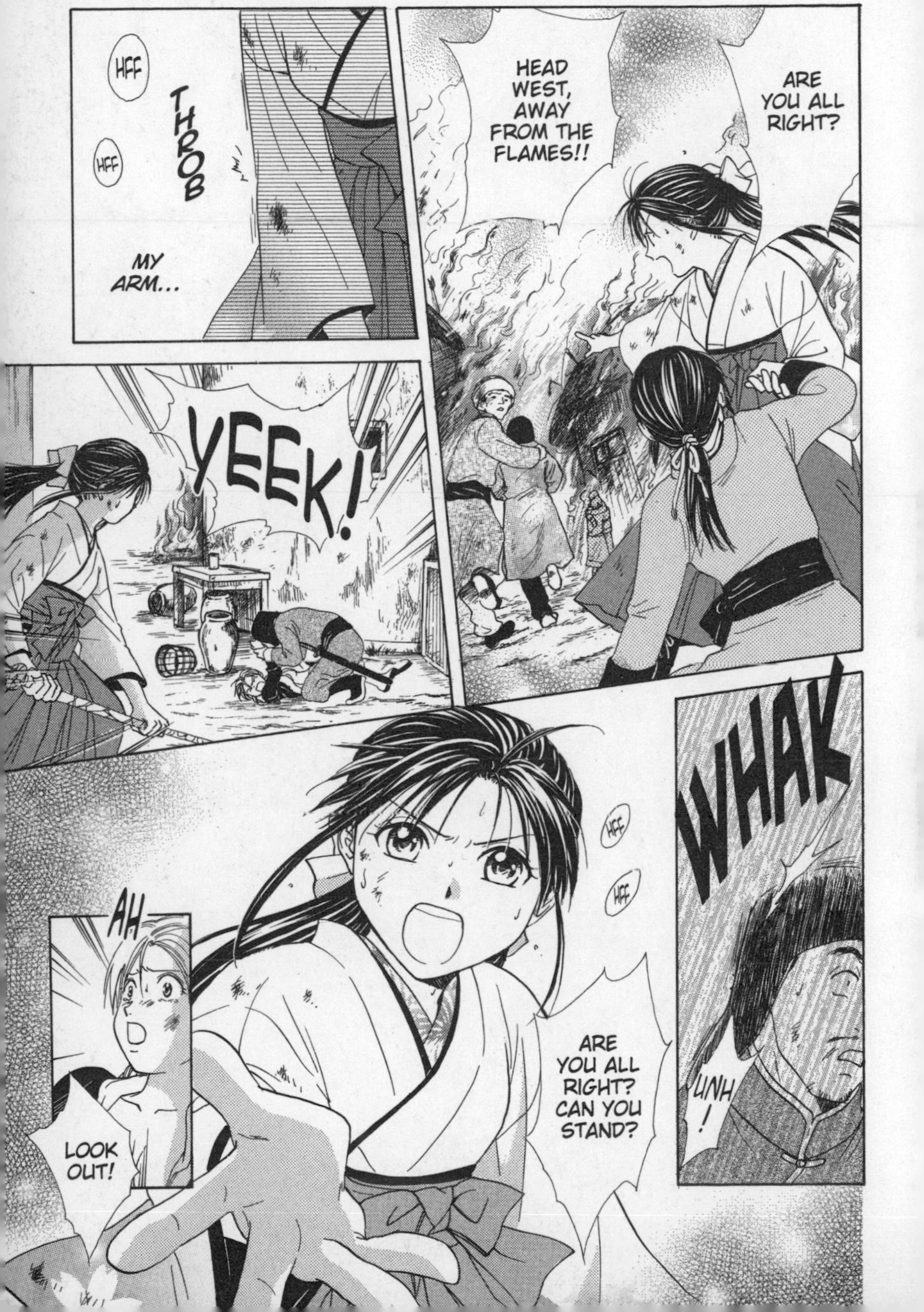
ARE YOU ALL RIGHT?
HEAD WEST, AWAY FROM THE FLAMES!!
HFF
HFF
THROB
MY ARM...
YEEK!
WHAK
UNH!
HFF
HFF
ARE YOU ALL RIGHT? CAN YOU STAND?
AH
LOOK OUT!

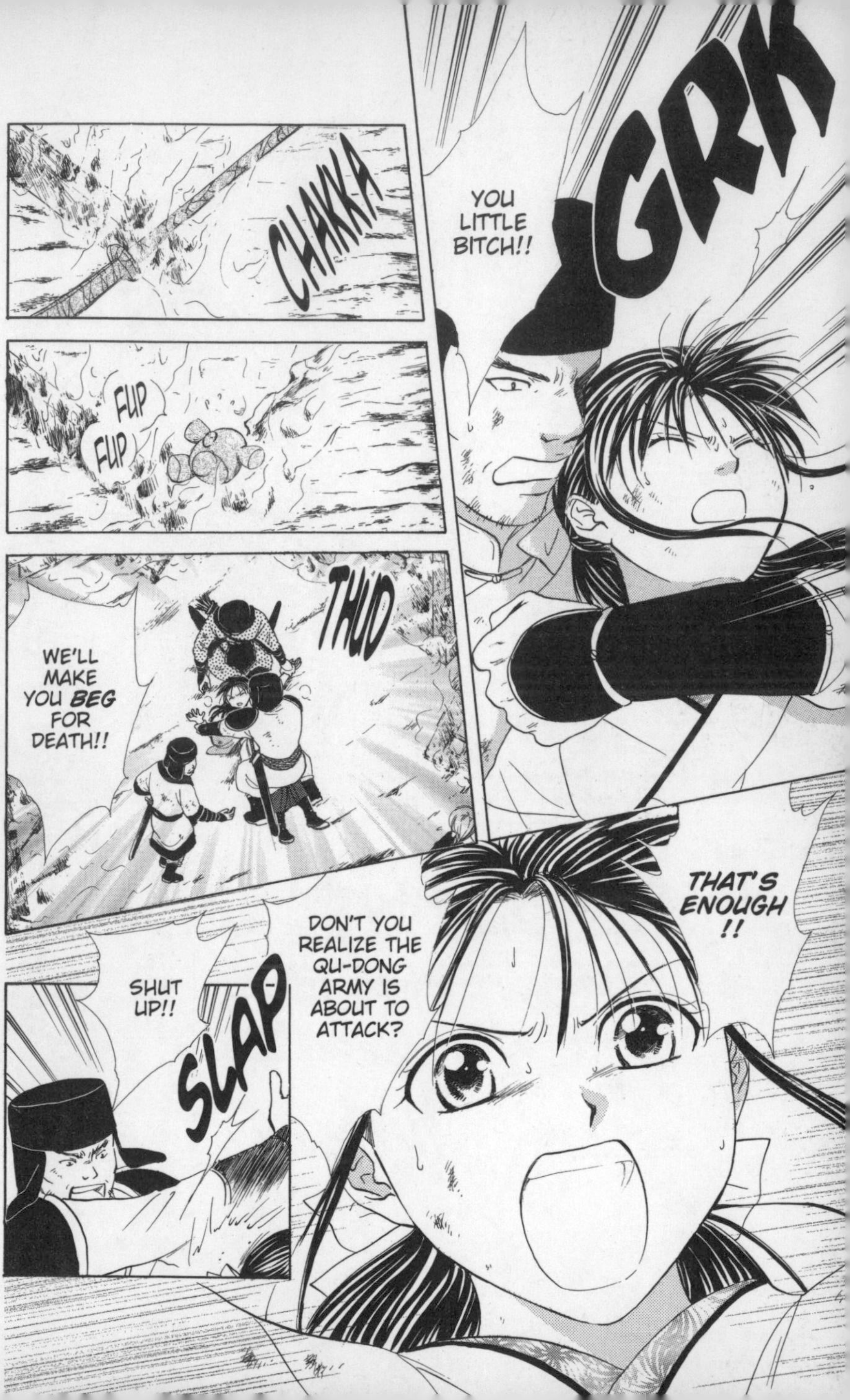
GRK
YOU LITTLE BITCH!!
CHAKKA
FUP
FUP
THUD
WE'LL MAKE YOU *BEG* FOR DEATH!!
THAT'S ENOUGH!!
DON'T YOU REALIZE THE QU-DONG ARMY IS ABOUT TO ATTACK?
SHUT UP!!
SLAP

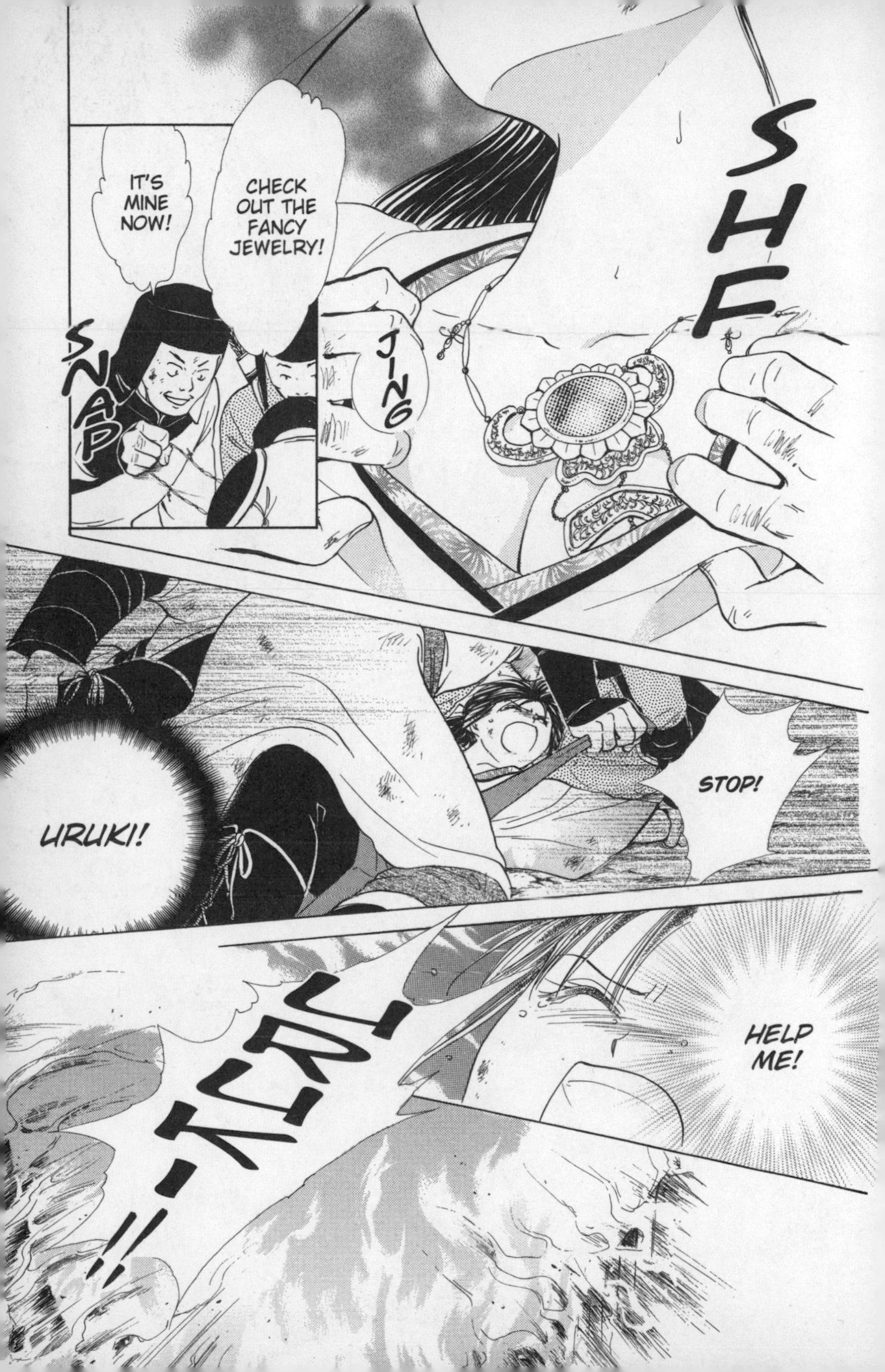
SHFF
JING
CHECK OUT THE FANCY JEWELRY!
IT'S MINE NOW!
SNAP
STOP!
URUKI!
HELP ME!
URUKI-!!

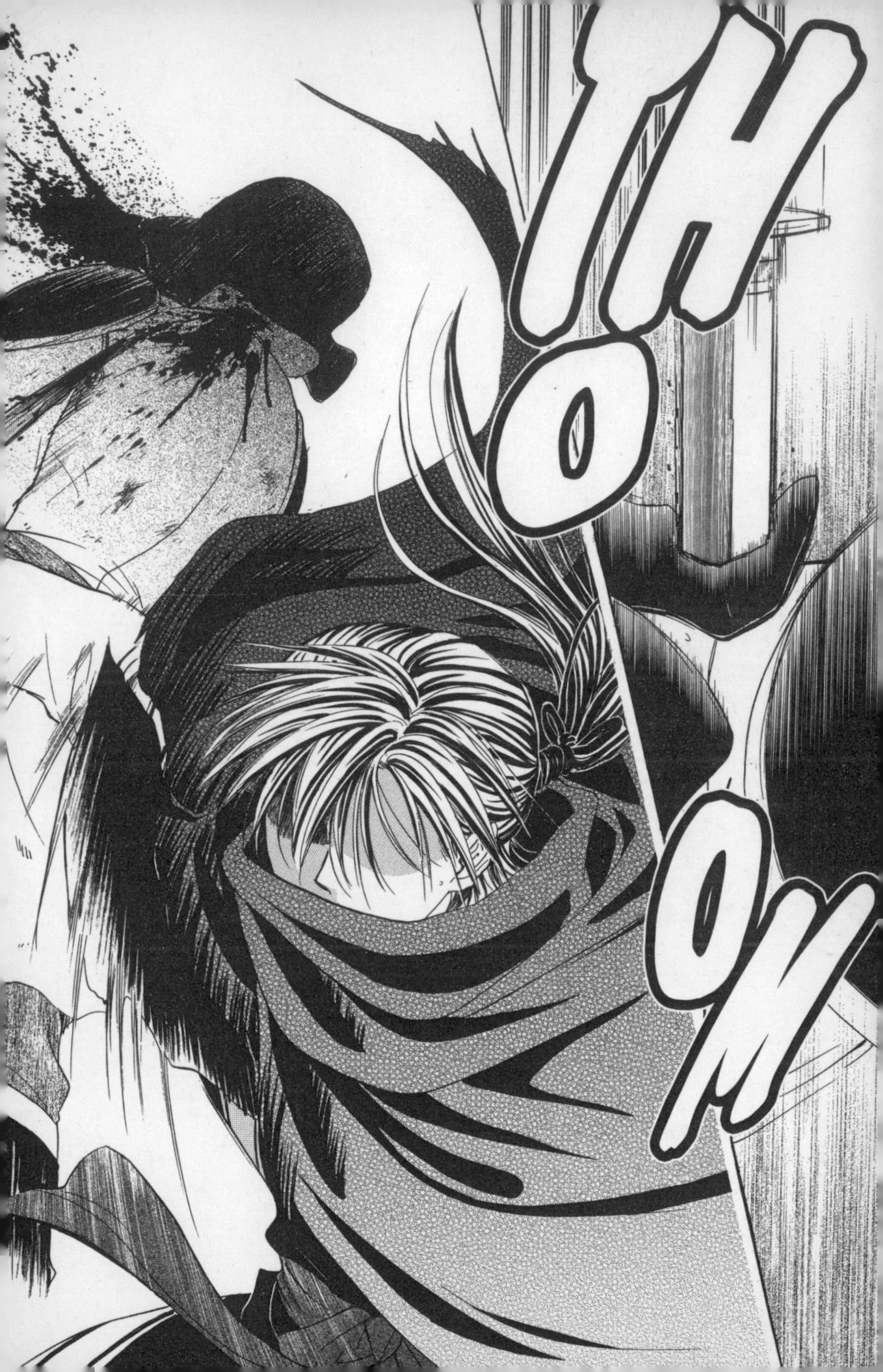

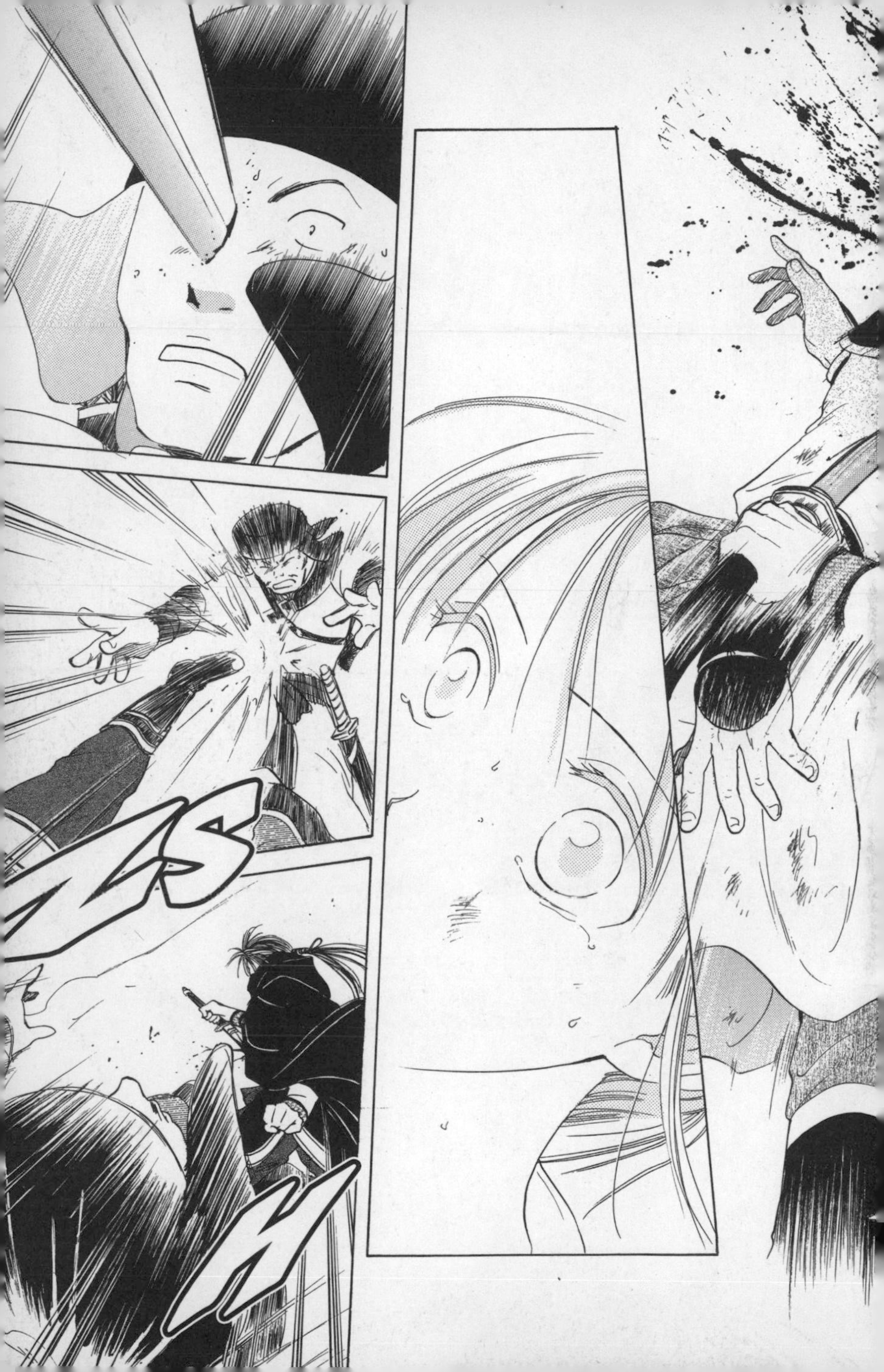

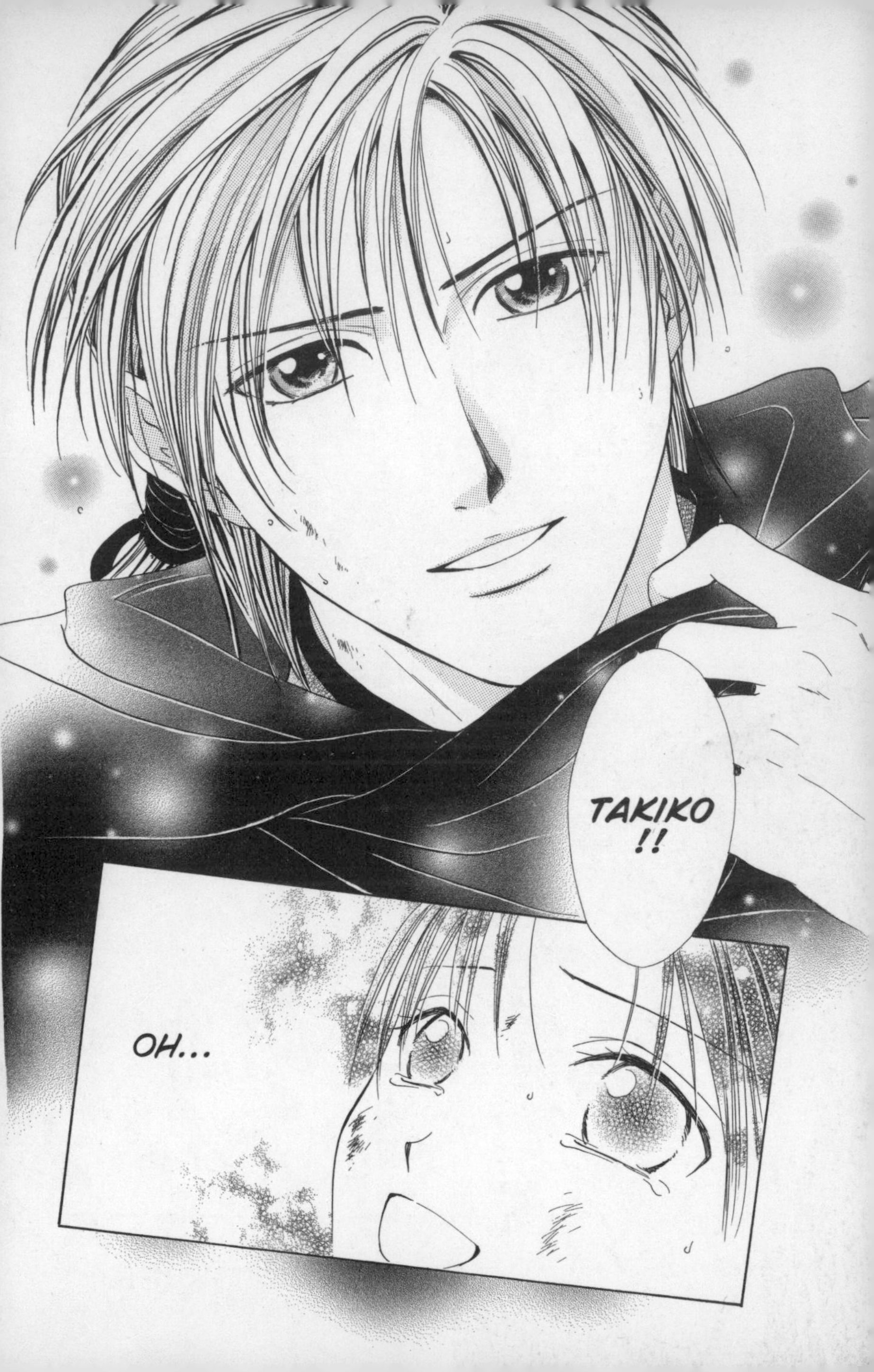
TAKIKO !!
OH...

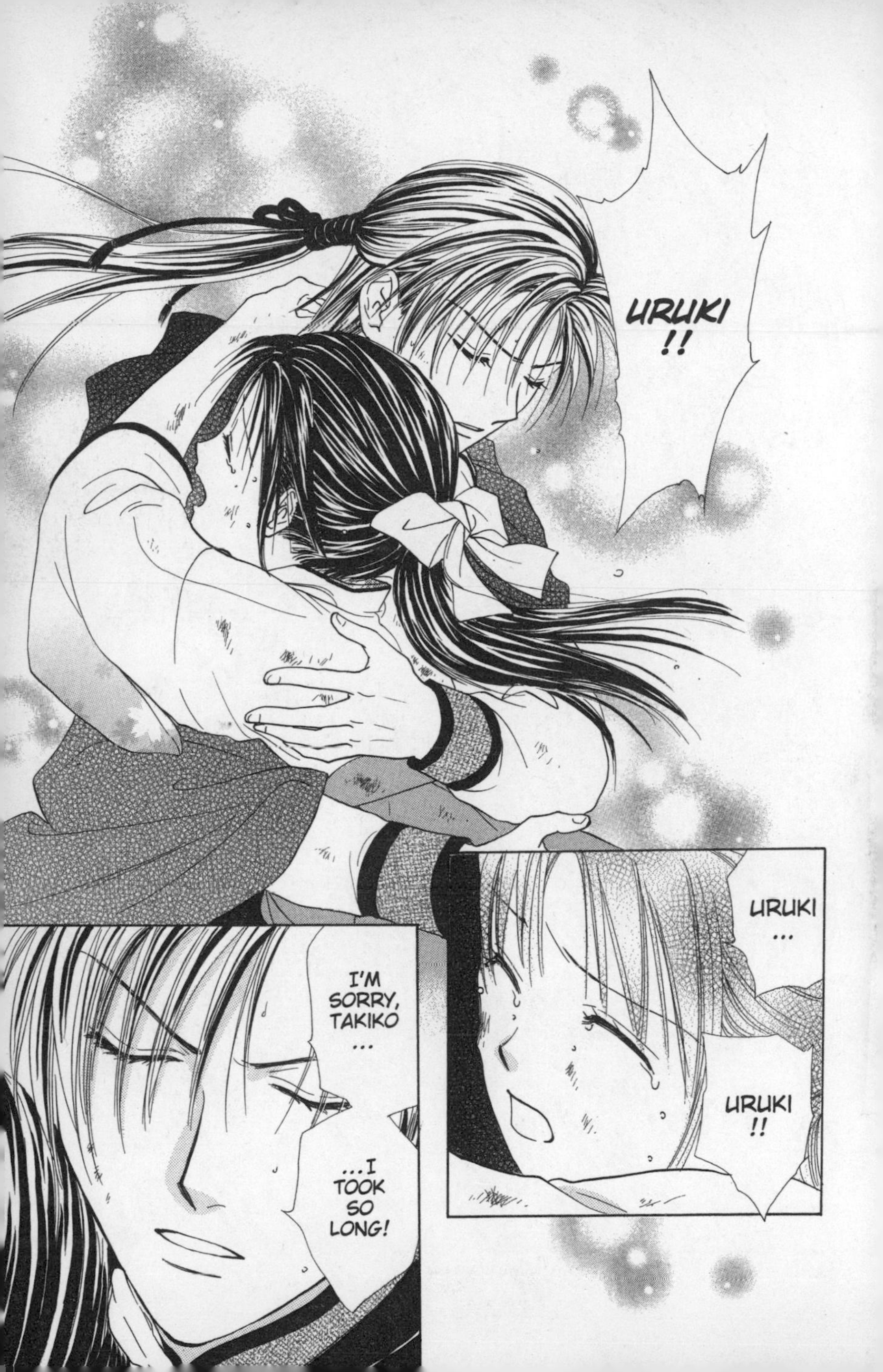
URUKI !!
URUKI ...
URUKI !!
I'M SORRY, TAKIKO ...
...I TOOK SO LONG!

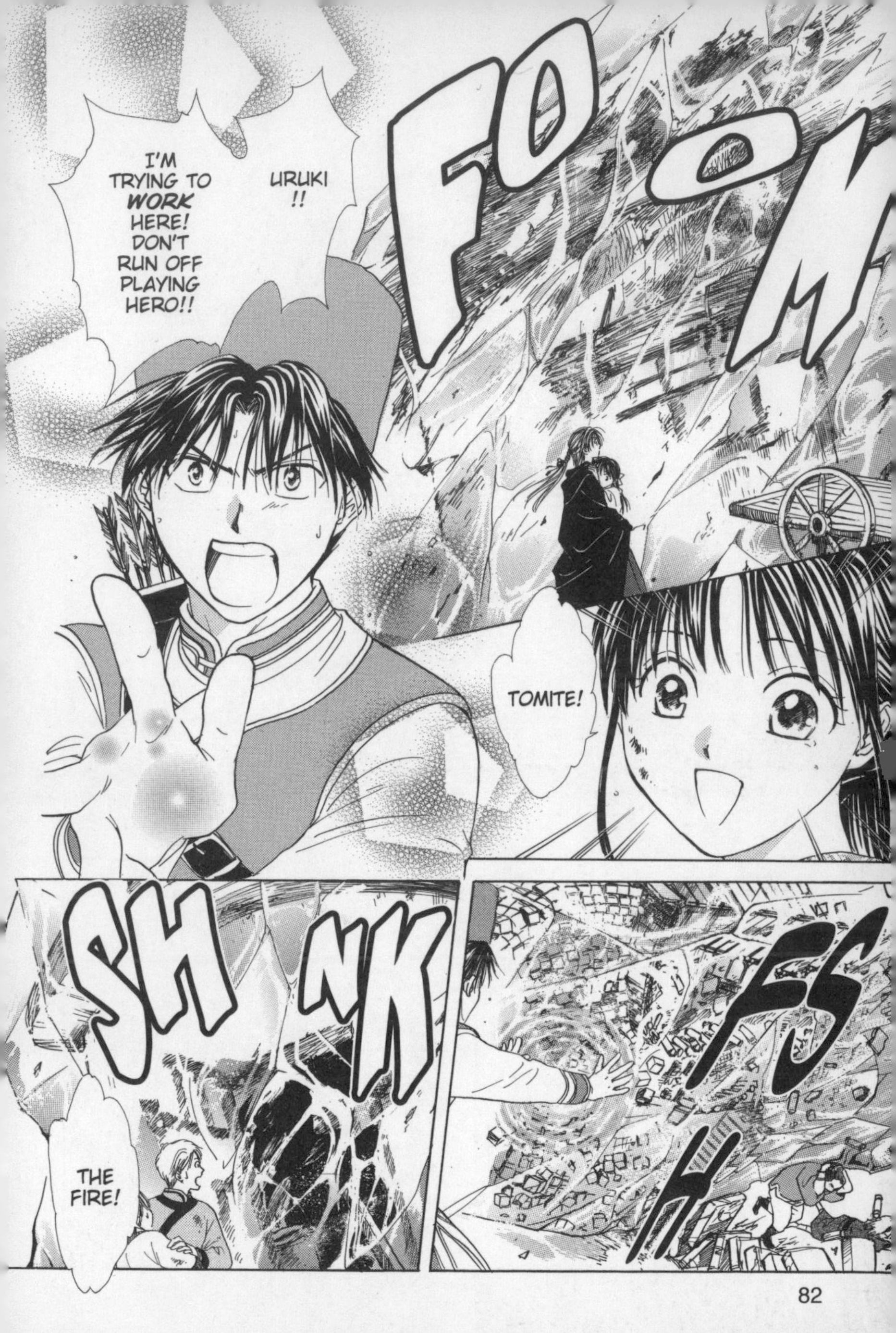
FOOM
TOMITE!
URUKI!!
I'M TRYING TO WORK HERE! DON'T RUN OFF PLAYING HERO!!
FSH
SH NK
THE FIRE!

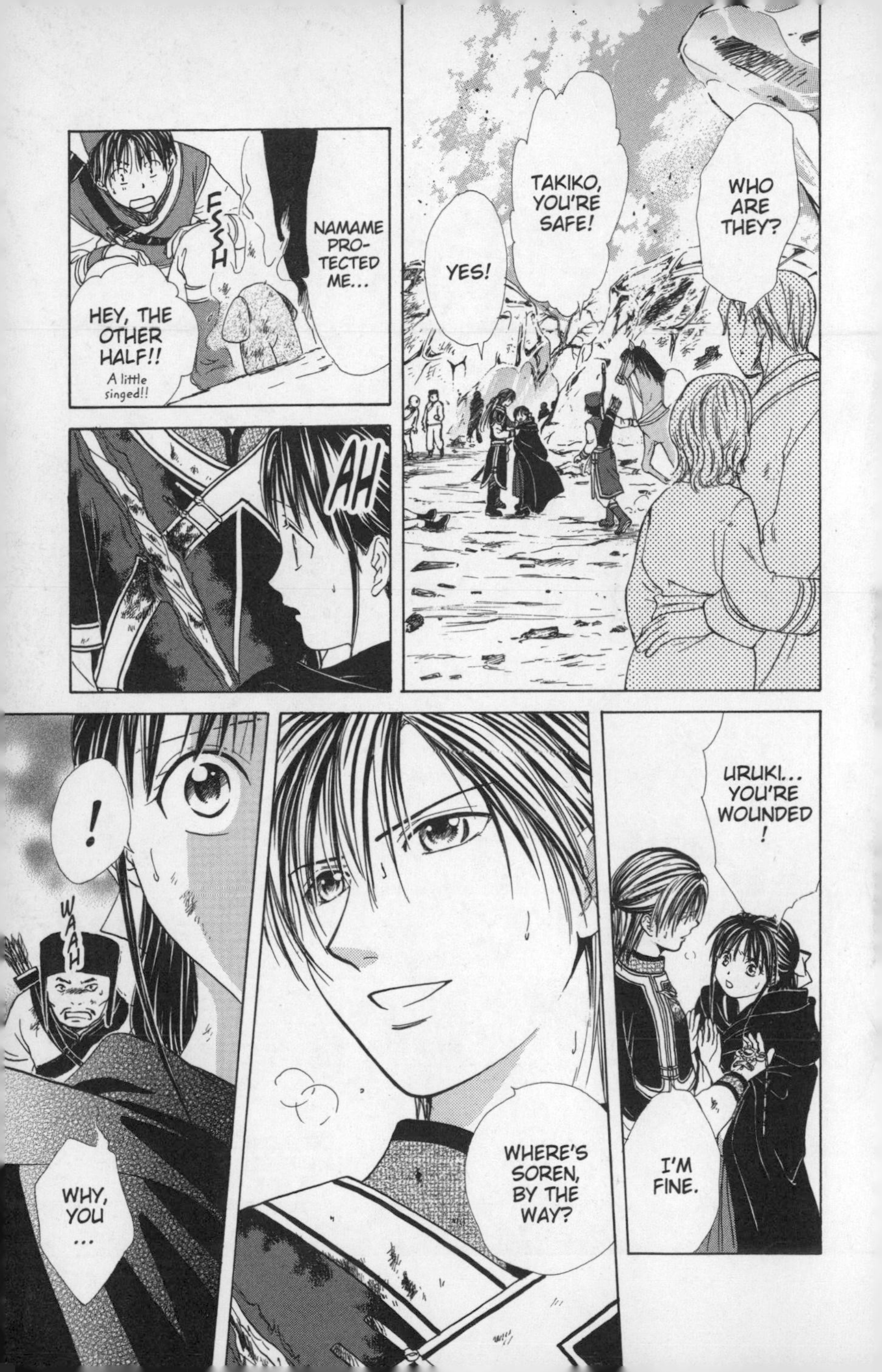
WHO ARE THEY?
TAKIKO, YOU'RE SAFE!
YES!
NAMAME PRO-TECTED ME...
FSSH
HEY, THE OTHER HALF!!
A little singed!!
AH
URUKI... YOU'RE WOUNDED!
I'M FINE.
WHERE'S SOREN, BY THE WAY?
!
WAAH
WHY, YOU ...

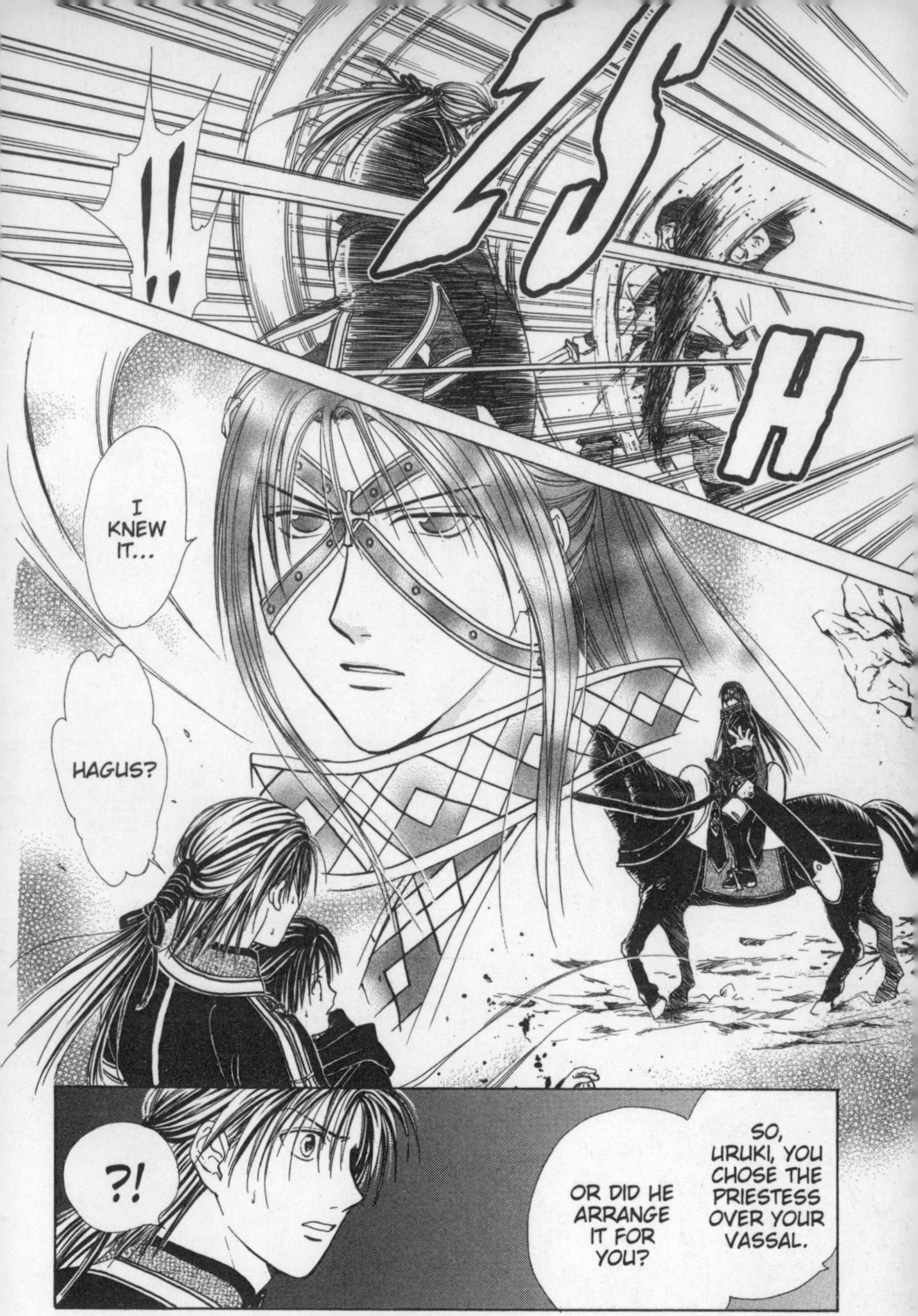
!!
I KNEW IT...
HAGUS?
SO, URUKI, YOU CHOSE THE PRIESTESS OVER YOUR VASSAL.
OR DID HE ARRANGE IT FOR YOU?
?!

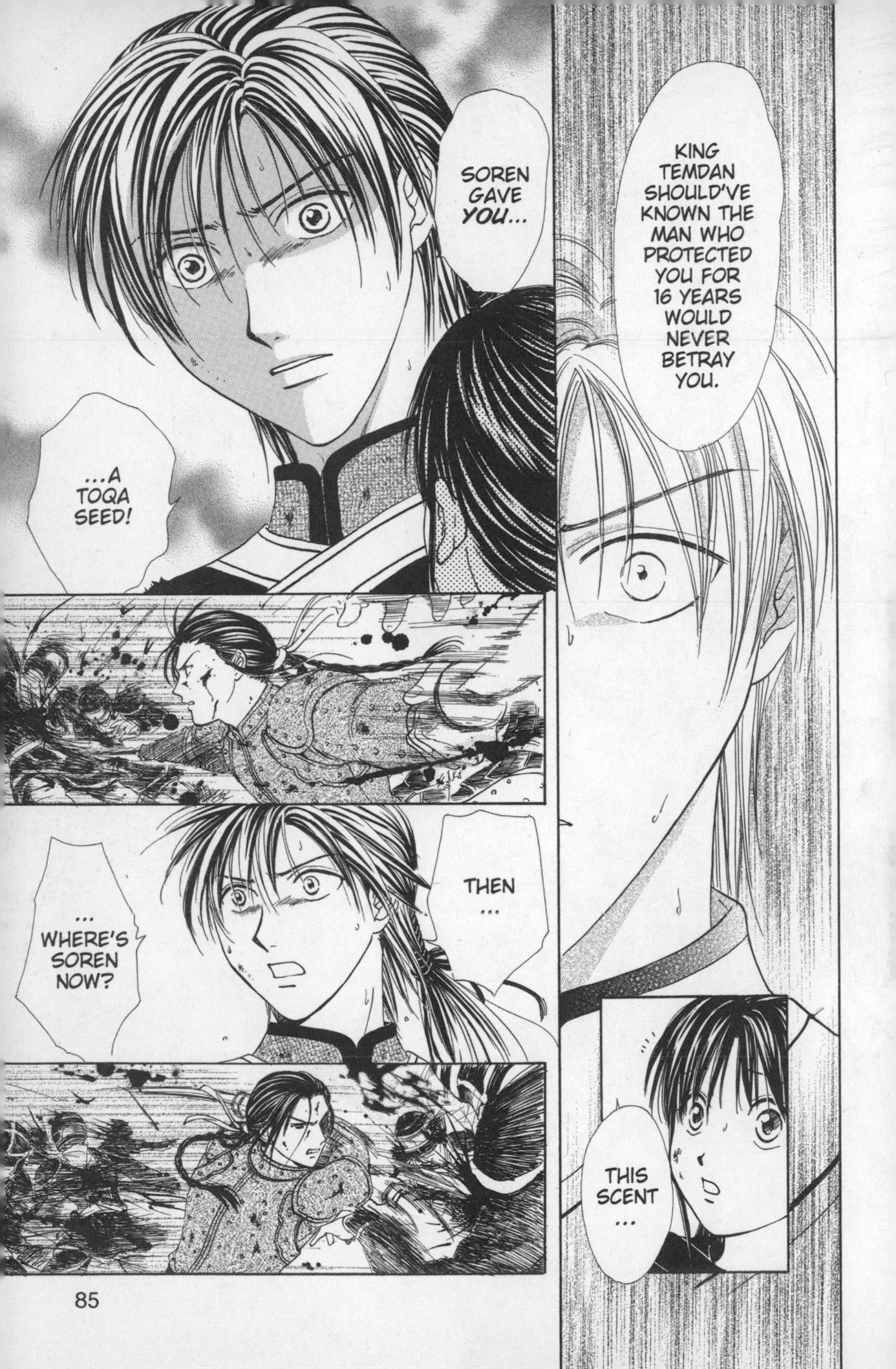
KING TEMDAN SHOULD'VE KNOWN THE MAN WHO PROTECTED YOU FOR 16 YEARS WOULD NEVER BETRAY YOU.
THIS SCENT ...
SOREN GAVE *YOU*...
...A TOQA SEED!
THEN ...
... WHERE'S SOREN NOW?

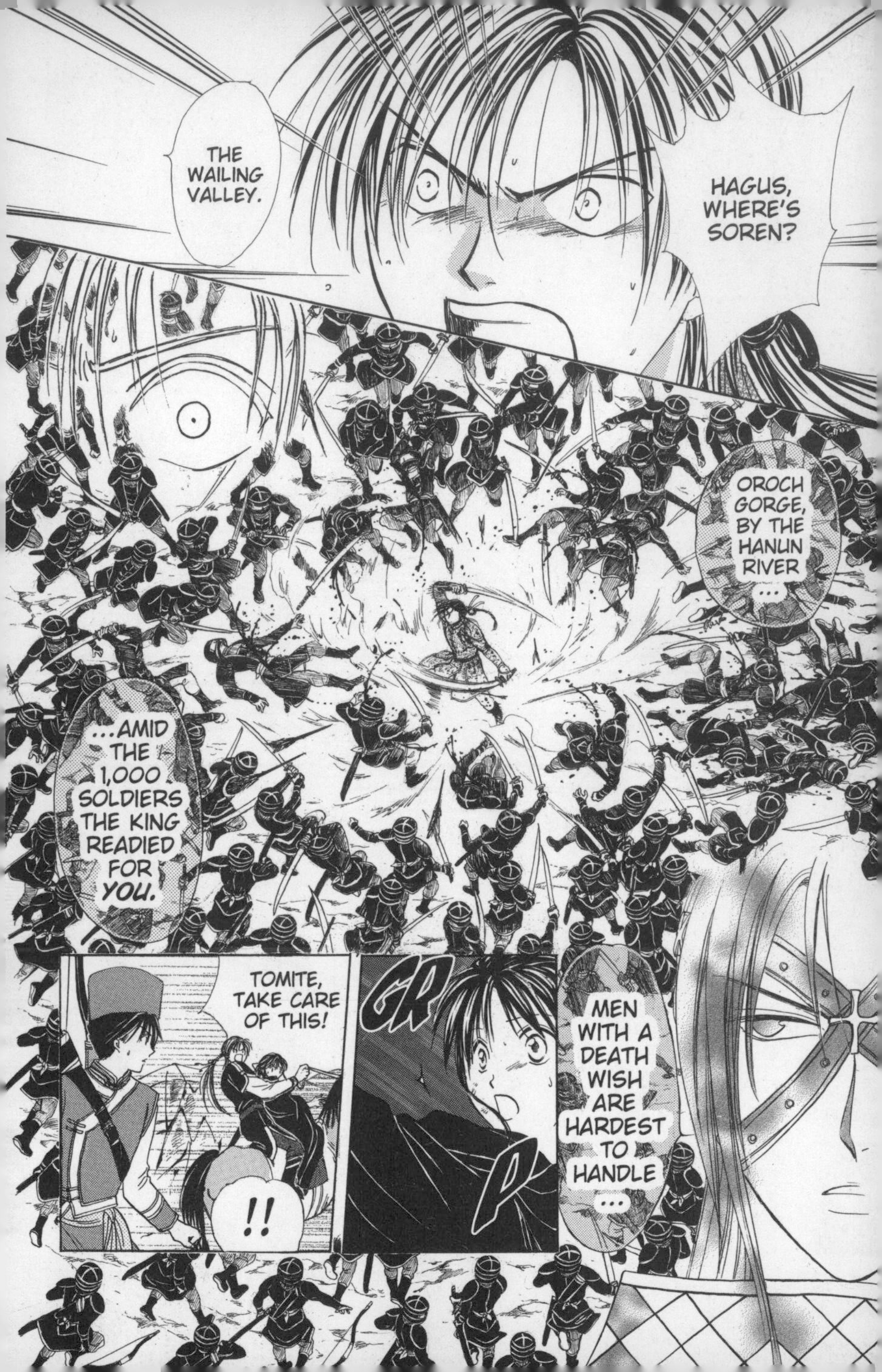
HAGUS, WHERE'S SOREN?
THE WAILING VALLEY.
OROCH GORGE, BY THE HANUN RIVER ...
...AMID THE 1,000 SOLDIERS THE KING READIED FOR YOU.
MEN WITH A DEATH WISH ARE HARDEST TO HANDLE ...
GR
TOMITE, TAKE CARE OF THIS!
!!

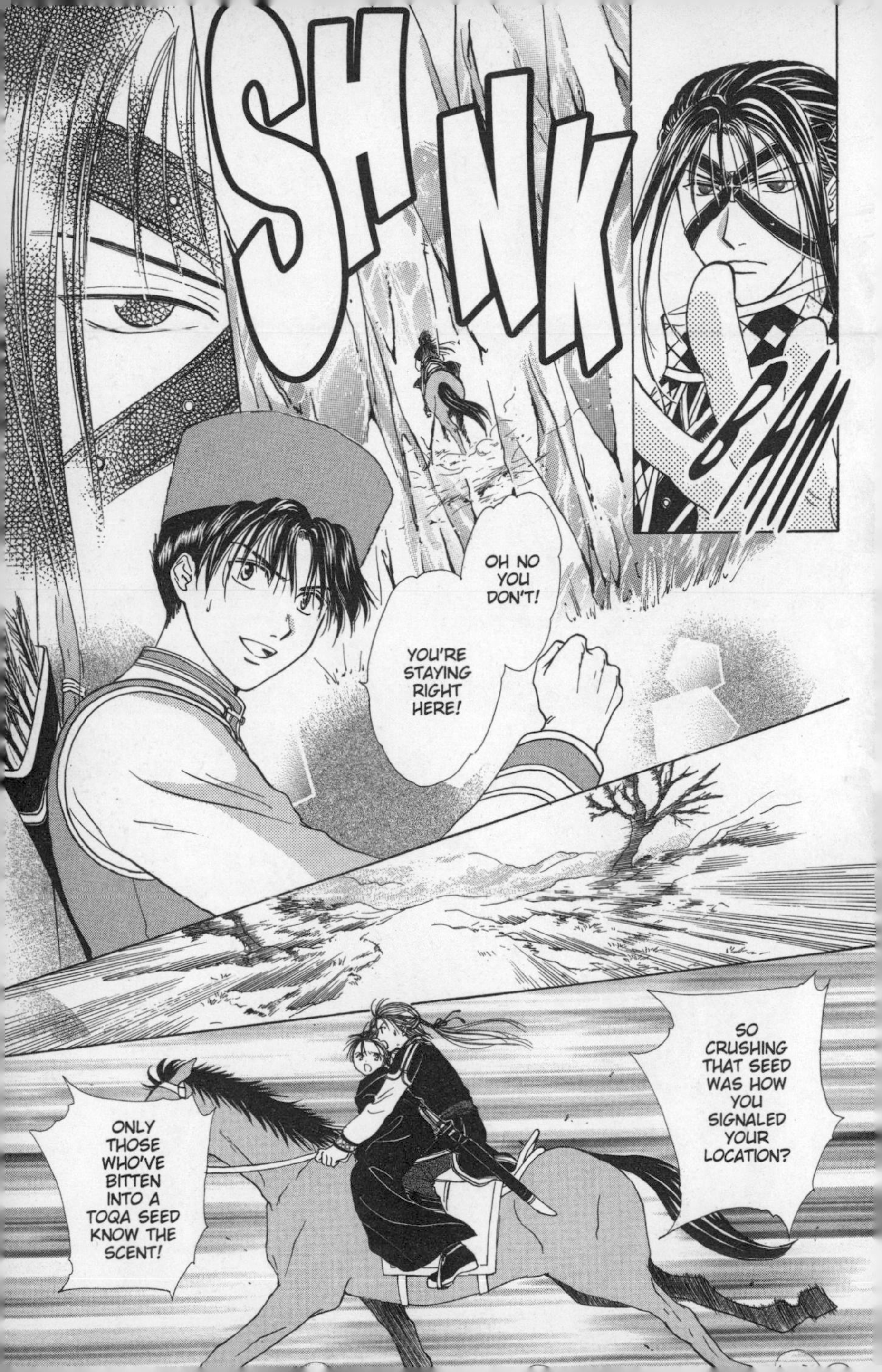
BAM
SHINK
OH NO YOU DON'T!
YOU'RE STAYING RIGHT HERE!
SO CRUSHING THAT SEED WAS HOW YOU SIGNALED YOUR LOCATION?
ONLY THOSE WHO'VE BITTEN INTO A TOQA SEED KNOW THE SCENT!

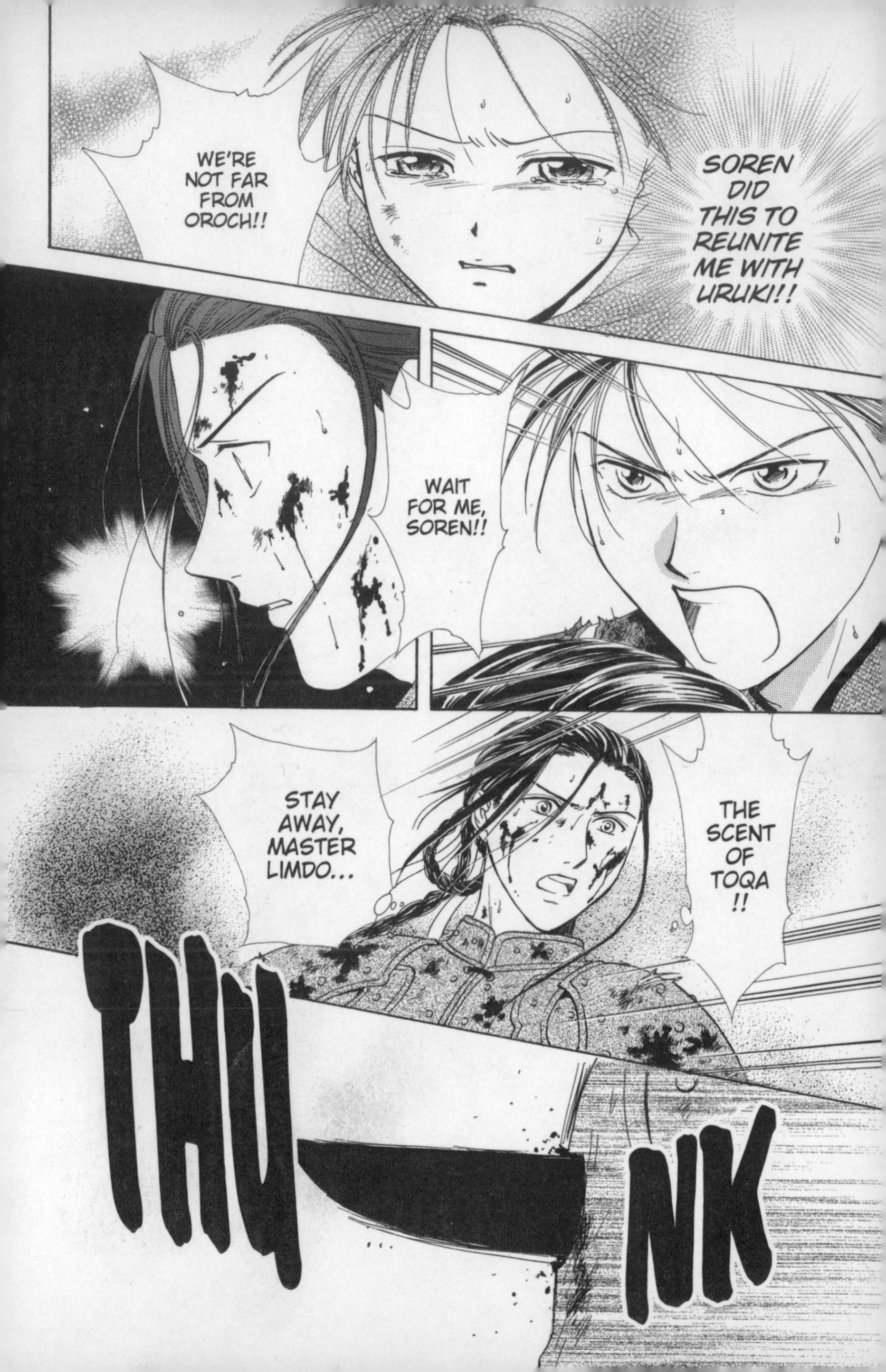
SOREN DID THIS TO REUNITE ME WITH URUKI!!
WE'RE NOT FAR FROM OROCH!!
WAIT FOR ME, SOREN!!
THE SCENT OF TOQA !!
STAY AWAY, MASTER LIMDO...
THU—NK

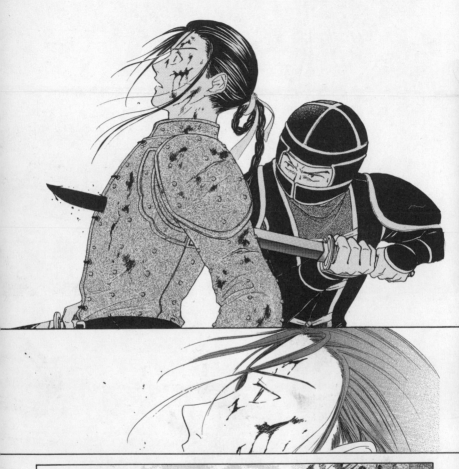

MASTER
LIMDO
...

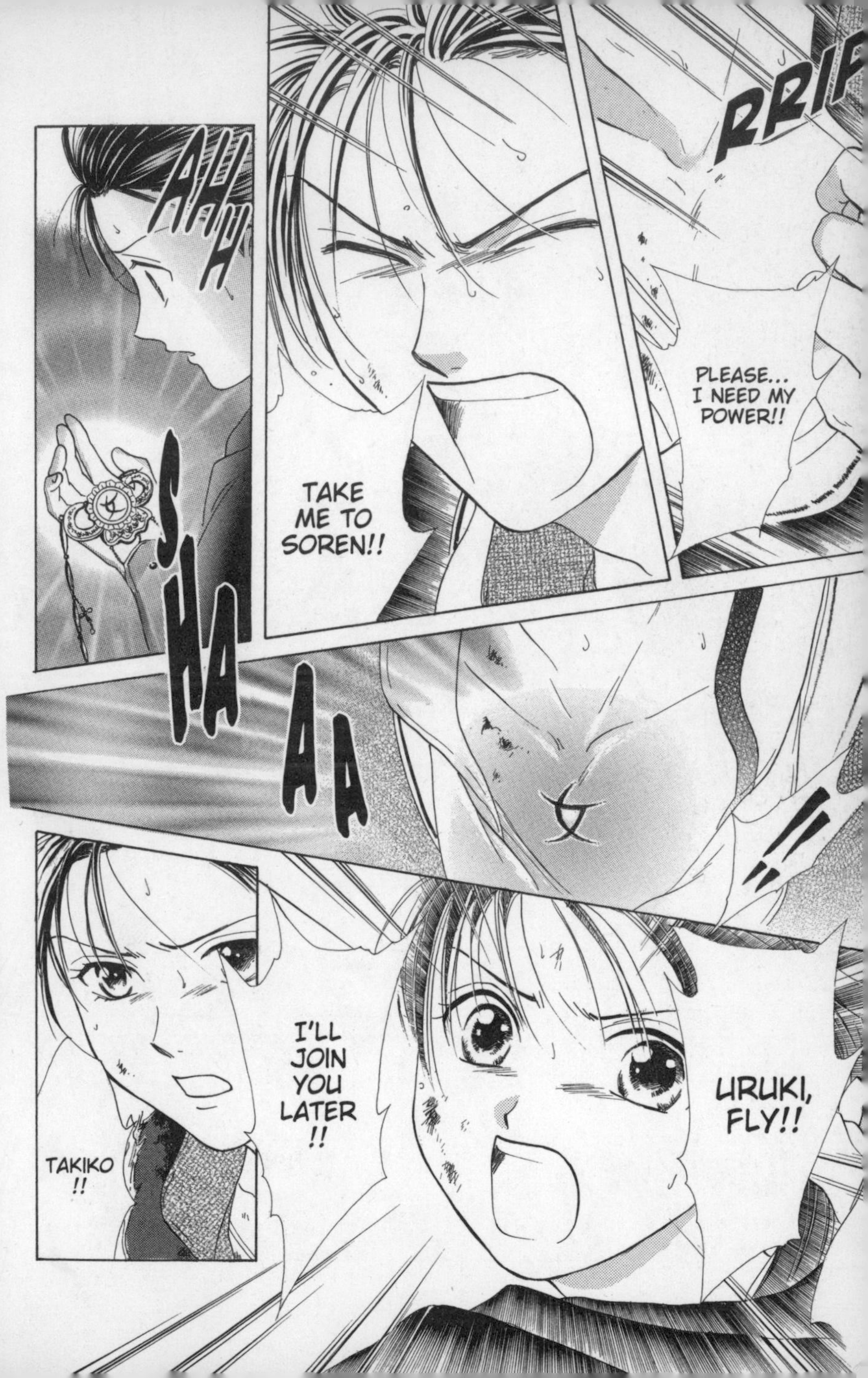
PLEASE... I NEED MY POWER!!
TAKE ME TO SOREN!!
AHH
SHAHAA
!!
URUKI, FLY!!
I'LL JOIN YOU LATER!!
TAKIKO!!

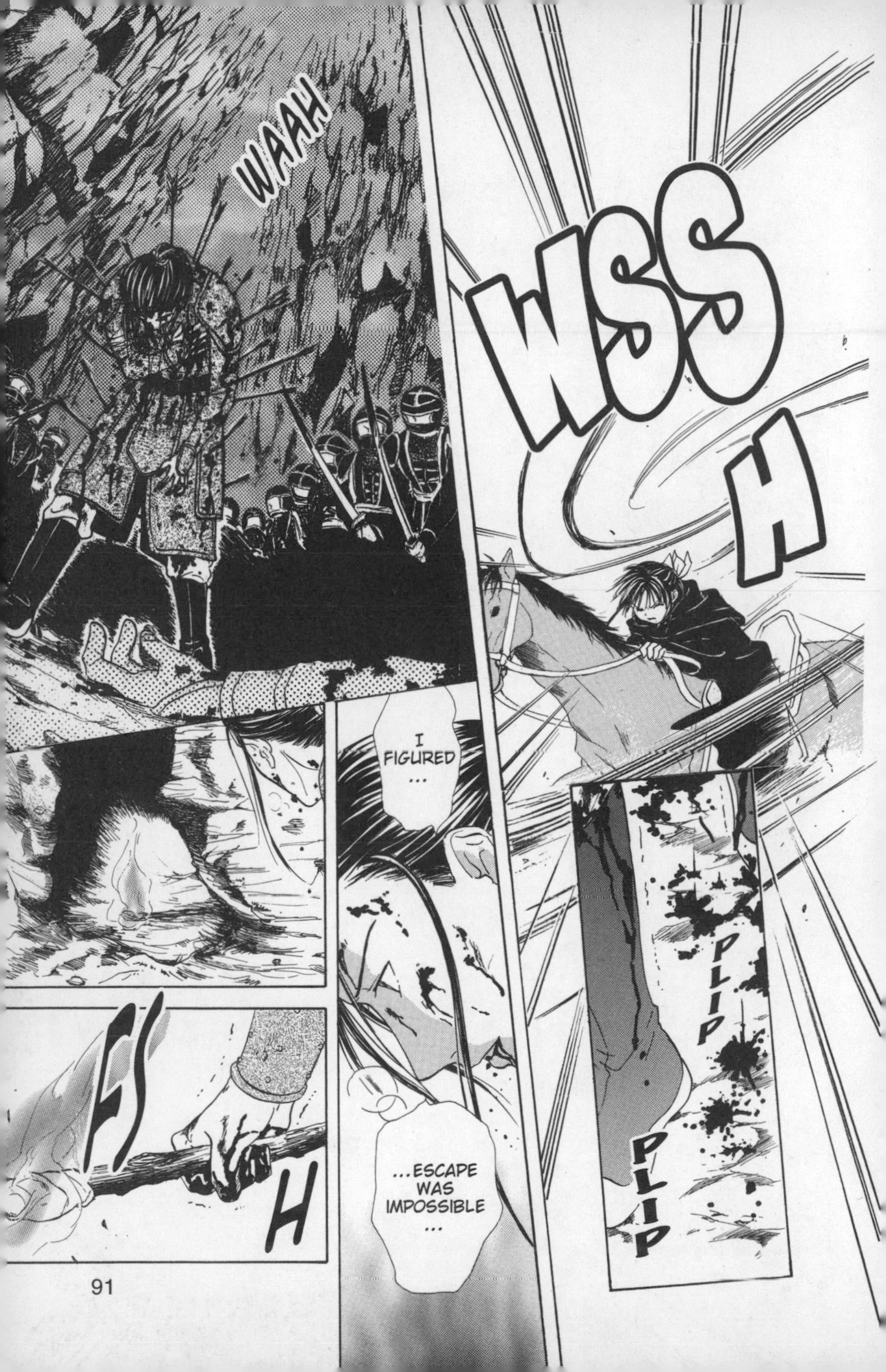
WSSH
WAAH
PLIP PLIP
I FIGURED ...
...ESCAPE WAS IMPOSSIBLE ...
FSH

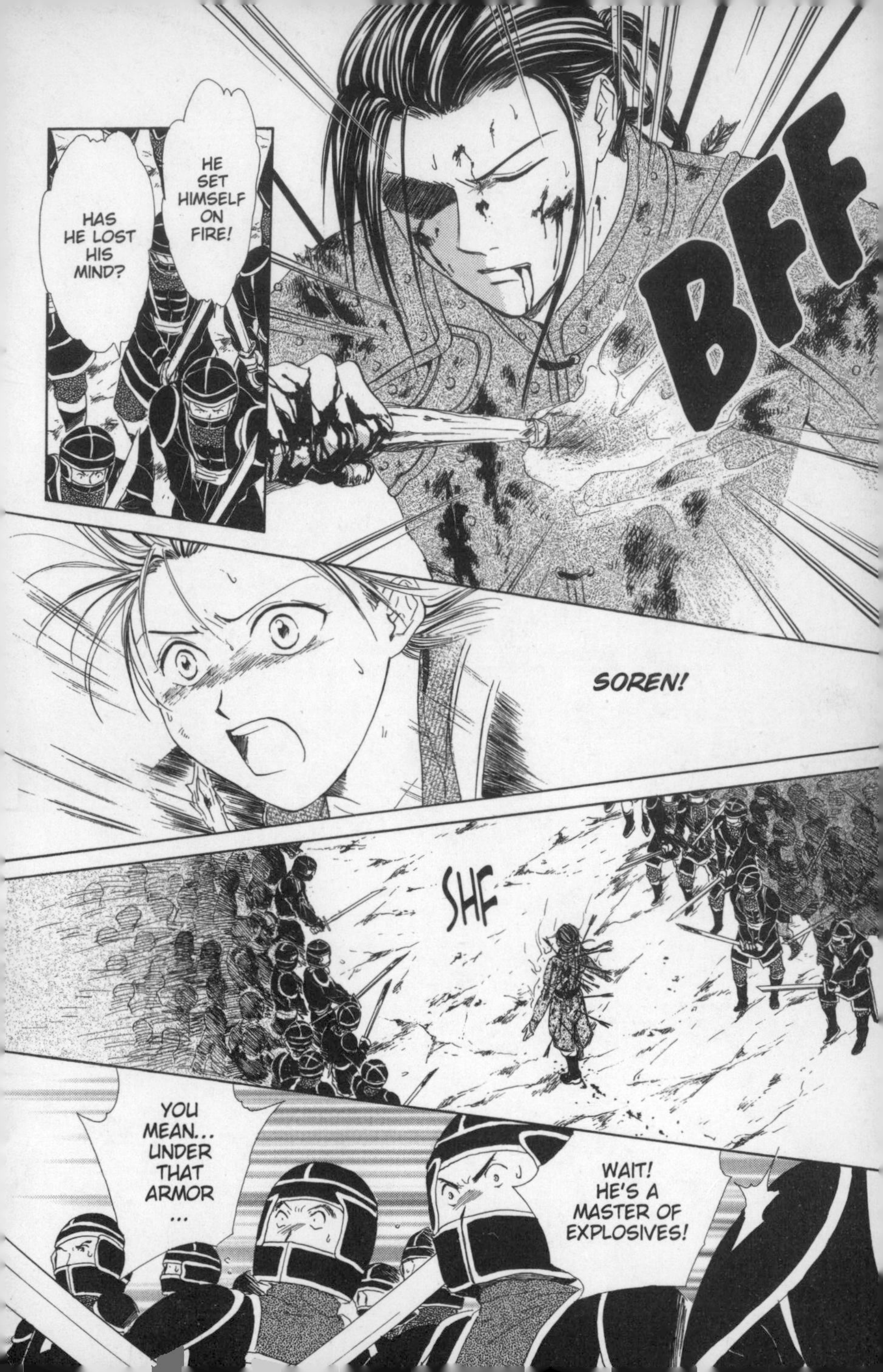
BFF
HE SET HIMSELF ON FIRE!
HAS HE LOST HIS MIND?
SOREN!
SHF
WAIT! HE'S A MASTER OF EXPLOSIVES!
YOU MEAN... UNDER THAT ARMOR ...

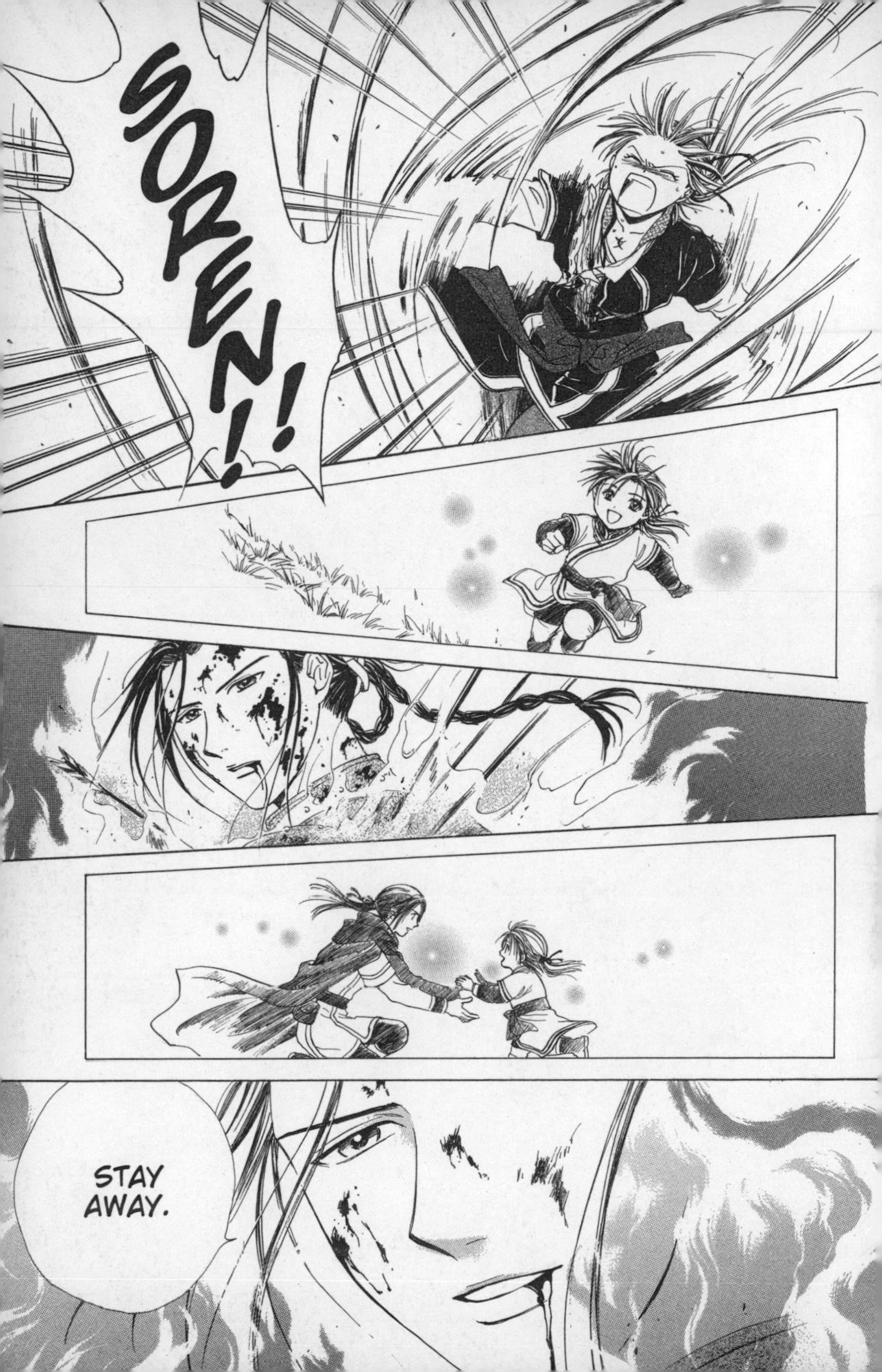
SOREN!!
STAY AWAY.

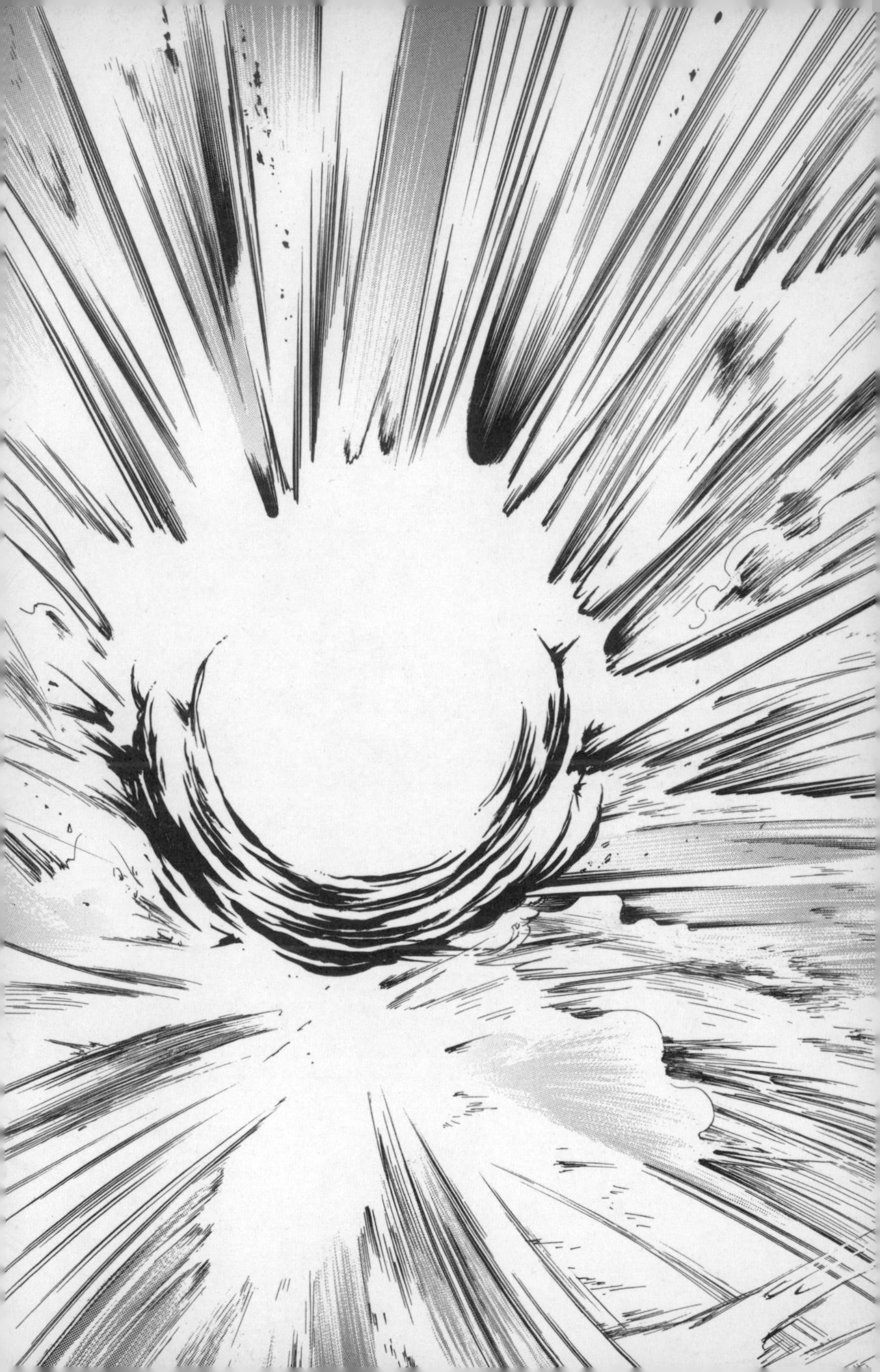

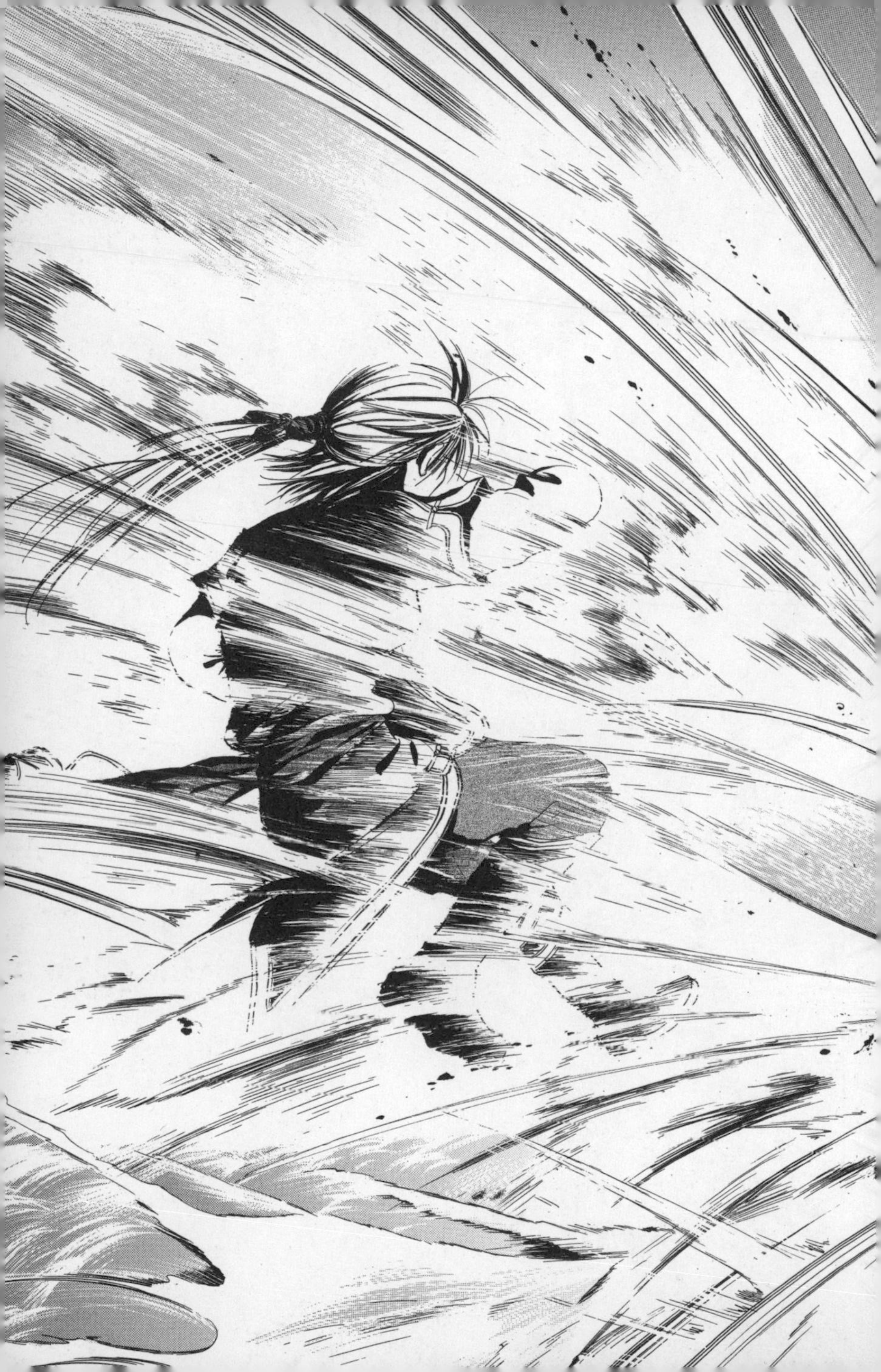

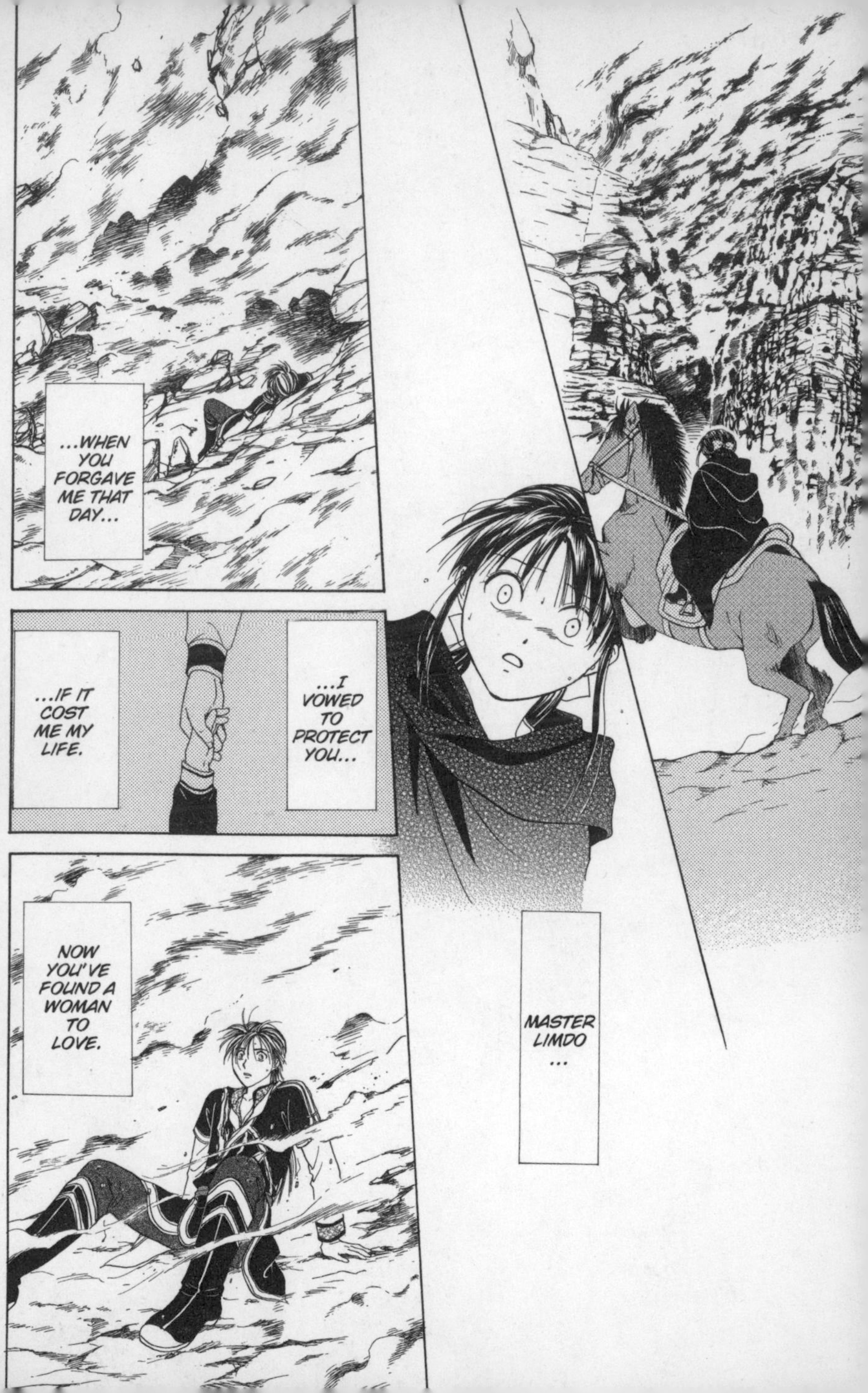
MASTER LIMDO ...
...WHEN YOU FORGAVE ME THAT DAY...
...I VOWED TO PROTECT YOU...
...IF IT COST ME MY LIFE.
NOW YOU'VE FOUND A WOMAN TO LOVE.

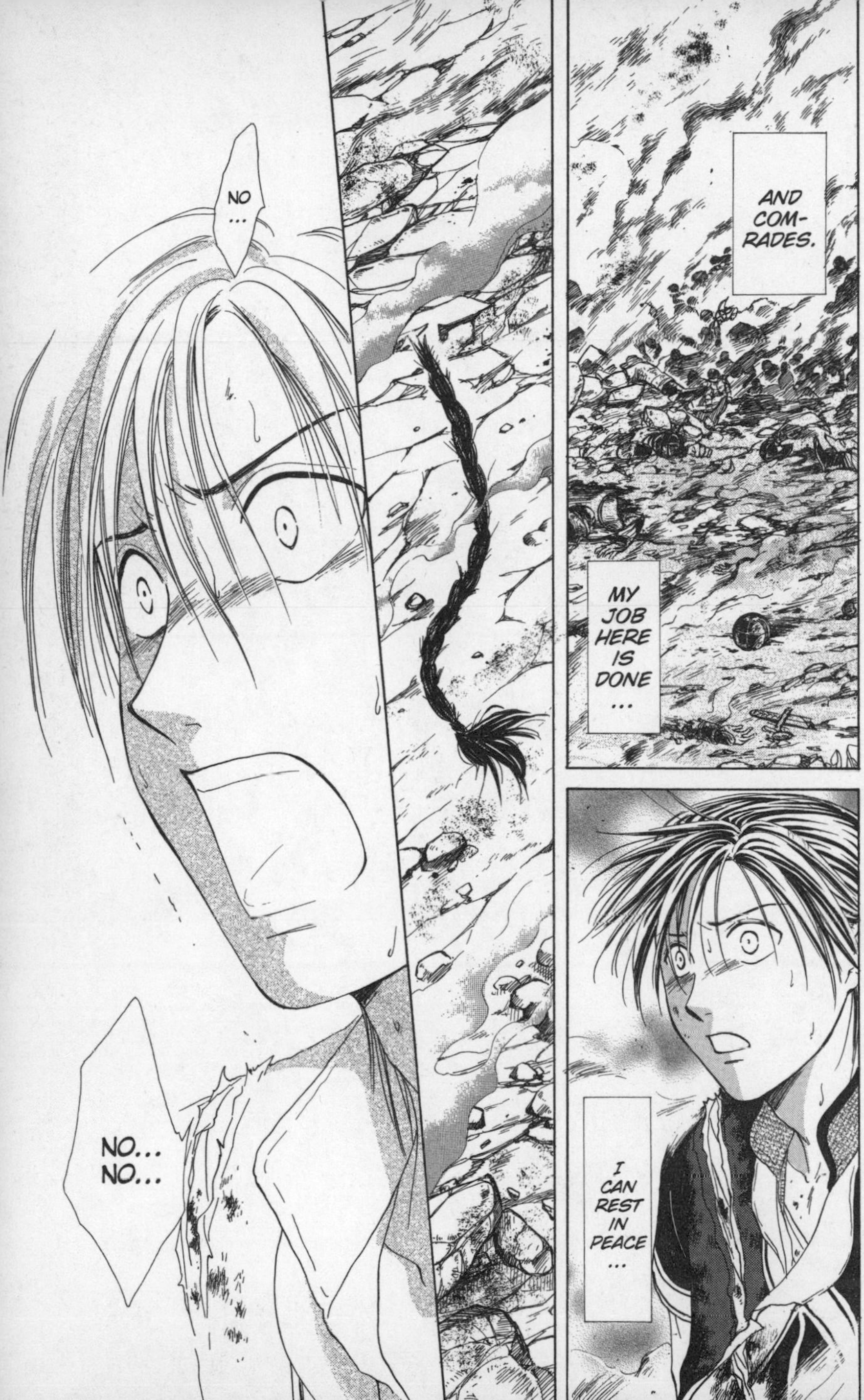
AND COM-RADES.
MY JOB HERE IS DONE...
I CAN REST IN PEACE...
NO...
NO... NO...

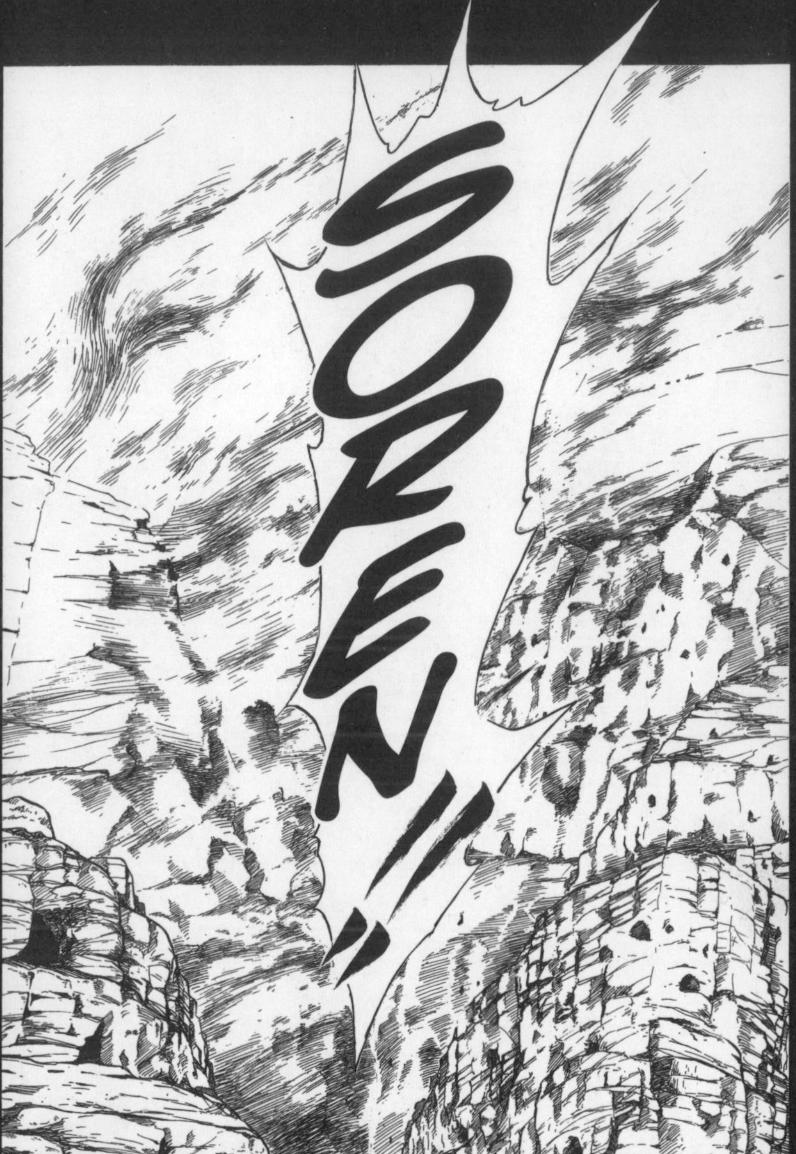
SOZEN!!

TWO HOWLS

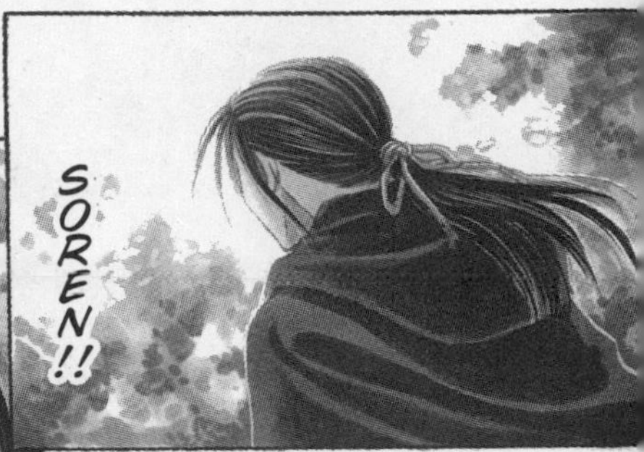
SOREN!!

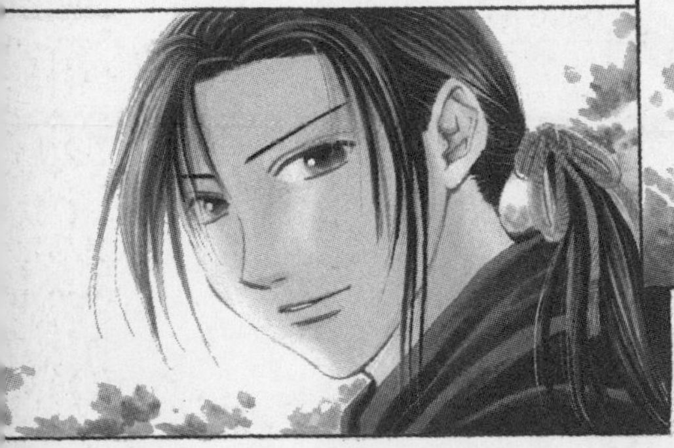

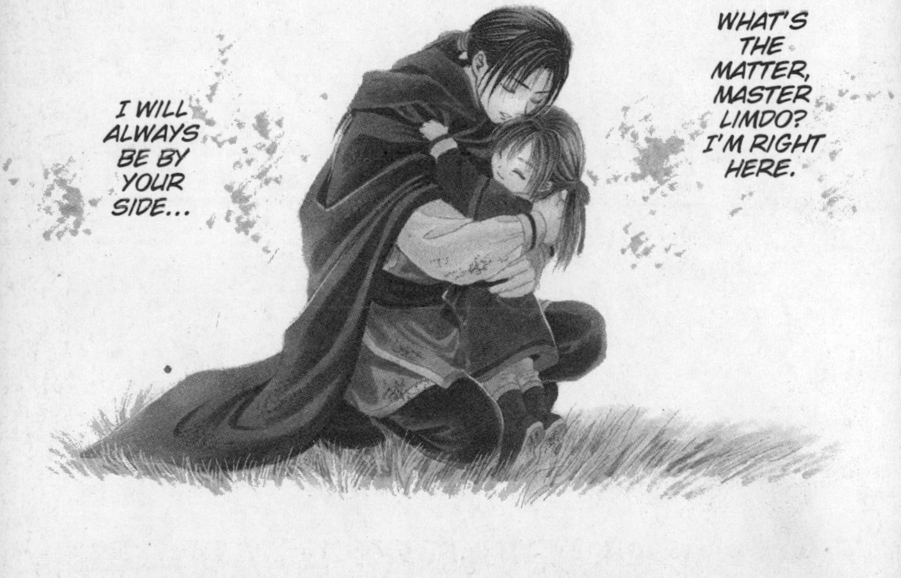
WHAT'S THE MATTER, MASTER LIMDO? I'M RIGHT HERE.
I WILL ALWAYS BE BY YOUR SIDE...

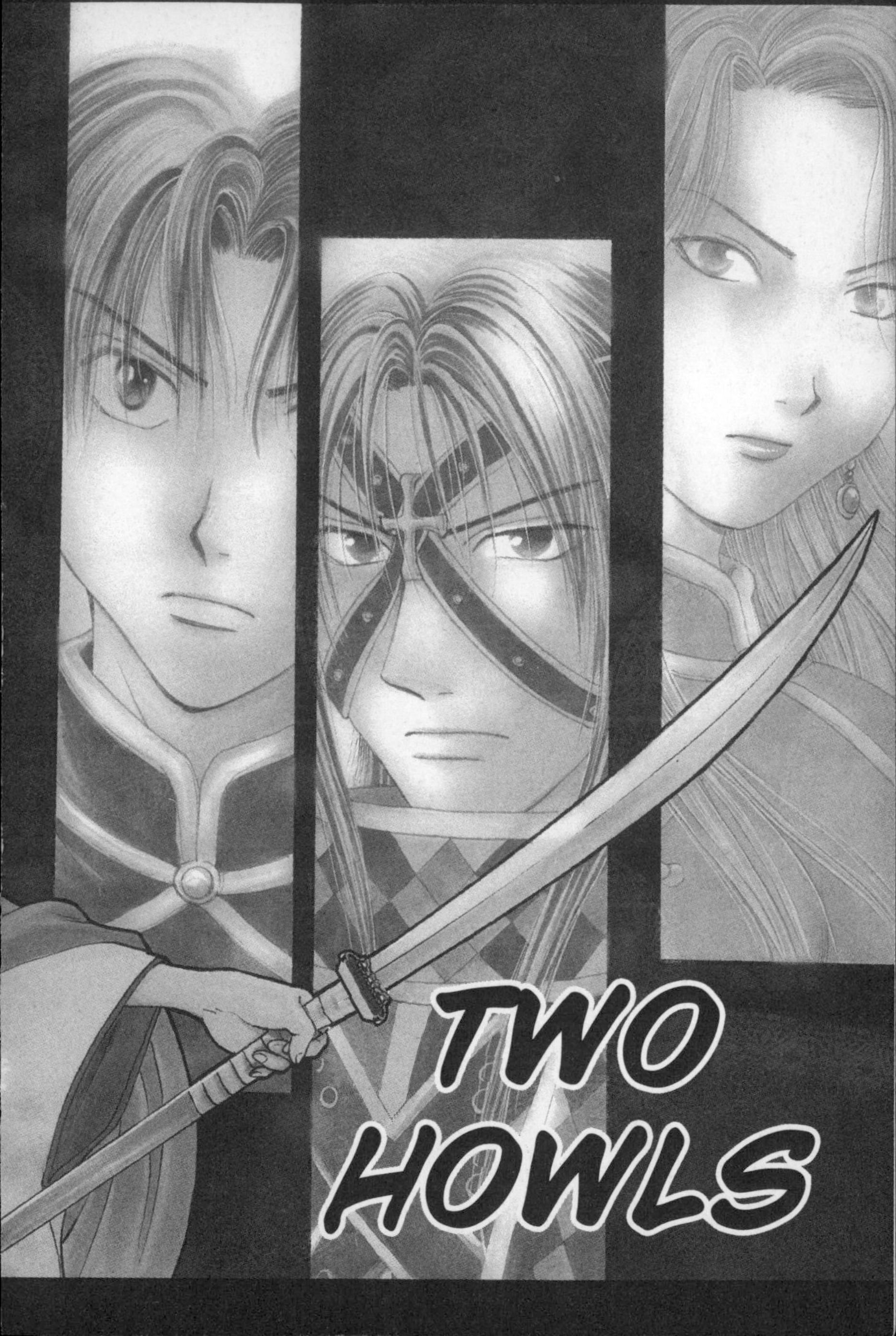
TWO
HOWLS

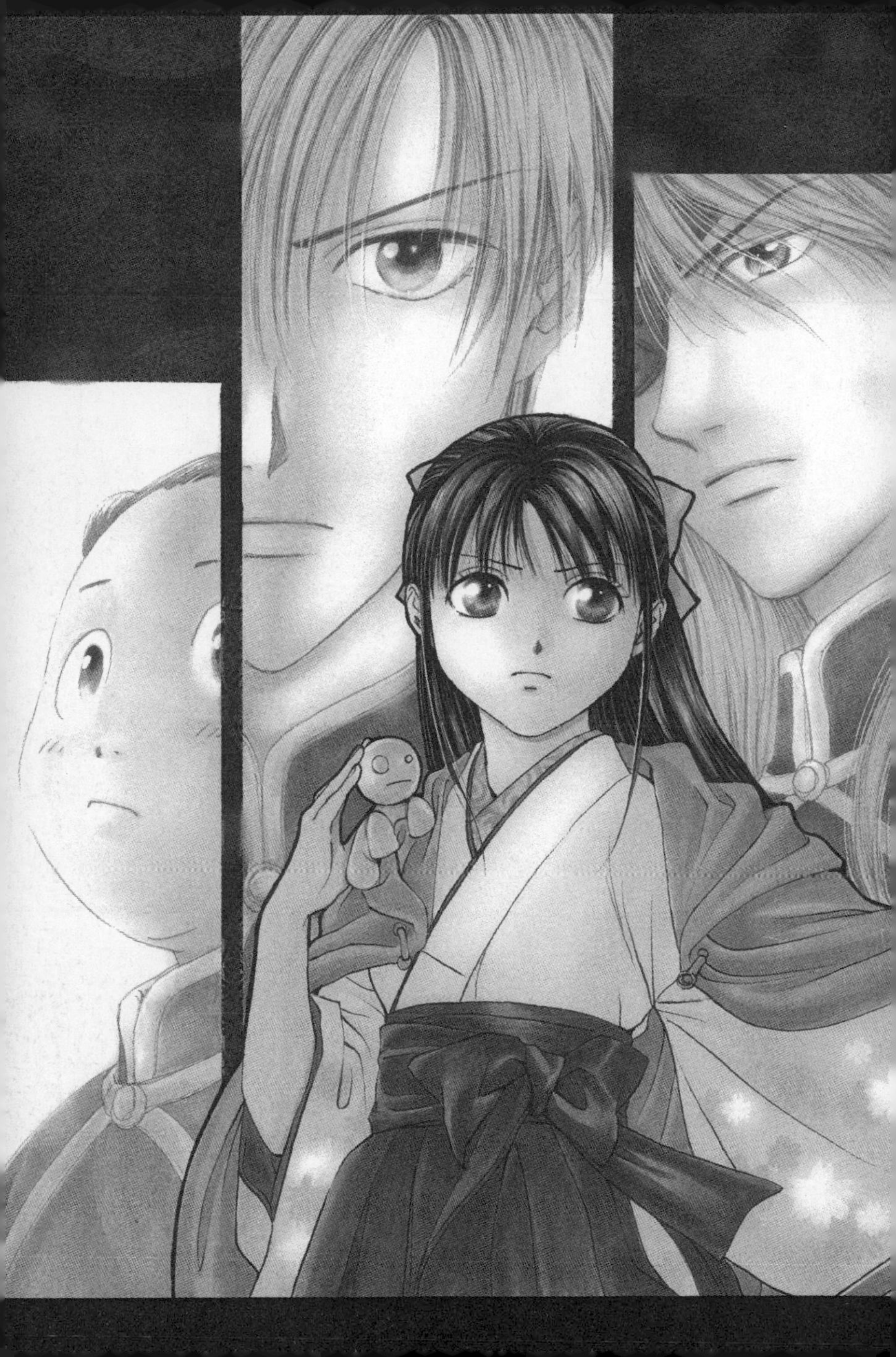

三

Urg... (--;

Uh-oh, I'm seriously losing willpower! I swear I've been feeling pretty good lately (except for my back)!! But it's early July 2007 as I'm writing this, so I've got plenty of time before this is due.

In this volume, Soren, one of my favorite characters, passed away. He wasn't a Celestial Warrior, but he had so much presence, and he was the guy everyone turned to... There goes my beloved master-servant relationship!! Well, this was the ultimate expression of his devotion, really...I'm not sure if it'll be out by the time this volume hits the shelves, but Shogakukan's Lululu Books is publishing a side novel about Limdo and Soren.

Working on this part was really tough because the deadline coincided with the deadline for the 100 pages of my new series, *Sakura-gari*, which I drew for *Rinka* a spinoff of the monthly magazine *Flowers*. Sigh.

The next issue of *Rinka* will be out around October 13. Thank goodness the deadlines are staggered this time...It seems a lot of opinions (or criticisms) are flying around among the fans who have read it. I bet a lot of people were just surprised by how totally different it is from my usual material. You can look forward to more surprises. The first graphic novel will come out in Japan in the spring of 2008, I think...*Perfect World* is published quarterly, but *Rinka* comes out three times a year. That means there will be one graphic novel a year. I'm happy to get feedback on anything, whether it's FY or not. Oh, the Japanese pocket edition of *Alice 19th* will also come out around October, so keep an eye out for it..

See you in Volume 8!

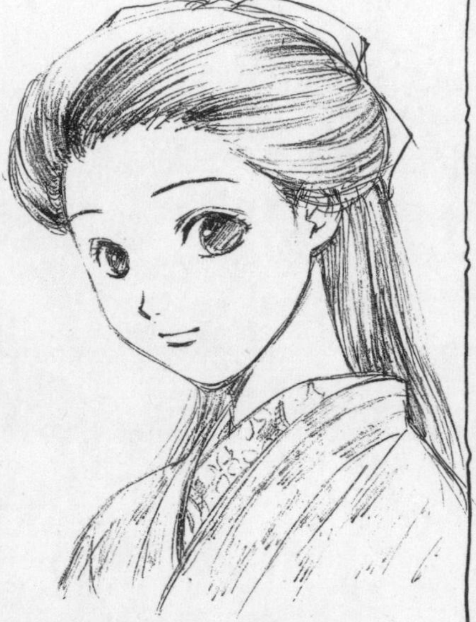

This is how Takiko would look in my *Sakura-gari* art style. :) Coincidentally, both stories are set during the Taisho period. But *Genbu* is fantasy, so they're not on the same level of realism. I adjust the realism for each story, you know.

Thanks to my assistants: M, H, A, the other H, K, the other K, I, T and K!

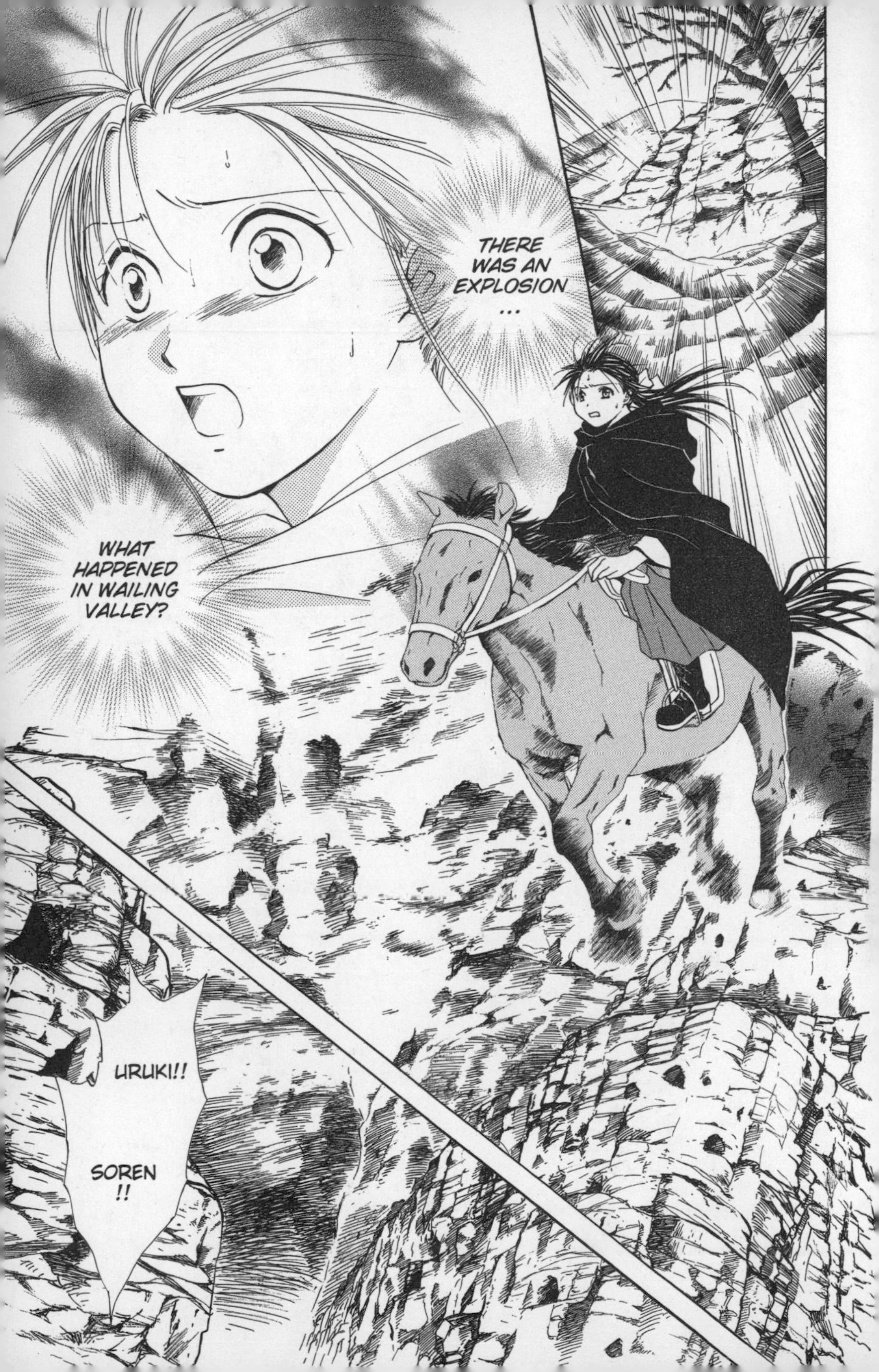
THERE WAS AN EXPLOSION ...
WHAT HAPPENED IN WAILING VALLEY?
URUKI!!
SOREN !!

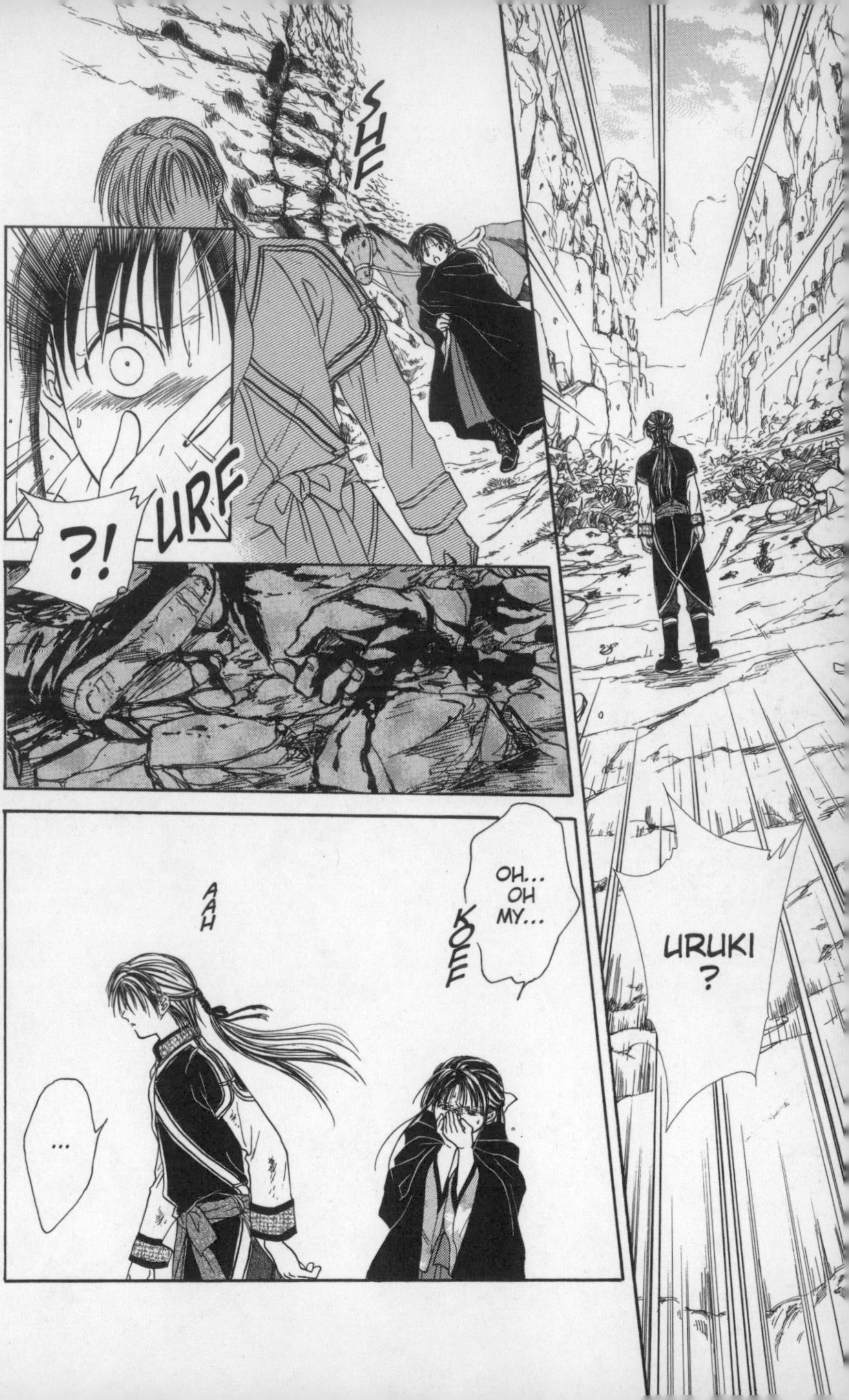
URUKI ?
SHFF
URF
?!
OH... OH MY...
KOFF
AAH
...

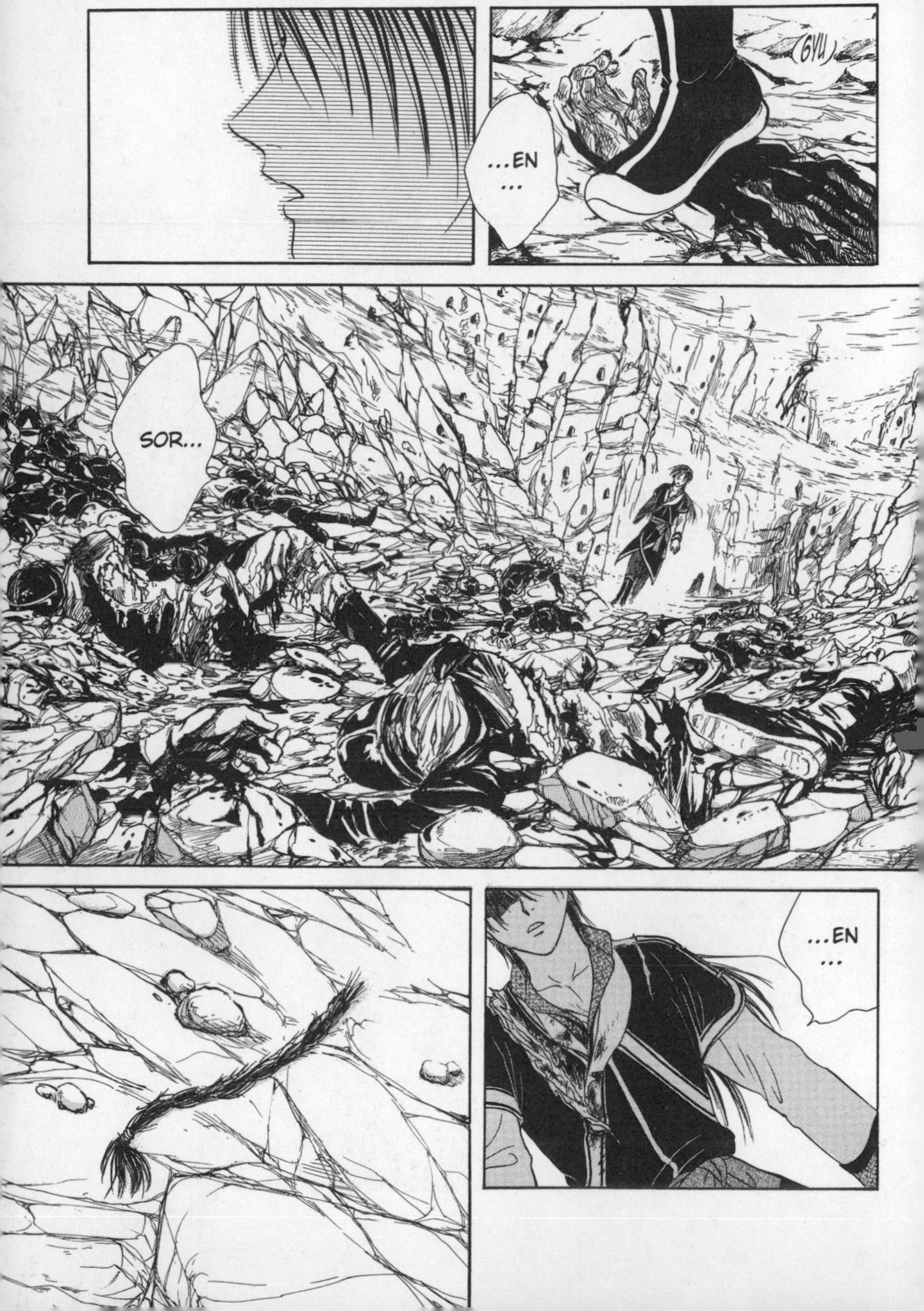
(GYU)
...EN ...
SOR...
...EN ...

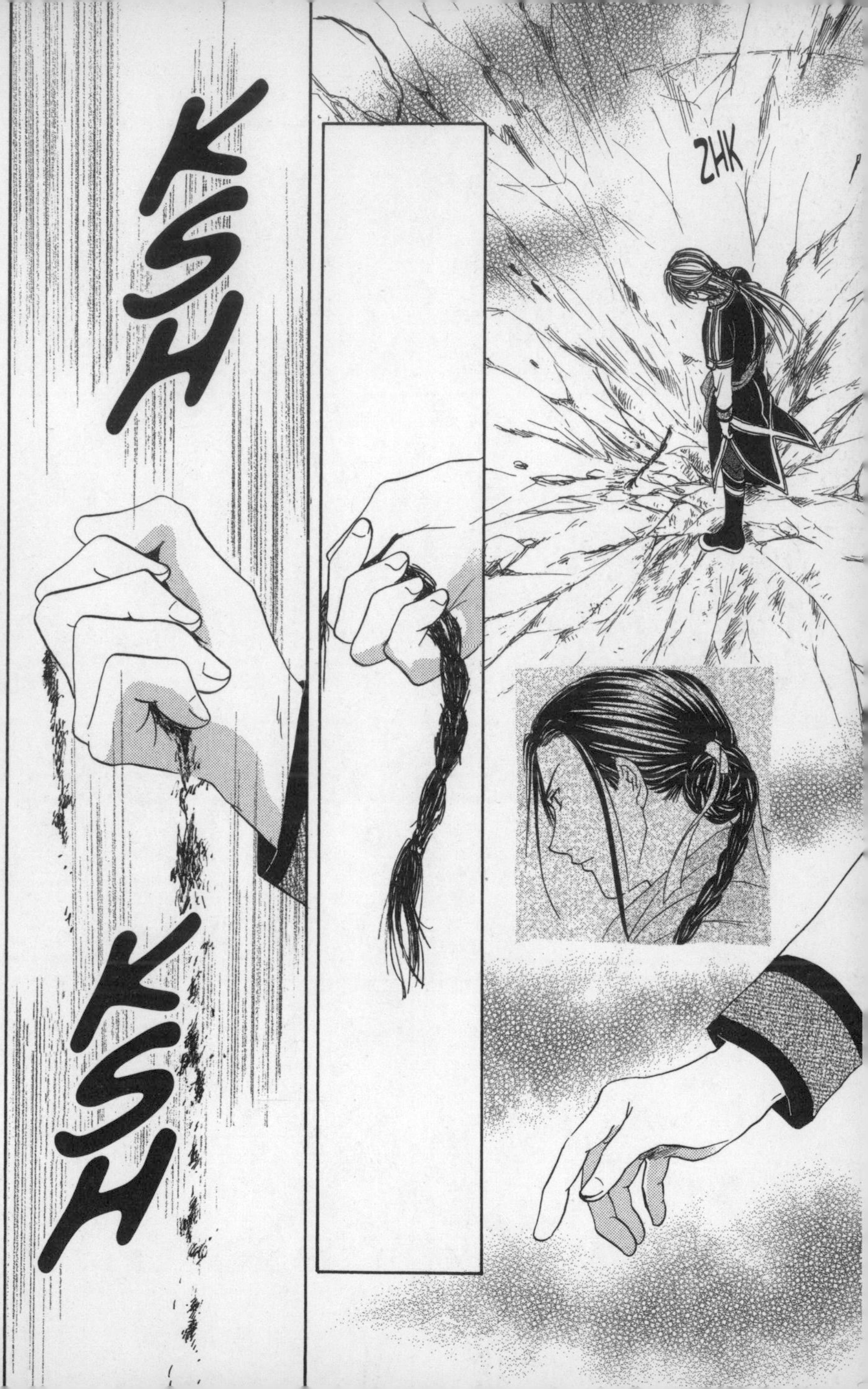
ZHK
KSH
KSH

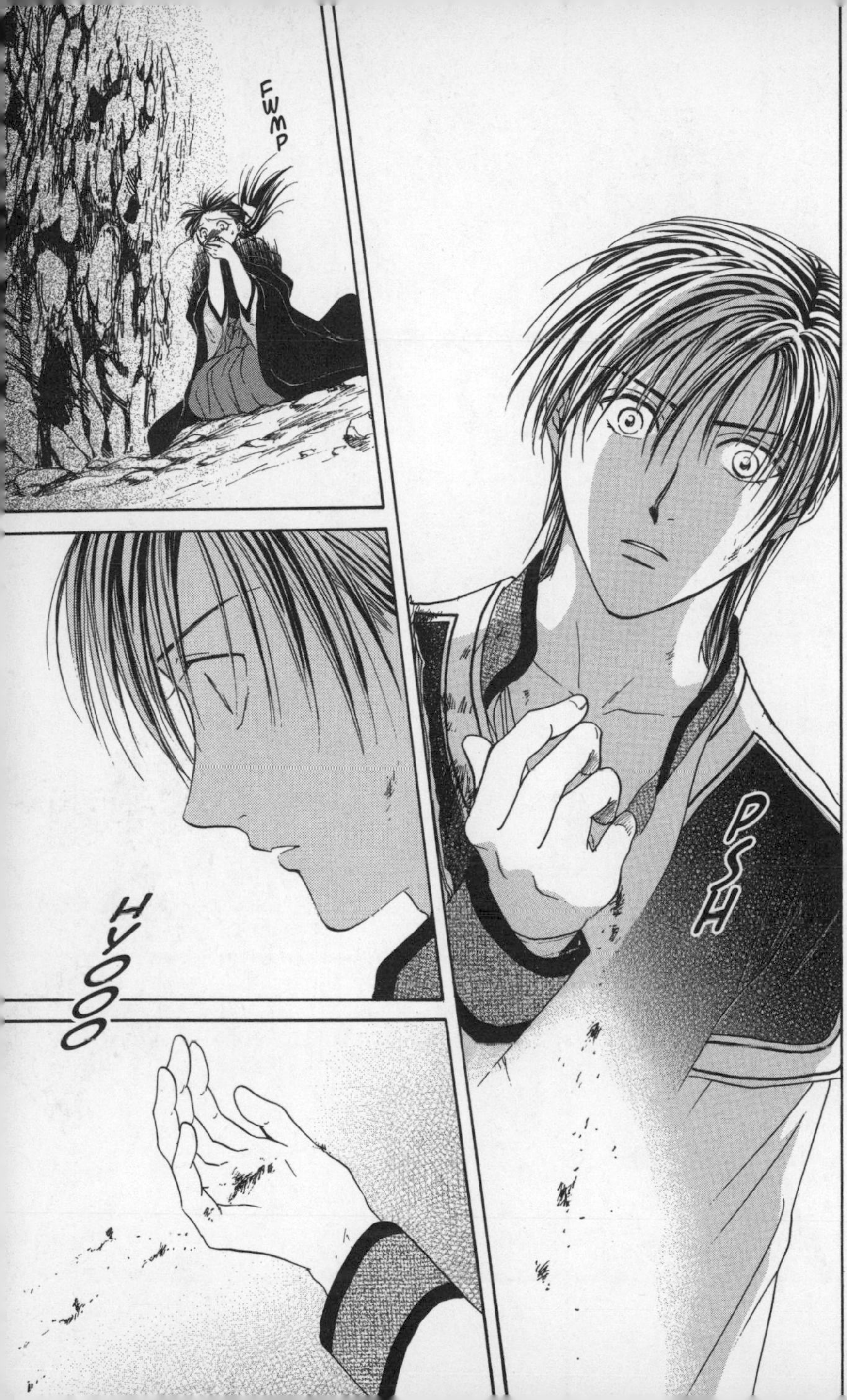
PSH
FWMP
HYOOO

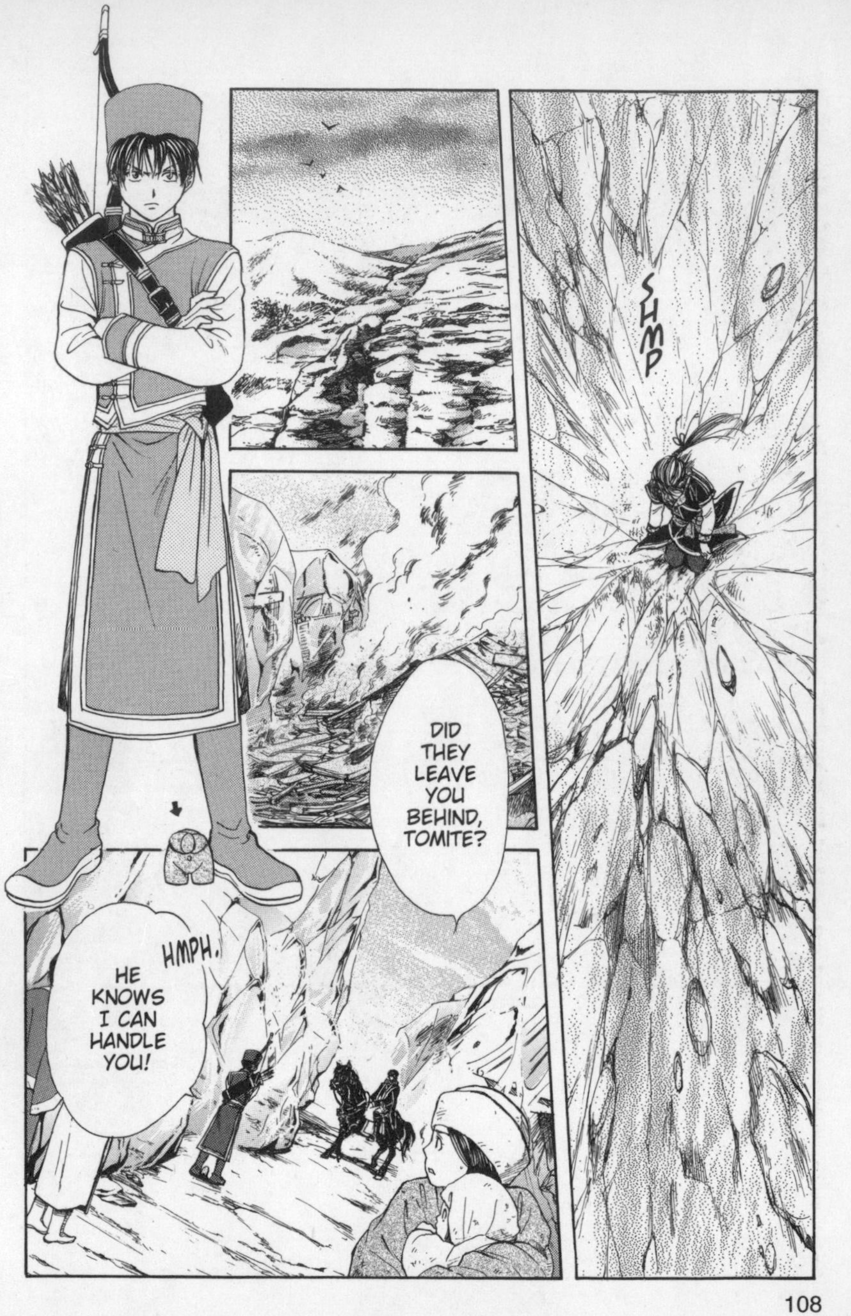
SHMP
DID THEY LEAVE YOU BEHIND, TOMITE?
HMPH.
HE KNOWS I CAN HANDLE YOU!

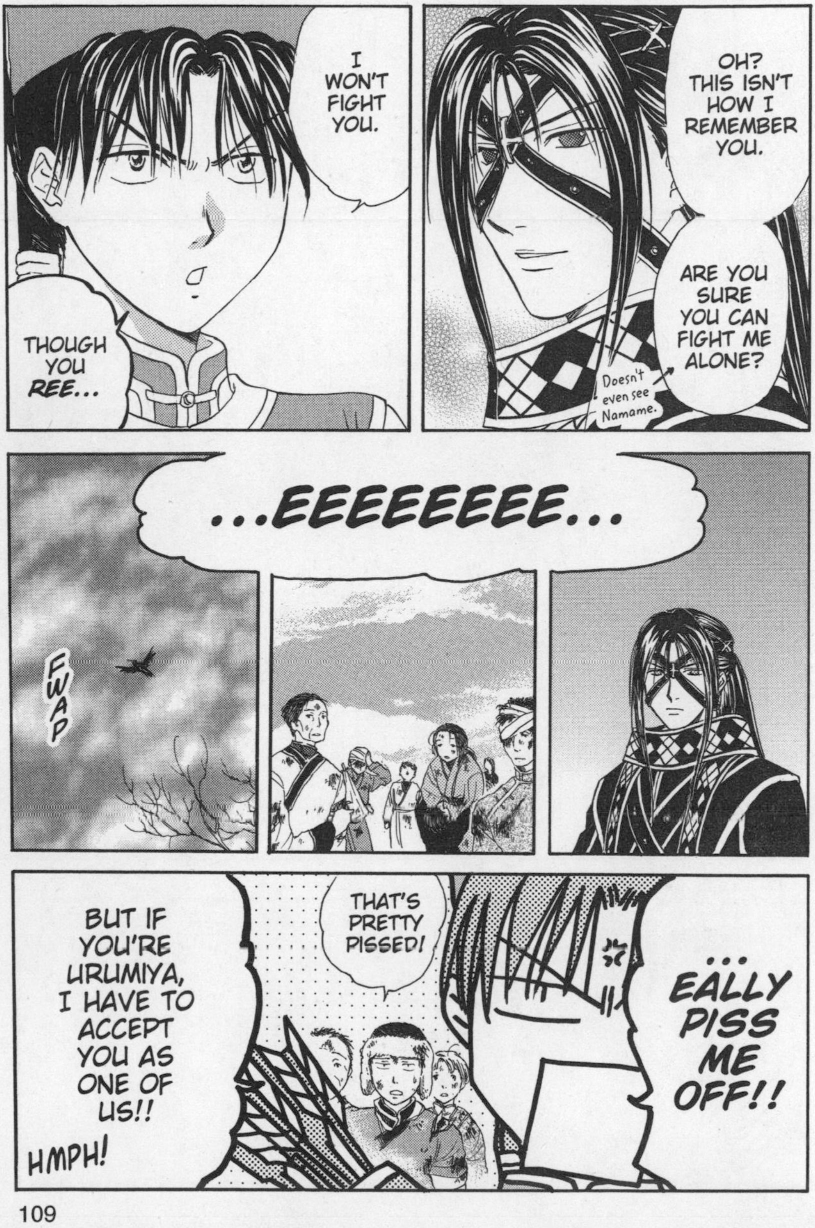
OH? THIS ISN'T HOW I REMEMBER YOU.
ARE YOU SURE YOU CAN FIGHT ME ALONE?
Doesn't even see Namame.
I WON'T FIGHT YOU.
THOUGH YOU REE...
...EEEEEEEEE...
FWAP
... EALLY PISS ME OFF!!
THAT'S PRETTY PISSED!
BUT IF YOU'RE URUMIYA, I HAVE TO ACCEPT YOU AS ONE OF US!!
HMPH!

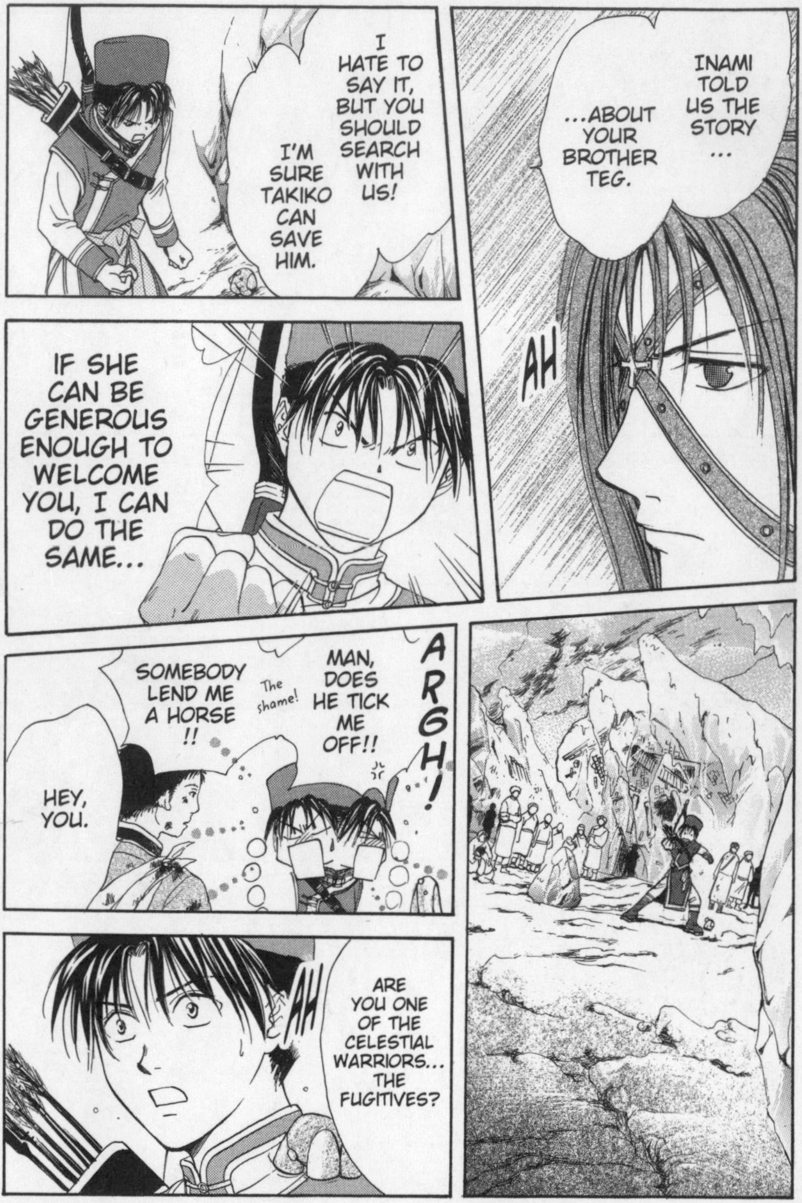
INAMI TOLD US THE STORY...
...ABOUT YOUR BROTHER TEG.
AH
I HATE TO SAY IT, BUT YOU SHOULD SEARCH WITH US!
I'M SURE TAKIKO CAN SAVE HIM.
IF SHE CAN BE GENEROUS ENOUGH TO WELCOME YOU, I CAN DO THE SAME...
ARGH!
MAN, DOES HE TICK ME OFF!!
The shame!
SOMEBODY LEND ME A HORSE!!
HEY, YOU.
AH
ARE YOU ONE OF THE CELESTIAL WARRIORS... THE FUGITIVES?

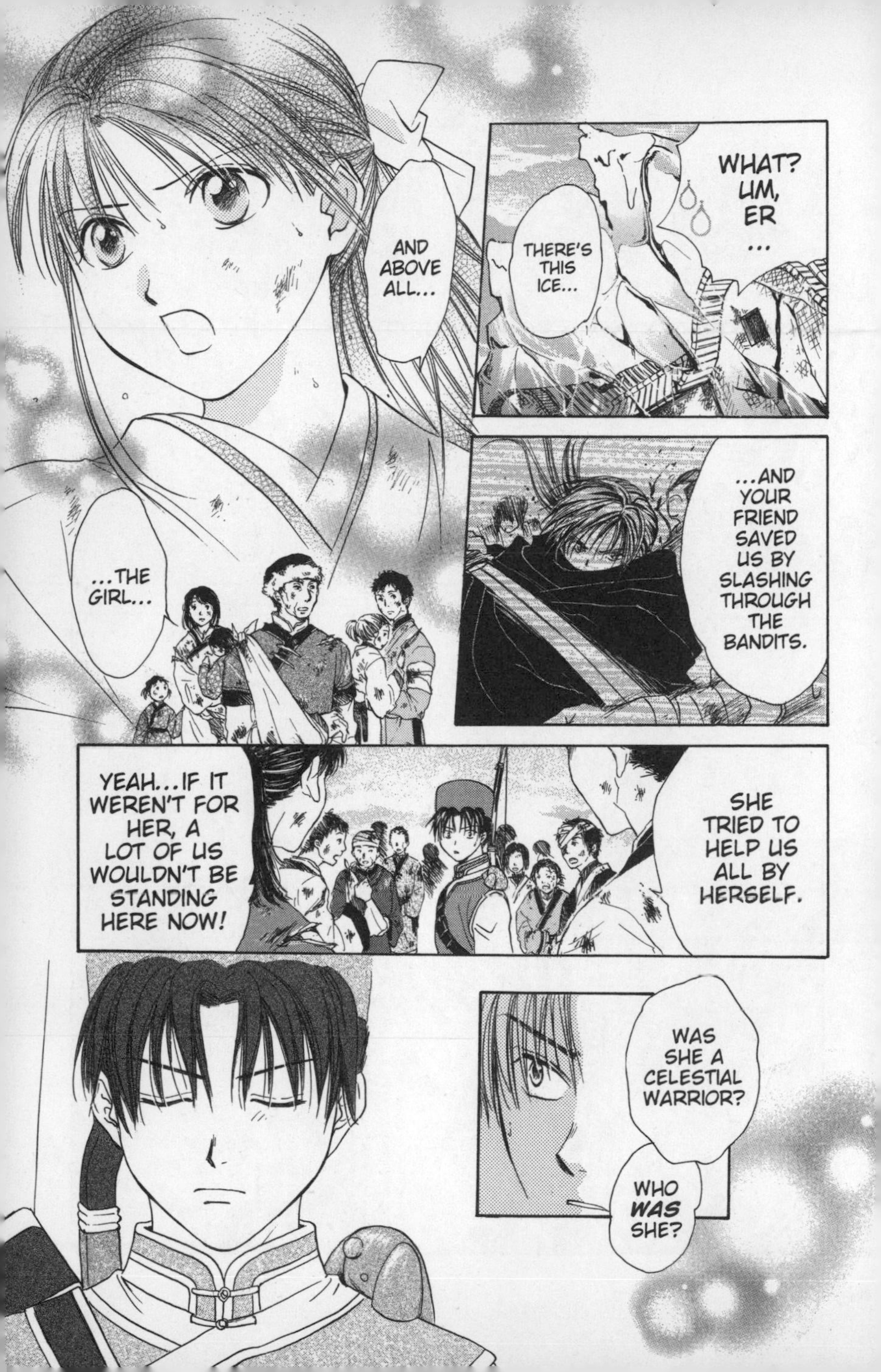
WHAT? UM, ER...
THERE'S THIS ICE...
AND ABOVE ALL...
...THE GIRL...
...AND YOUR FRIEND SAVED US BY SLASHING THROUGH THE BANDITS.
SHE TRIED TO HELP US ALL BY HERSELF.
YEAH...IF IT WEREN'T FOR HER, A LOT OF US WOULDN'T BE STANDING HERE NOW!
WAS SHE A CELESTIAL WARRIOR?
WHO **WAS** SHE?

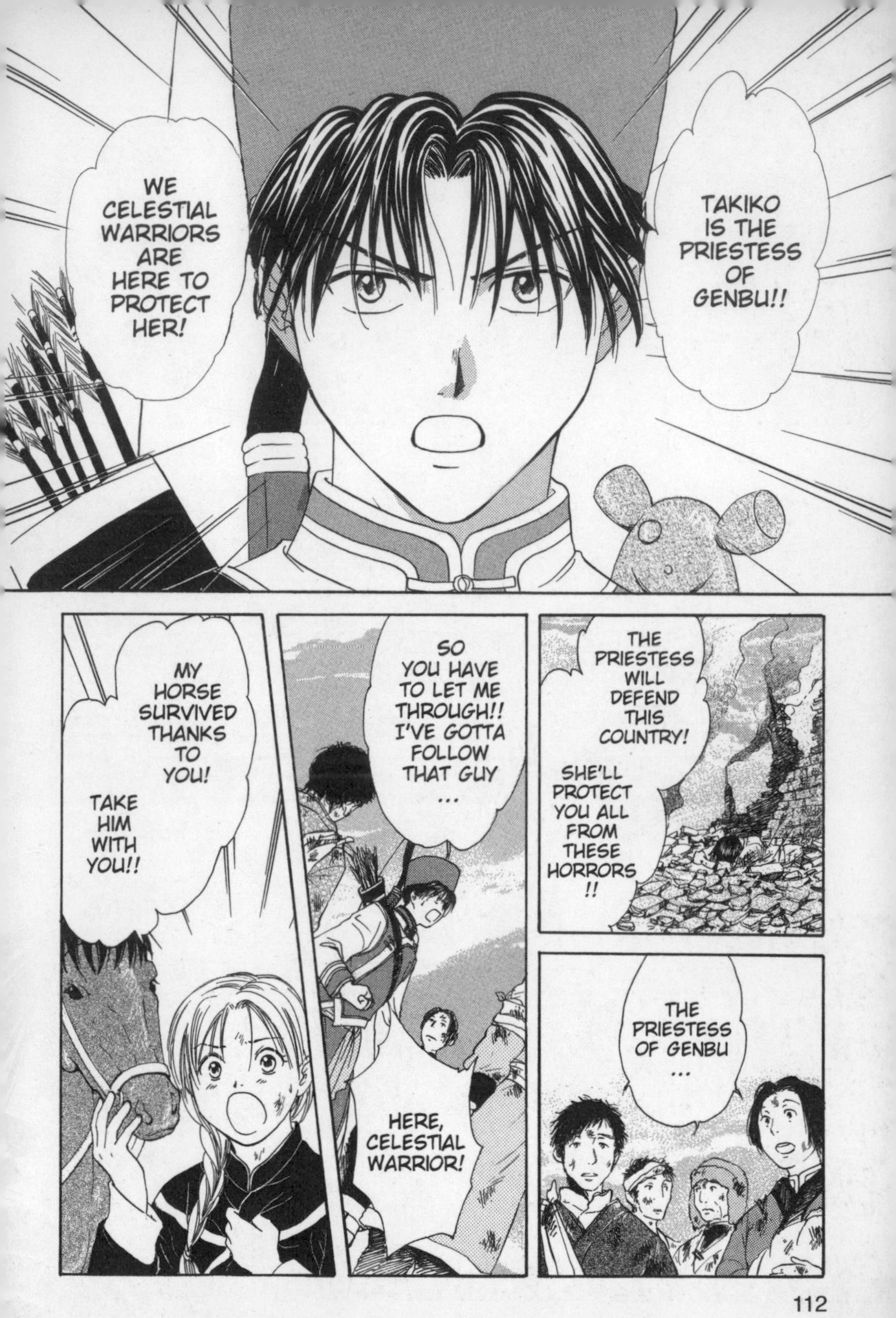
TAKIKO IS THE PRIESTESS OF GENBU!!
WE CELESTIAL WARRIORS ARE HERE TO PROTECT HER!
THE PRIESTESS WILL DEFEND THIS COUNTRY!
SHE'LL PROTECT YOU ALL FROM THESE HORRORS!!
THE PRIESTESS OF GENBU...
SO YOU HAVE TO LET ME THROUGH!! I'VE GOTTA FOLLOW THAT GUY...
HERE, CELESTIAL WARRIOR!
MY HORSE SURVIVED THANKS TO YOU!
TAKE HIM WITH YOU!!

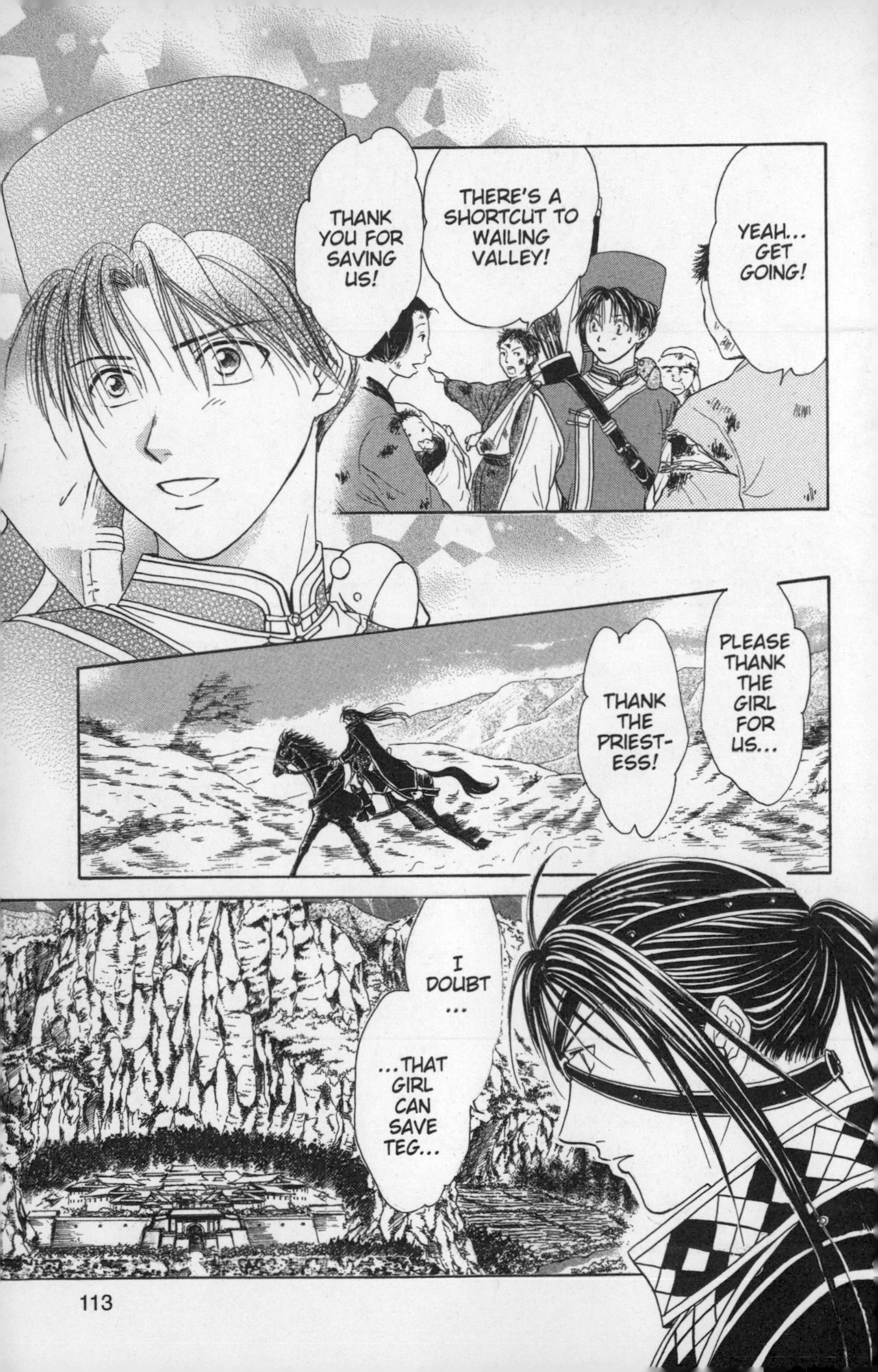
YEAH... GET GOING!
THERE'S A SHORTCUT TO WAILING VALLEY!
THANK YOU FOR SAVING US!
PLEASE THANK THE GIRL FOR US...
THANK THE PRIEST-ESS!
I DOUBT ...
...THAT GIRL CAN SAVE TEG...

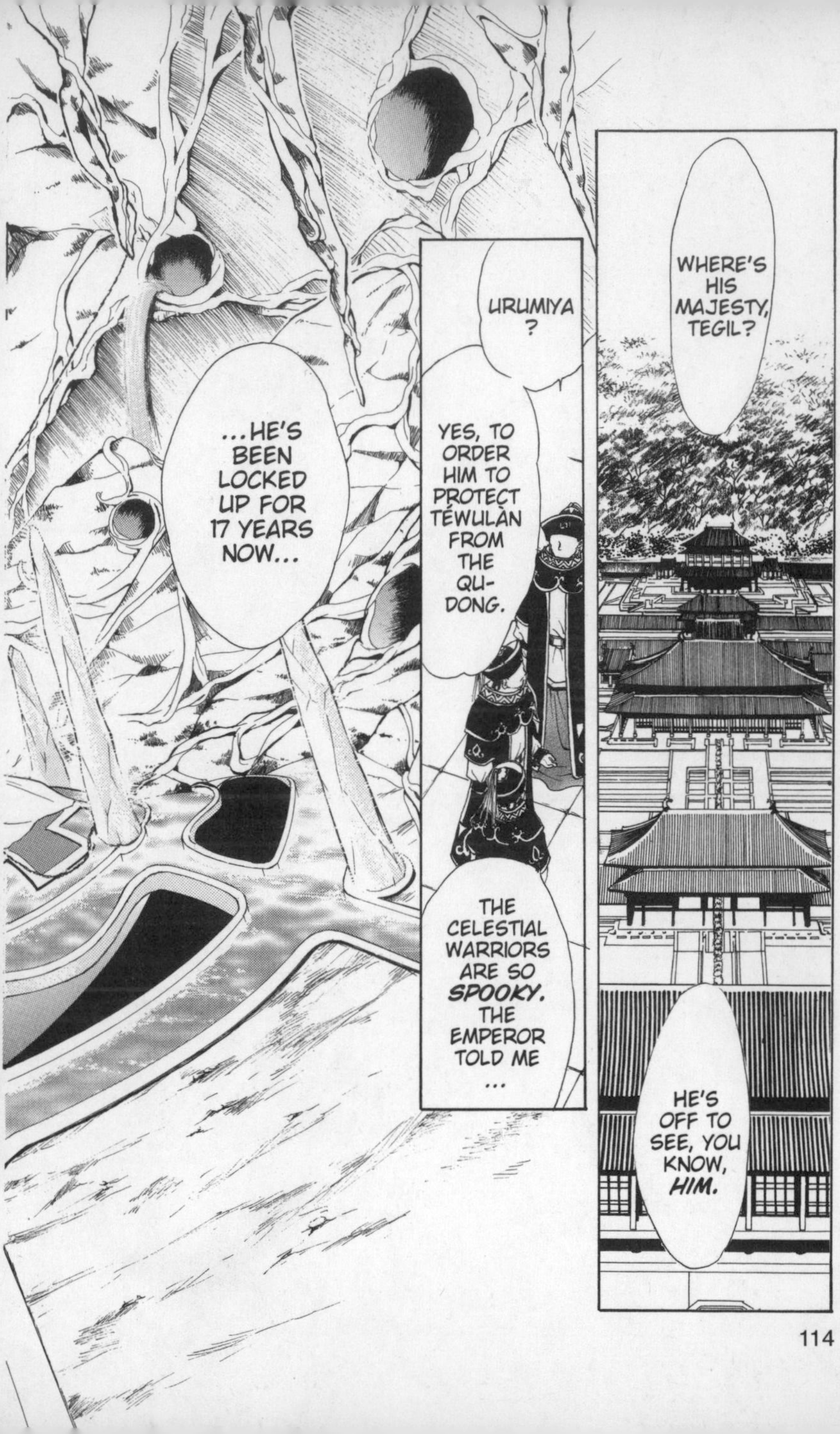
WHERE'S HIS MAJESTY, TEGIL?
HE'S OFF TO SEE, YOU KNOW, *HIM.*
URUMIYA?
YES, TO ORDER HIM TO PROTECT TÉWULÀN FROM THE QU-DONG.
THE CELESTIAL WARRIORS ARE SO *SPOOKY.* THE EMPEROR TOLD ME...
...HE'S BEEN LOCKED UP FOR 17 YEARS NOW...

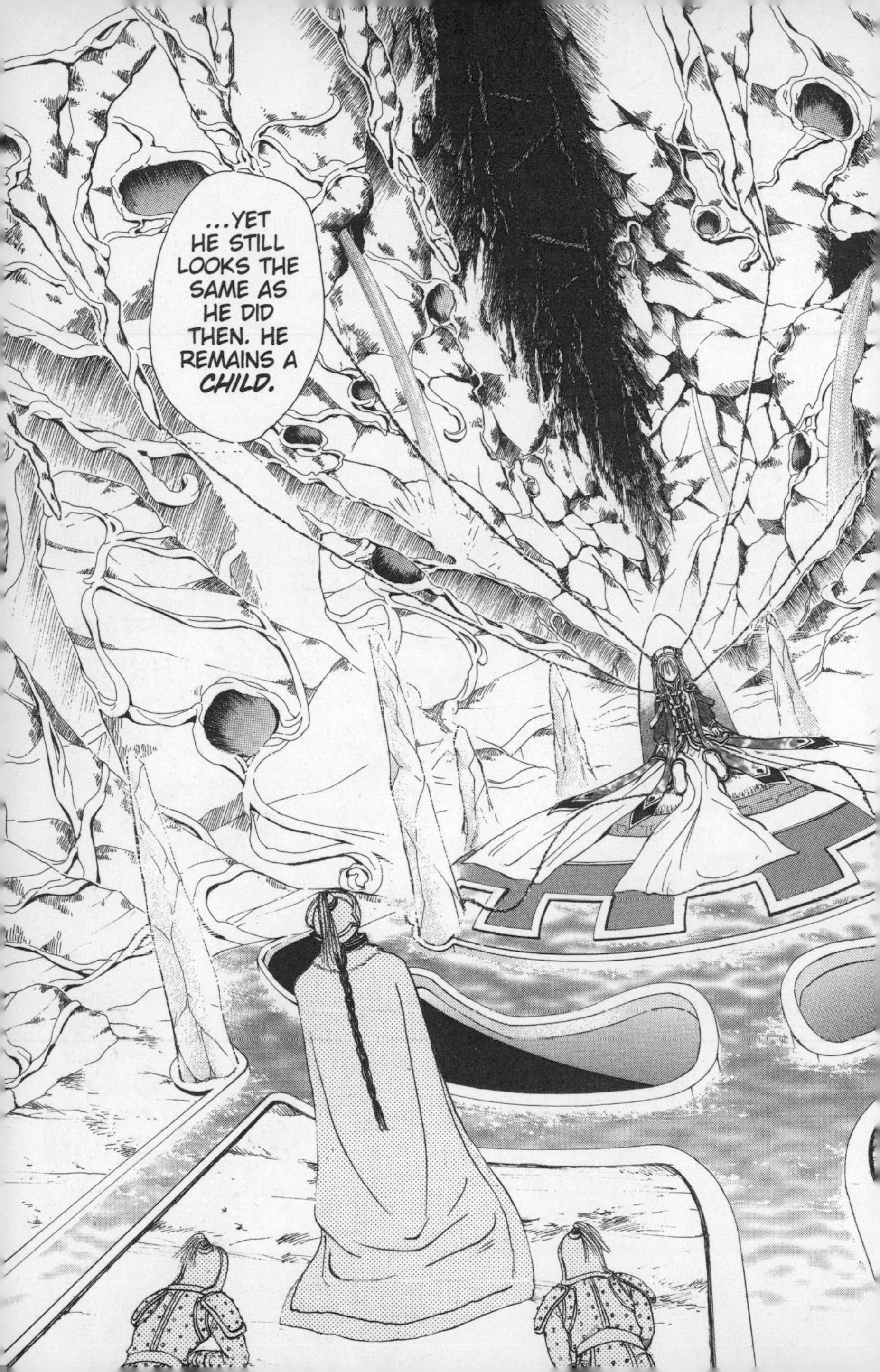
...YET HE STILL LOOKS THE SAME AS HE DID THEN. HE REMAINS A CHILD.

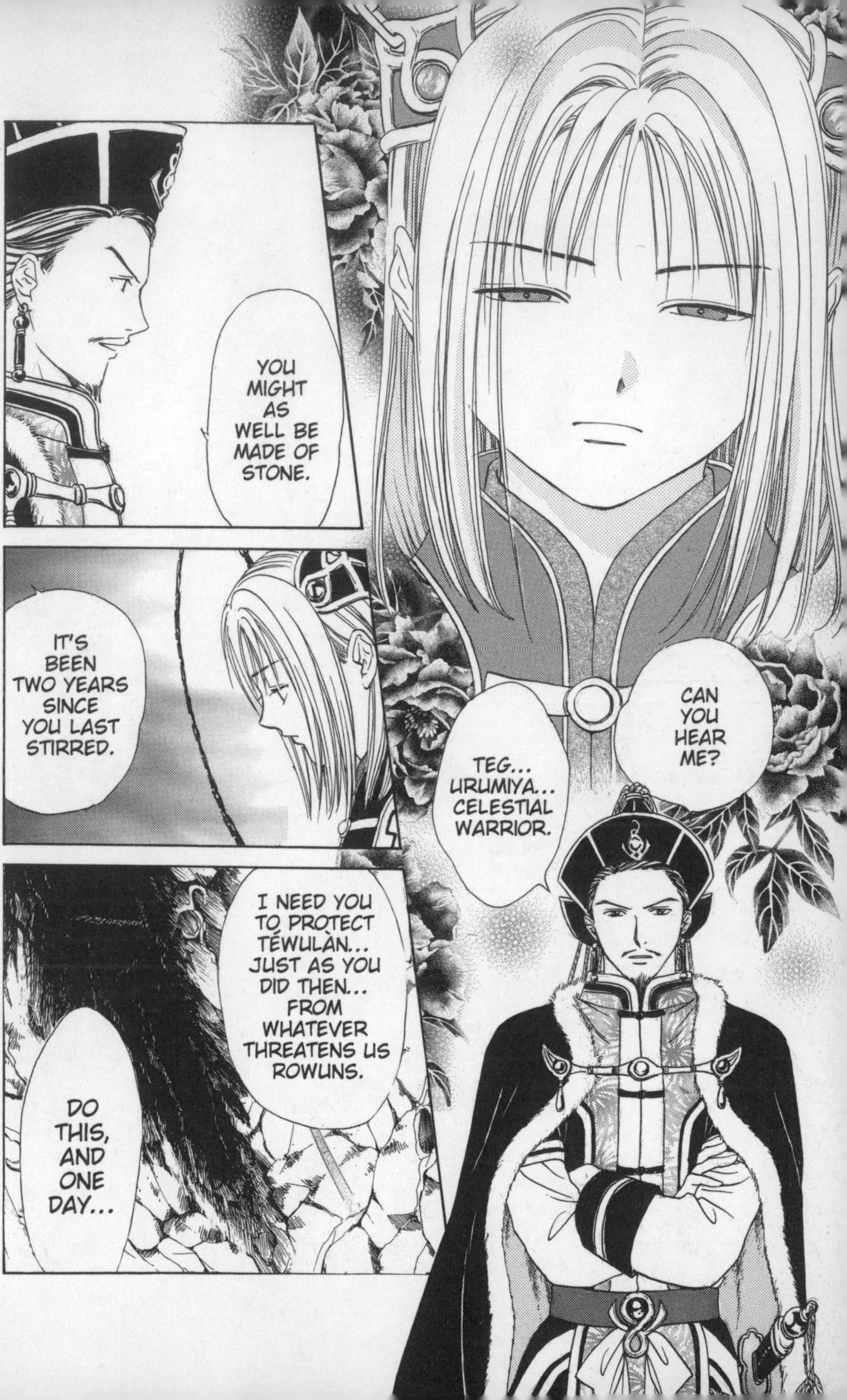
CAN YOU HEAR ME?
TEG... URUMIYA... CELESTIAL WARRIOR.
YOU MIGHT AS WELL BE MADE OF STONE.
IT'S BEEN TWO YEARS SINCE YOU LAST STIRRED.
I NEED YOU TO PROTECT TÉWULÀN... JUST AS YOU DID THEN... FROM WHATEVER THREATENS US ROWUNS.
DO THIS, AND ONE DAY...

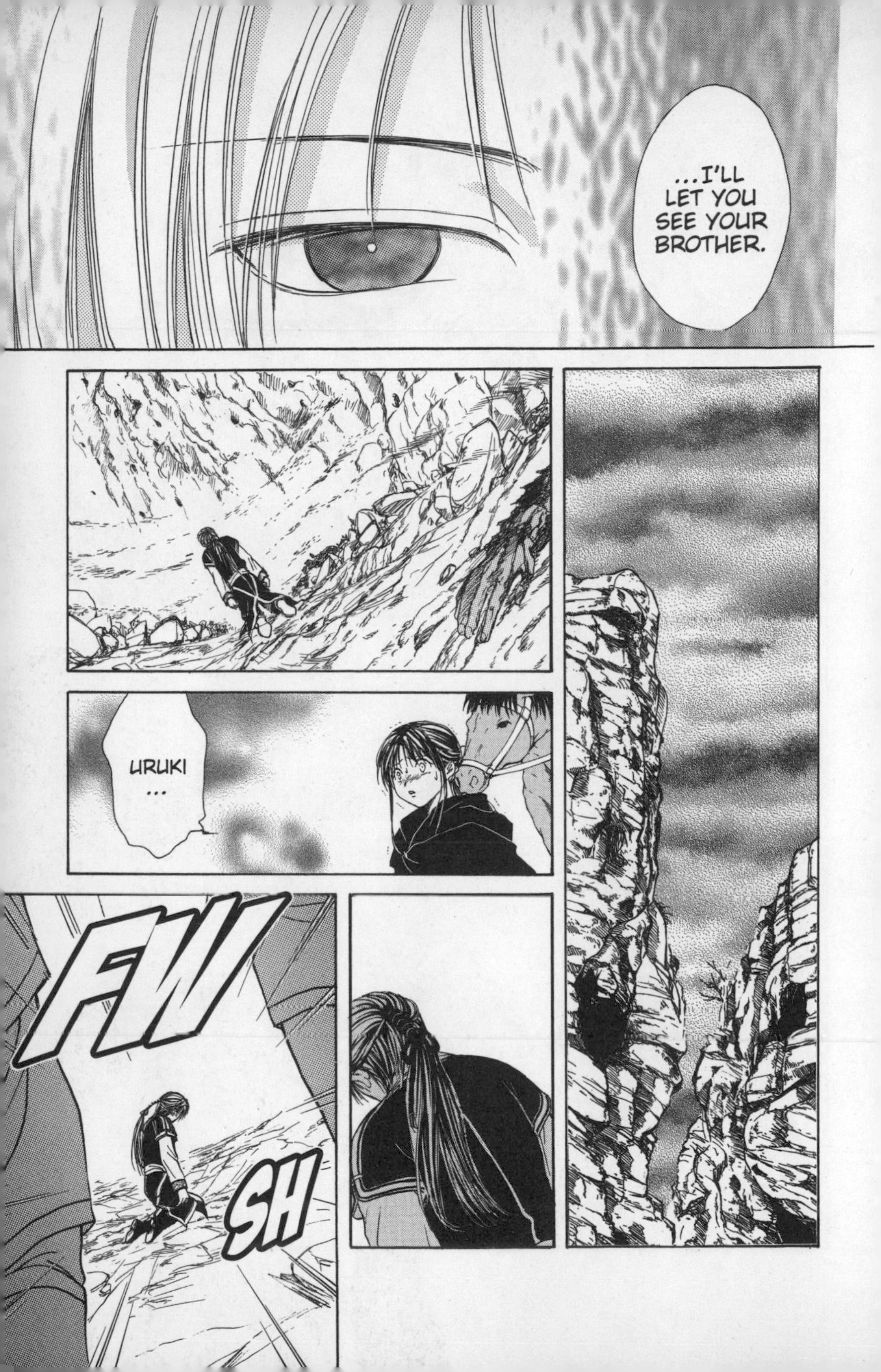
...I'LL LET YOU SEE YOUR BROTHER.
URUKI ...
FWSH

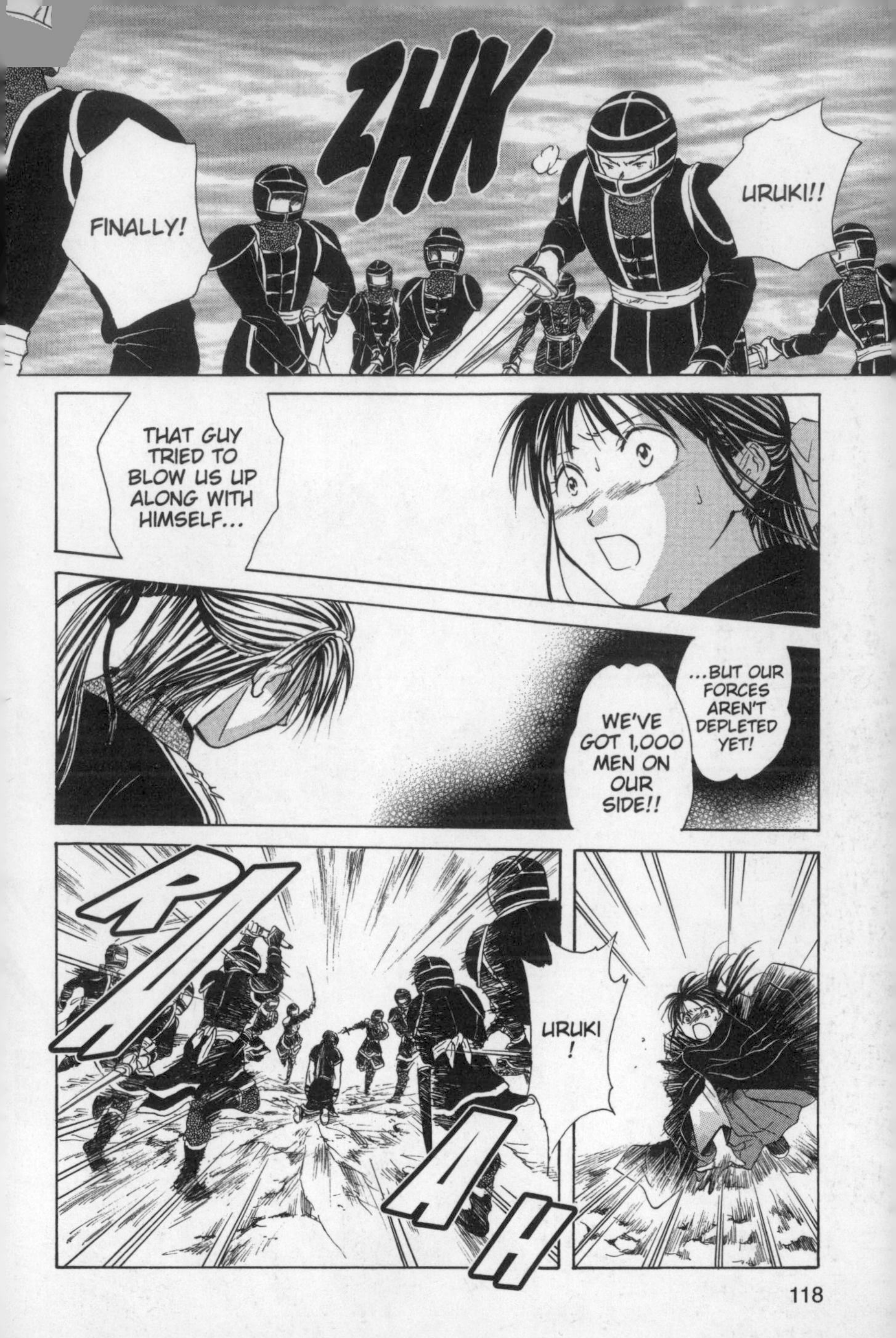
URUKI!!
ZHN
FINALLY!
THAT GUY TRIED TO BLOW US UP ALONG WITH HIMSELF...
...BUT OUR FORCES AREN'T DEPLETED YET!
WE'VE GOT 1,000 MEN ON OUR SIDE!!
URUKI!
RA
AAH

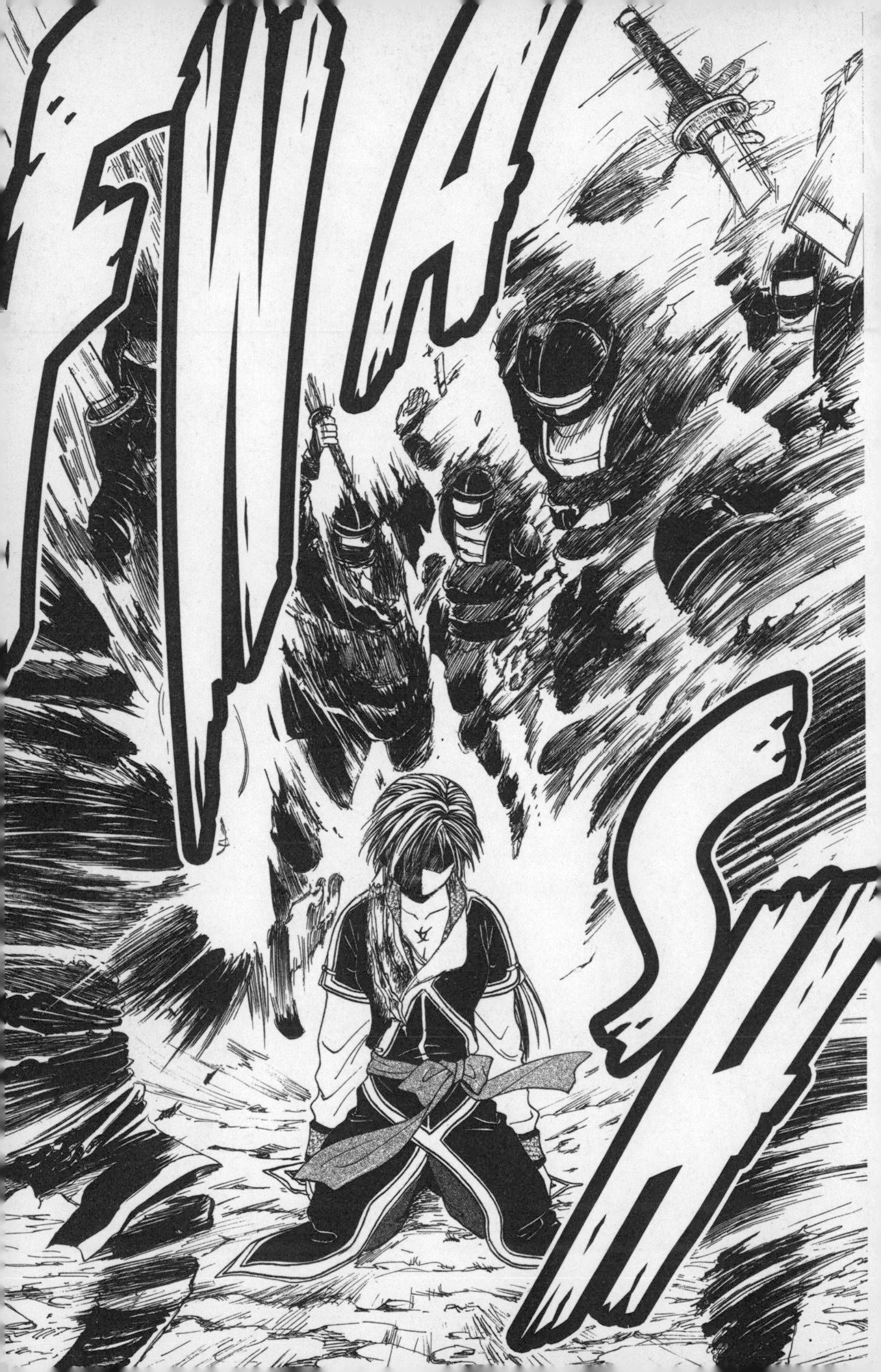
FWASH

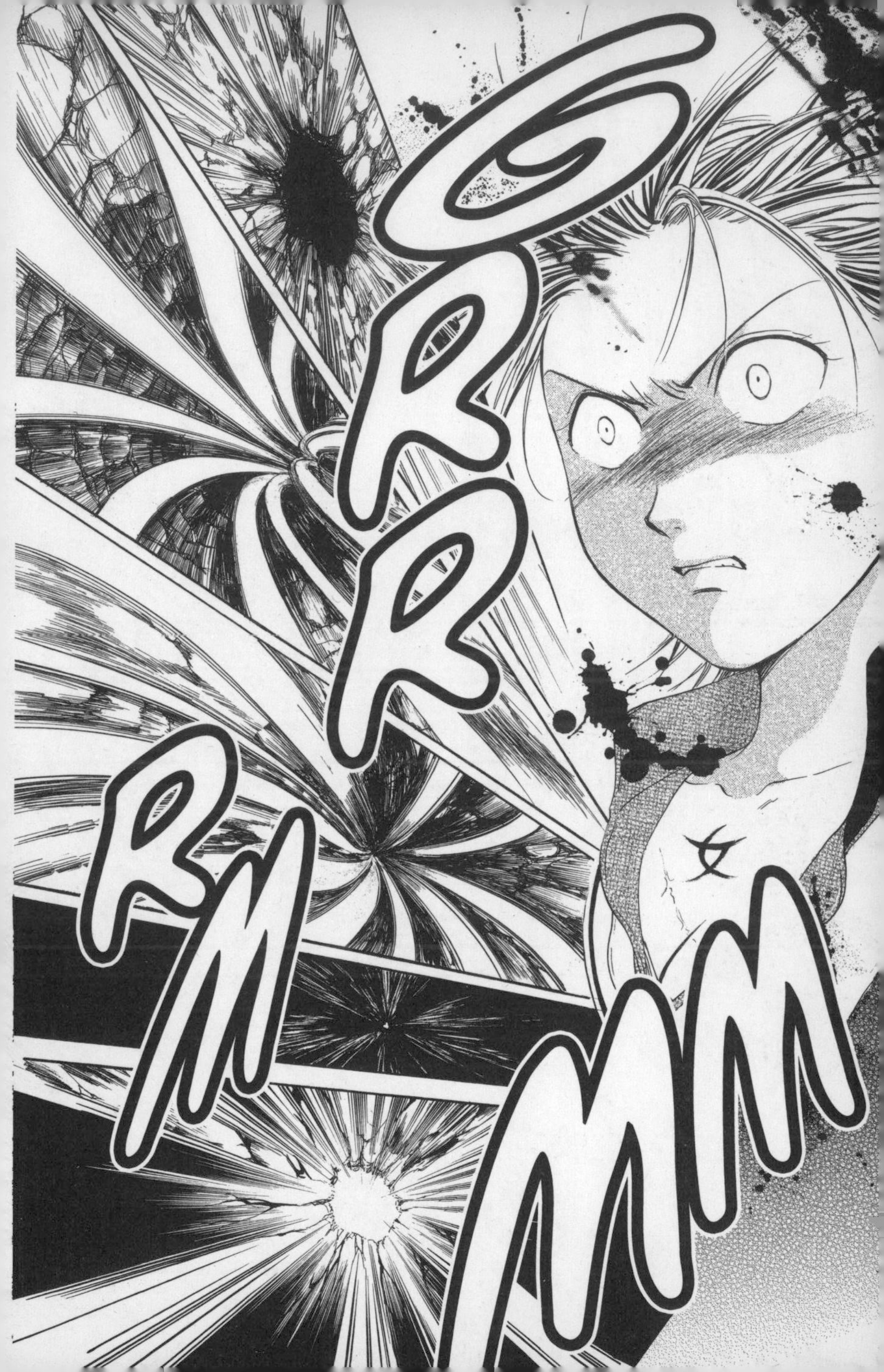
GRRRMMMM

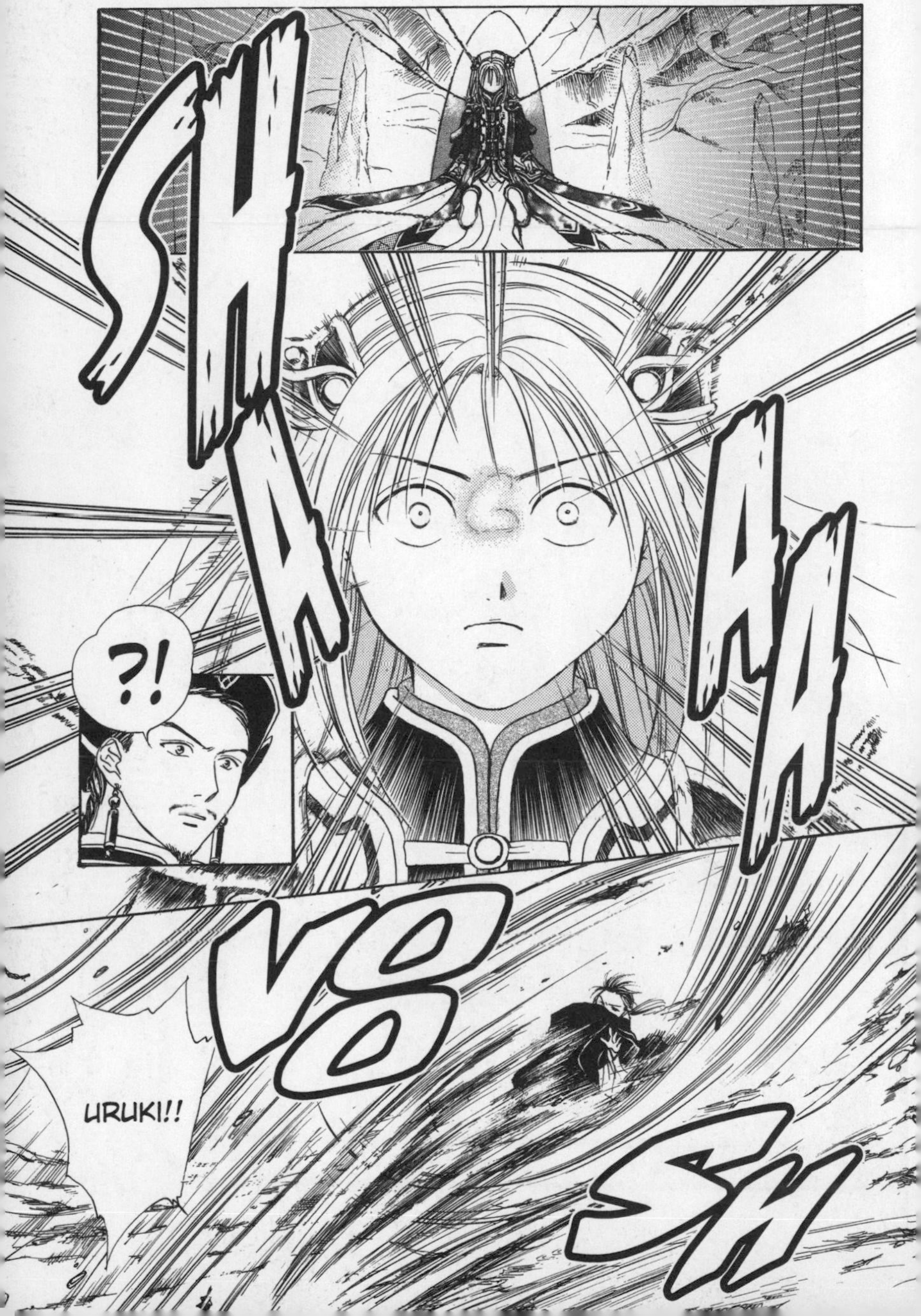

SHAAA
?!
VSSH
URUKI!!

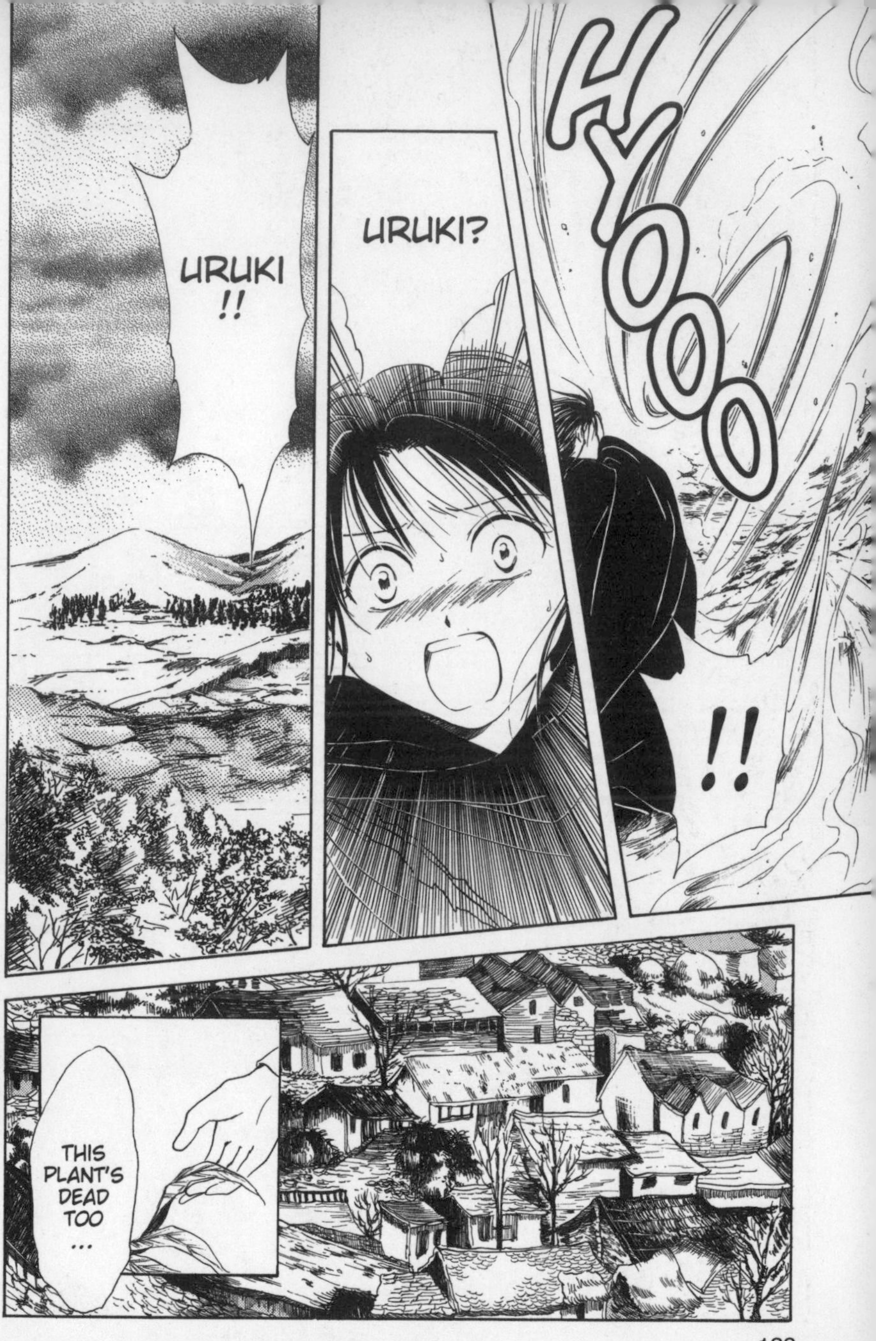
HYOOO
!!
URUKI?
URUKI !!
THIS PLANT'S DEAD TOO ...

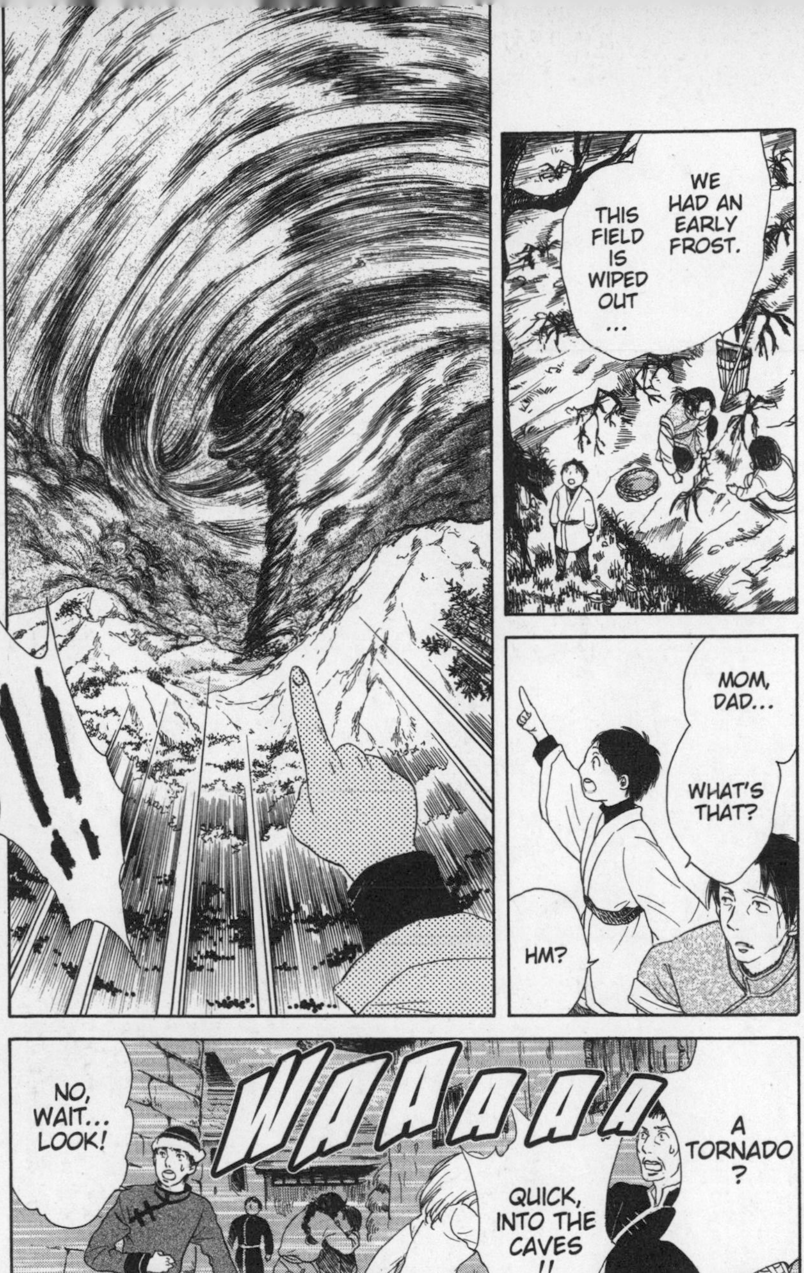
WE HAD AN EARLY FROST.
THIS FIELD IS WIPED OUT ...
MOM, DAD...
WHAT'S THAT?
HM?
!!
A TORNADO?
QUICK, INTO THE CAVES !!
WAAAAAA
NO, WAIT... LOOK!

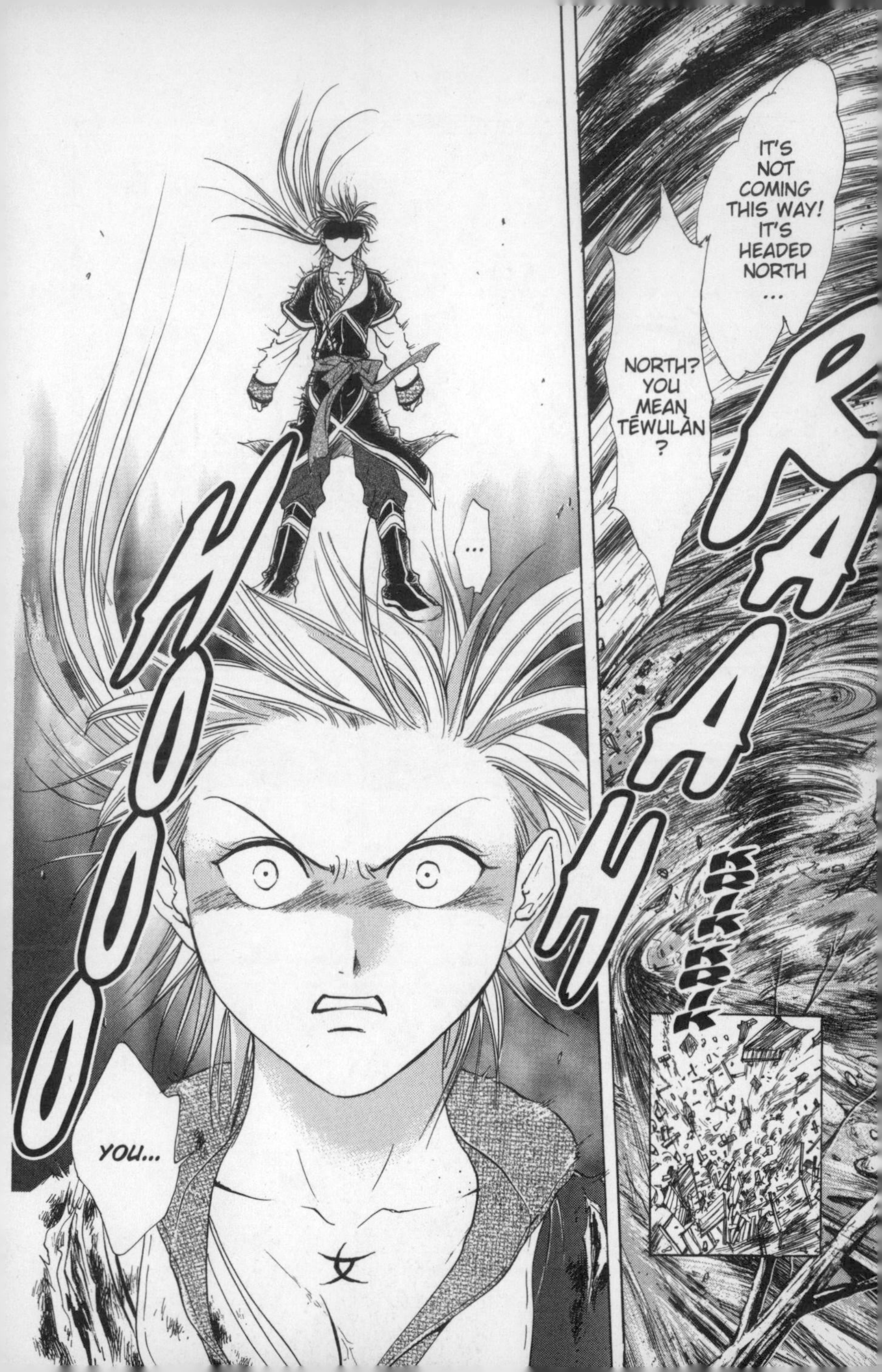
IT'S NOT COMING THIS WAY! IT'S HEADED NORTH...
NORTH? YOU MEAN TĒWULÀN?
...
HOOOO
YOU...

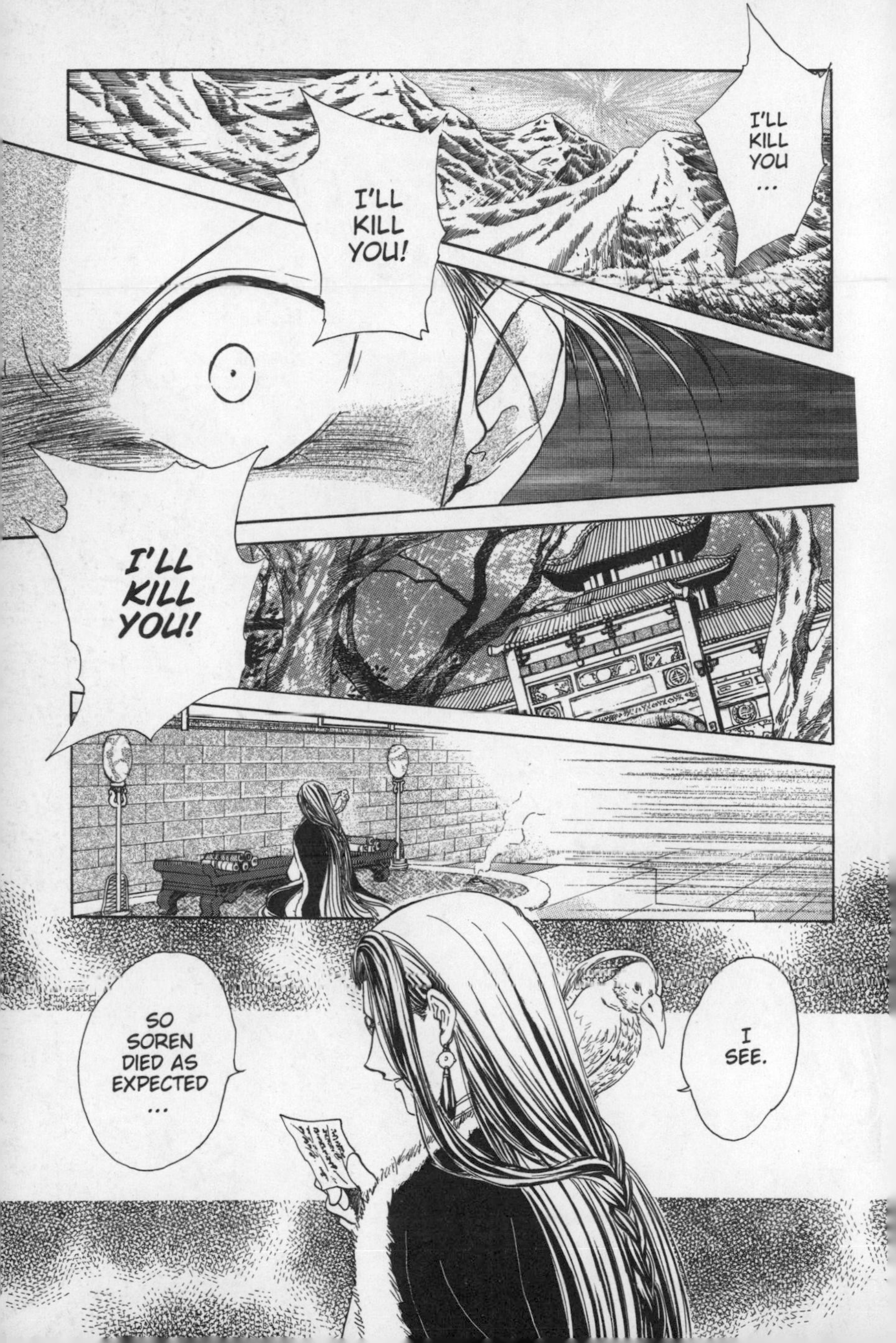
I'LL KILL YOU ...
I'LL KILL YOU!
I'LL KILL YOU!
I SEE.
SO SOREN DIED AS EXPECTED ...

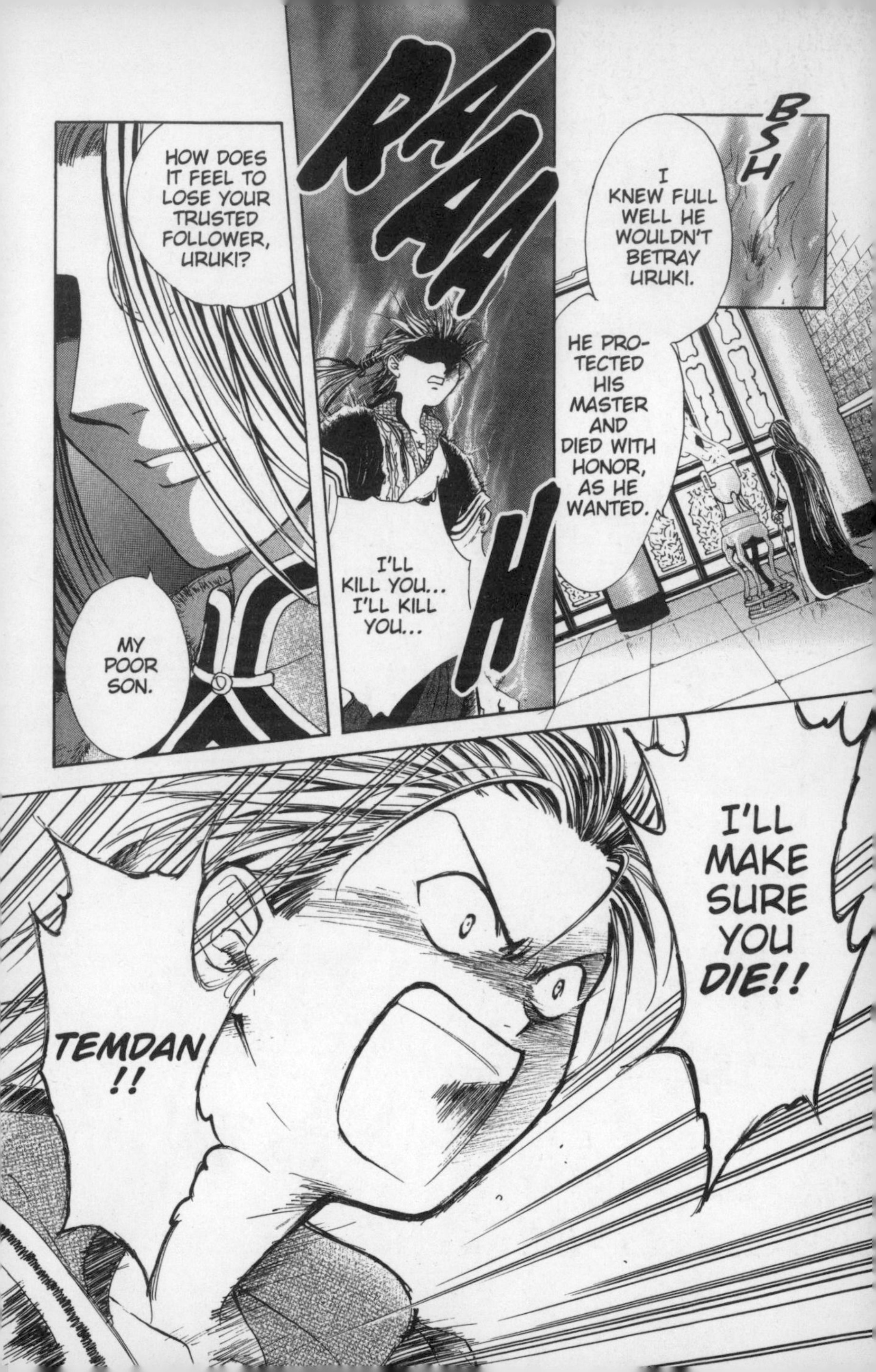
BSH
I KNEW FULL WELL HE WOULDN'T BETRAY URUKI.
HE PROTECTED HIS MASTER AND DIED WITH HONOR, AS HE WANTED.
RAAAH
I'LL KILL YOU... I'LL KILL YOU...
HOW DOES IT FEEL TO LOSE YOUR TRUSTED FOLLOWER, URUKI?
MY POOR SON.
I'LL MAKE SURE YOU DIE!!
TEMDAN!!

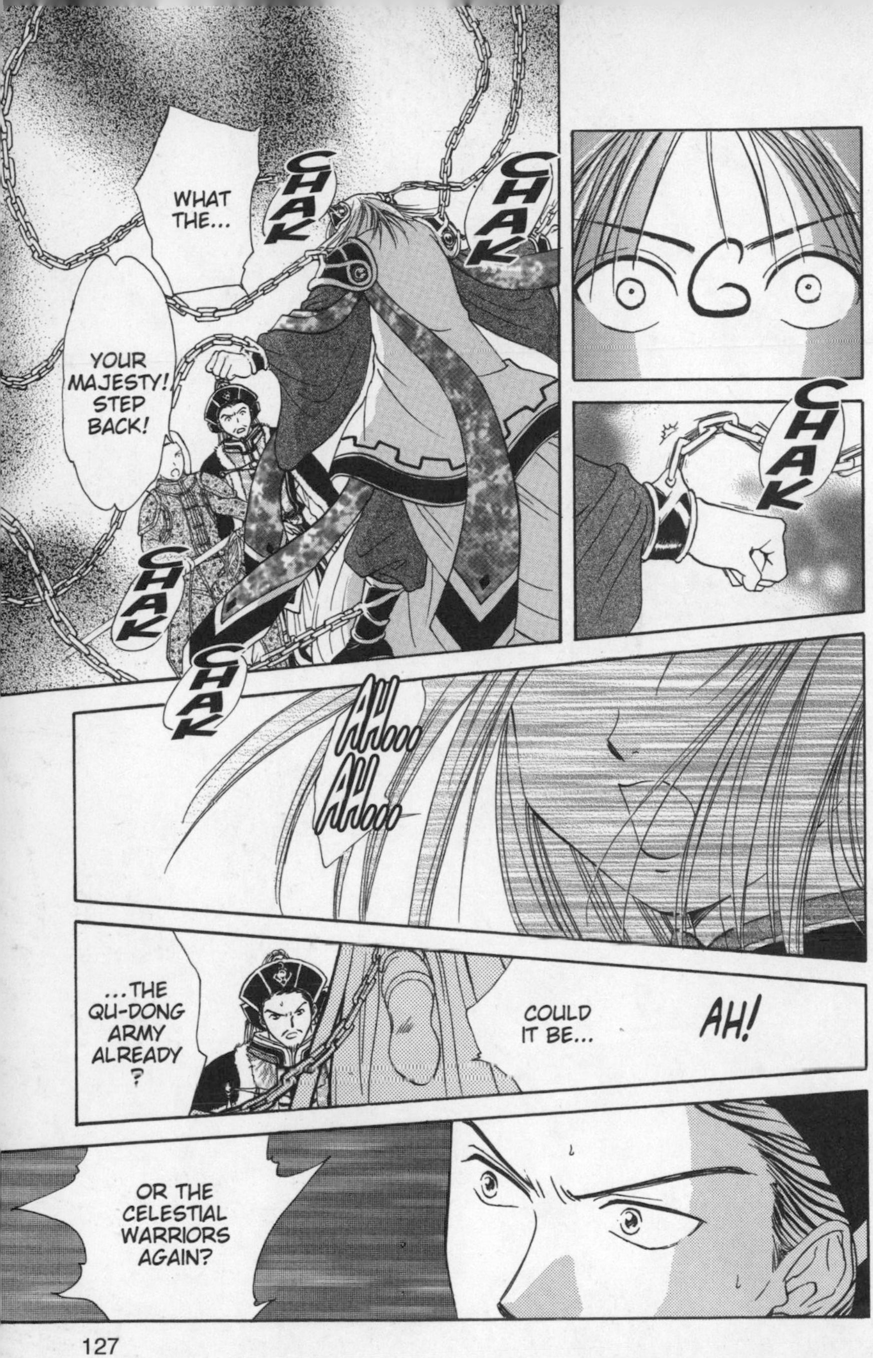
CHAK
CHAK
CHAK
WHAT THE...
YOUR MAJESTY! STEP BACK!
CHAK
CHAK
AHooo AHooo
AH!
COULD IT BE...
...THE QU-DONG ARMY ALREADY?
OR THE CELESTIAL WARRIORS AGAIN?

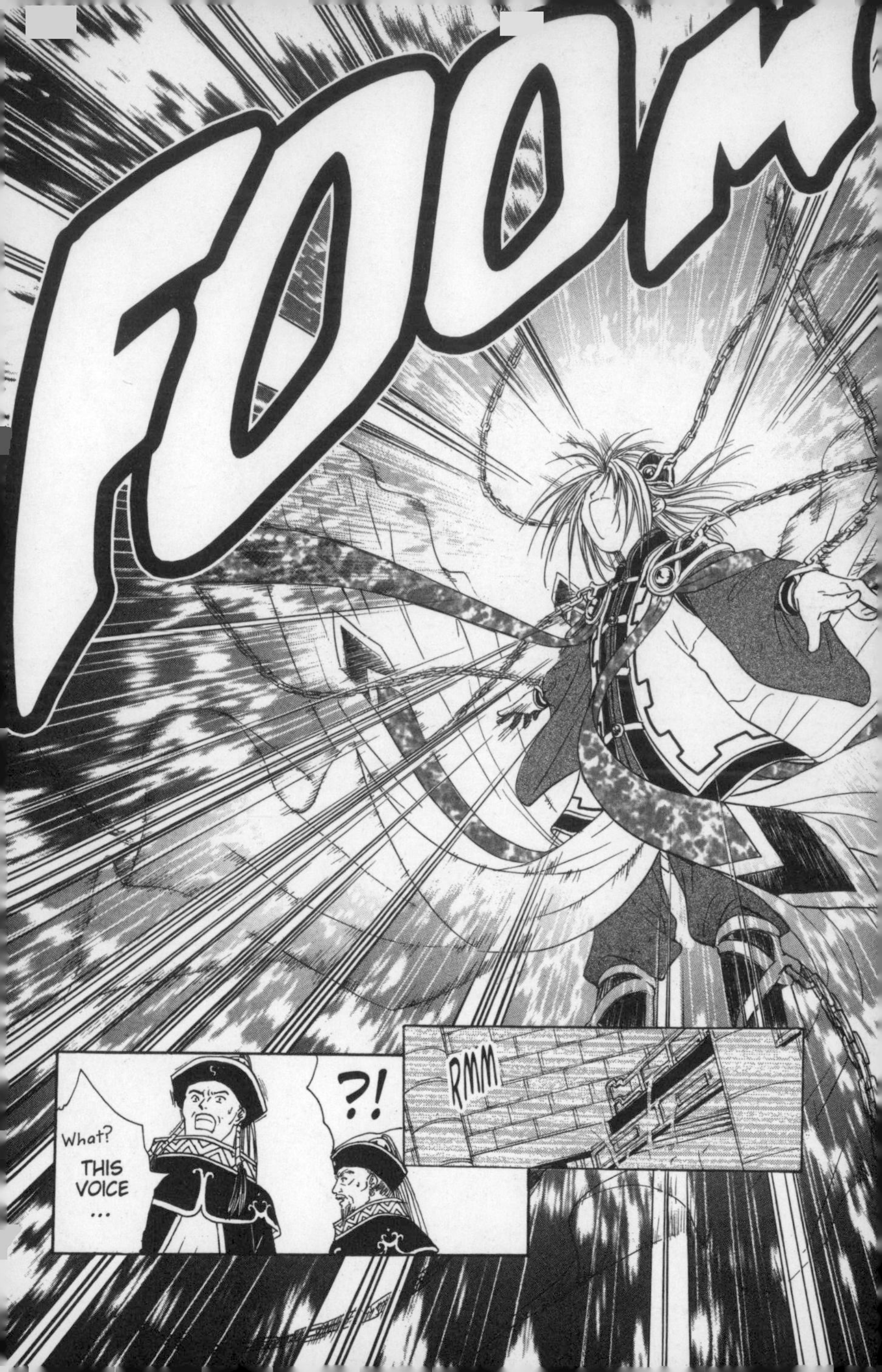
FOOM
RMM
?!
What?
THIS VOICE
...

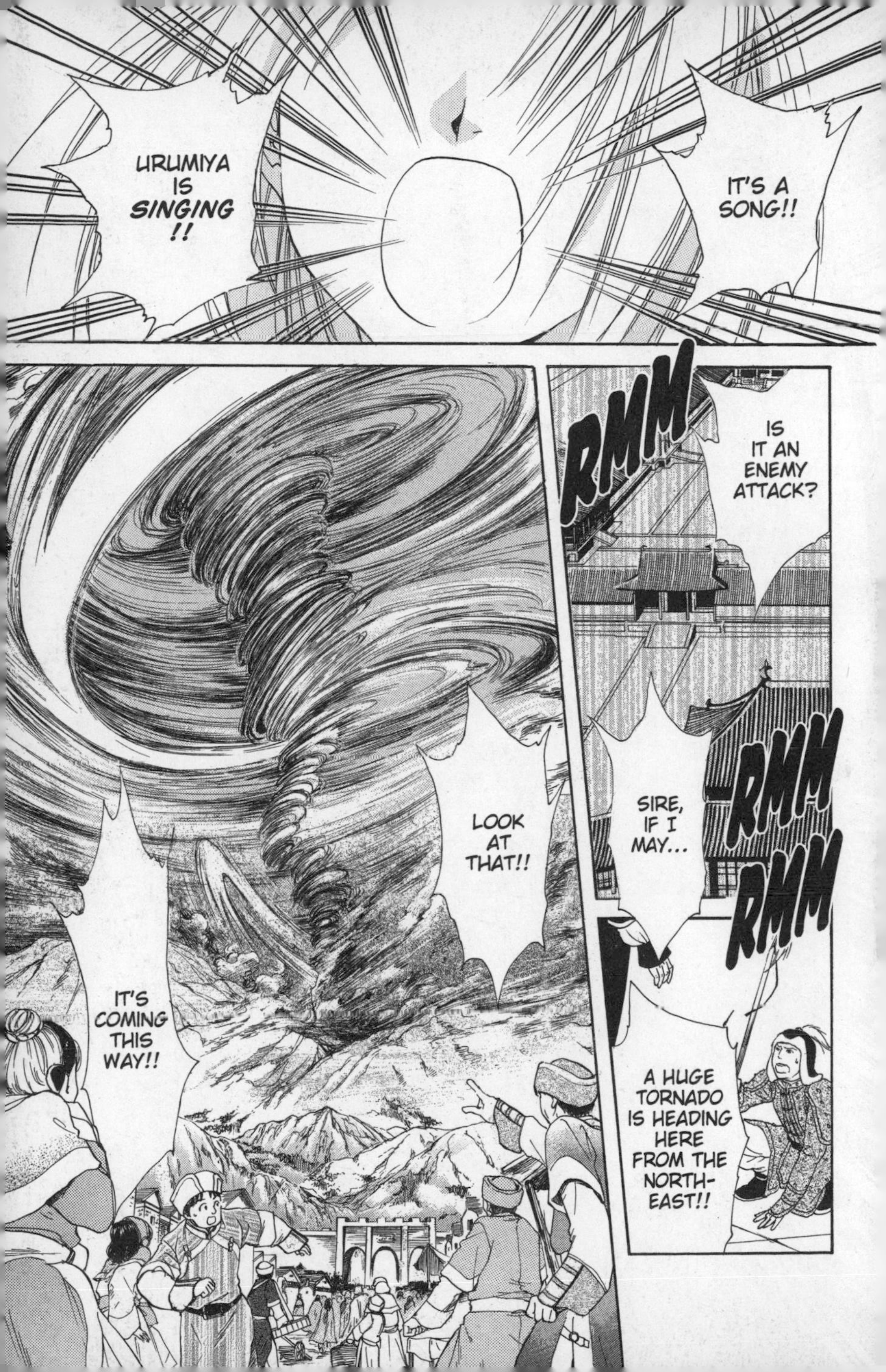
IT'S A SONG!!
URUMIYA IS SINGING!!
IS IT AN ENEMY ATTACK?
RMM
RMM
RMM
SIRE, IF I MAY...
A HUGE TORNADO IS HEADING HERE FROM THE NORTH-EAST!!
LOOK AT THAT!!
IT'S COMING THIS WAY!!

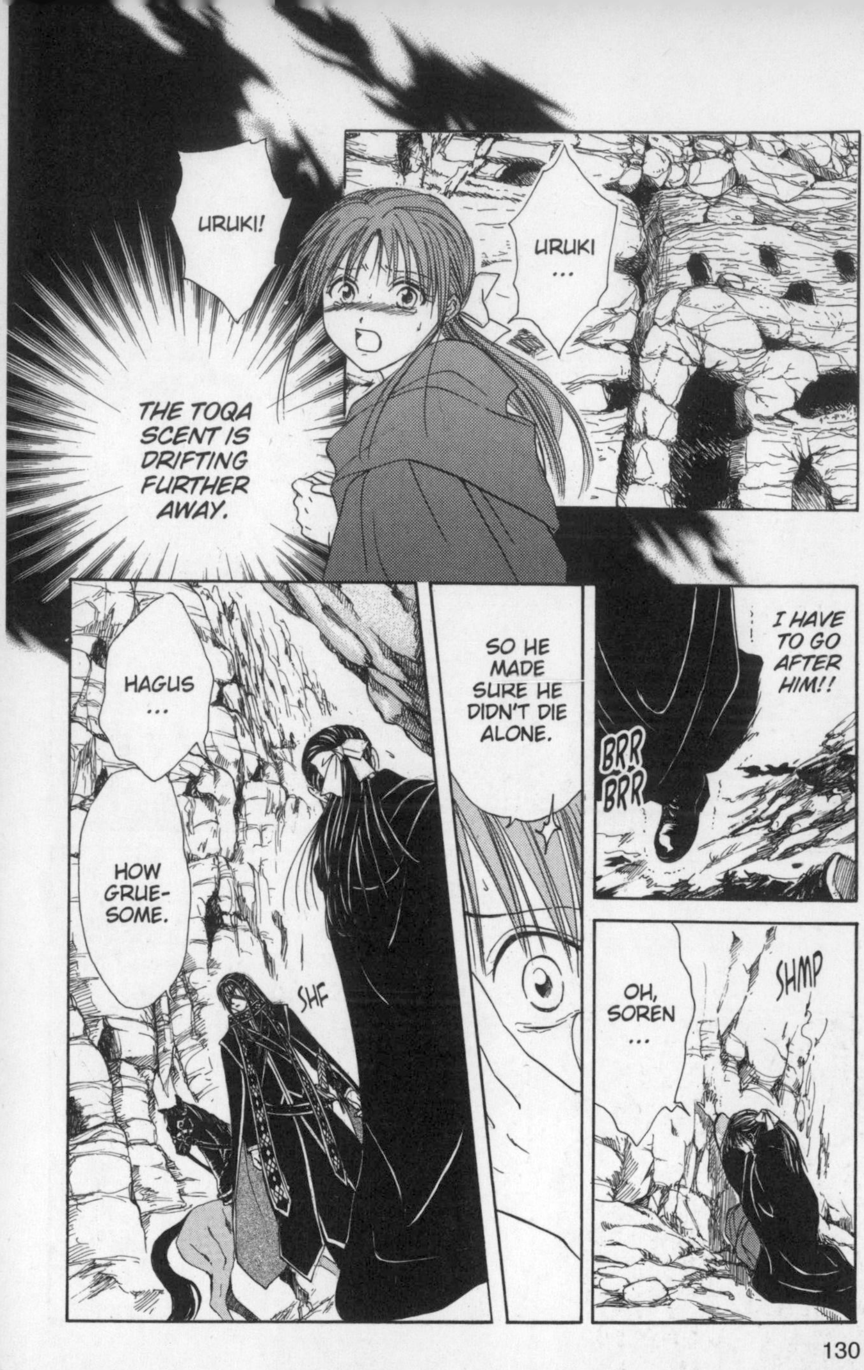
URUKI ...
URUKI!
THE TOQA SCENT IS DRIFTING FURTHER AWAY.
I HAVE TO GO AFTER HIM!!
BRR BRR
OH, SOREN ...
SHMP
SO HE MADE SURE HE DIDN'T DIE ALONE.
HAGUS ...
HOW GRUE-SOME.
SHF

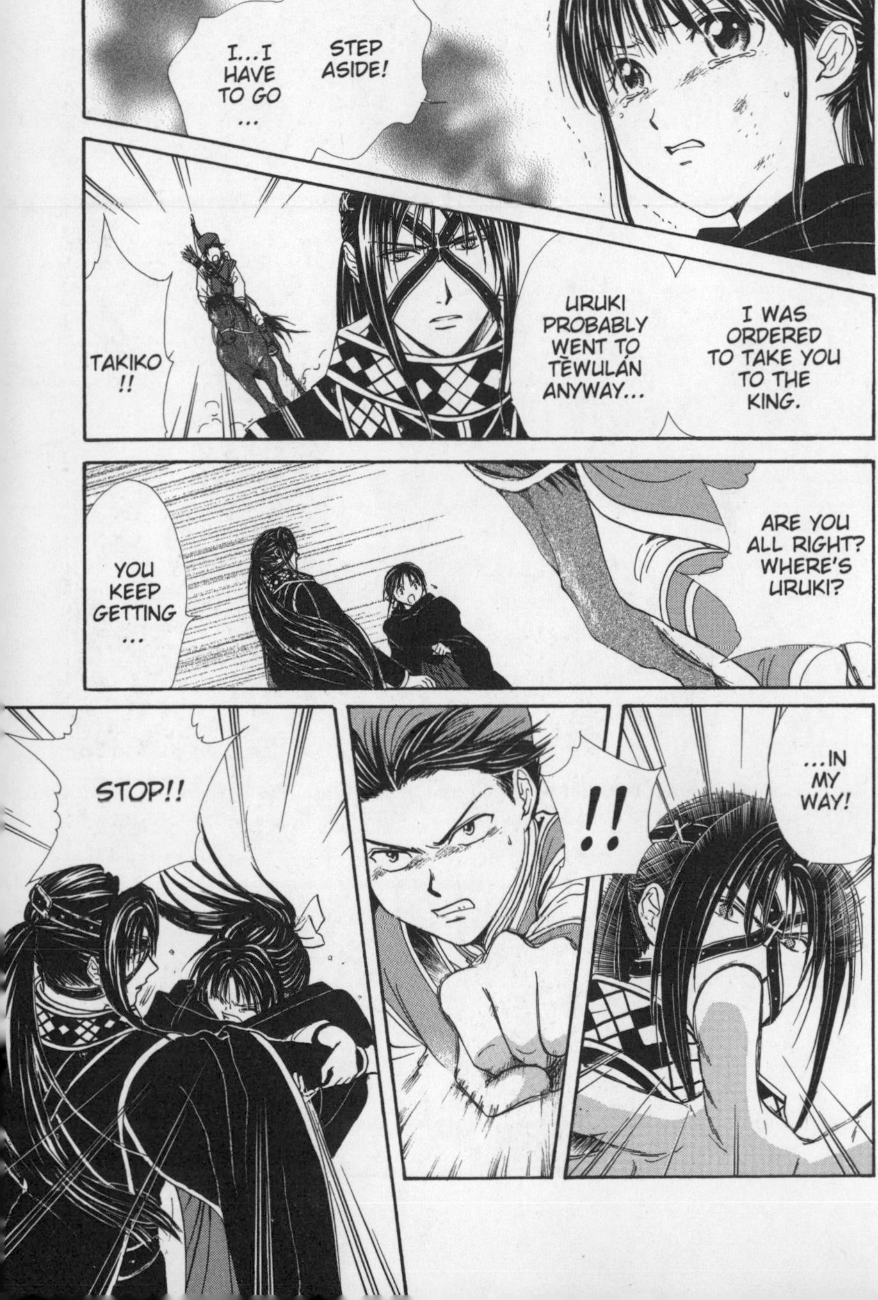
STEP ASIDE!
I...I HAVE TO GO...
I WAS ORDERED TO TAKE YOU TO THE KING.
URUKI PROBABLY WENT TO TÈWULÁN ANYWAY...
TAKIKO!!
ARE YOU ALL RIGHT? WHERE'S URUKI?
YOU KEEP GETTING...
...IN MY WAY!
!!
STOP!!

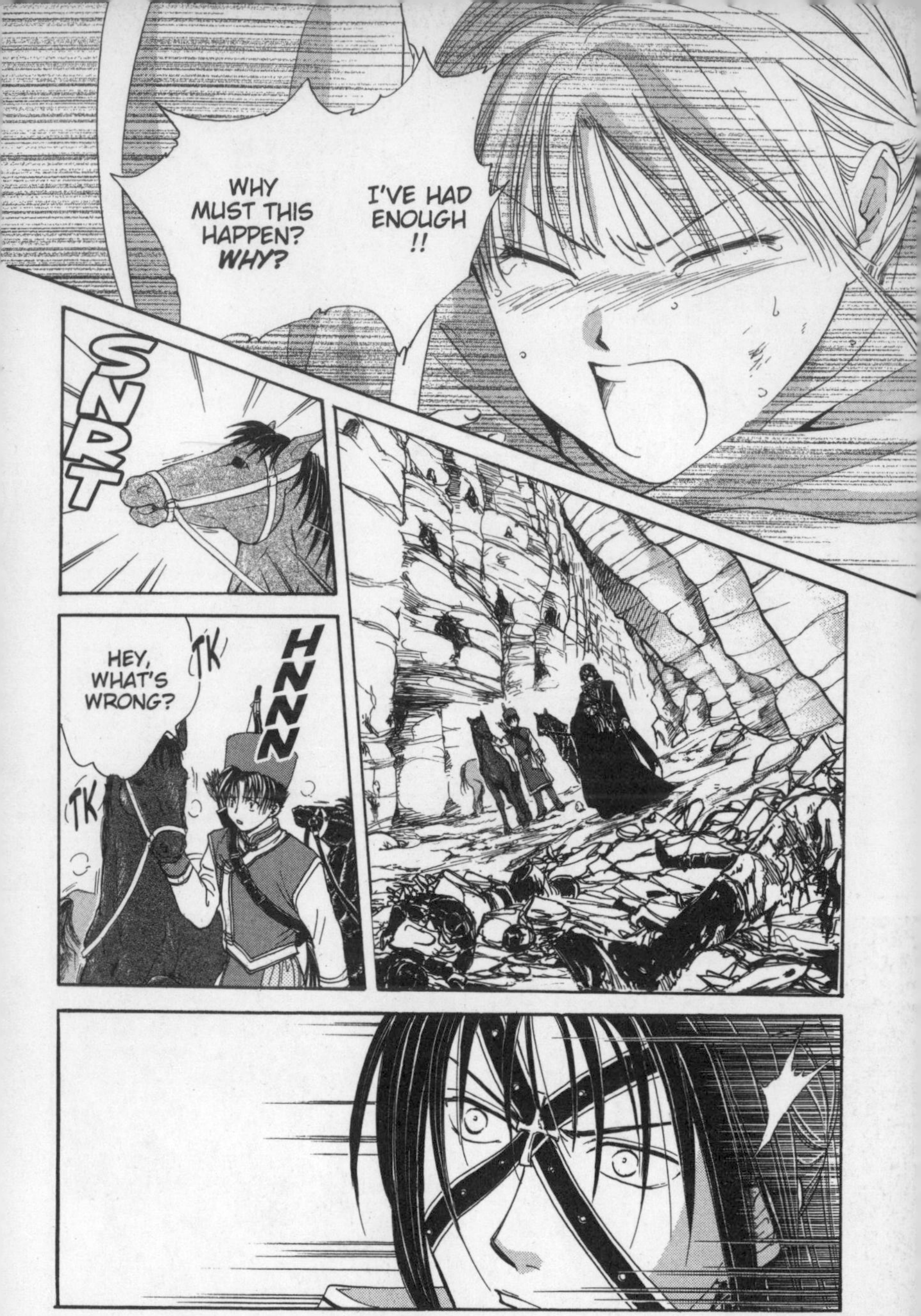
I'VE HAD ENOUGH !!
WHY MUST THIS HAPPEN? *WHY?*
SNRT
TK
HNNN
HEY, WHAT'S WRONG?
TK

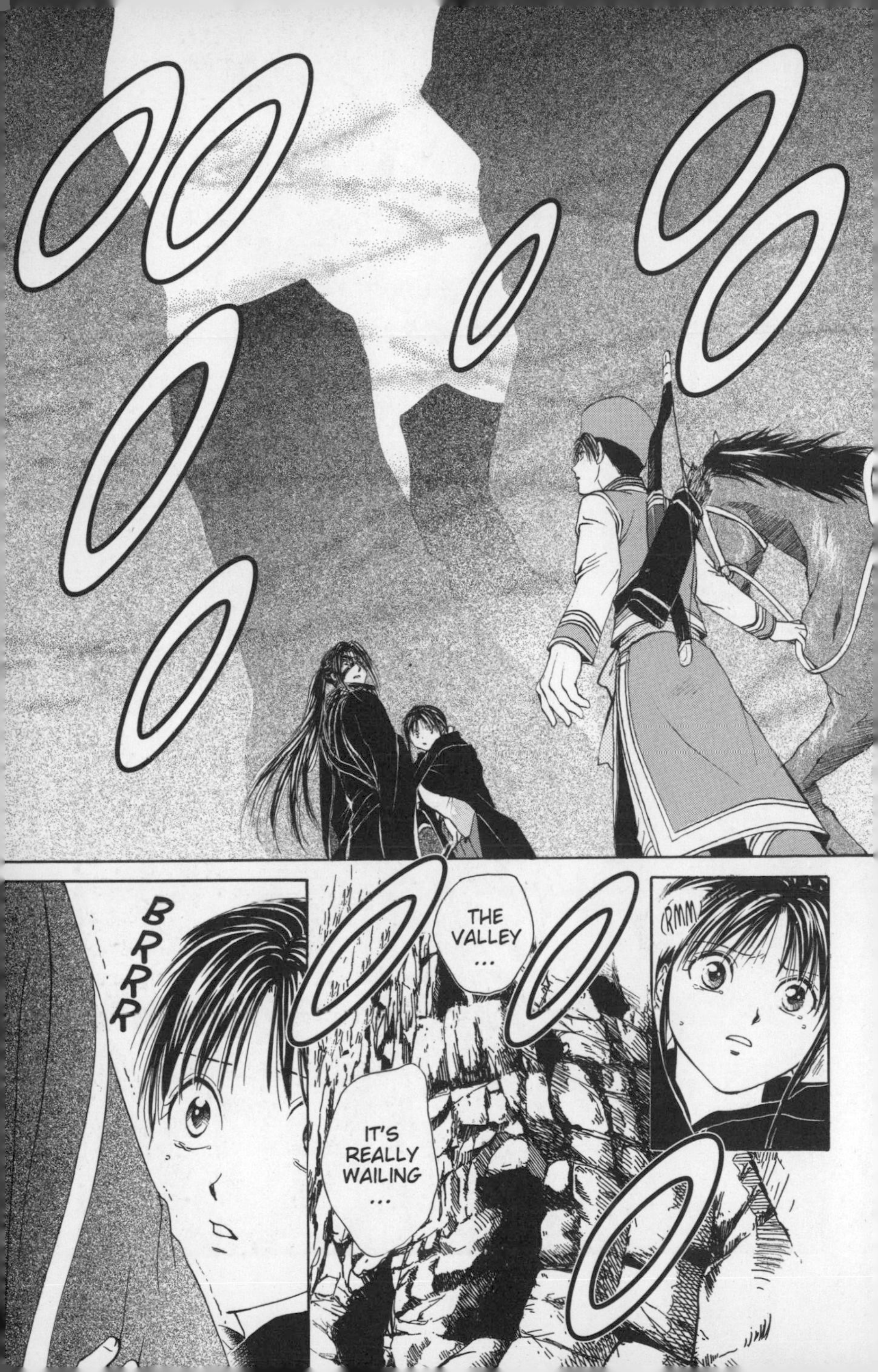
RMM
THE VALLEY...
IT'S REALLY WAILING...
BRRR

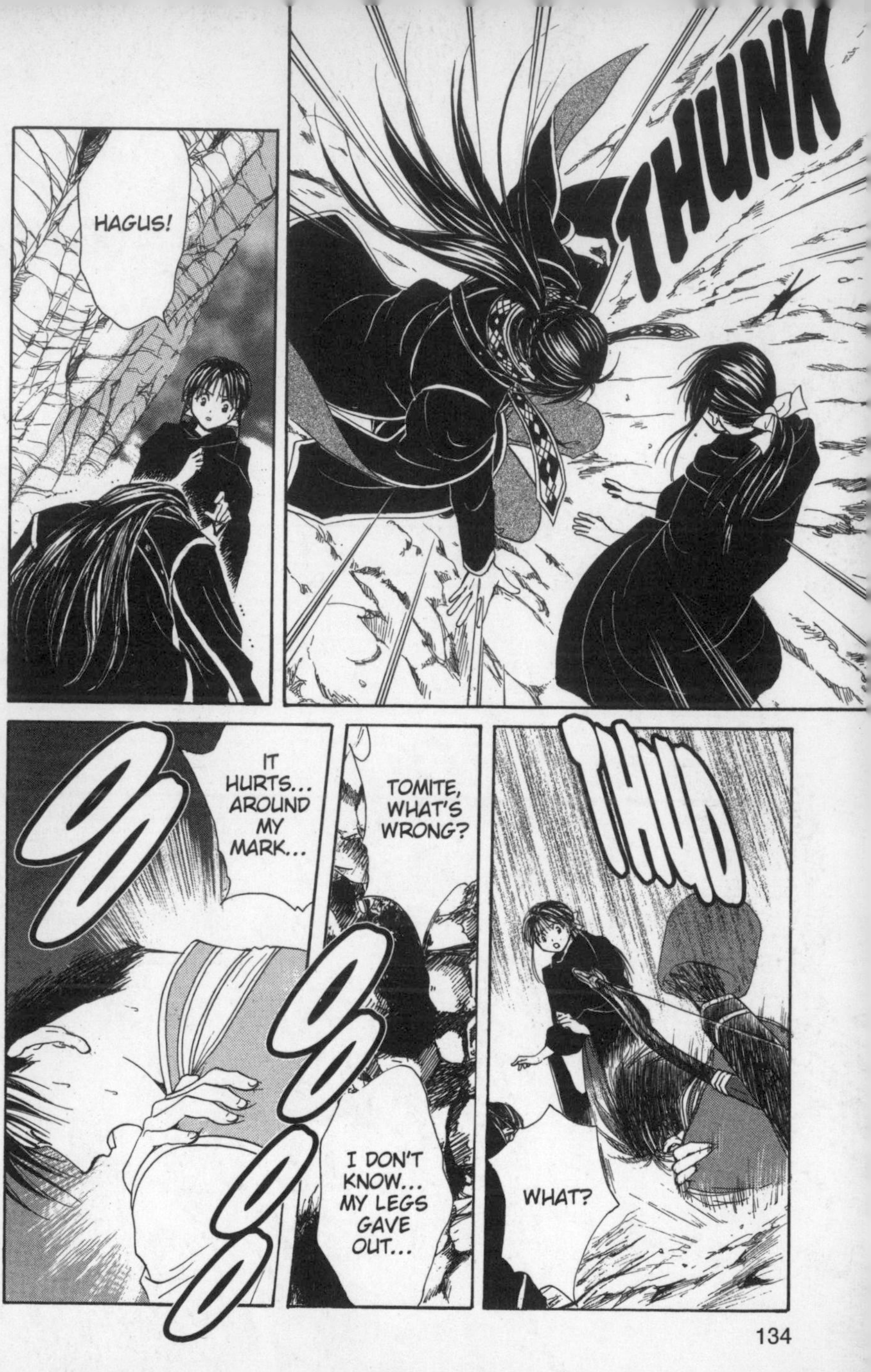
THUNK
HAGUS!
THUD
WHAT?
TOMITE, WHAT'S WRONG?
I DON'T KNOW... MY LEGS GAVE OUT...
IT HURTS... AROUND MY MARK...

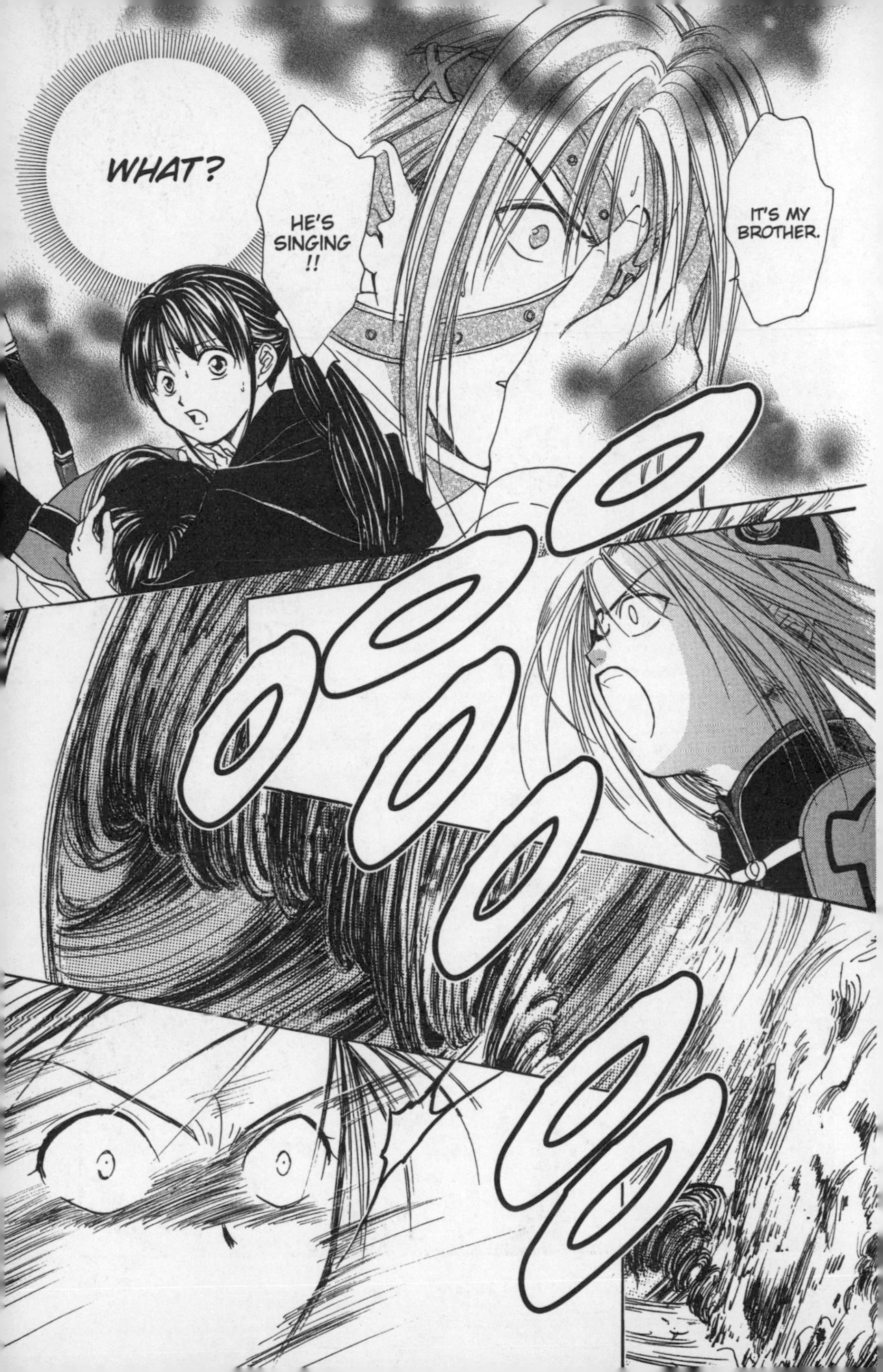
IT'S MY BROTHER.
HE'S SINGING !!
WHAT?

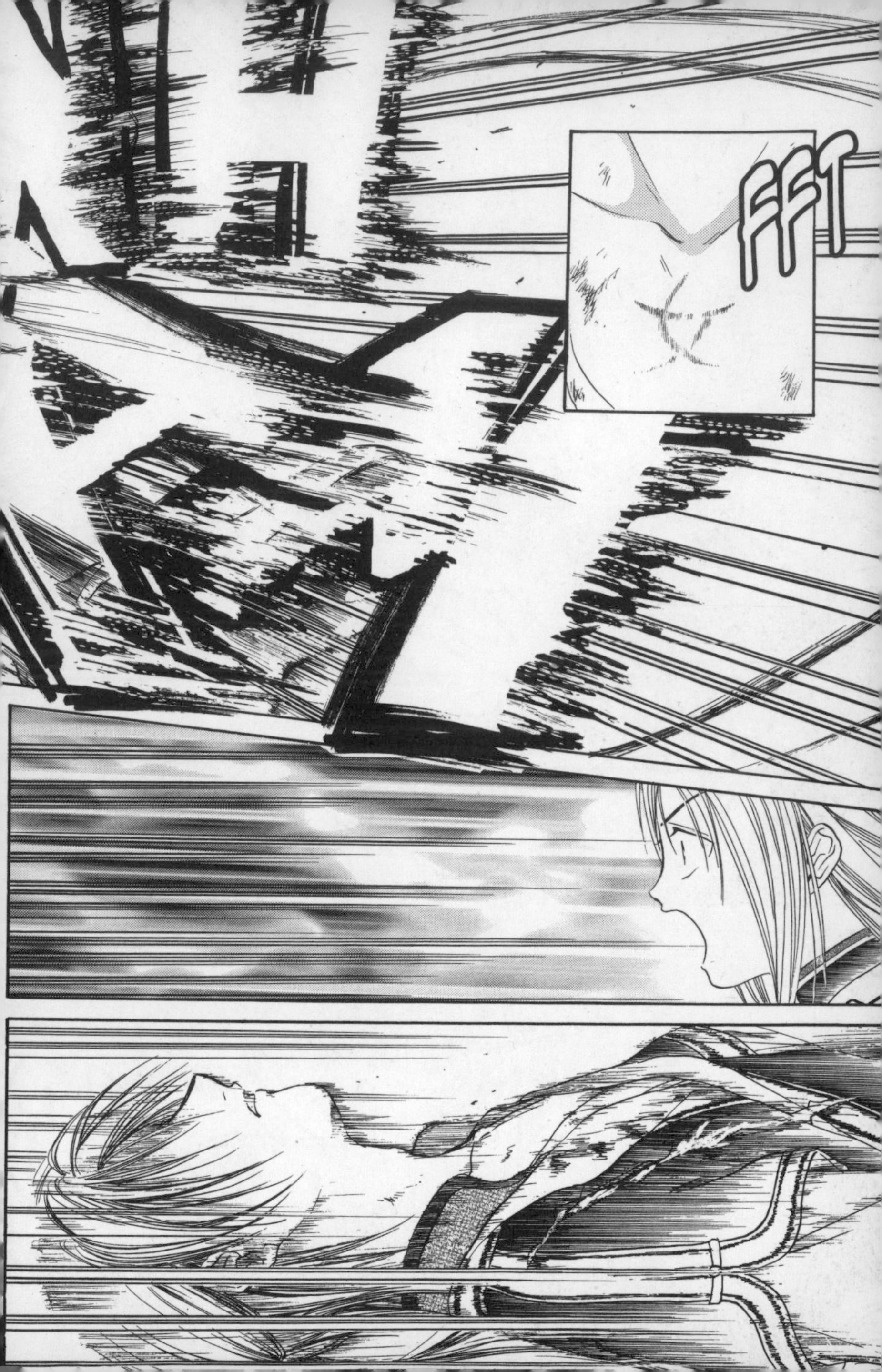
FFT

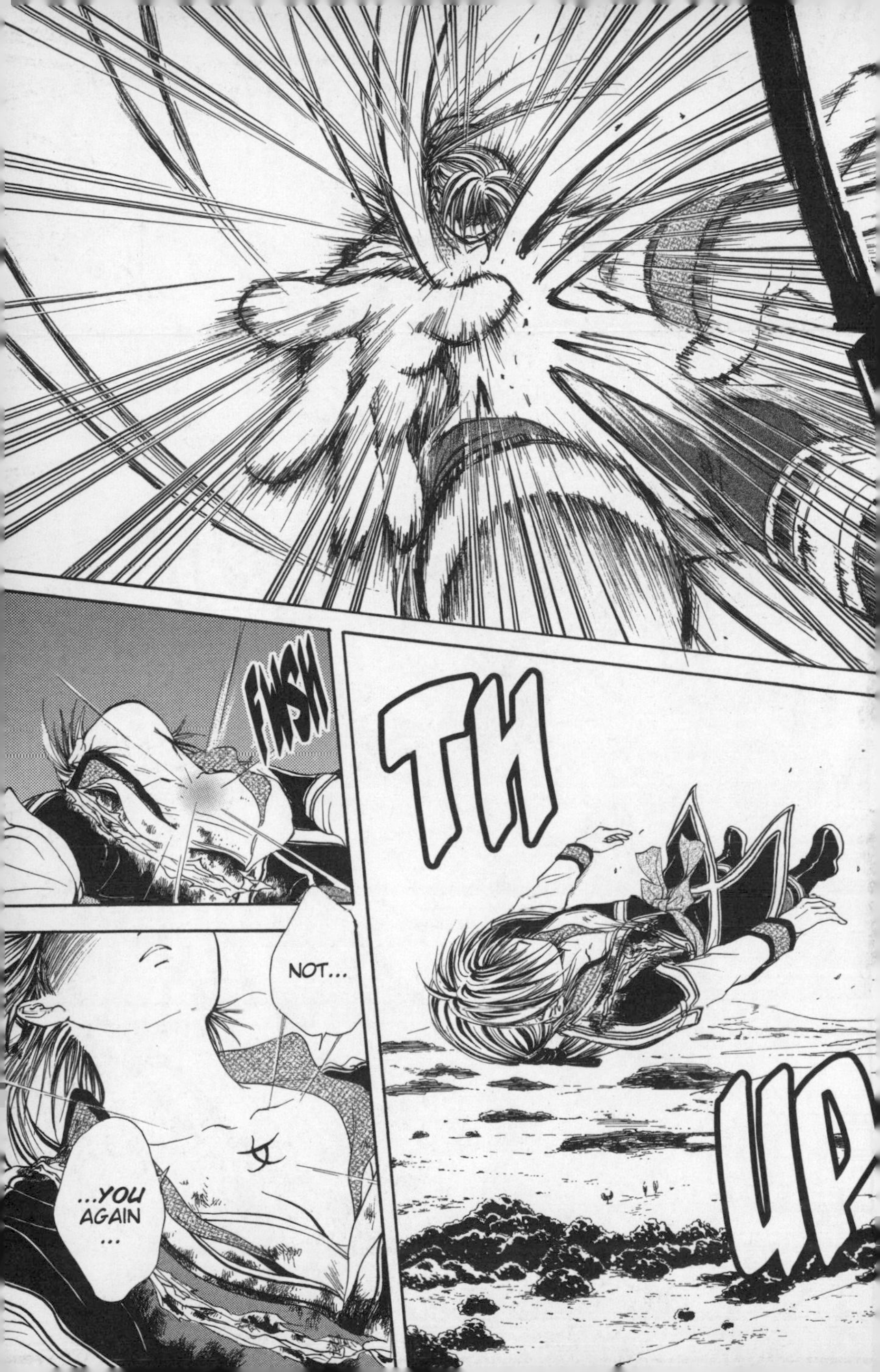
TH
UP
FWSH
NOT...
...YOU AGAIN ...

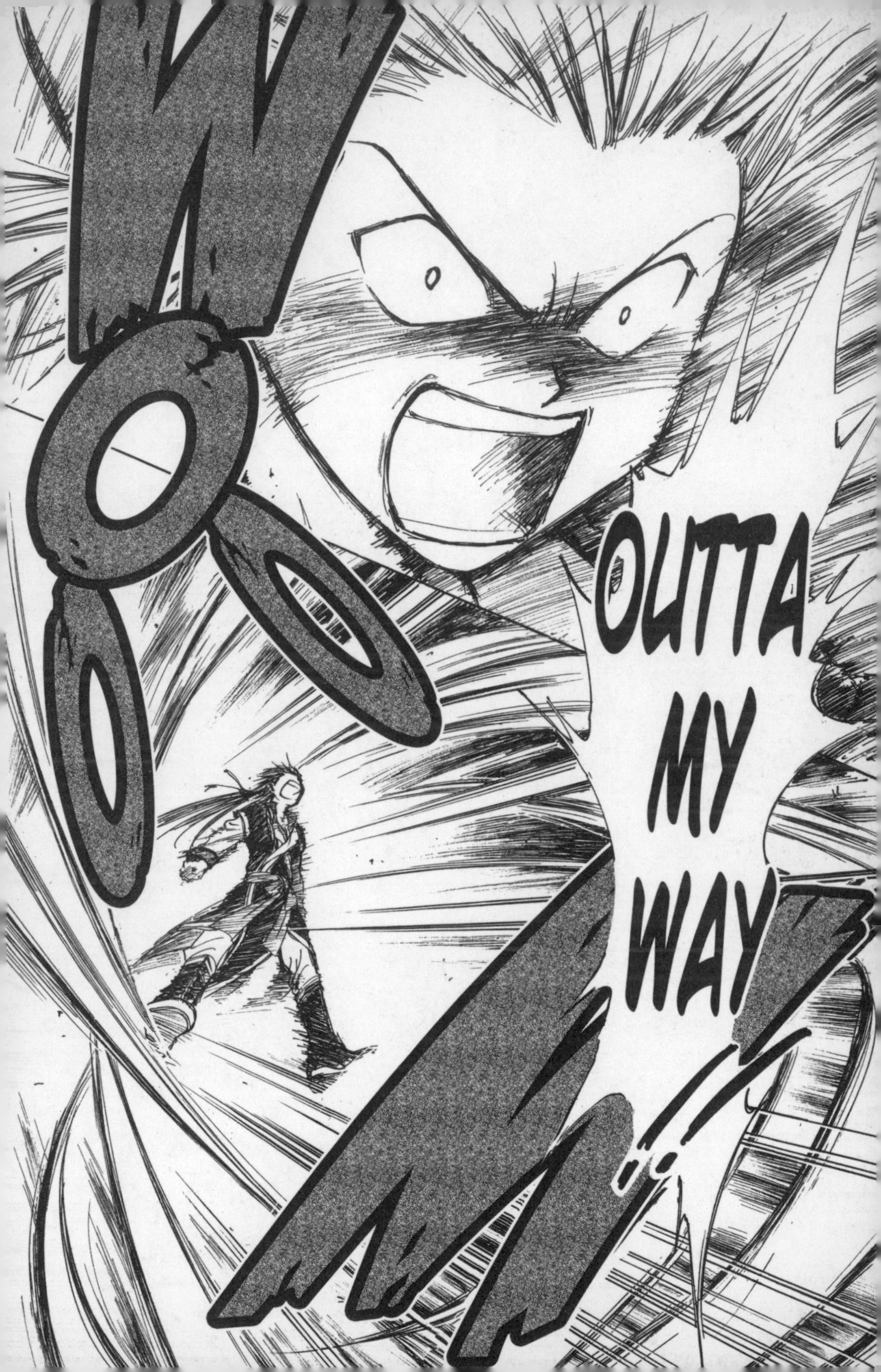
OUTTA MY WAY!!

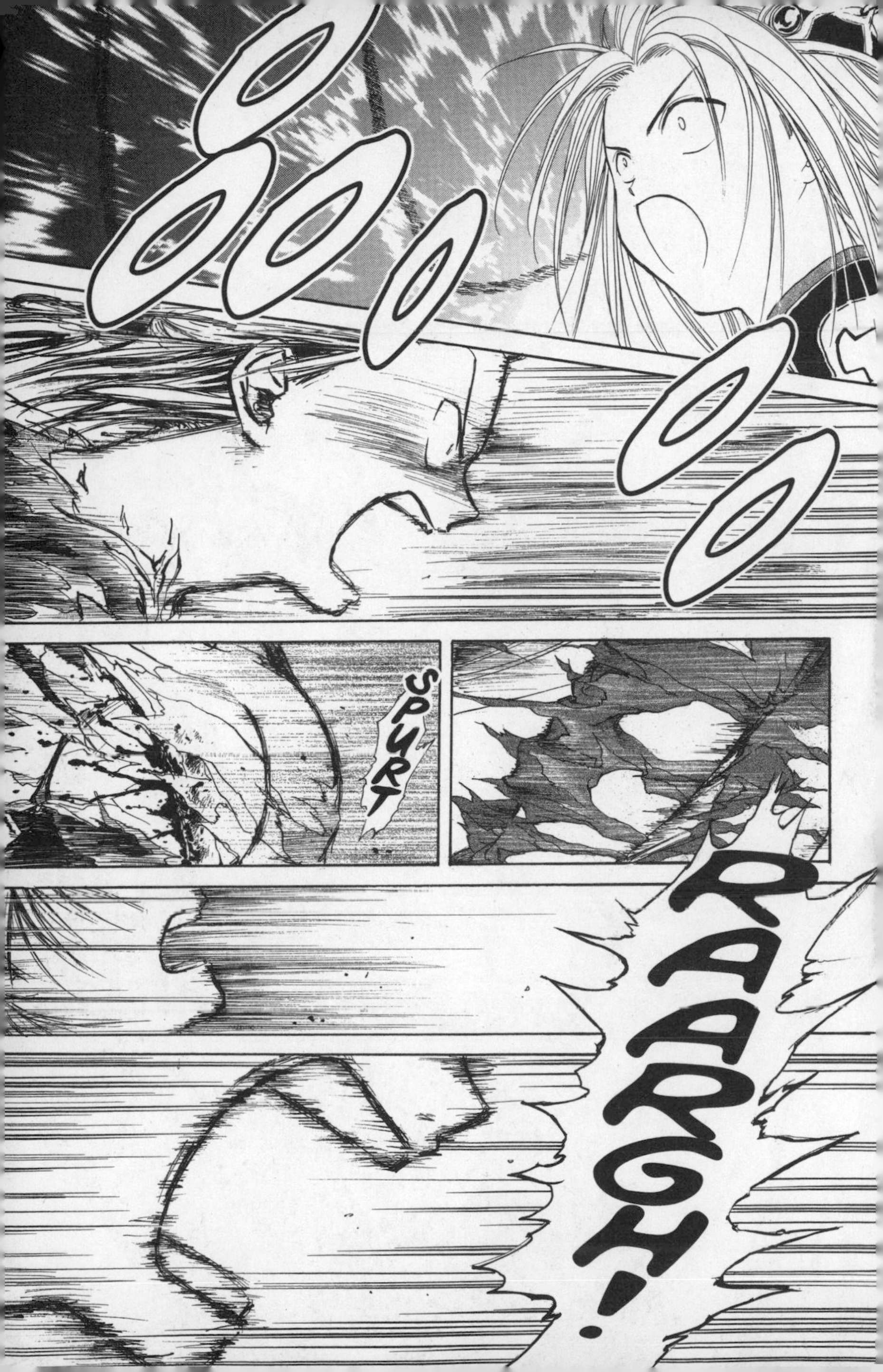
SPURT
RAARGH!

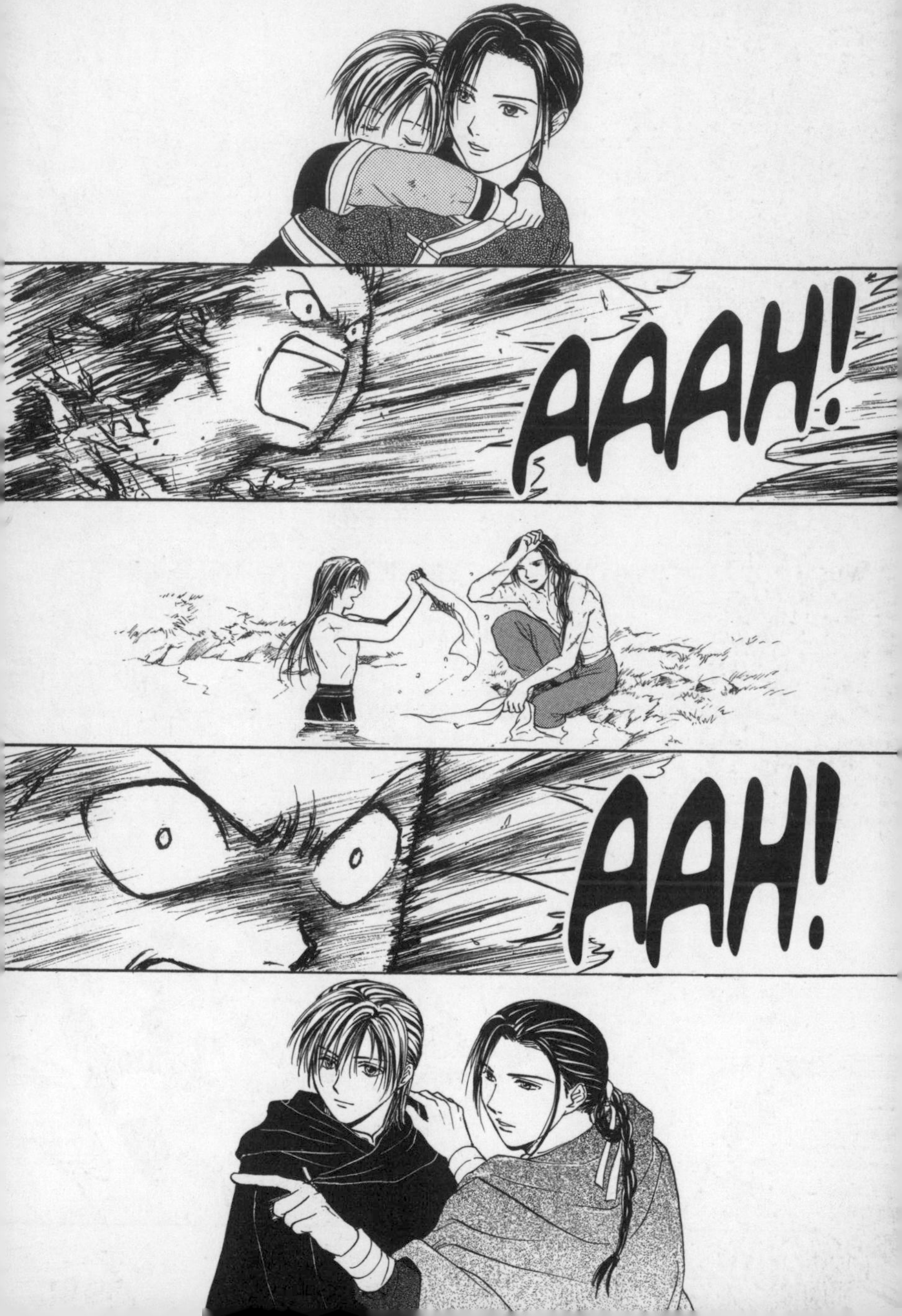
AAAH!
AAH!

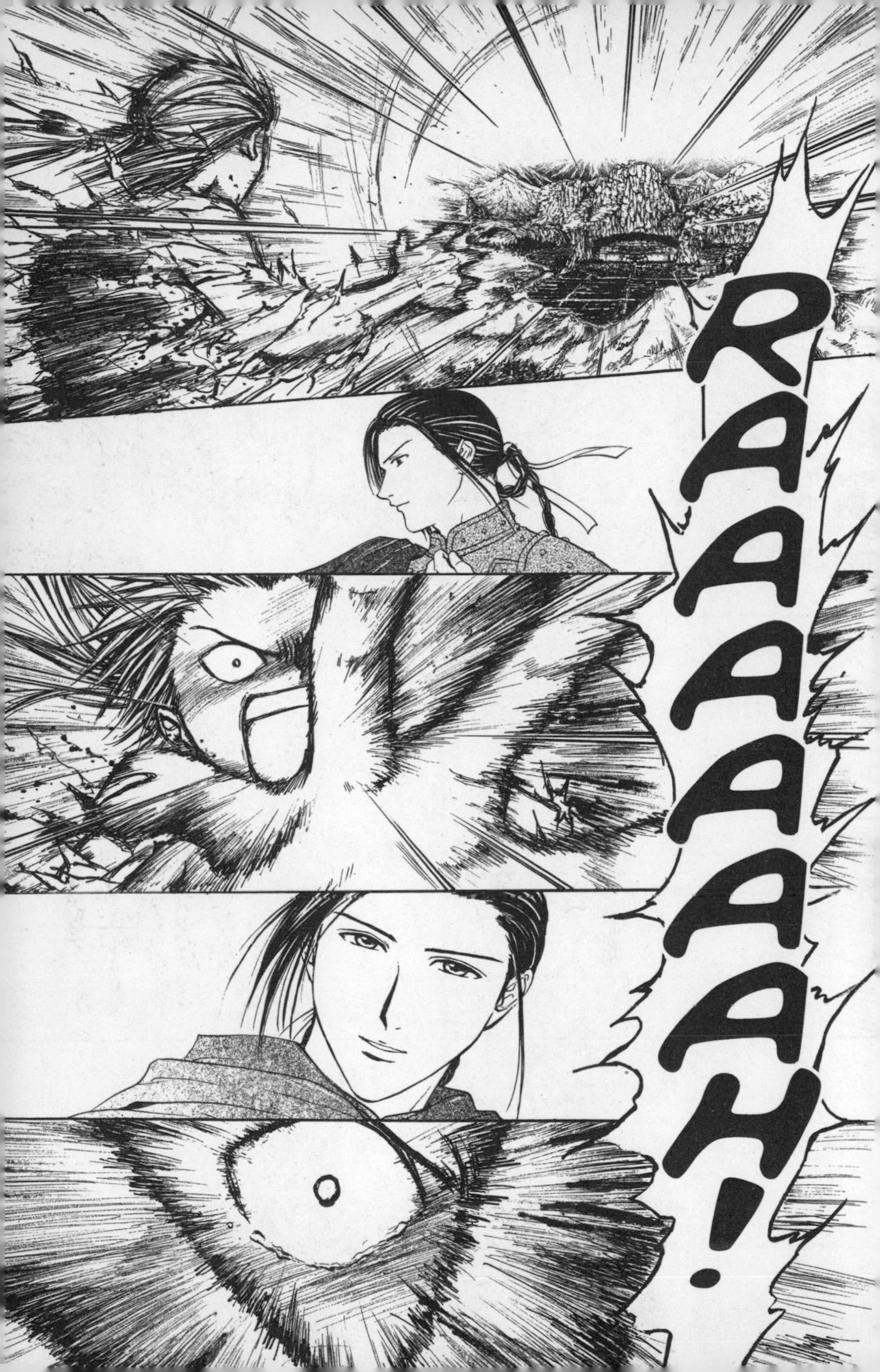
RAAAAAAAAH!!

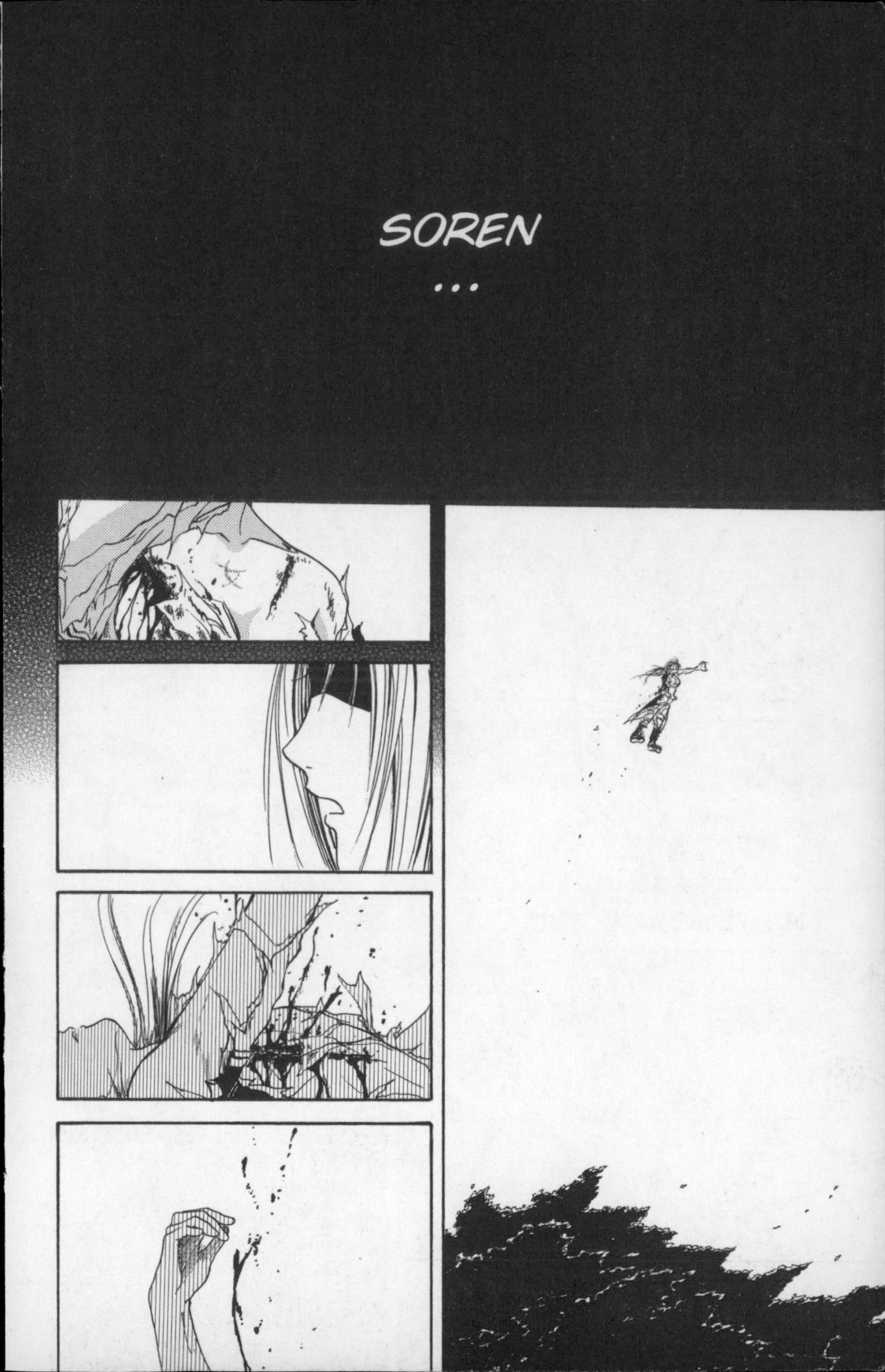
SOREN
...

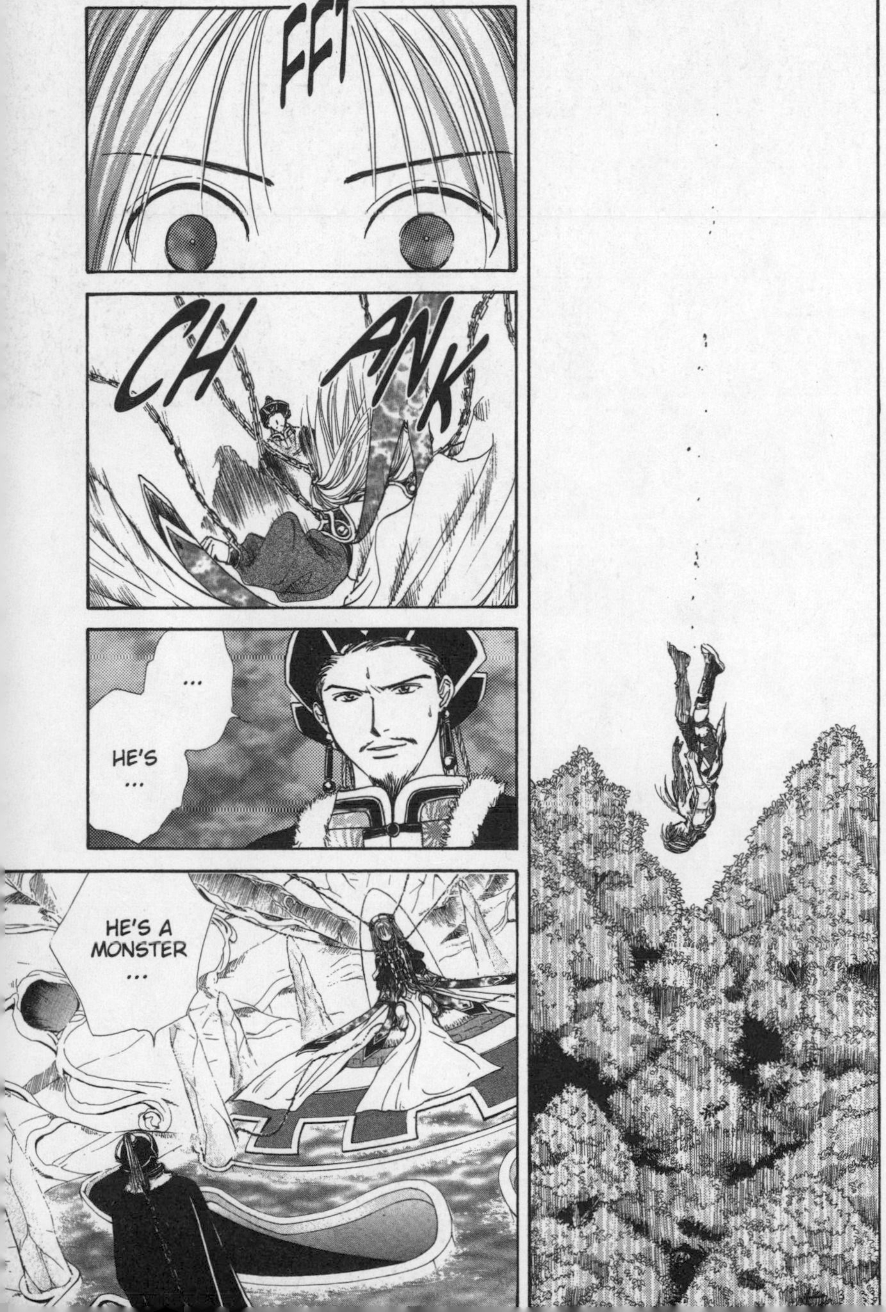
FFT
CHANK
...
HE'S ...
HE'S A MONSTER ...

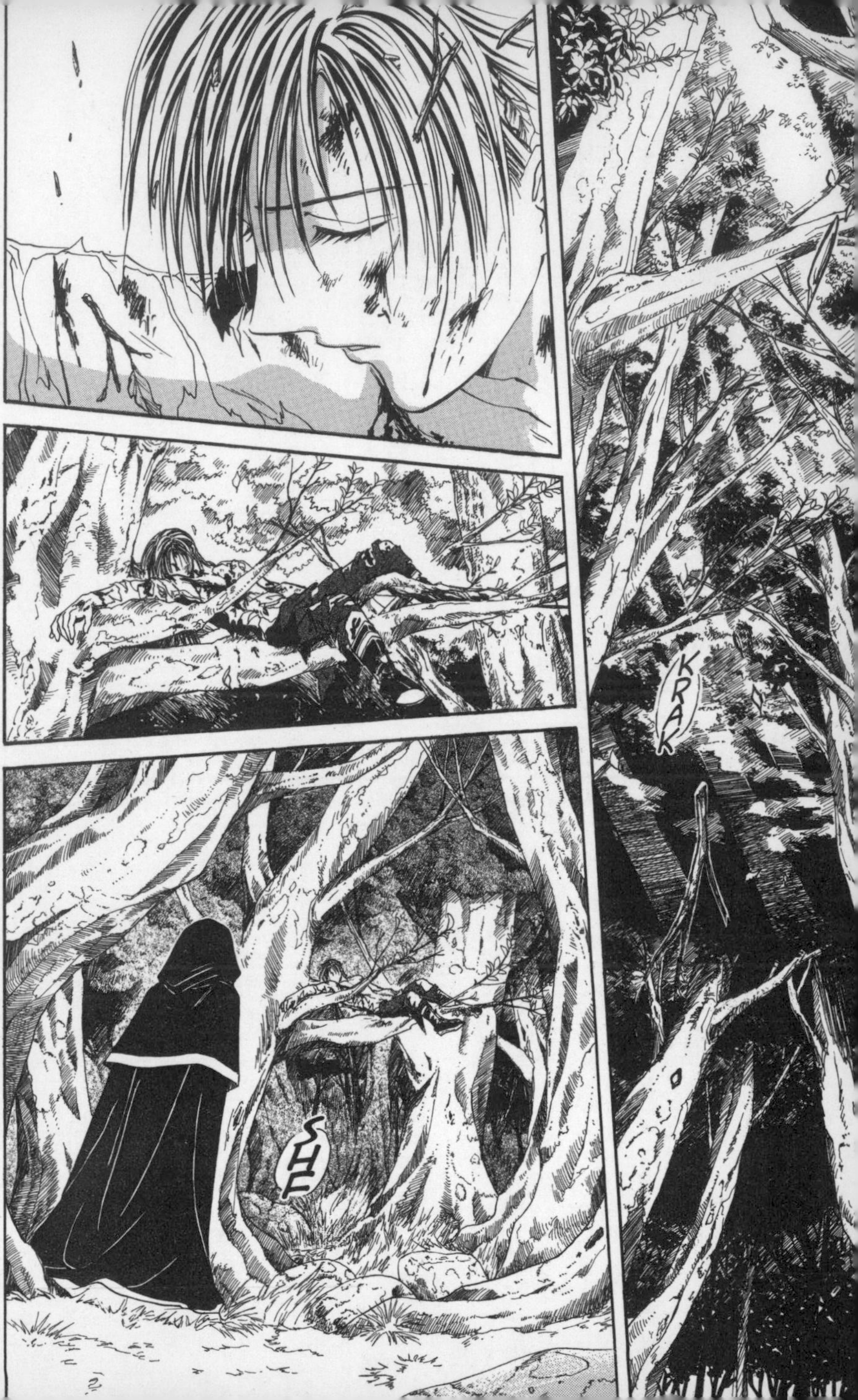
KRAK
SHF

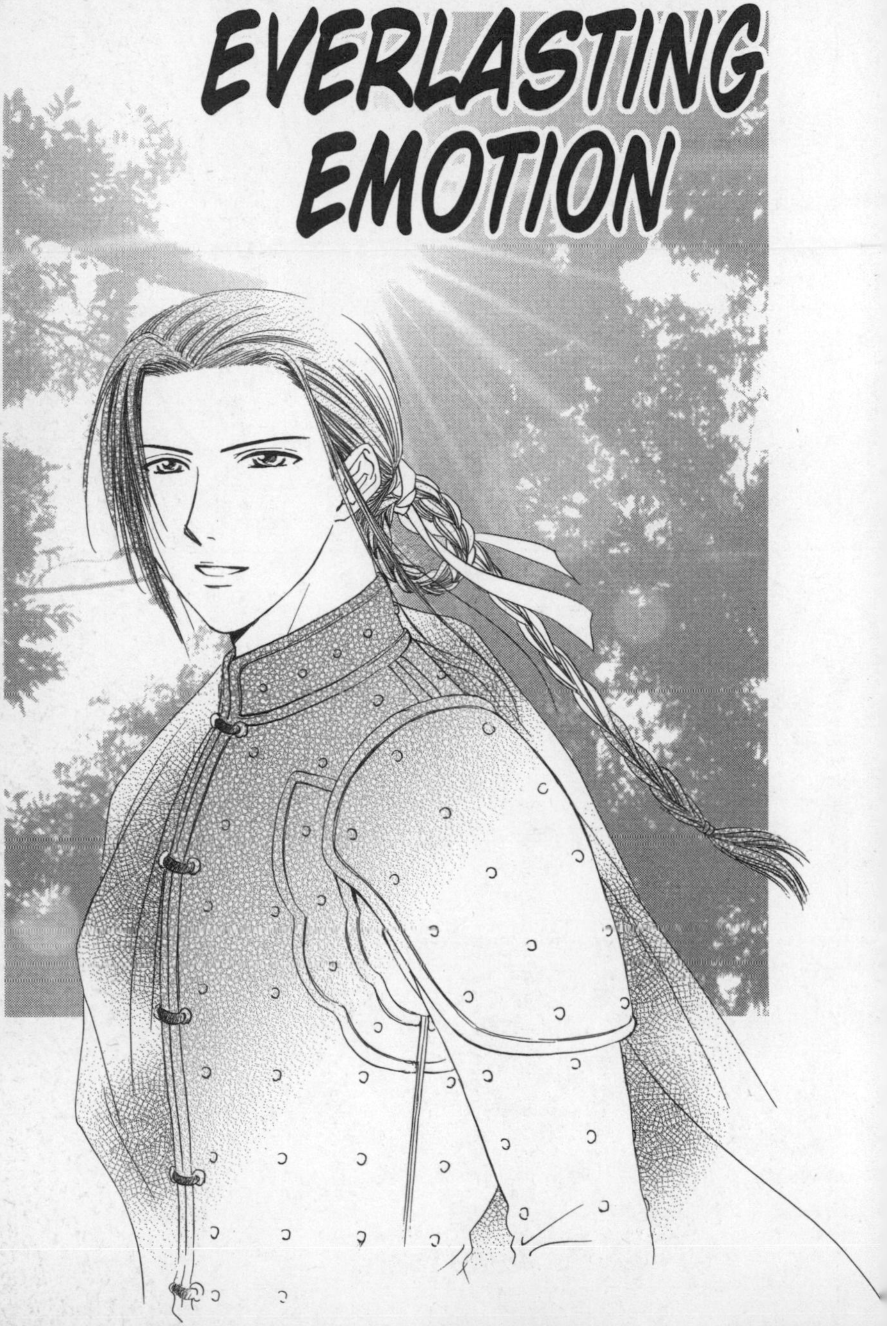
EVERLASTING
EMOTION

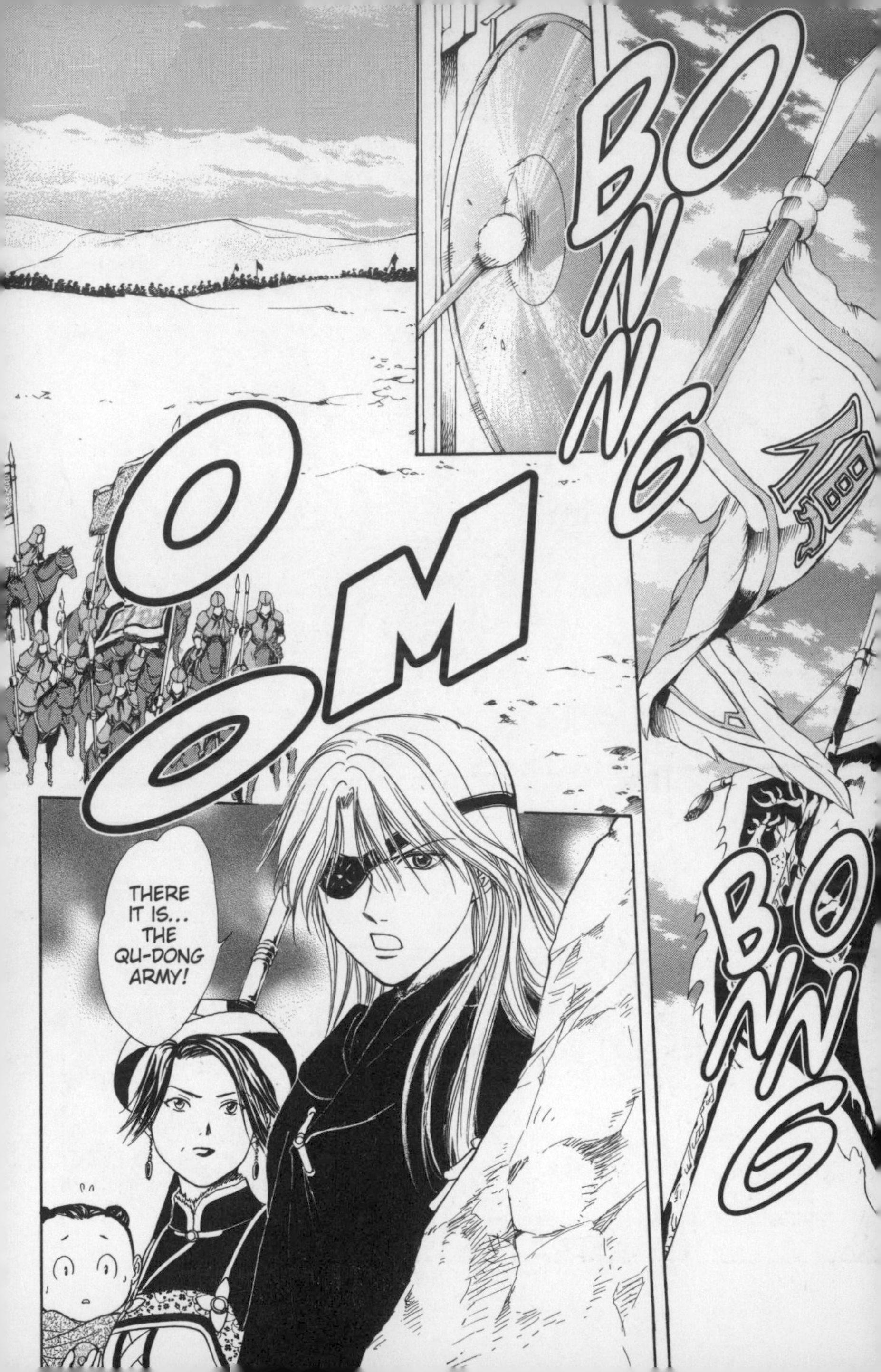

BONNG
OOM
BONNG
THERE IT IS... THE QU-DONG ARMY!

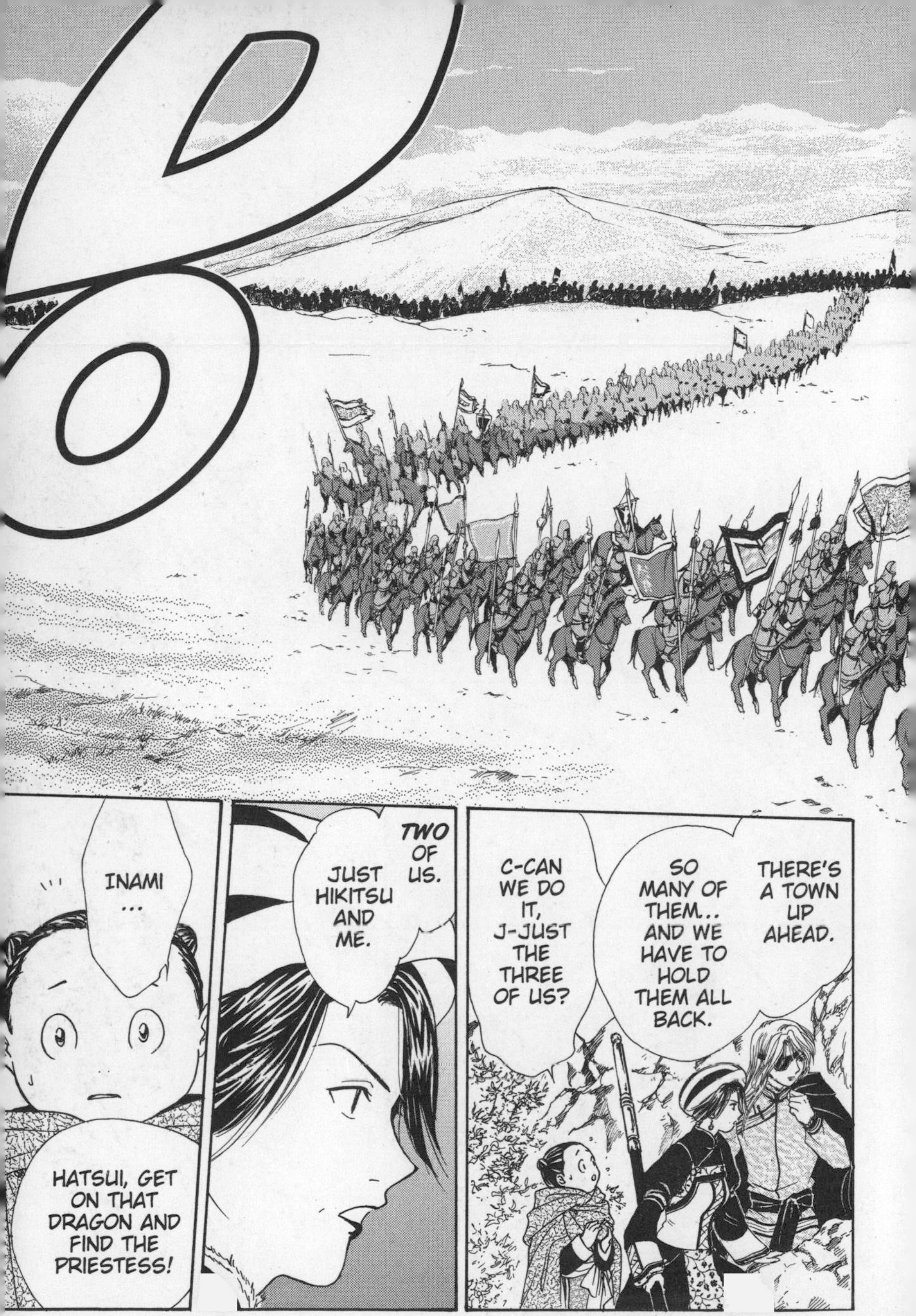
THERE'S A TOWN UP AHEAD.
SO MANY OF THEM... AND WE HAVE TO HOLD THEM ALL BACK.
C-CAN WE DO IT, J-JUST THE THREE OF US?
TWO OF US.
JUST HIKITSU AND ME.
INAMI ...
HATSUI, GET ON THAT DRAGON AND FIND THE PRIESTESS!

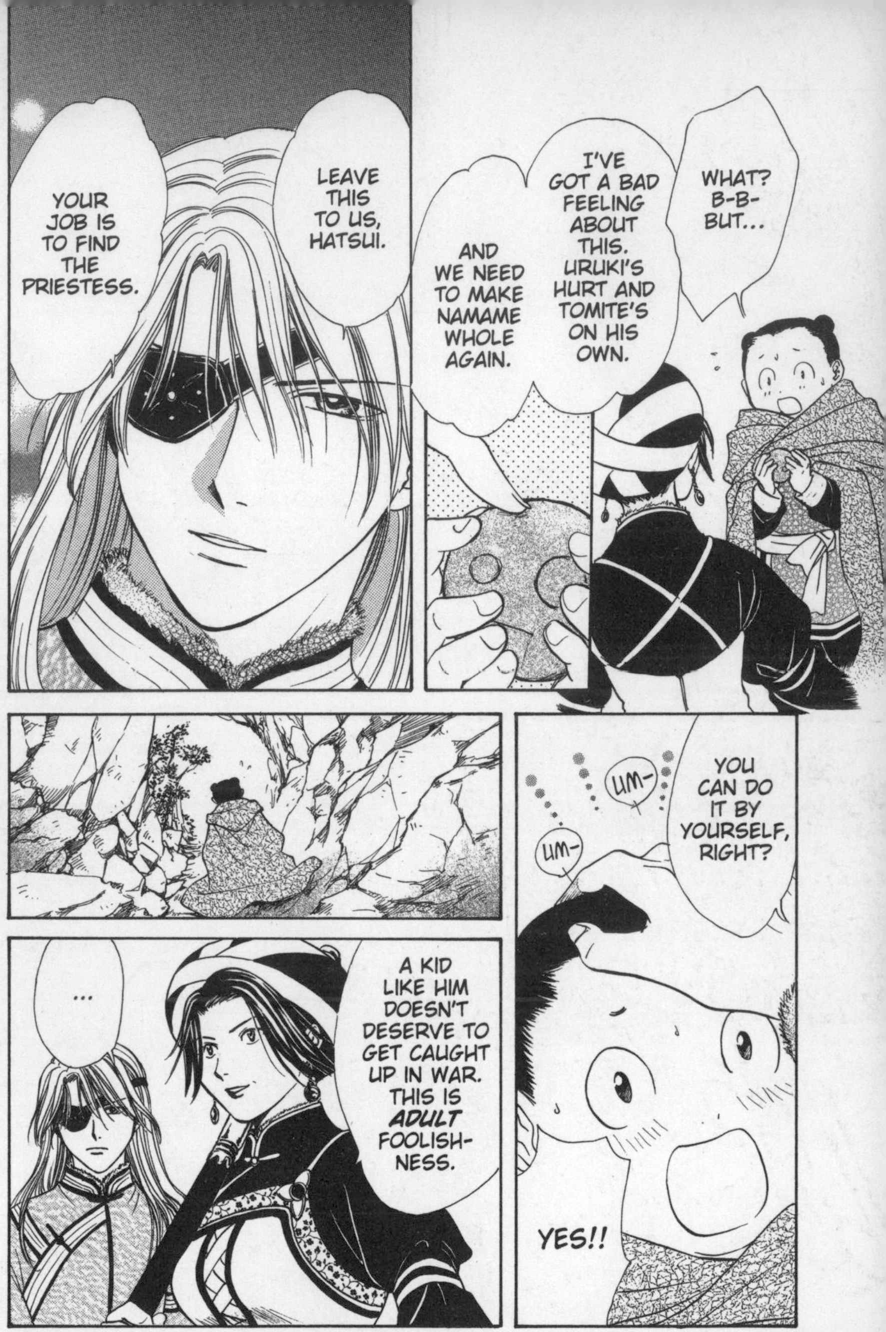
WHAT? B-B-BUT...
I'VE GOT A BAD FEELING ABOUT THIS. URUKI'S HURT AND TOMITE'S ON HIS OWN.
AND WE NEED TO MAKE NAMAME WHOLE AGAIN.
LEAVE THIS TO US, HATSUI.
YOUR JOB IS TO FIND THE PRIESTESS.
YOU CAN DO IT BY YOURSELF, RIGHT?
UM-
UM-
YES!!
A KID LIKE HIM DOESN'T DESERVE TO GET CAUGHT UP IN WAR. THIS IS *ADULT* FOOLISHNESS.
...

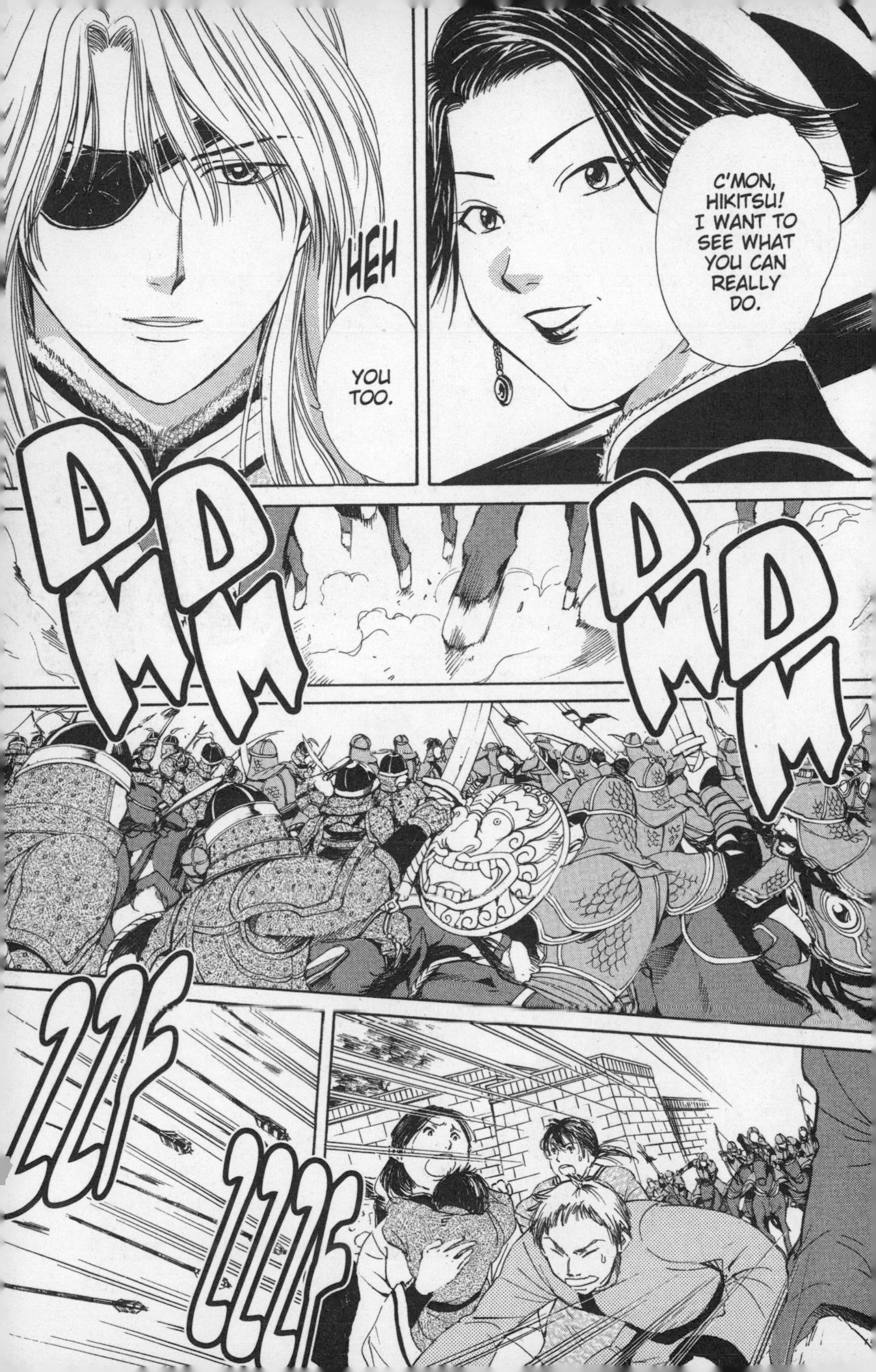
C'MON, HIKITSU! I WANT TO SEE WHAT YOU CAN REALLY DO.
HEH
YOU TOO.

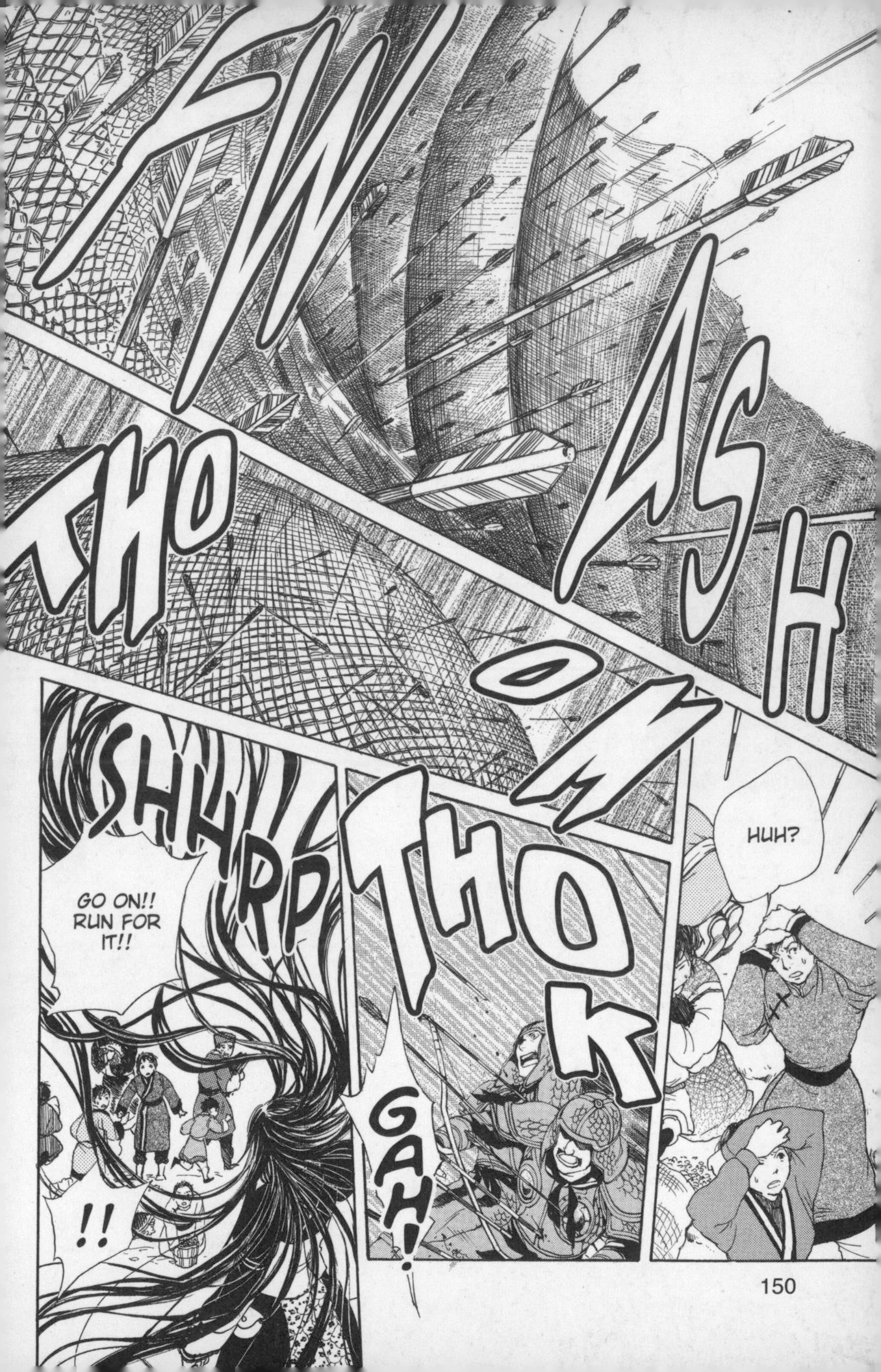
FWASH
THOOM
HUH?
THOK
GAH!
SHHRP
GO ON!! RUN FOR IT!!
!!

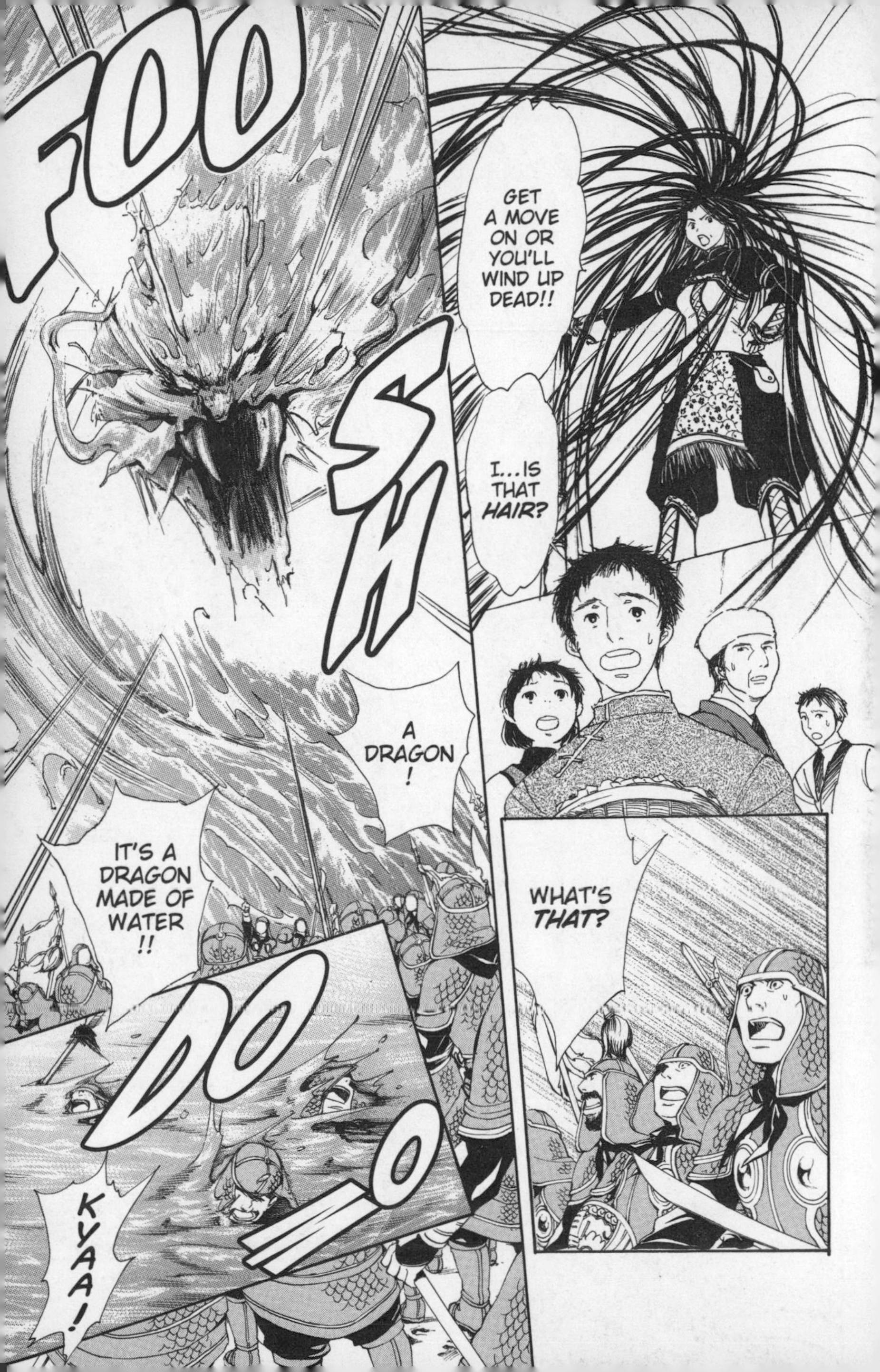
GET A MOVE ON OR YOU'LL WIND UP DEAD!!
I...IS THAT HAIR?
WHAT'S THAT?
FOO
SHH
A DRAGON!
IT'S A DRAGON MADE OF WATER!!
DOO
KYAAA!

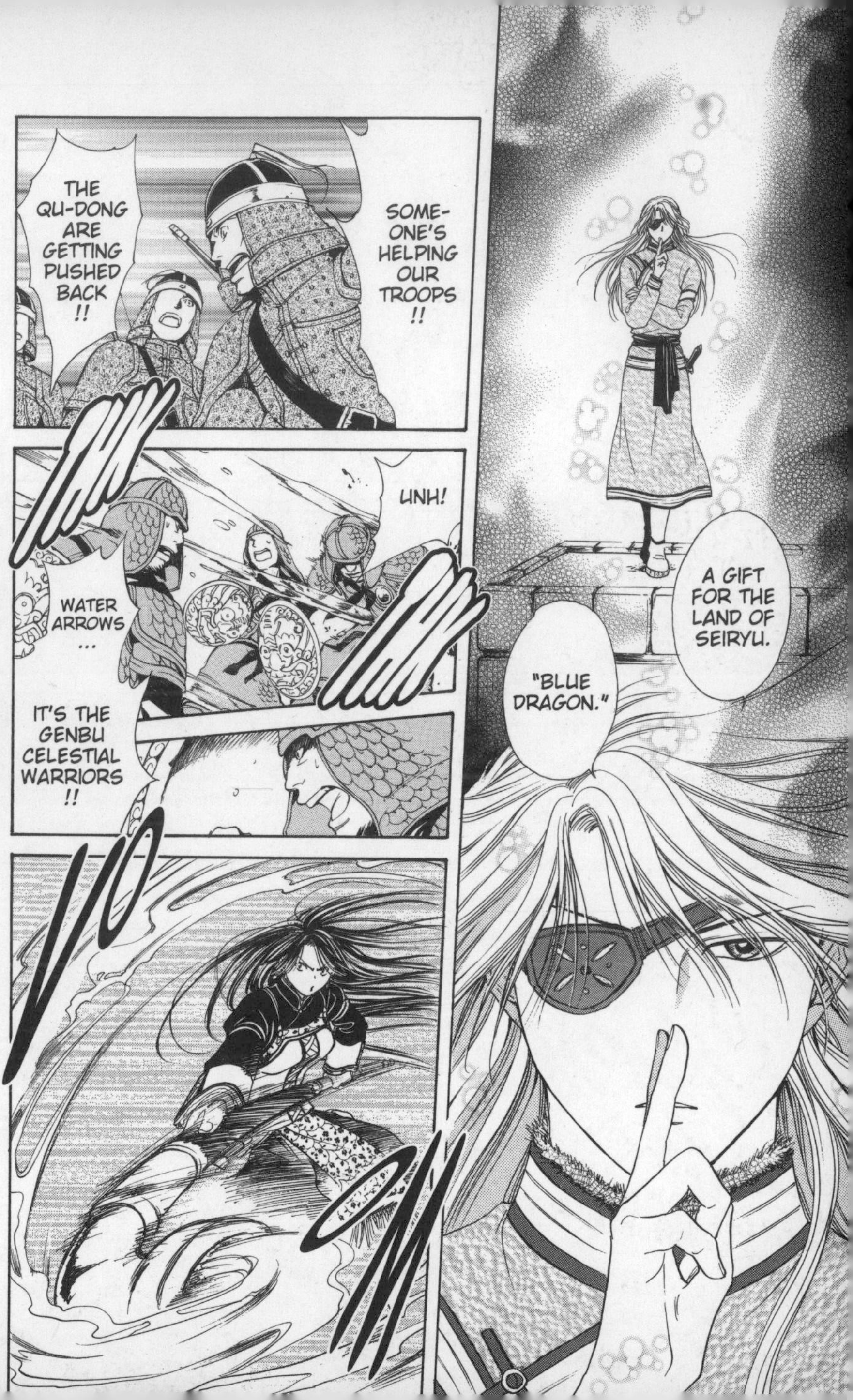
A GIFT FOR THE LAND OF SEIRYU.
"BLUE DRAGON."
SOME-ONE'S HELPING OUR TROOPS!!
THE QU-DONG ARE GETTING PUSHED BACK!!
UNH!
WATER ARROWS...
IT'S THE GENBU CELESTIAL WARRIORS!!

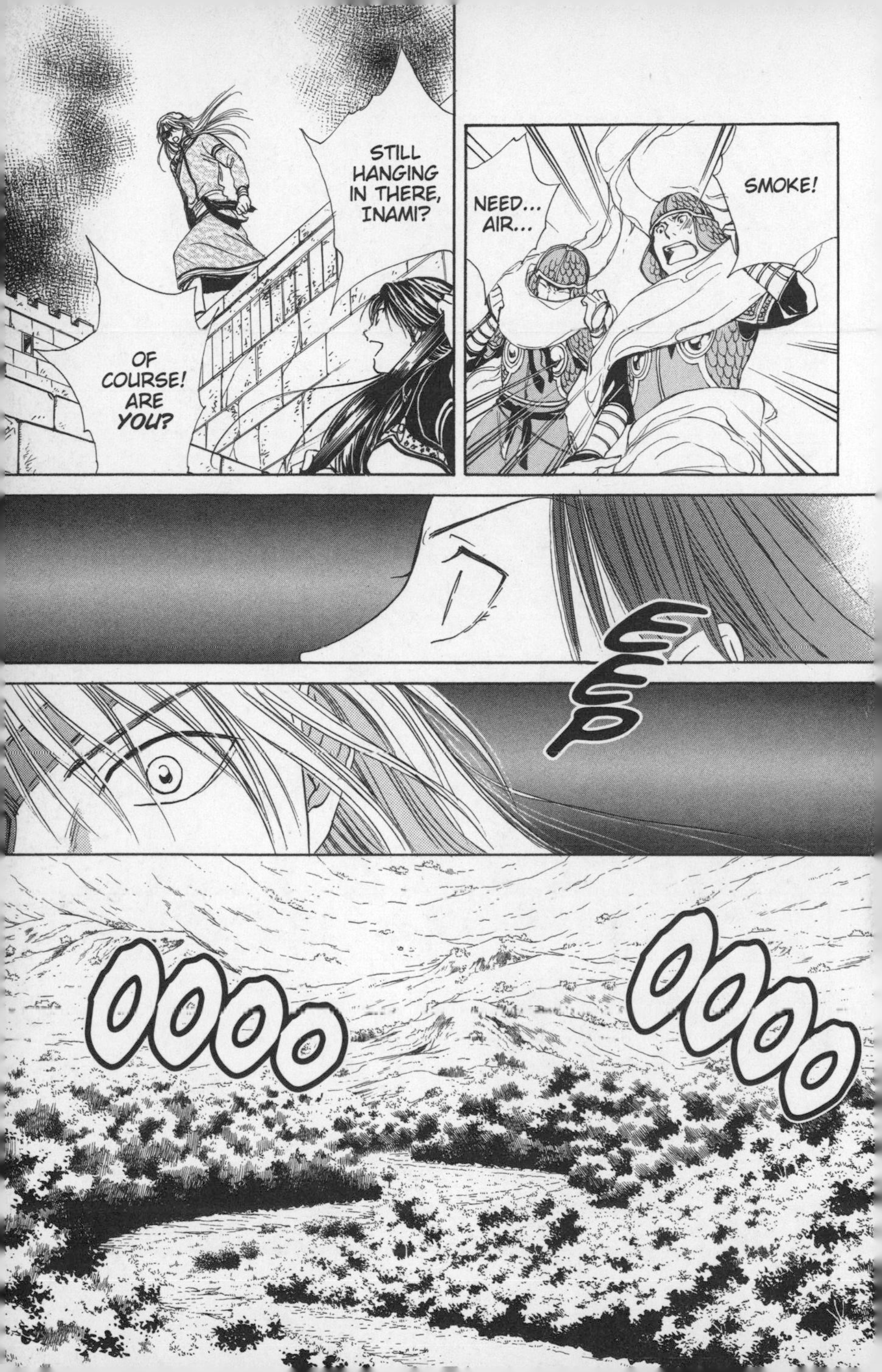
SMOKE!
NEED... AIR...
STILL HANGING IN THERE, INAMI?
OF COURSE! ARE *YOU?*
EEP
OOOO
OOOOO

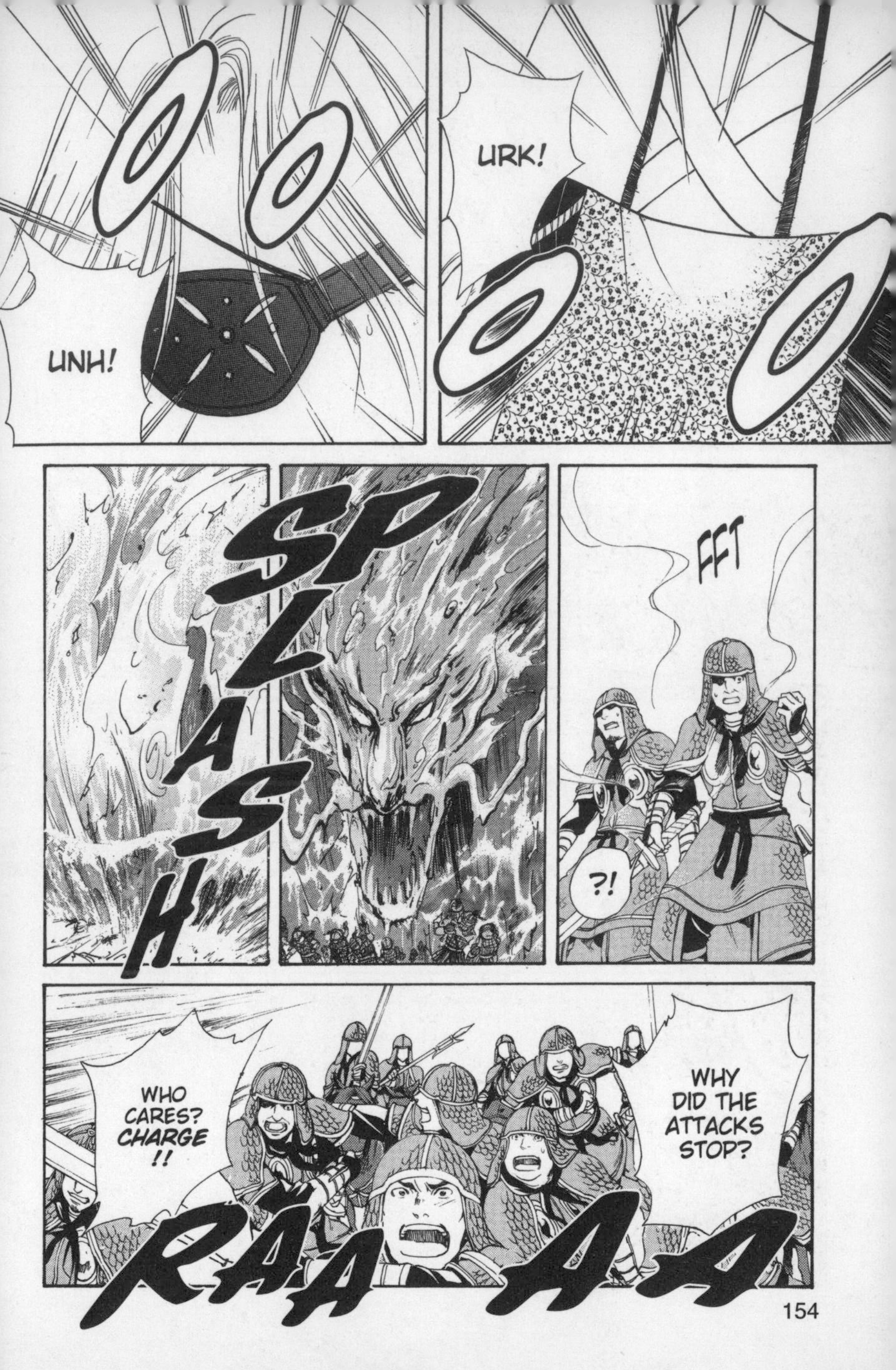
URK!
UNH!
FFT
?!
SPLASH
WHY DID THE ATTACKS STOP?
WHO CARES? CHARGE !!
RAAAAA

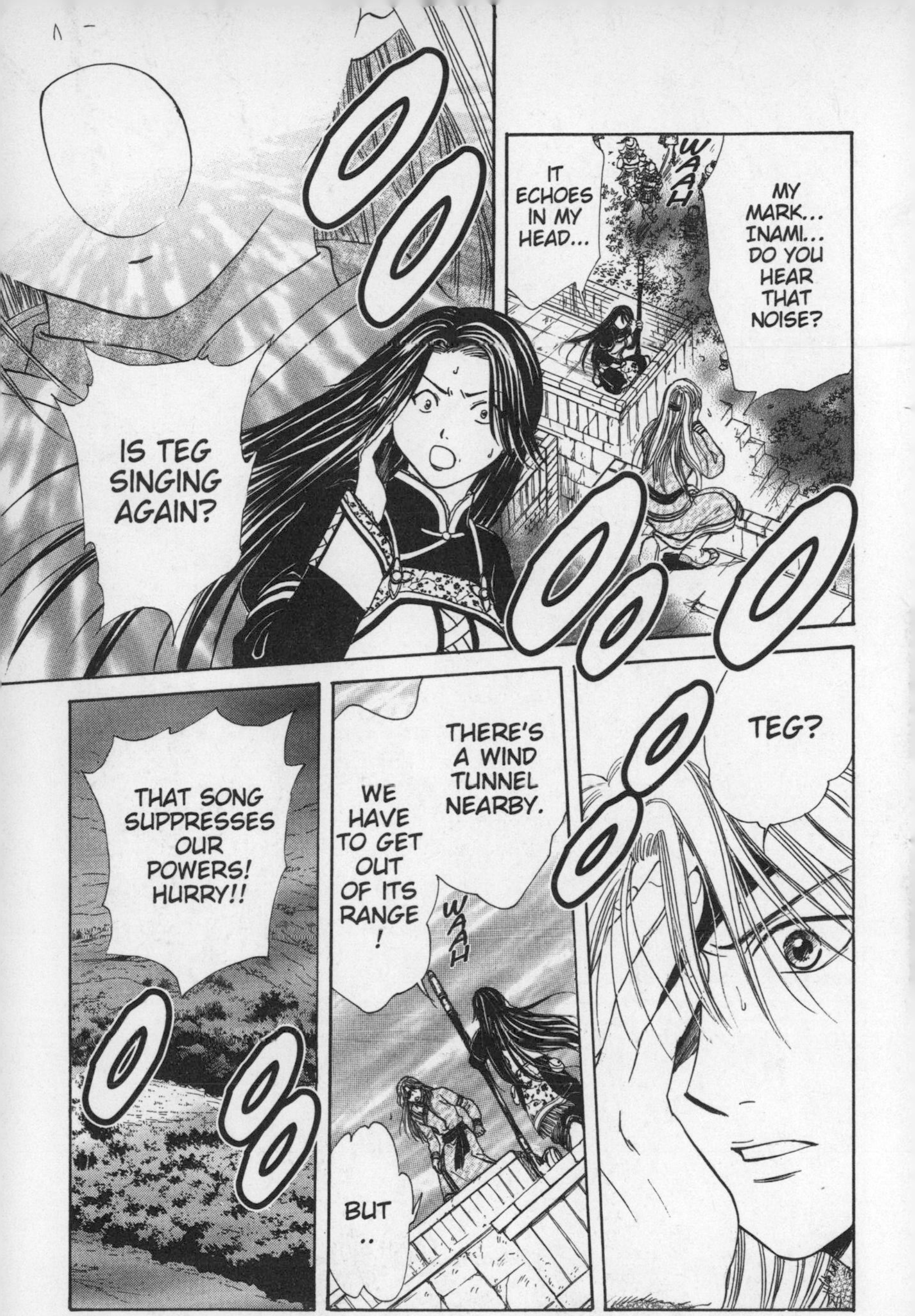
MY MARK... INAMI... DO YOU HEAR THAT NOISE?
WAAH
IT ECHOES IN MY HEAD...
IS TEG SINGING AGAIN?
TEG?
THERE'S A WIND TUNNEL NEARBY.
WE HAVE TO GET OUT OF ITS RANGE!
WAAH
BUT ..
THAT SONG SUPPRESSES OUR POWERS! HURRY!!

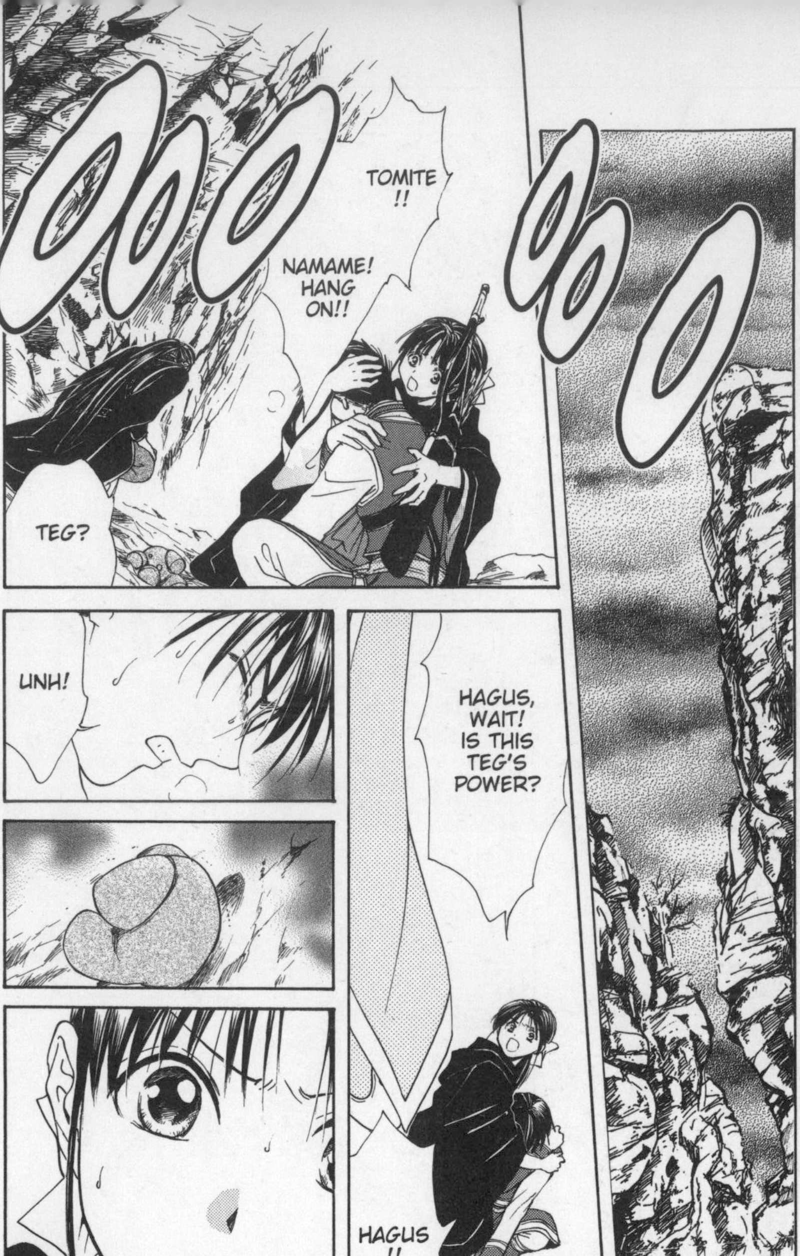
TOMITE !!
NAMAME! HANG ON!!
TEG?
HAGUS, WAIT! IS THIS TEG'S POWER?
HAGUS !!
UNH!

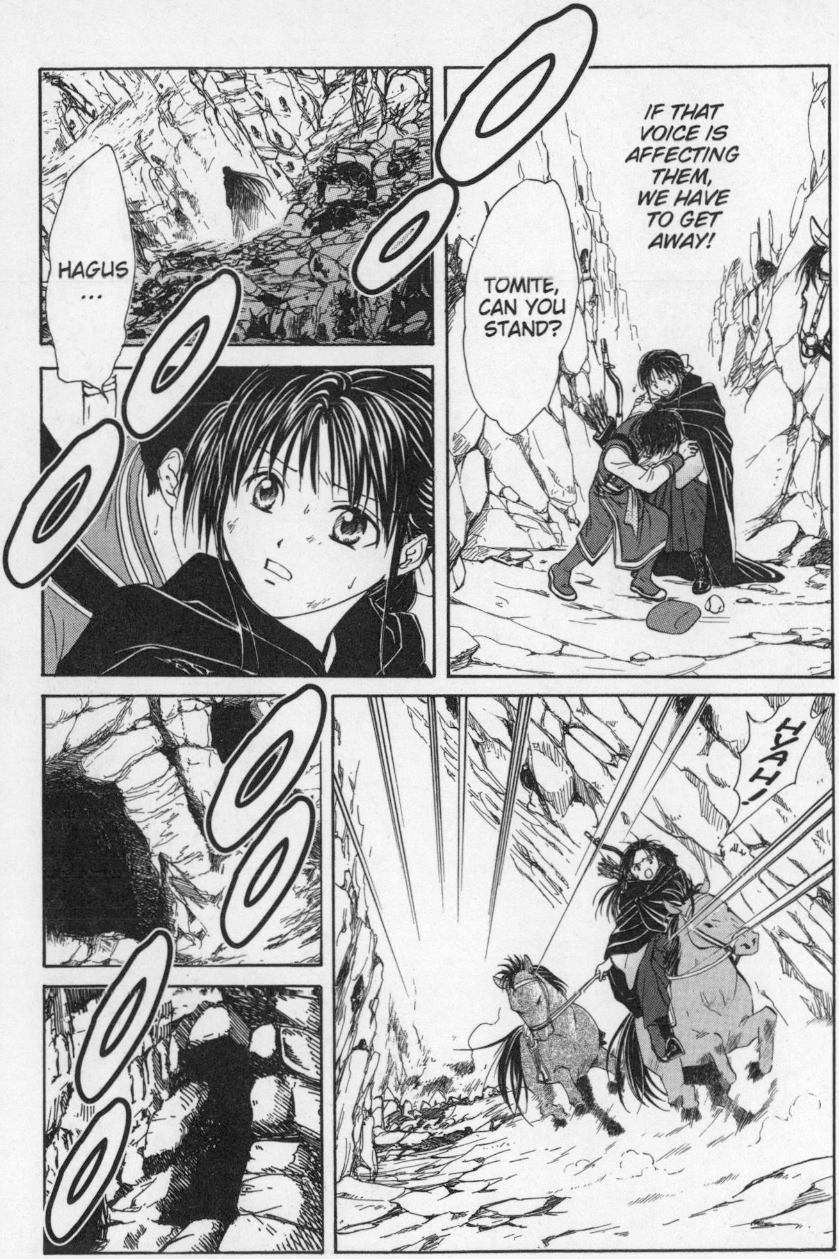
IF THAT VOICE IS AFFECTING THEM, WE HAVE TO GET AWAY!
TOMITE, CAN YOU STAND?
HAGUS ...
HYAH!

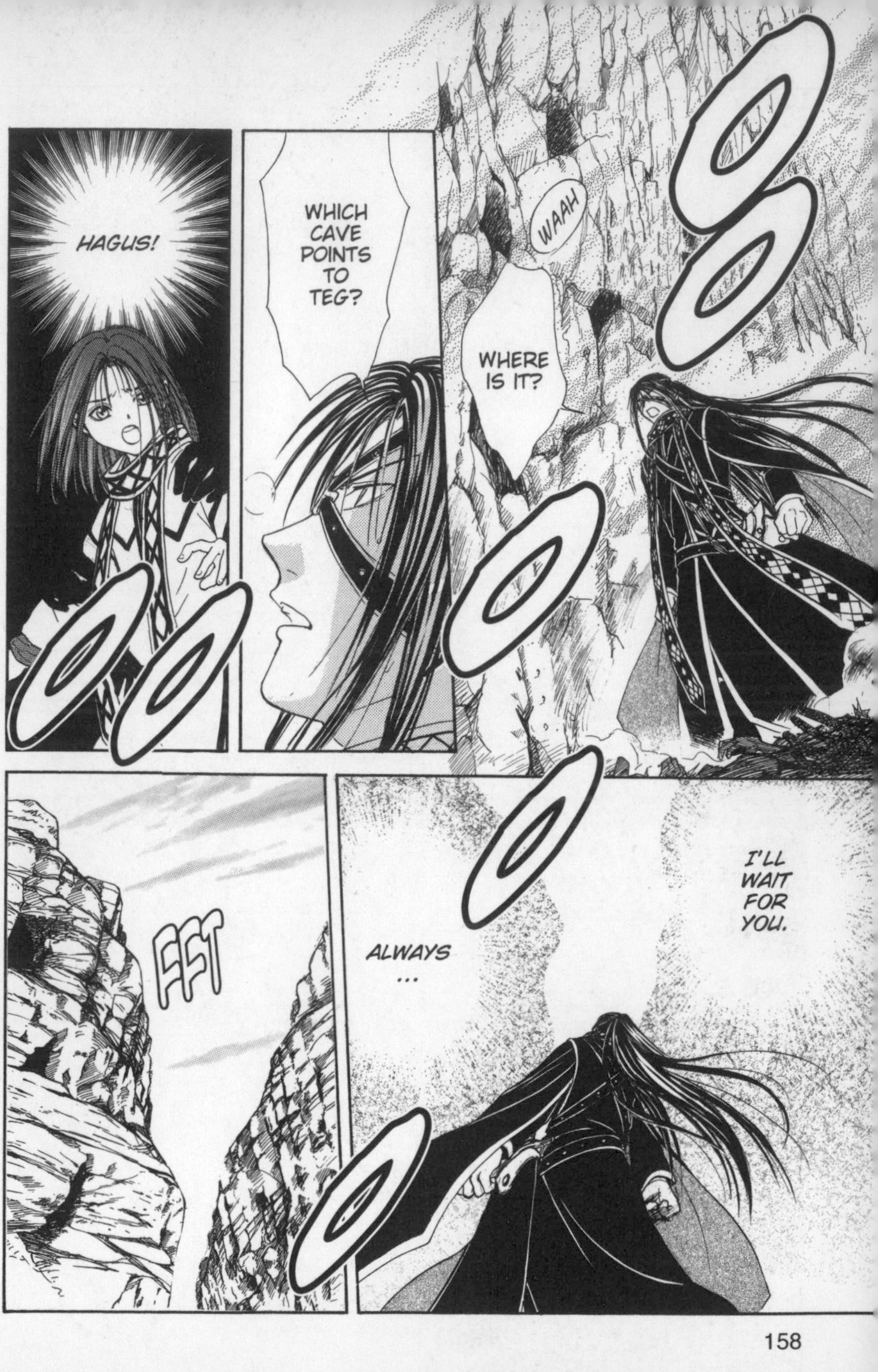
WAAH
WHERE IS IT?
WHICH CAVE POINTS TO TEG?
HAGUS!
I'LL WAIT FOR YOU.
ALWAYS ...
FFT

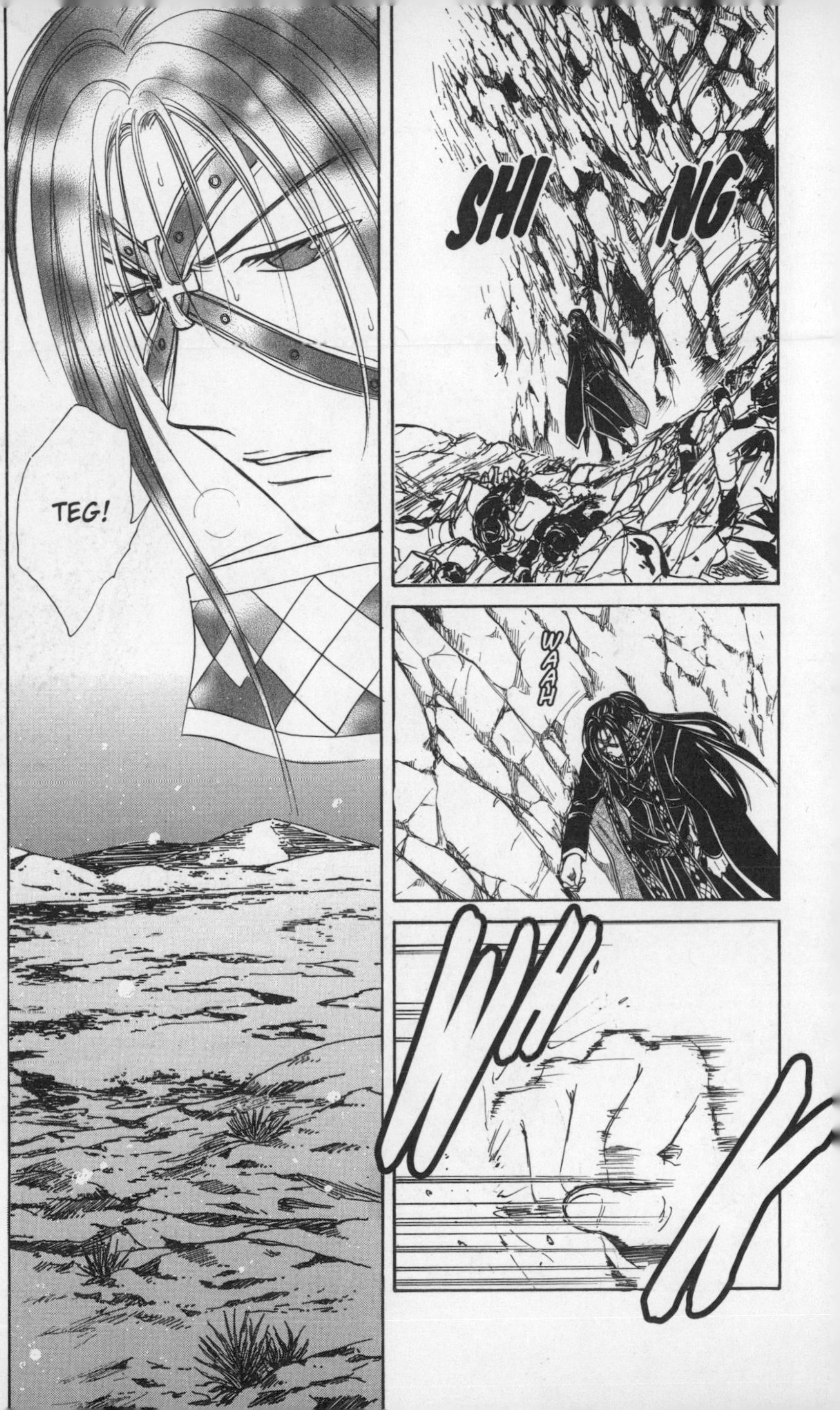
SHI NG
WAAH
WH
TEG!

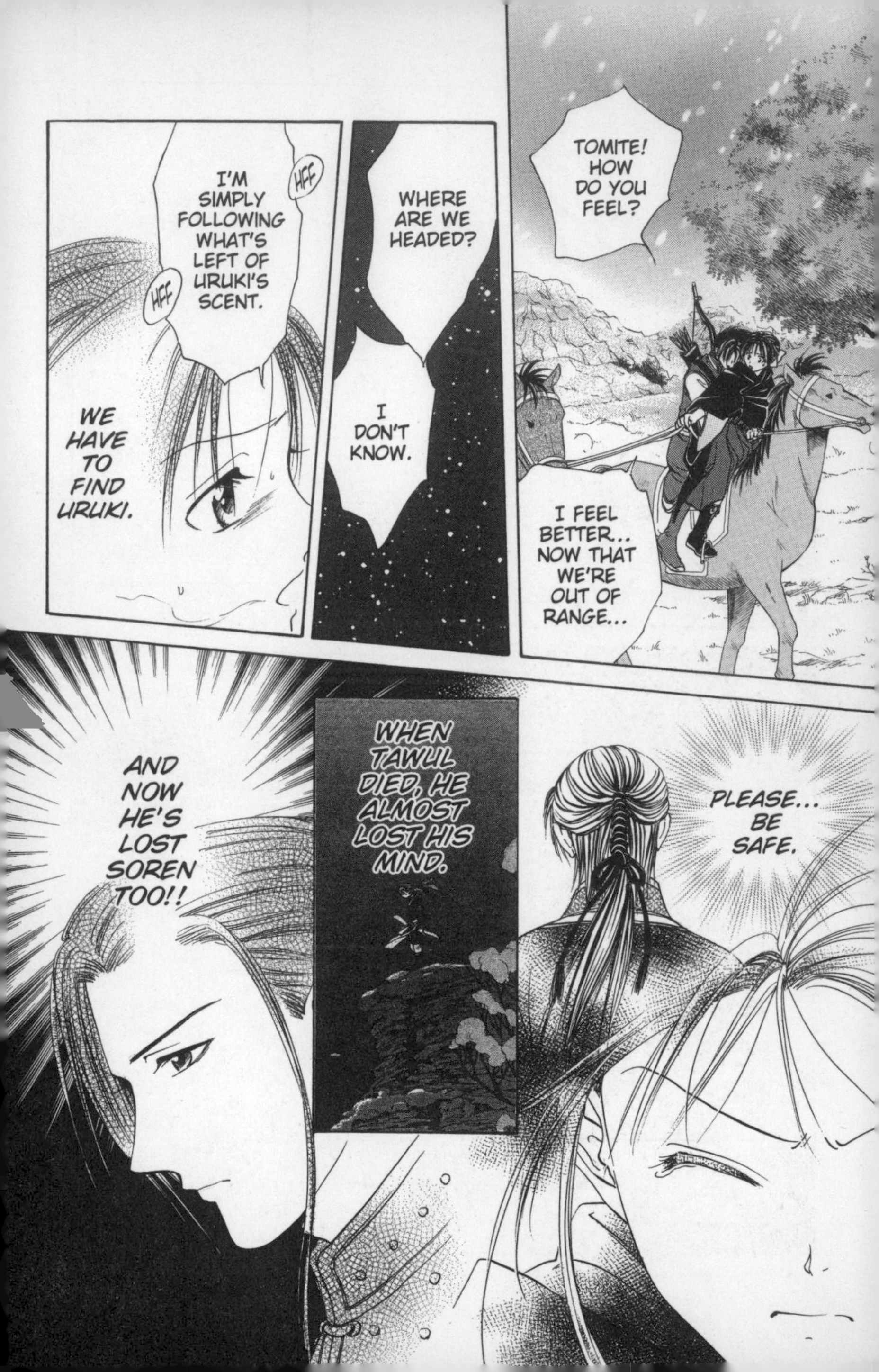
TOMITE! HOW DO YOU FEEL?
I FEEL BETTER... NOW THAT WE'RE OUT OF RANGE...
WHERE ARE WE HEADED?
I DON'T KNOW.
HFF
I'M SIMPLY FOLLOWING WHAT'S LEFT OF URUKI'S SCENT.
HFF
WE HAVE TO FIND URUKI.
PLEASE... BE SAFE.
WHEN TAWUL DIED, HE ALMOST LOST HIS MIND.
AND NOW HE'S LOST SOREN TOO!!

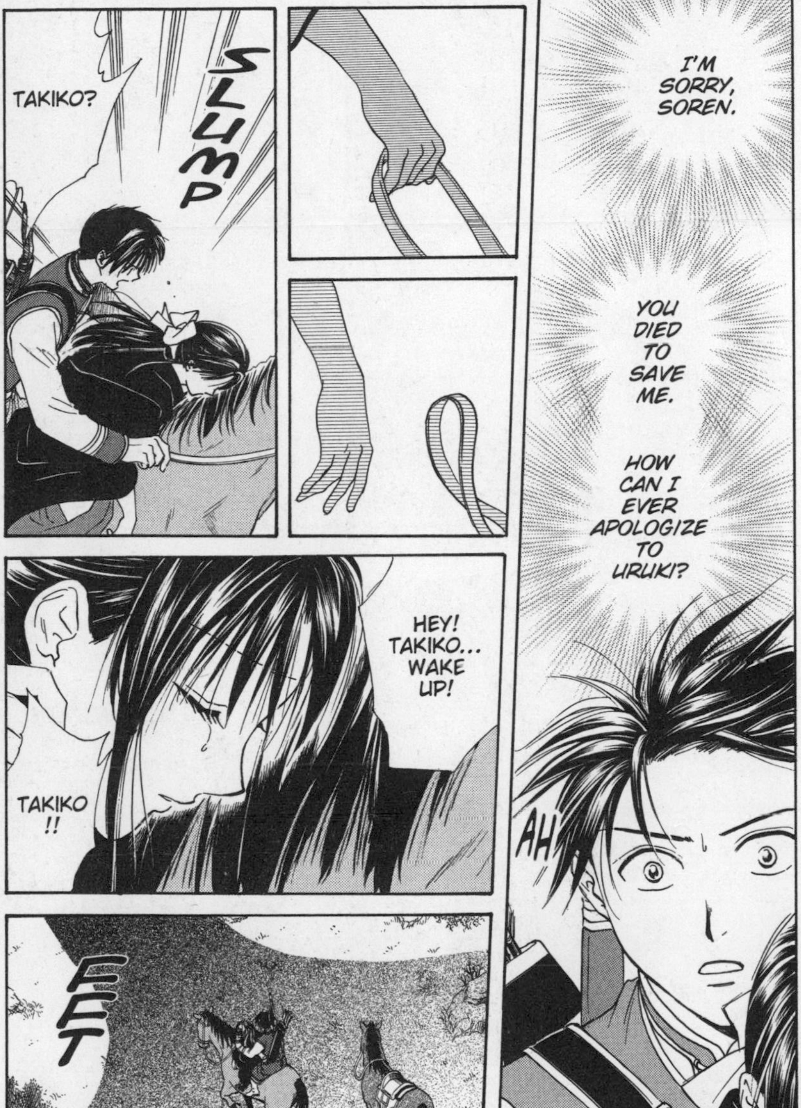
I'M SORRY, SOREN.
YOU DIED TO SAVE ME.
HOW CAN I EVER APOLOGIZE TO URUKI?
AH
SLUMP
TAKIKO?
HEY! TAKIKO... WAKE UP!
TAKIKO !!
EET

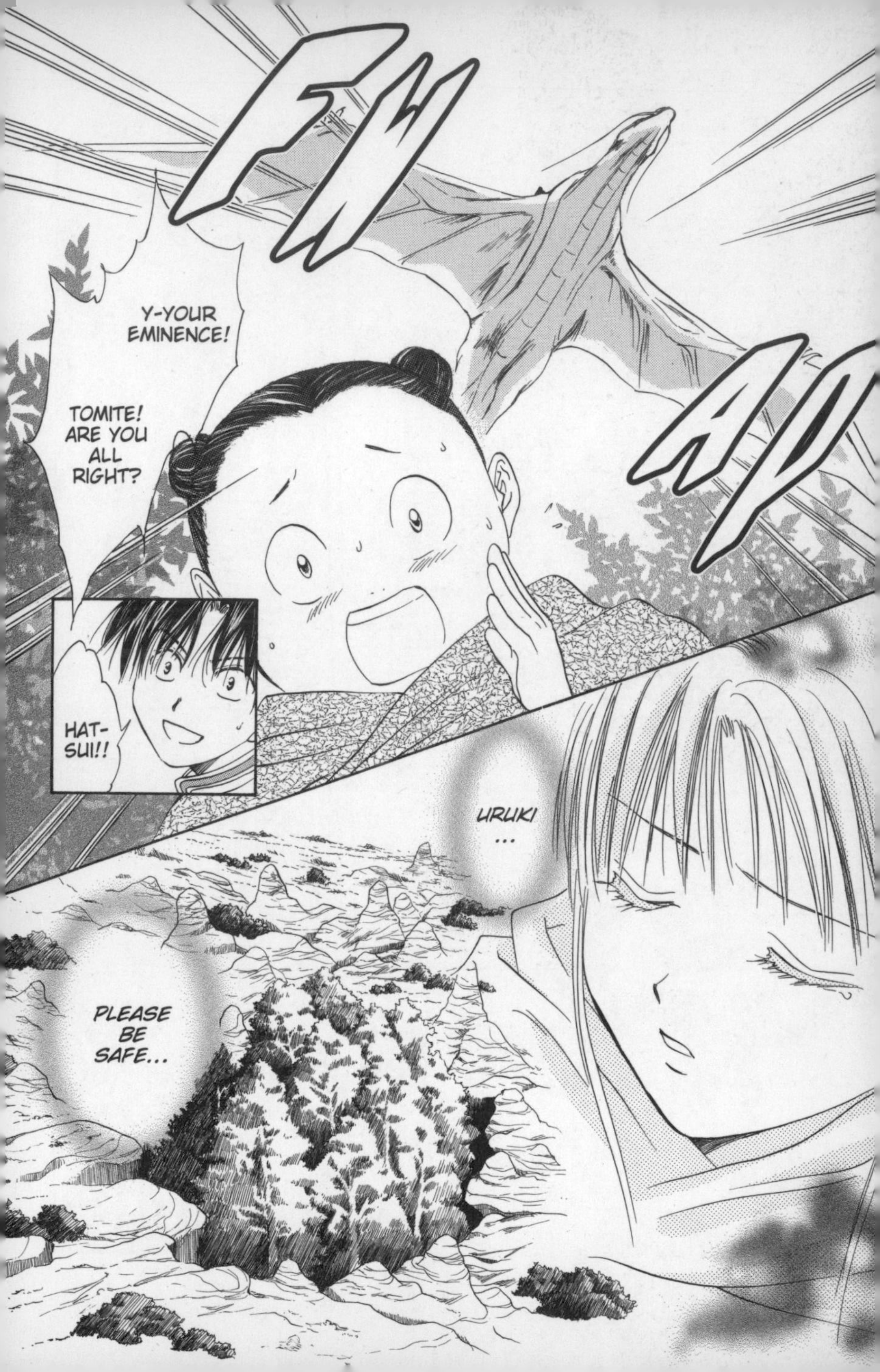
FWAP
Y-YOUR EMINENCE!
TOMITE! ARE YOU ALL RIGHT?
HAT-SUI!!
URUKI...
PLEASE BE SAFE...

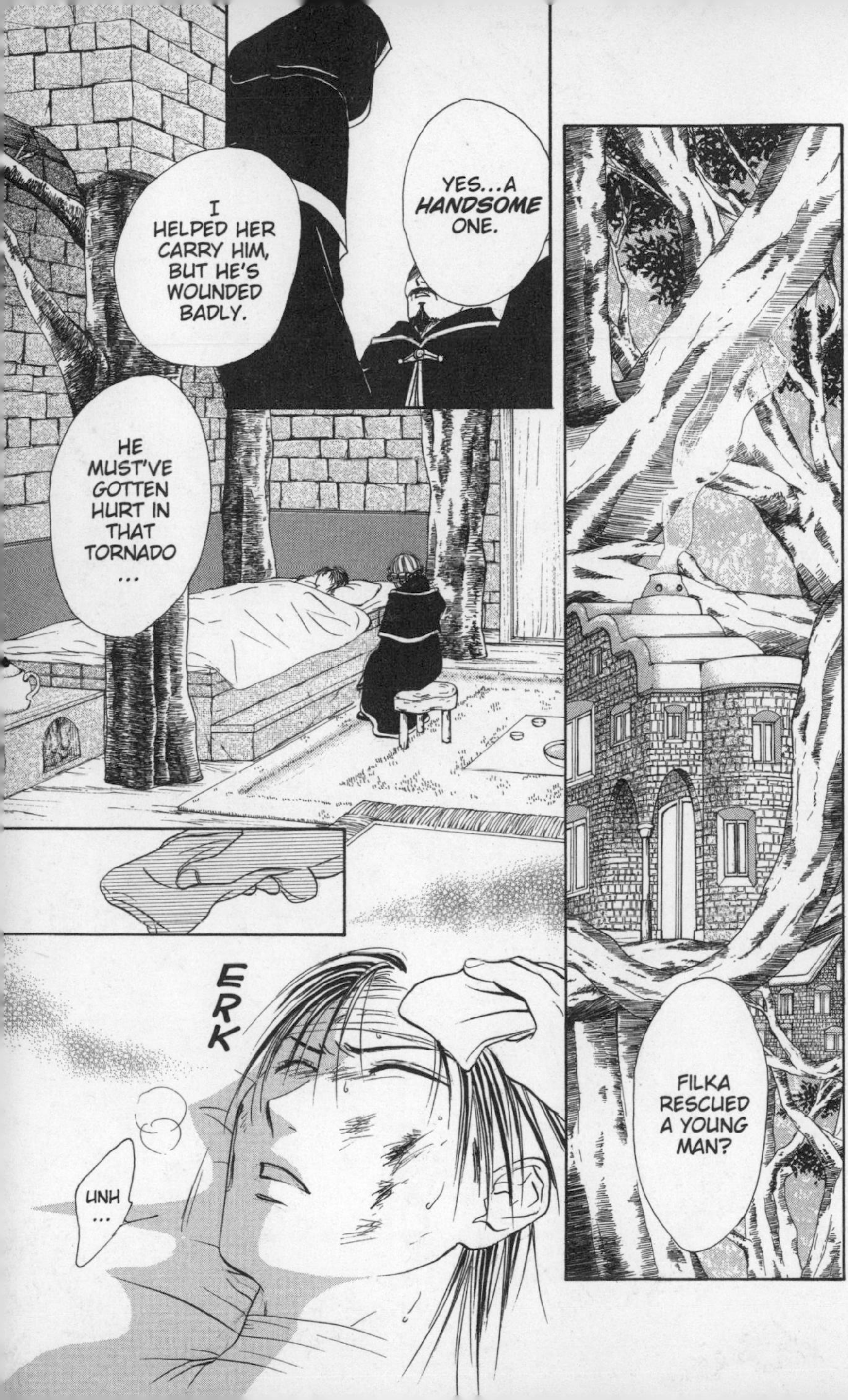
FILKA RESCUED A YOUNG MAN?
YES...A *HANDSOME* ONE.
I HELPED HER CARRY HIM, BUT HE'S WOUNDED BADLY.
HE MUST'VE GOTTEN HURT IN THAT TORNADO ...
ERK
UNH ...

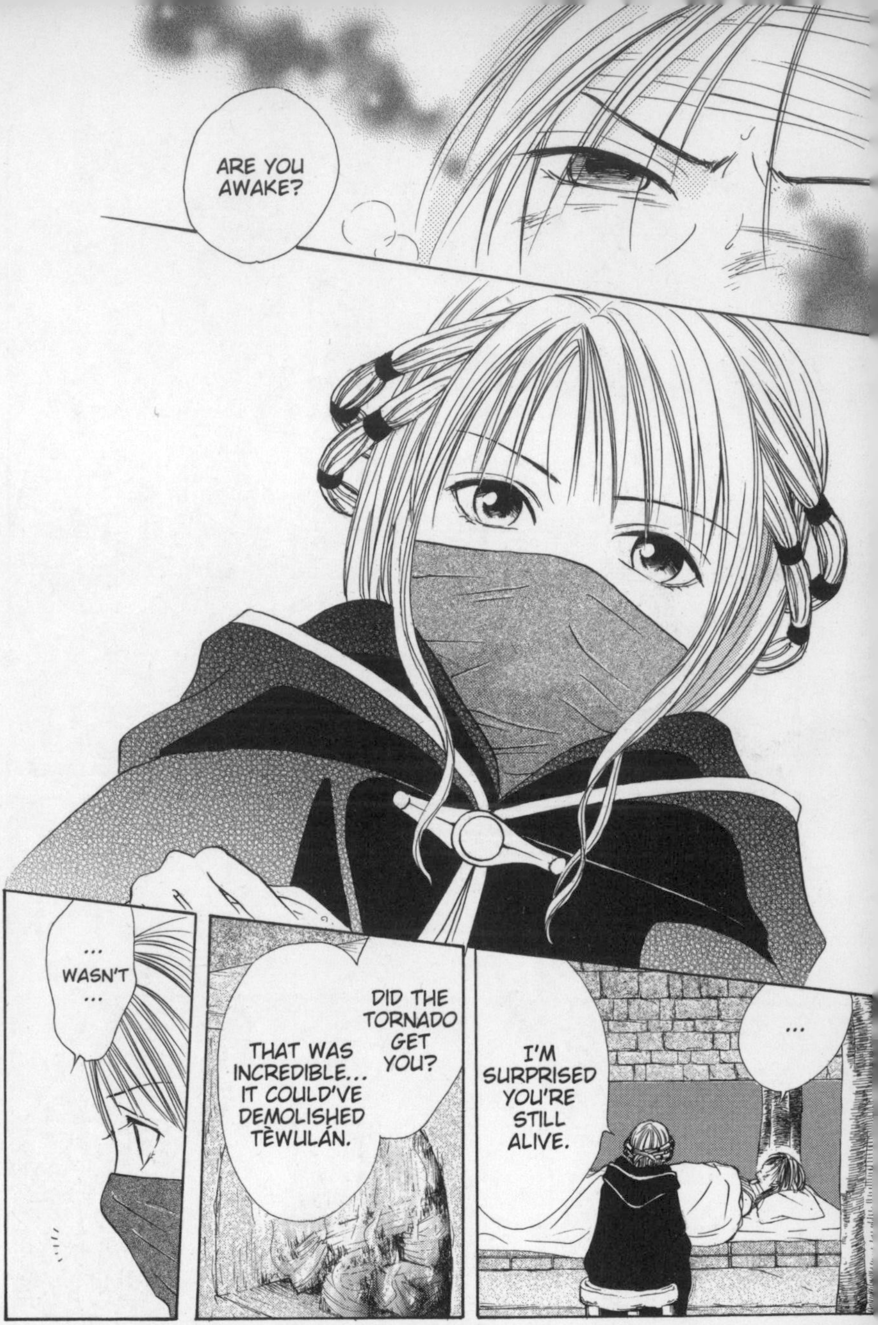
ARE YOU AWAKE?
...
I'M SURPRISED YOU'RE STILL ALIVE.
DID THE TORNADO GET YOU?
THAT WAS INCREDIBLE... IT COULD'VE DEMOLISHED TÈWULÁN.
... WASN'T ...

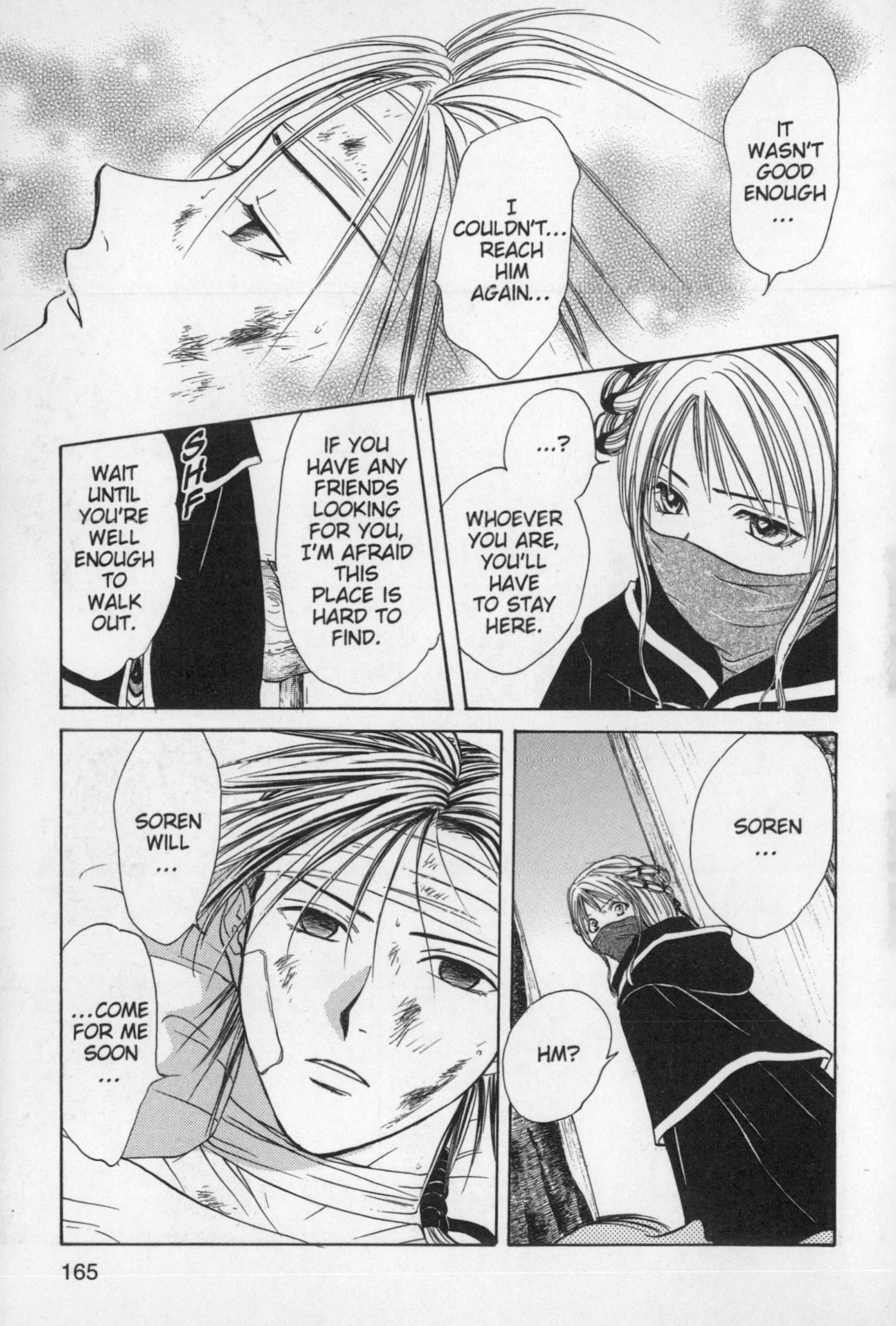

IT WASN'T GOOD ENOUGH ...
I COULDN'T... REACH HIM AGAIN...
...?
WHOEVER YOU ARE, YOU'LL HAVE TO STAY HERE.
IF YOU HAVE ANY FRIENDS LOOKING FOR YOU, I'M AFRAID THIS PLACE IS HARD TO FIND.
SHF
WAIT UNTIL YOU'RE WELL ENOUGH TO WALK OUT.
SOREN ...
HM?
SOREN WILL ...
...COME FOR ME SOON ...

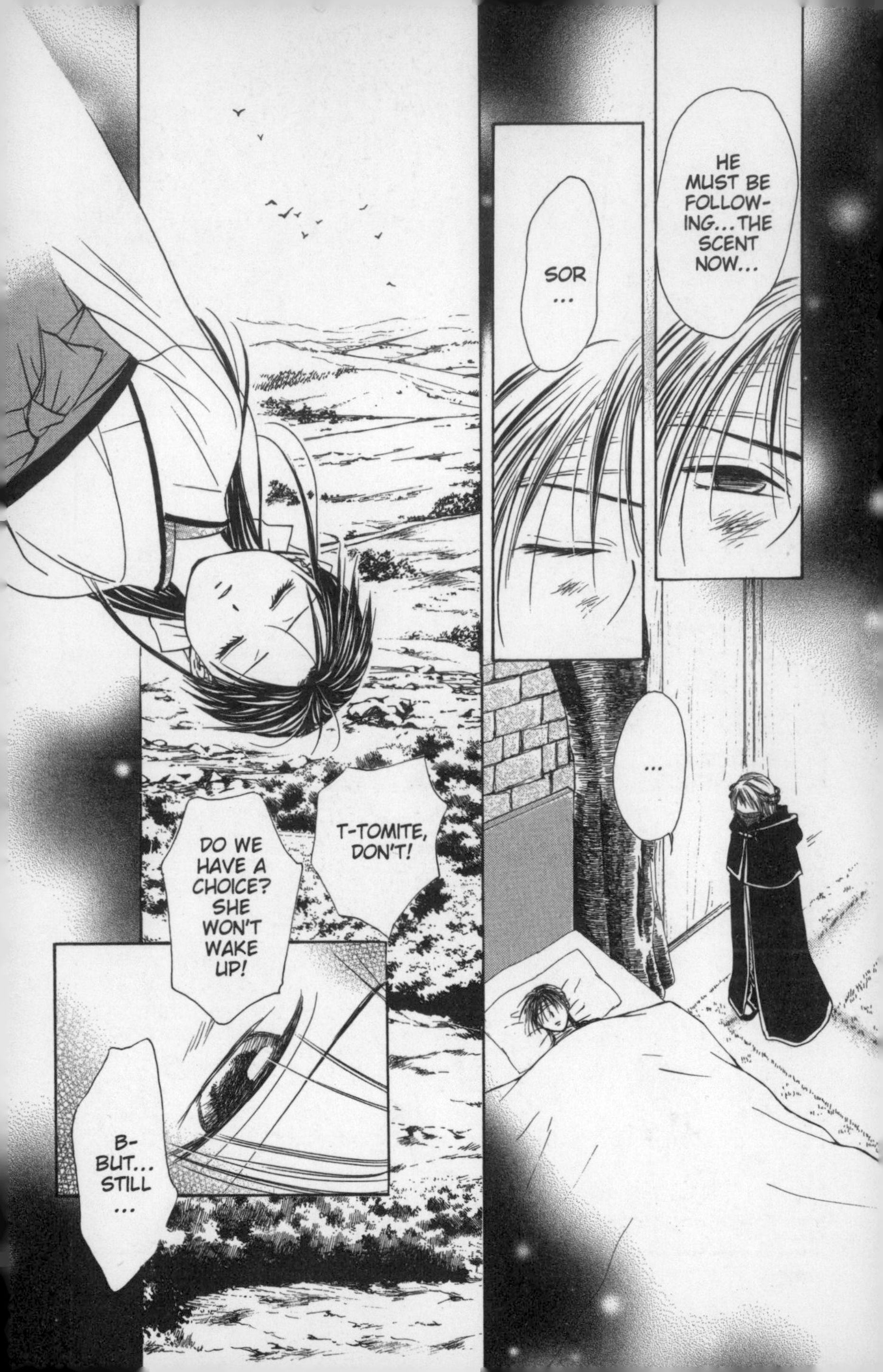
HE MUST BE FOLLOWING... THE SCENT NOW...
SOR...
...
T-TOMITE, DON'T!
DO WE HAVE A CHOICE? SHE WON'T WAKE UP!
B-BUT... STILL...

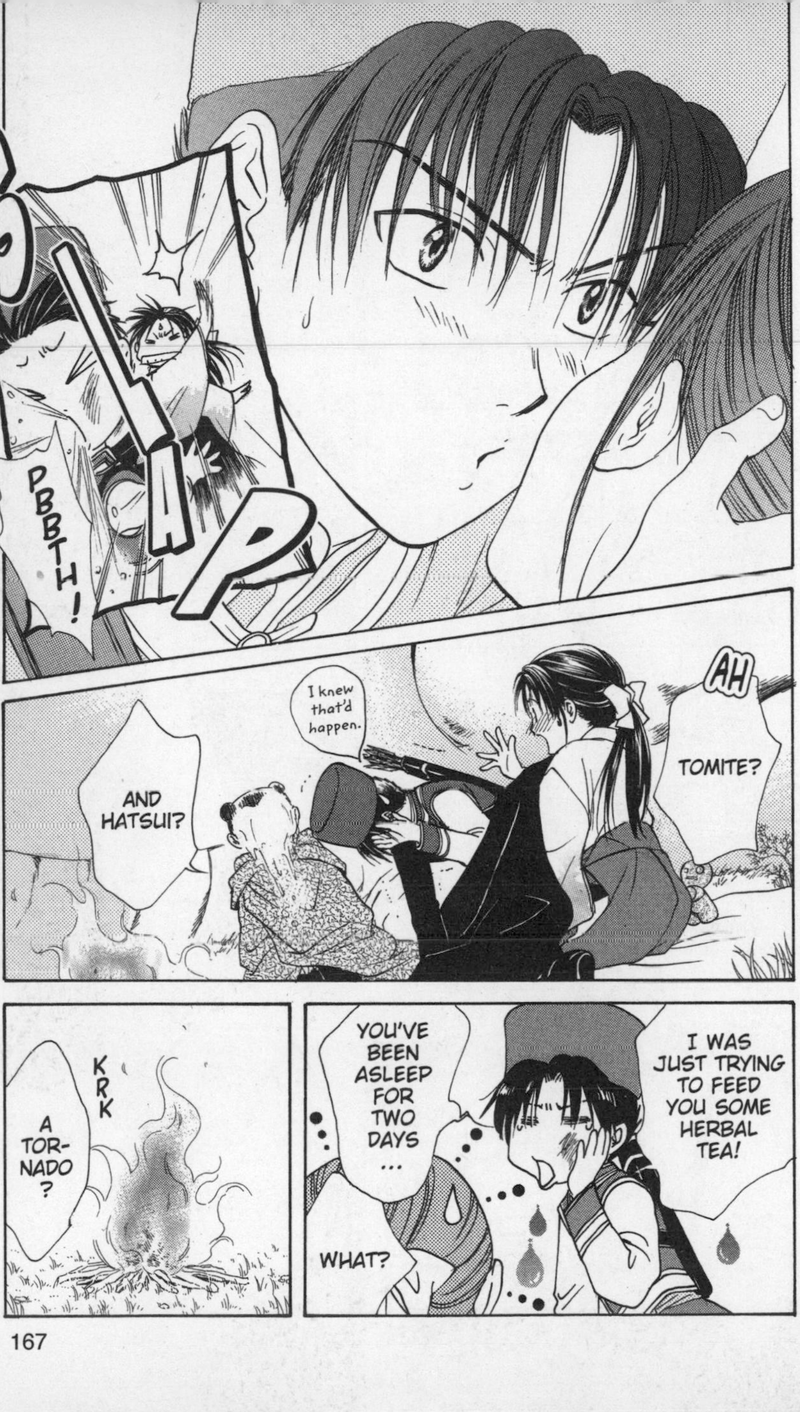
SLAP
PBBTH!
AH
TOMITE?
I knew that'd happen.
AND HATSUI?
I WAS JUST TRYING TO FEED YOU SOME HERBAL TEA!
YOU'VE BEEN ASLEEP FOR TWO DAYS ...
WHAT?
KRK
A TOR-NADO?

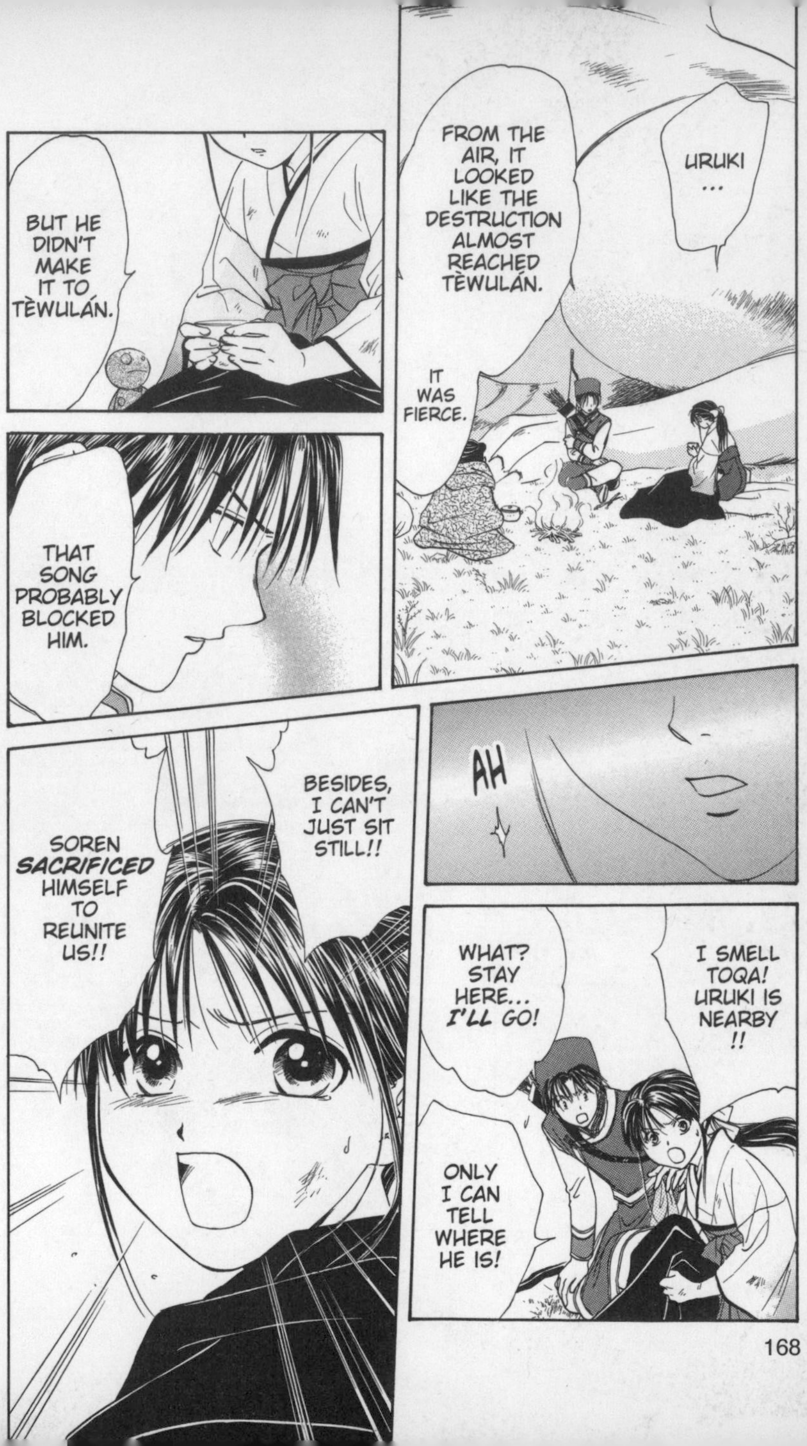
URUKI ...
FROM THE AIR, IT LOOKED LIKE THE DESTRUCTION ALMOST REACHED TÈWULÁN.
IT WAS FIERCE.
BUT HE DIDN'T MAKE IT TO TÈWULÁN.
THAT SONG PROBABLY BLOCKED HIM.
AH
I SMELL TOQA! URUKI IS NEARBY!!
WHAT? STAY HERE... *I'LL* GO!
ONLY I CAN TELL WHERE HE IS!
BESIDES, I CAN'T JUST SIT STILL!!
SOREN *SACRIFICED* HIMSELF TO REUNITE US!!

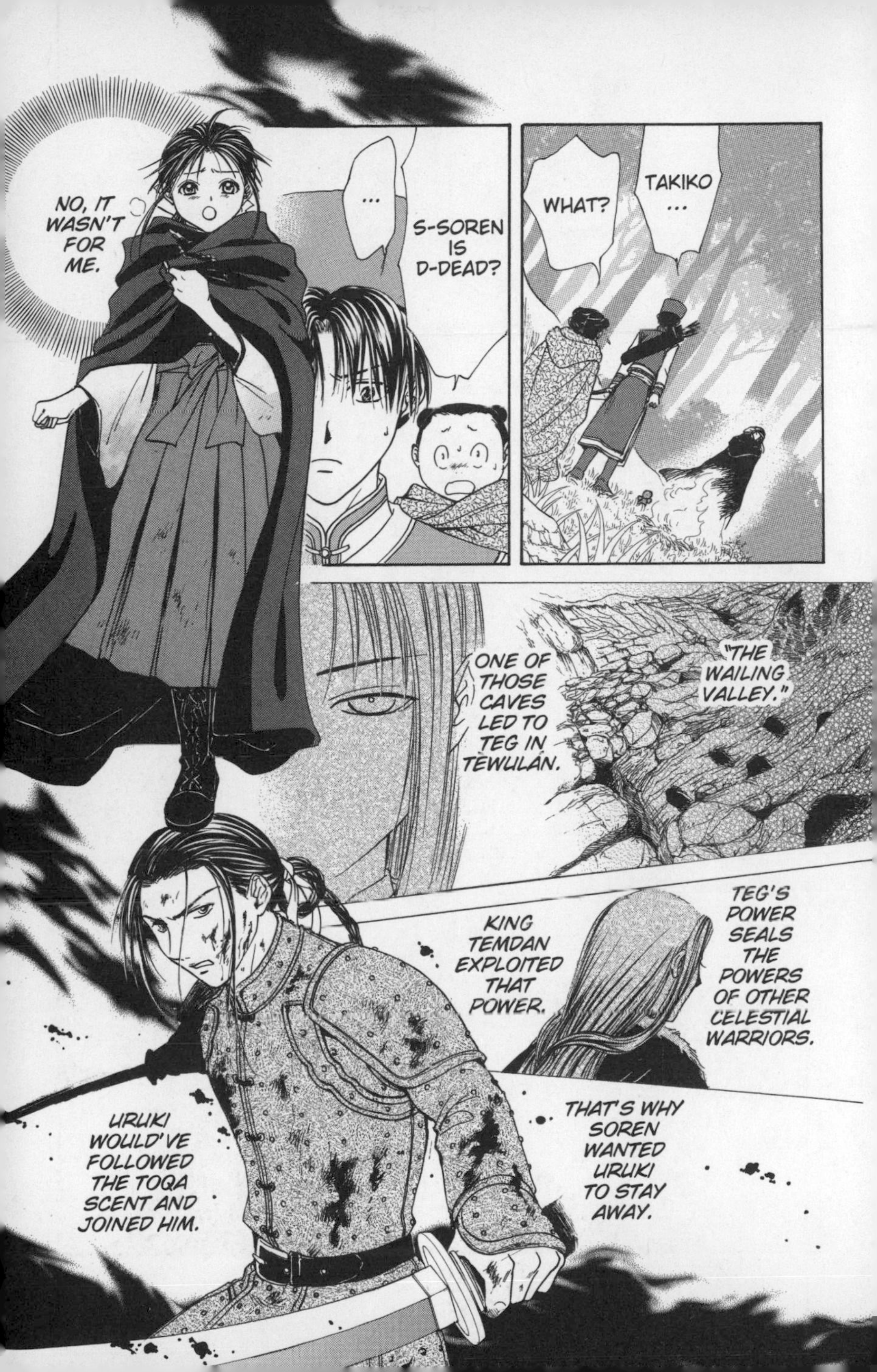
TAKIKO ...
WHAT?
...
S-SOREN IS D-DEAD?
NO, IT WASN'T FOR ME.
"THE WAILING VALLEY."
ONE OF THOSE CAVES LED TO TEG IN TEWULAN.
TEG'S POWER SEALS THE POWERS OF OTHER CELESTIAL WARRIORS.
KING TEMDAN EXPLOITED THAT POWER.
THAT'S WHY SOREN WANTED URUKI TO STAY AWAY.
URUKI WOULD'VE FOLLOWED THE TOQA SCENT AND JOINED HIM.

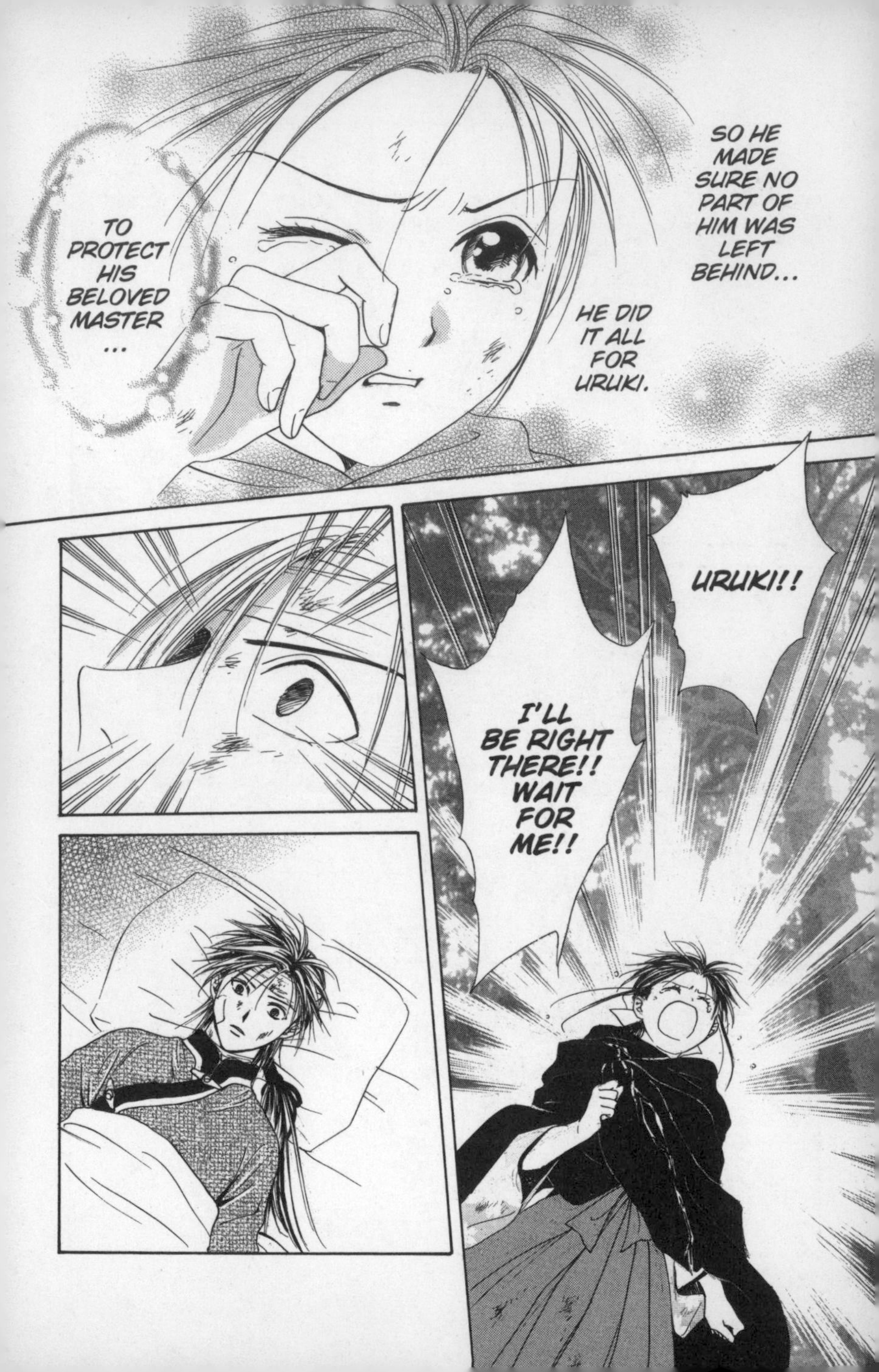
SO HE MADE SURE NO PART OF HIM WAS LEFT BEHIND...
HE DID IT ALL FOR URUKI.
TO PROTECT HIS BELOVED MASTER ...
URUKI!!
I'LL BE RIGHT THERE!! WAIT FOR ME!!

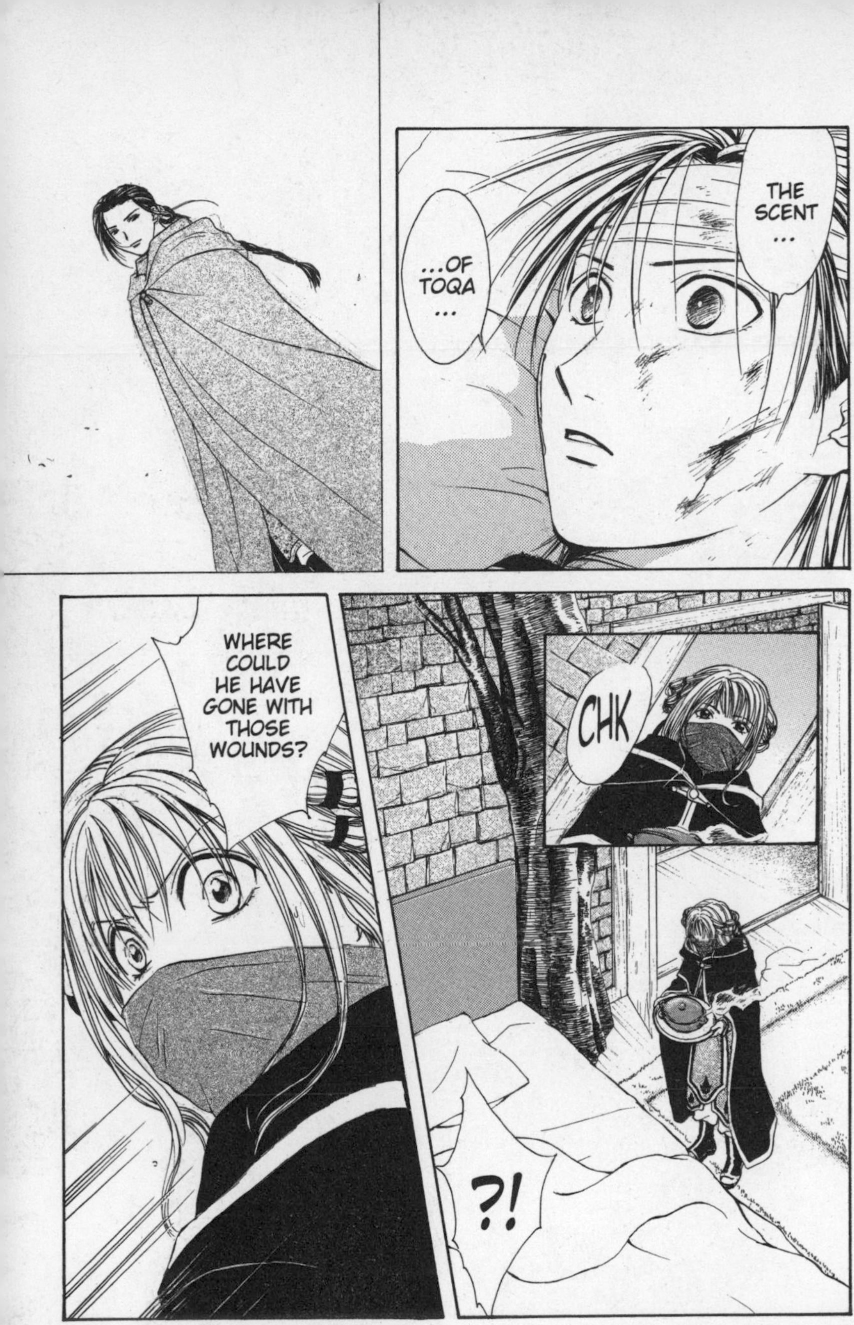
THE SCENT ...
...OF TOQA ...
CHK
?!
WHERE COULD HE HAVE GONE WITH THOSE WOUNDS?

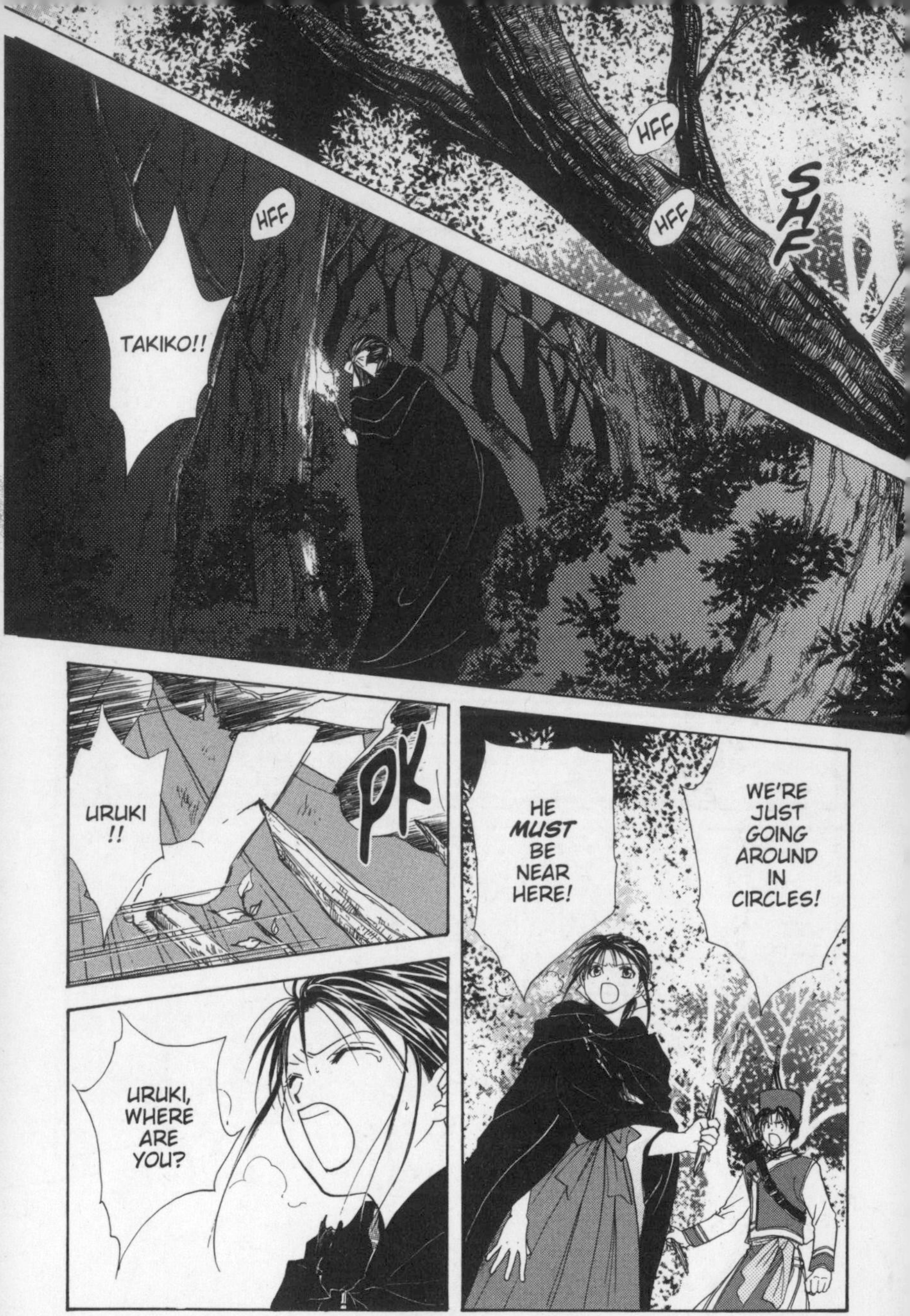
HFF
SHF
HFF
HFF
TAKIKO!!
WE'RE JUST GOING AROUND IN CIRCLES!
HE *MUST* BE NEAR HERE!
PK
URUKI !!
URUKI, WHERE ARE YOU?

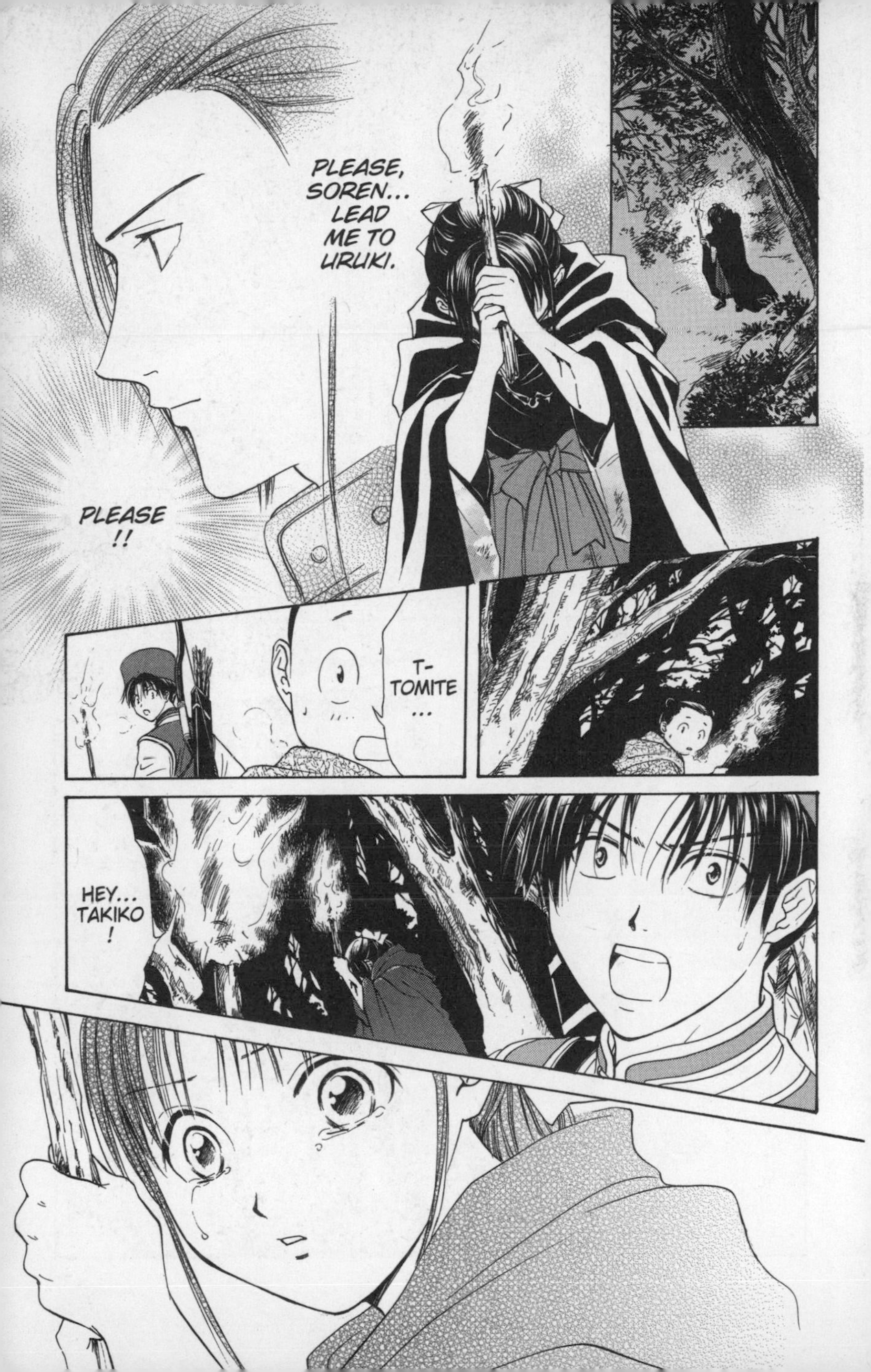
PLEASE, SOREN... LEAD ME TO URUKI.
PLEASE !!
T-TOMITE ...
HEY... TAKIKO !

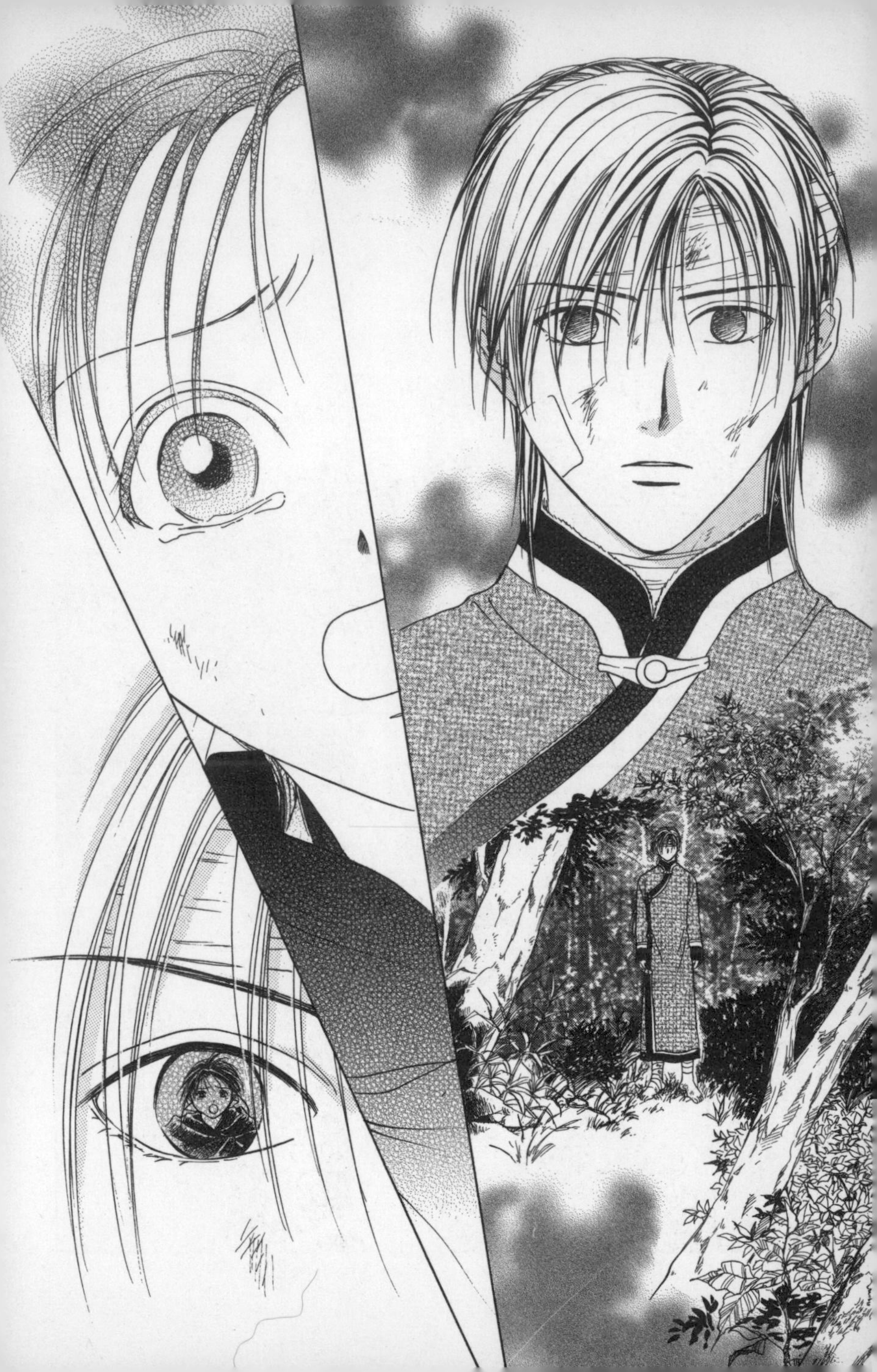

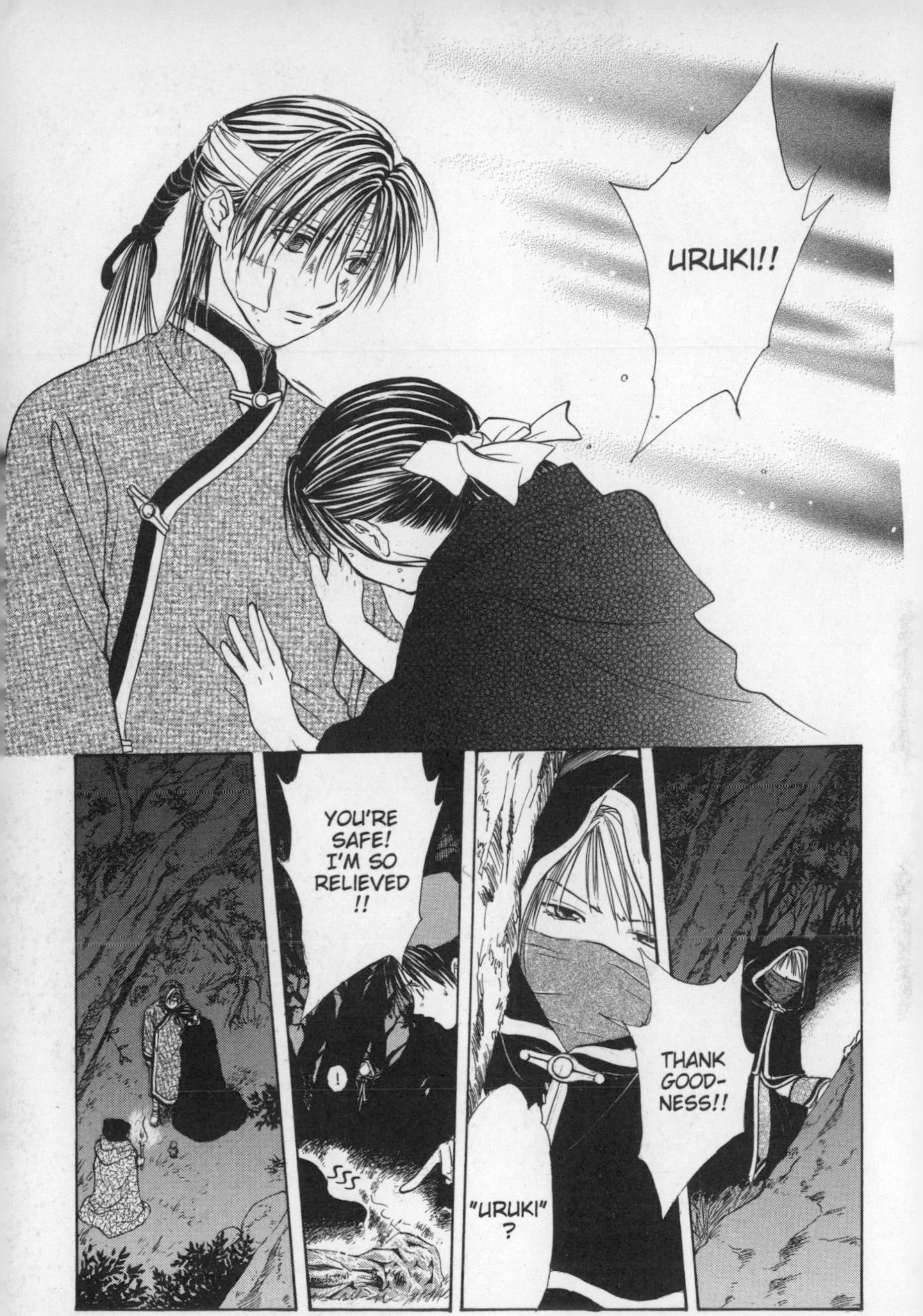
URUKI!!
THANK GOODNESS!!
"URUKI"?
YOU'RE SAFE! I'M SO RELIEVED!!
SSS
!

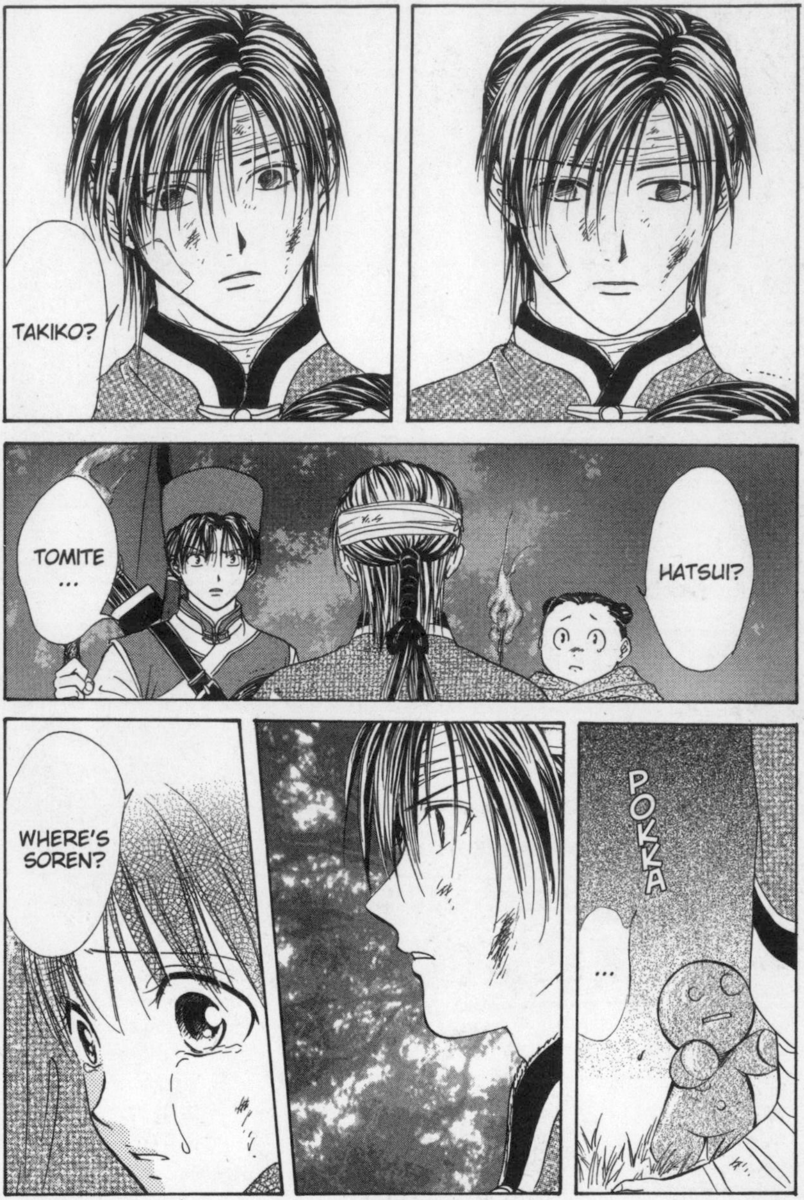
TAKIKO?
HATSUI?
TOMITE ...
POKKA
...
WHERE'S SOREN?

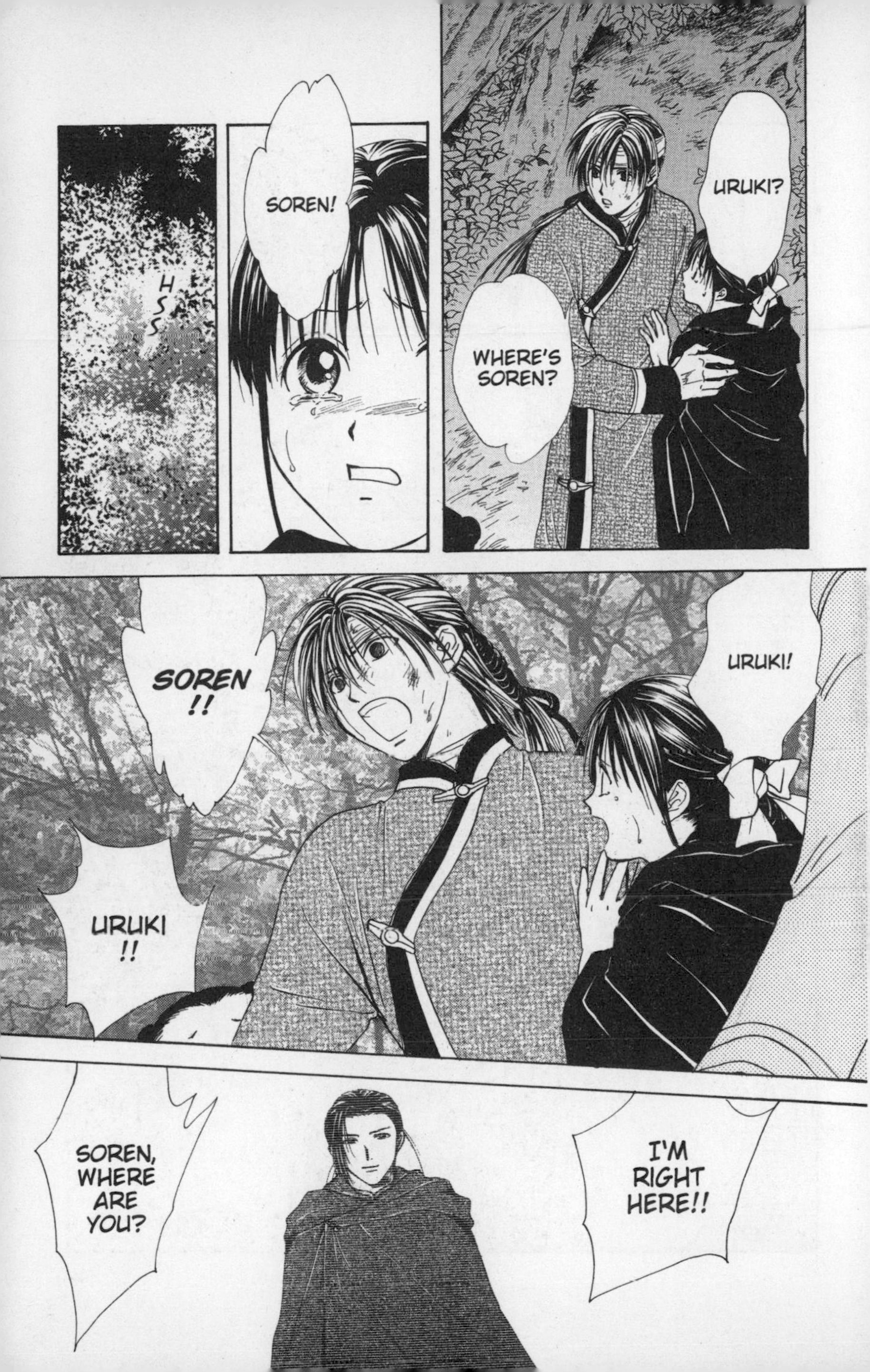
URUKI?
WHERE'S SOREN?
SOREN!
HSS
URUKI!
SOREN !!
URUKI !!
I'M RIGHT HERE!!
SOREN, WHERE ARE YOU?

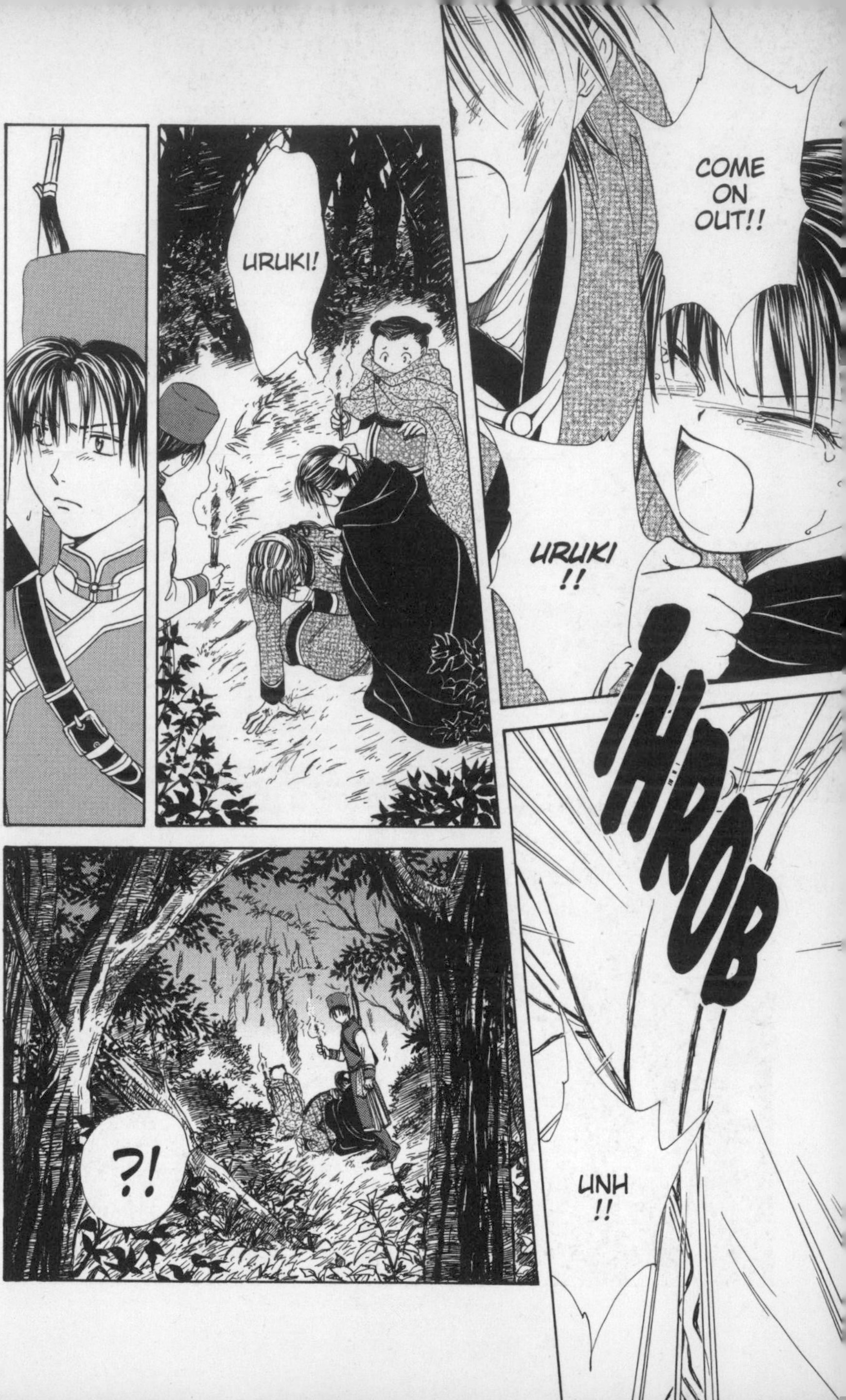
COME ON OUT!!
URUKI !!
THROB
UNH !!
URUKI!
?!

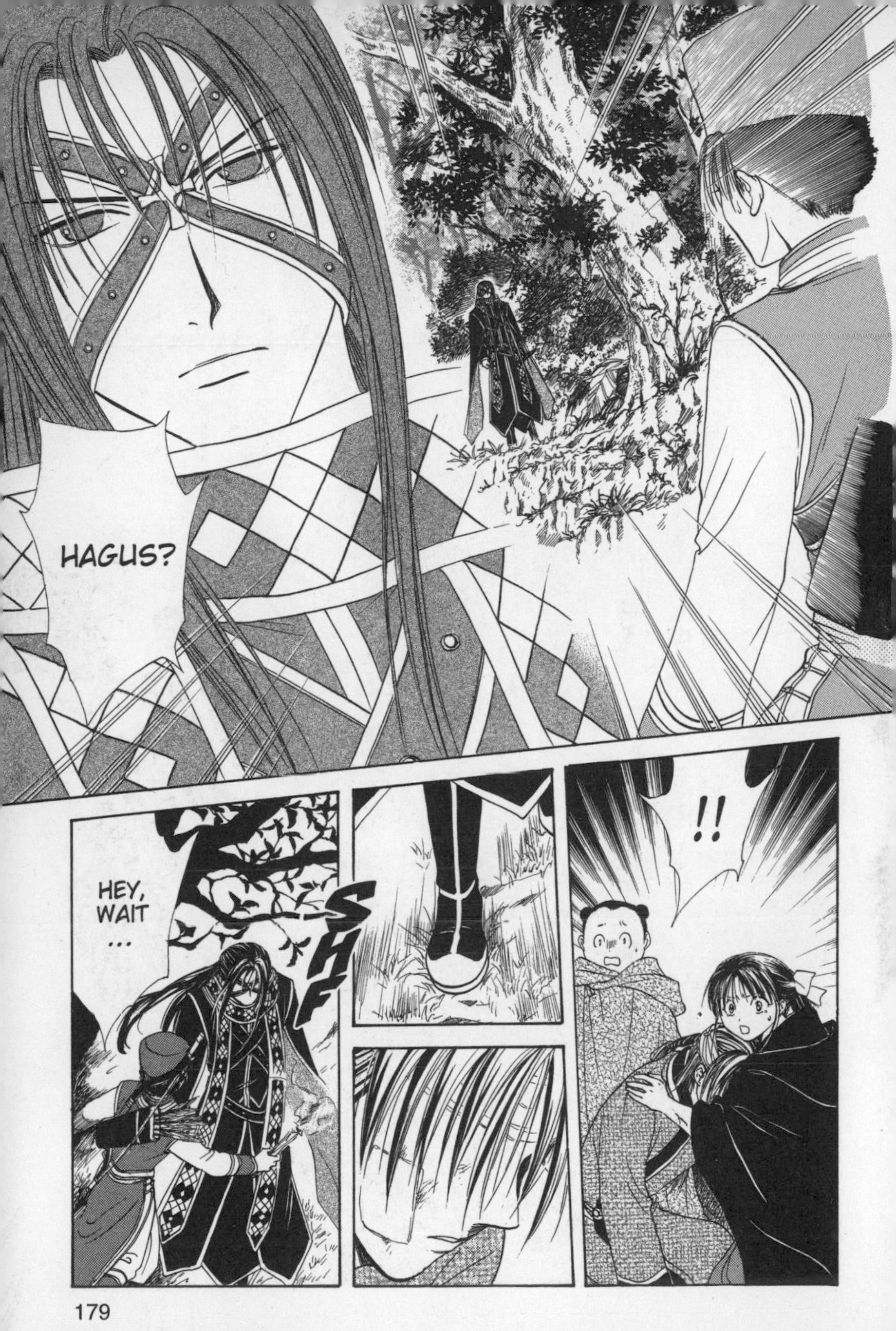
HAGUS?
!!
HEY, WAIT ...
SHF

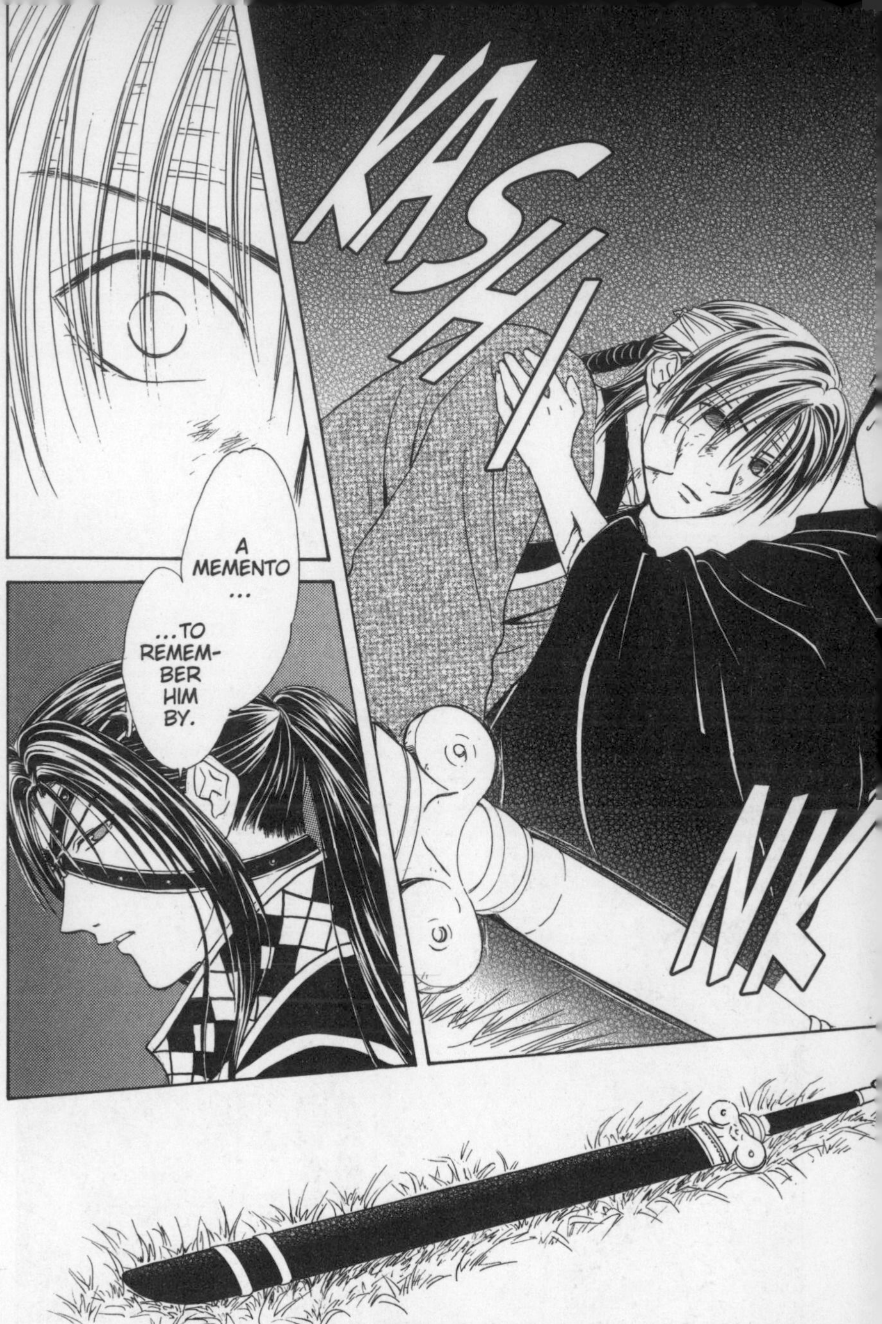
KASHA
NK
A MEMENTO ...
...TO REMEMBER HIM BY.

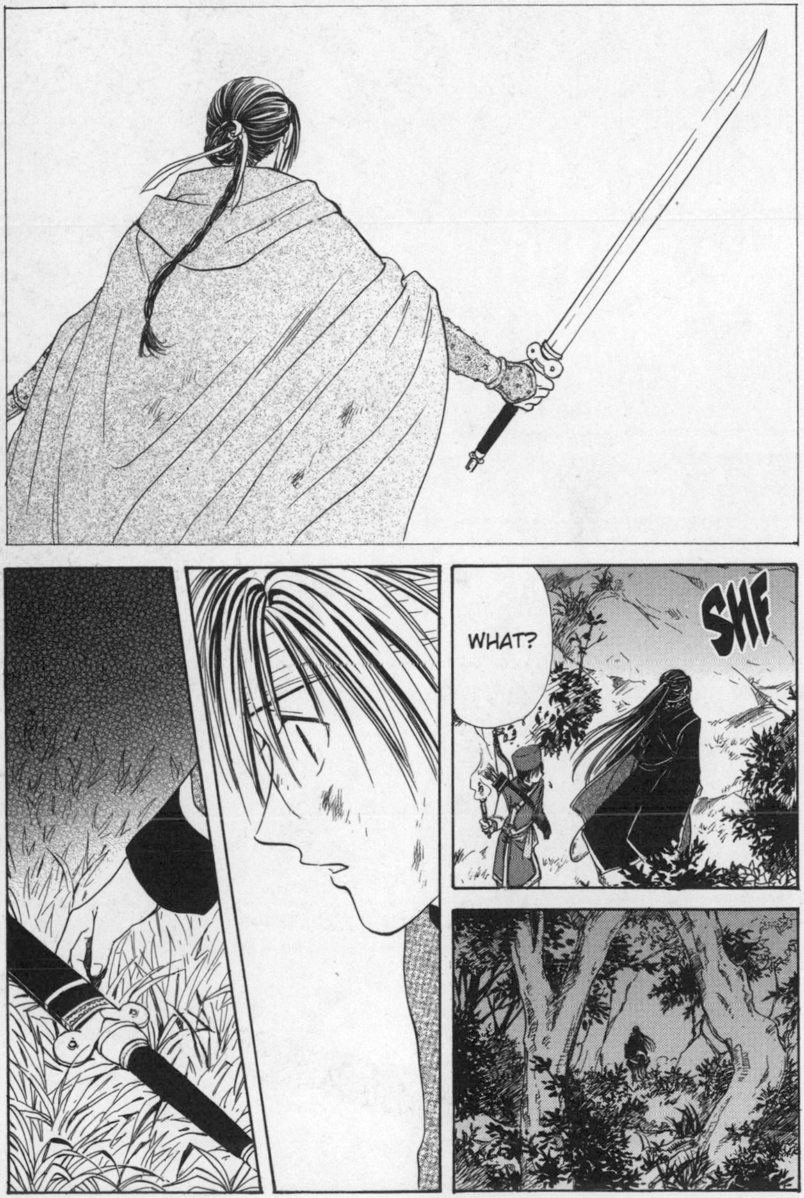
SHF
WHAT?

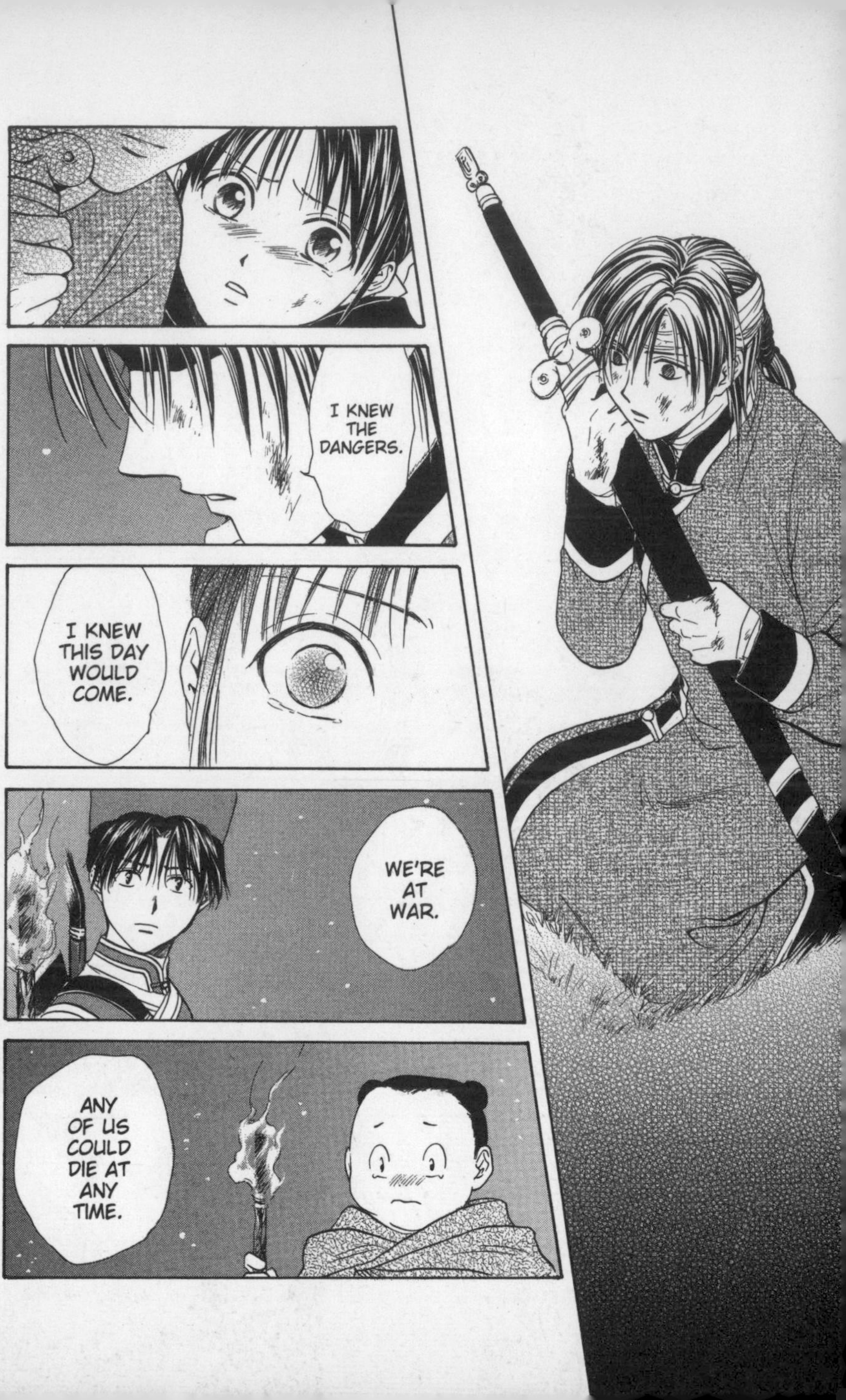
I KNEW THE DANGERS.
I KNEW THIS DAY WOULD COME.
WE'RE AT WAR.
ANY OF US COULD DIE AT ANY TIME.

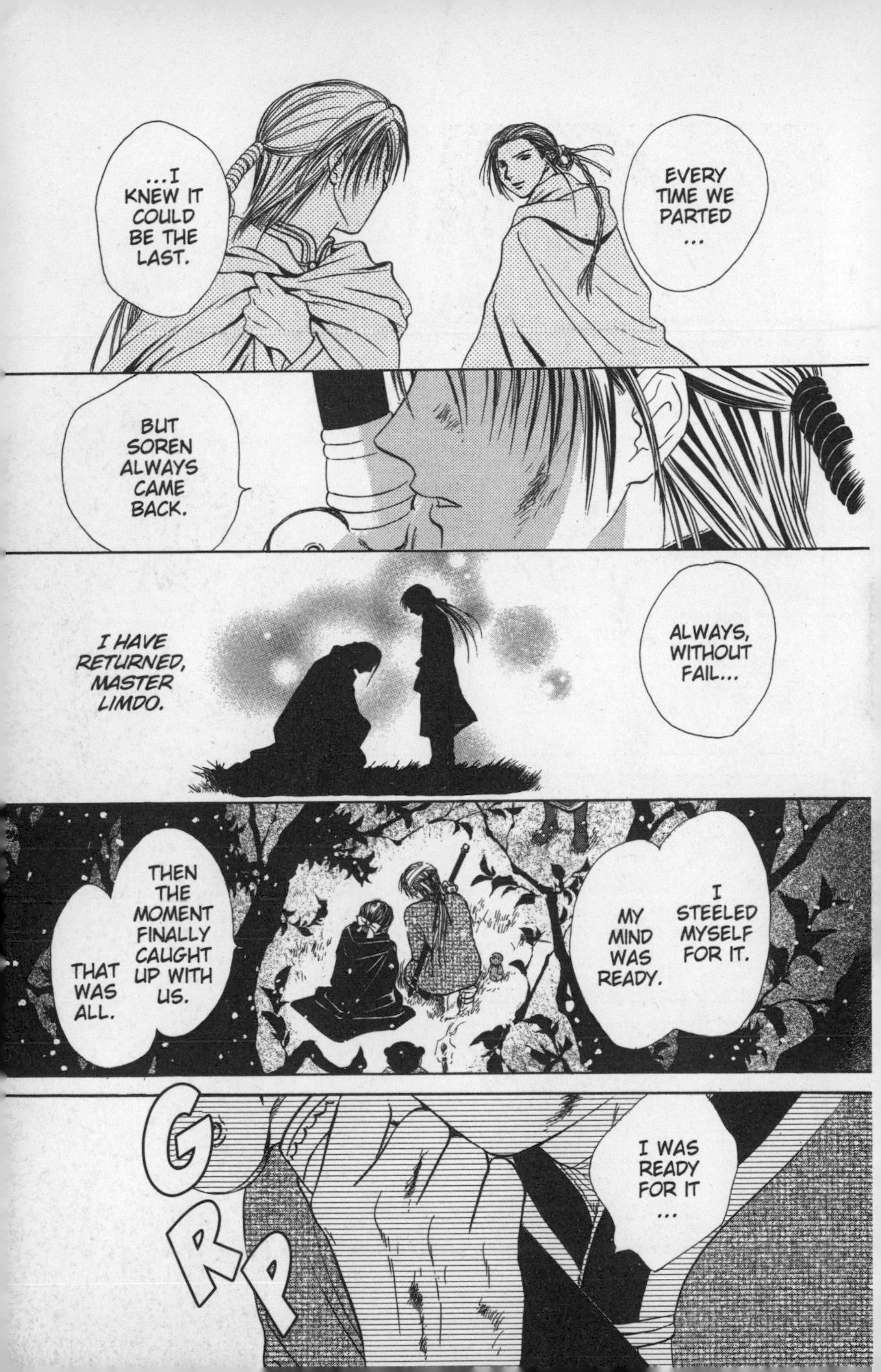
EVERY TIME WE PARTED ...
...I KNEW IT COULD BE THE LAST.
BUT SOREN ALWAYS CAME BACK.
ALWAYS, WITHOUT FAIL...
I HAVE RETURNED, MASTER LIMDO.
I STEELED MYSELF FOR IT.
MY MIND WAS READY.
THEN THE MOMENT FINALLY CAUGHT UP WITH US.
THAT WAS ALL.
I WAS READY FOR IT ...
GRP

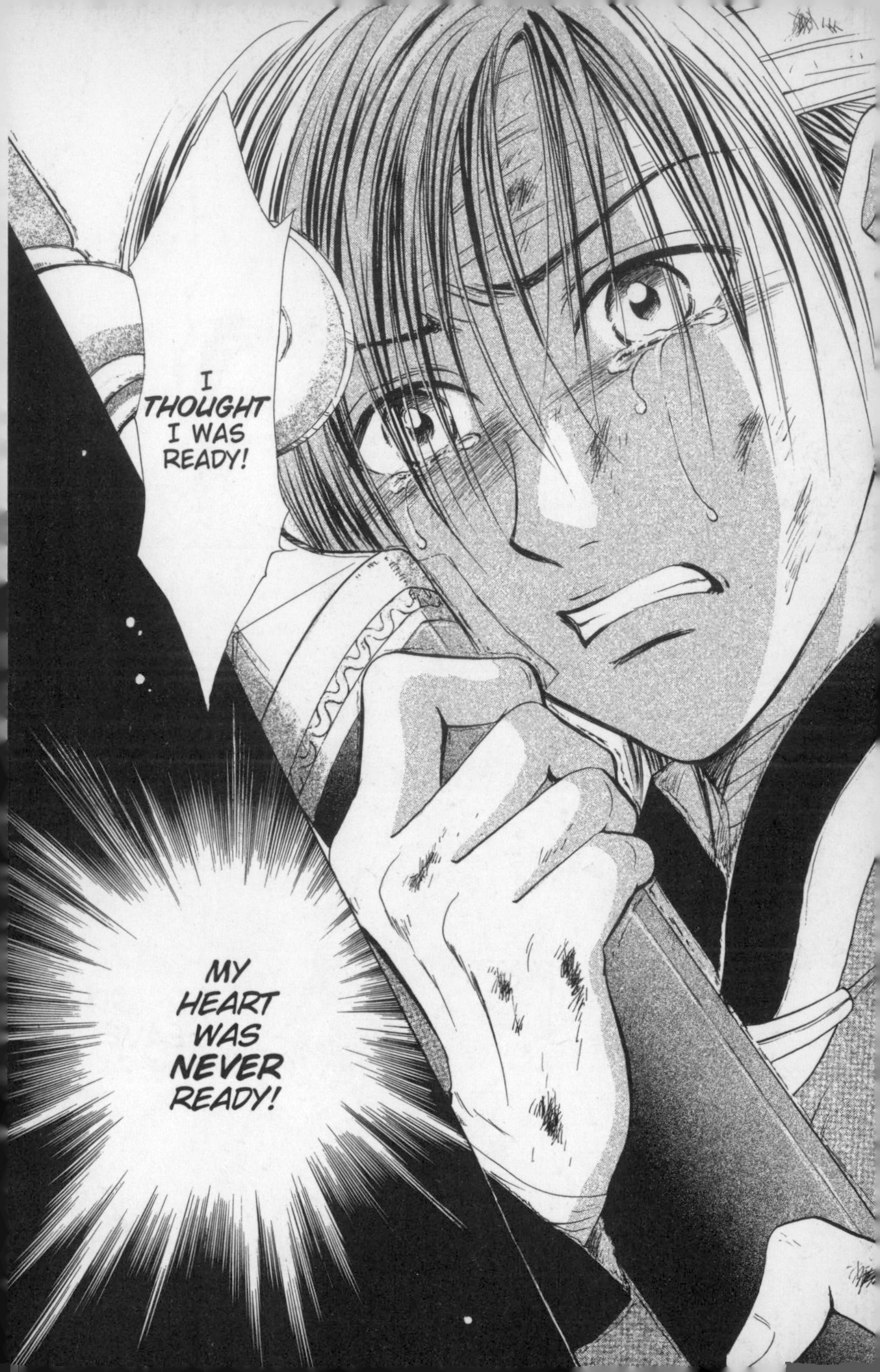
I THOUGHT I WAS READY!
MY HEART WAS NEVER READY!

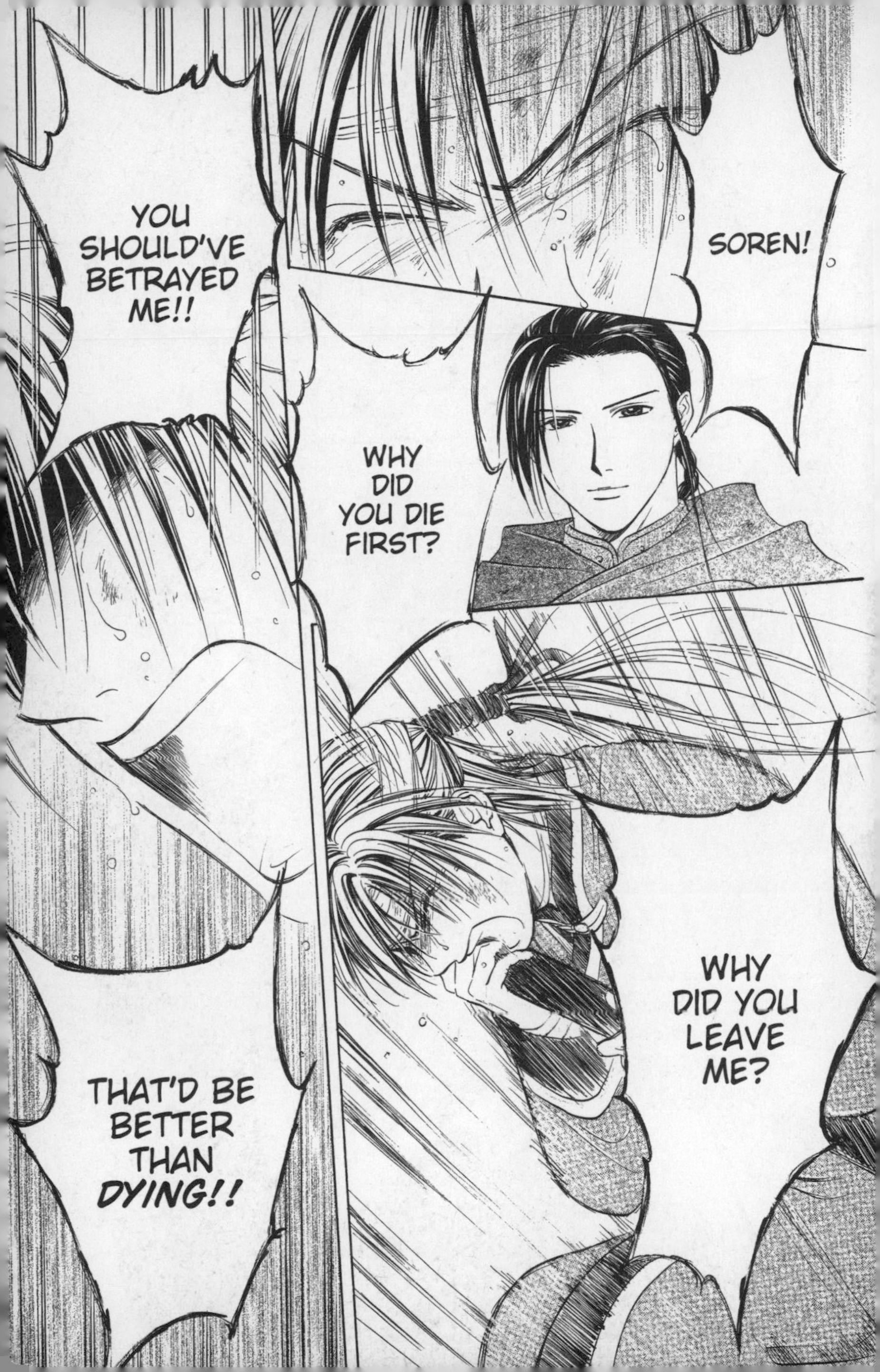
SOREN!
WHY DID YOU DIE FIRST?
WHY DID YOU LEAVE ME?
YOU SHOULD'VE BETRAYED ME!!
THAT'D BE BETTER THAN *DYING!!*

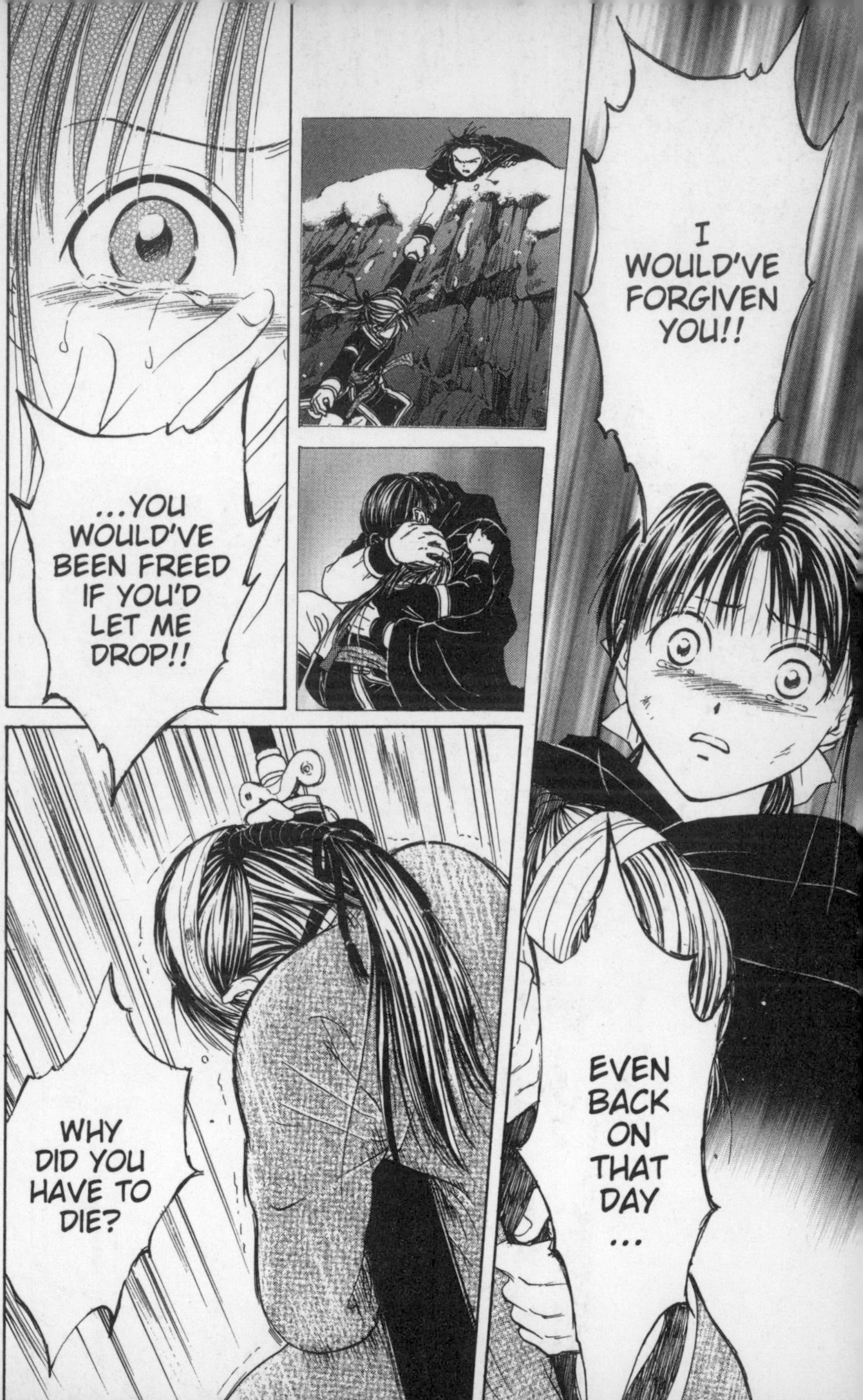
I WOULD'VE FORGIVEN YOU!!
EVEN BACK ON THAT DAY ...
...YOU WOULD'VE BEEN FREED IF YOU'D LET ME DROP!!
WHY DID YOU HAVE TO DIE?

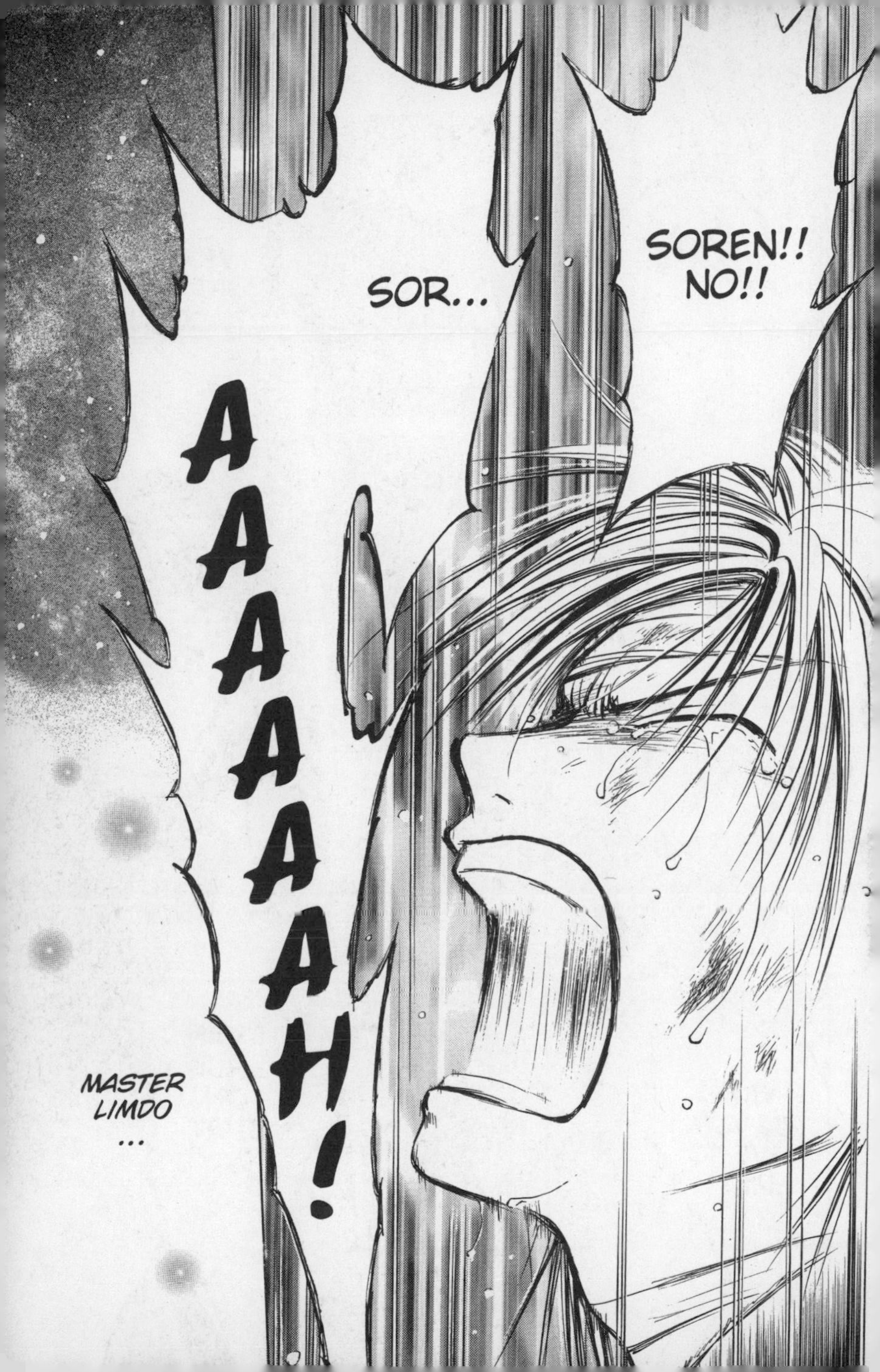
SOREN!! NO!!
SOR...
AAAAAAH!
MASTER LIMDO ...

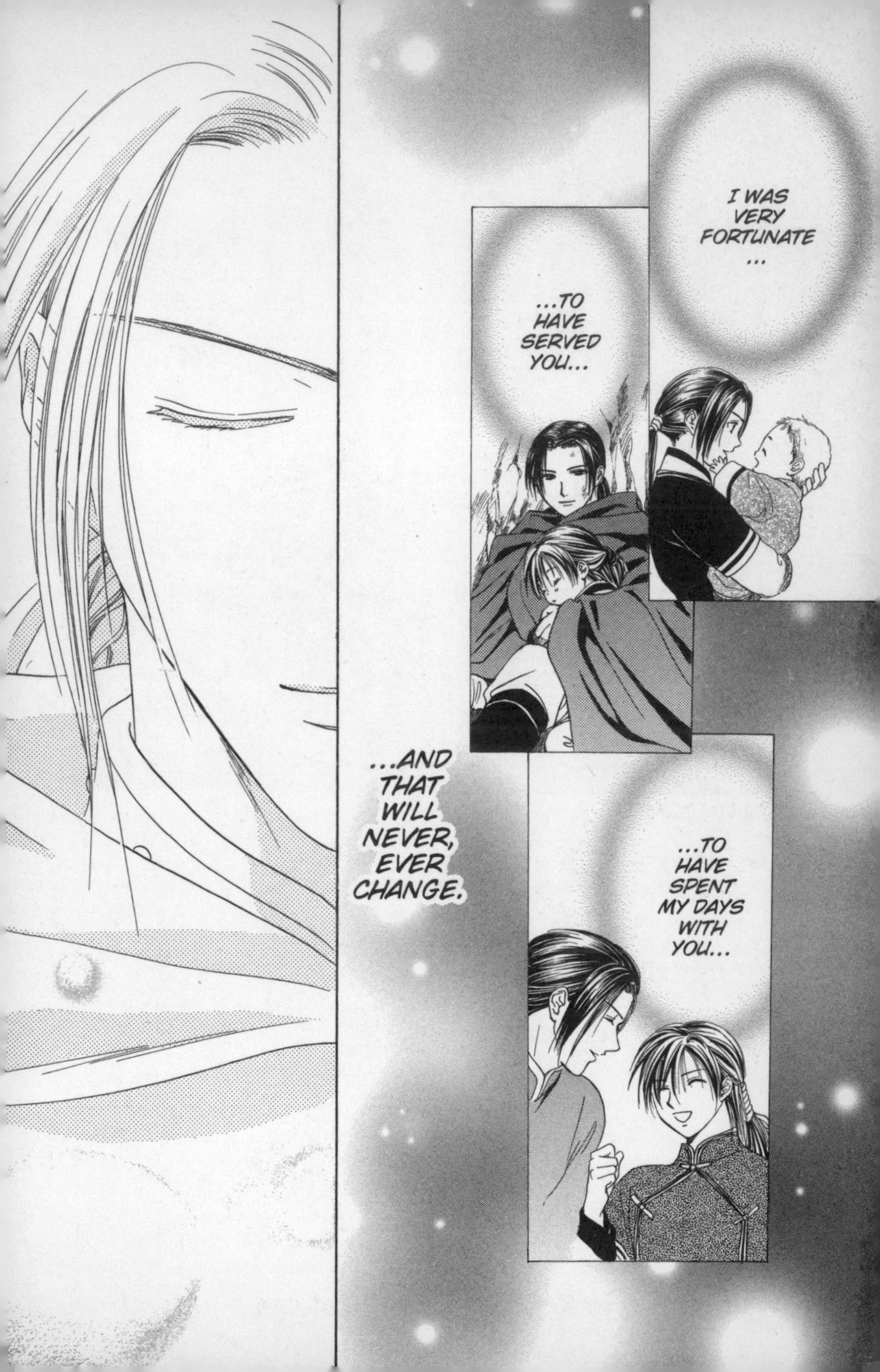
I WAS VERY FORTUNATE ...
...TO HAVE SERVED YOU...
...TO HAVE SPENT MY DAYS WITH YOU...
...AND THAT WILL NEVER, EVER CHANGE.

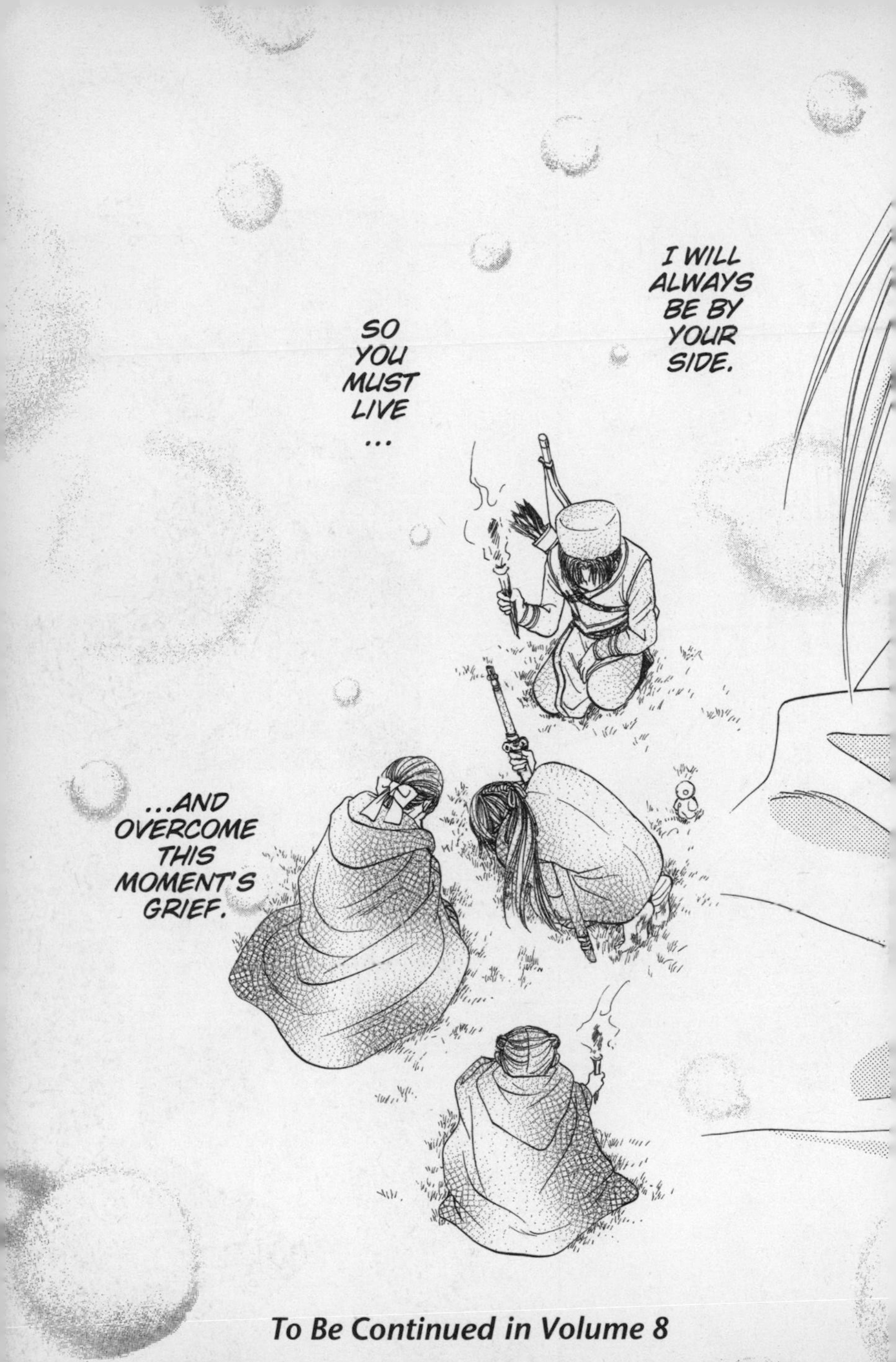
I WILL ALWAYS BE BY YOUR SIDE.
SO YOU MUST LIVE ...
...AND OVERCOME THIS MOMENT'S GRIEF.

To Be Continued in Volume 8

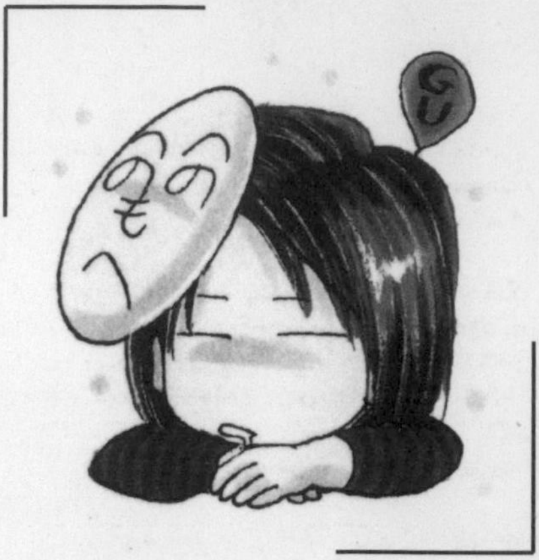
GU

Yuu Watase was born on March 5 in a town near Osaka, Japan. She was raised there before moving to Tokyo to follow her dream of creating manga. In the decade since her debut short story, *Pajama De Ojama* (An Intrusion in Pajamas), she has produced more than 50 volumes of short stories and continuing series. Her latest work, *Absolute Boyfriend*, appeared in Japan in the anthology magazine *Shôjo Comic* and is currently serialized in English in *Shojo Beat* magazine. Watase's other beloved series, *Alice 19th*, *Imadoki!*, and *Ceres: Celestial Legend*, are available in North America in English editions published by VIZ Media.

Fushigi Yûgi:
Genbu Kaiden Vol. 7

The Shojo Beat Manga Edition

STORY AND ART BY
YUU WATASE

Translation/Lillian Olsen
Touch-up Art & Lettering/Rina Mapa
Design/Izumi Hirayama
Editor/Shaenon K. Garrity

Editor in Chief, Books/Alvin Lu
Editor in Chief, Magazines/Marc Weidenbaum
VP, Publishing Licensing/Rika Inouye
VP, Sales and Product Marketing/Gonzalo Ferreyra
VP, Creative/Linda Espinosa
Publisher/Hyoe Narita

Printed in Canada

Published by VIZ Media, LLC
P.O. Box 77010
San Francisco, CA 94107

Shojo Beat Manga Edition
10 9 8 7 6 5 4 3 2 1
First printing, November 2008

www.viz.com

store.viz.com

Tell us wh
about Sho

Our survey is now available online. Go to:

shojobeat.com/mangasurvey

Help us make our product offerings better!

viz media

Shojo Beat
MANGA from the HEART
THE REAL DRAMA BEGINS IN...